D1561788

A HISTORY OF NEPAL

Nepal emerged as a unified state over 200 years ago, centred on the Kathmandu Valley with its 2000 years of urban civilisation. While John Whelpton's history focuses on the period since the overthrow of the Rana family autocracy in 1950–1, the early chapters are devoted to the origins of the kingdom and the evolving relations of its diverse peoples. By drawing on recent research on Nepal's environment, society and political institutions from the earliest times, the author portrays a country of extraordinary contrasts, which has been constantly buffeted through history by its neighbours, the two Asian giants, China and India. Economic and political turmoil over the last fifty years came to a climax in the massacre of the royal family in 2001, when the country erupted into civil war. The book represents the first widely available one-volume treatment in English of the whole span of Nepalese history to appear for over a generation. Its comprehensive and accessible approach will appeal to students, professionals and those visiting the region for the first time.

JOHN WHELPTON, who works as a teacher in Hong Kong, is a historian and linguist. He has worked and travelled extensively in Nepal, and has written numerous articles and books on the country. These include *People, Politics and Ideology: Democracy and Social Change in Nepal* (1999, with the late Martin Hoftun and William Raeper) and *Kings, Soldiers and Priests: Nepalese Politics and the Rise of Jang Bahadur Rana, 1830–1857* (1991).

A HISTORY OF NEPAL

JOHN WHELPTON

CAMBRIDGE
UNIVERSITY PRESS

PUBLISHED BY THE PRESS SYNDICATE OF THE UNIVERSITY OF CAMBRIDGE
The Pitt Building, Trumpington Street, Cambridge, United Kingdom

CAMBRIDGE UNIVERSITY PRESS
The Edinburgh Building, Cambridge, CB2 2RU, UK
40 West 20th Street, New York, NY 10011-4211, USA
477 Williamstown Road, Port Melbourne, VIC 3207, Australia
Ruiz de Alarcón 13, 28014 Madrid, Spain
Dock House, The Waterfront, Cape Town 8001, South Africa

http://www.cambridge.org

First published 2005

Printed in the United Kingdom at the University Press, Cambridge

Typeface Adobe Garamond 11/12.5 pt.   *System* LaTeX 2_ε [TB]

A catalogue record for this book is available from the British Library

Library of Congress Cataloguing in Publication data
Whelpton, John.
A History of Nepal / John Whelpton.
p.   cm.
Includes bibliographical references and index.
ISBN 0 521 80026 9 (hb.) – ISBN 0 521 80470 1 (pbk.)
1. Nepal – History.
DS494 5.W43   2005
954.96 – dc22   2004051856

ISBN 0 521 80026 9 hardback
ISBN 0 521 80470 1 paperback

The publisher has used its best endeavours to ensure that the URLs for external websites referred to in
this book are correct and active at the time of going to press. However, the publisher has no
responsibility for the websites and can make no guarantee that a site will remain live or that the
content is or will remain appropriate.

Contents

Illustrations

Maps

Tables

Key events

BC

130,000?   Hand-axe man in Dang and Satpati
c. 1700?   Beginning of Indo-Aryan movement into the
                  Indian subcontinent
c. 400?   Birth of the Buddha at Lumbini

AD

465   Changu Narayan inscription of King Manadeva
647   Nepalese troops assist Chinese envoy in punitive
                  expedition against an Indian state
879   Beginning of Nepal Era
1097   Nanyadeva of Karnataka takes control of Mithila
c. 1100   Establishment of Khasa empire in western Nepal
1200   Commencement of Malla period in Kathmandu
                  Valley
1349   Shams ud-din Ilyas Shah of Bengal raids
                  Kathmandu Valley
1382   Jayasthiti Malla gains control of Kathmandu Valley
1482   Death of Yaksha Malla, last sole king of Kathmandu
                  Valley
c. 1533   Migration of Sherpas from Kham (Tibet) into
                  Solukhumbu
1559   Drabya Shah seizes Gorkha
1628   Jesuit John Cabral is first European to visit the
                  Nepal Valley
1650 (or earlier) Treaty with Tibet gives Kathmandu joint control
                  over the Kuti and Kirong Passes, the right to mint
                  Tibet's coinage and permission for Newars to open
                  trading houses in Lhasa
1715   Establishment of Capuchin mission in Kathmandu

1743	Prithvi Narayan Shah crowned king of Gorkha
1768–9	Gorkhali conquest of Kathmandu Valley
1786	First Nepal–Tibet War
1791	Second Nepal–Tibet War
1792	Chinese invasion of Nepal
1793	Kirkpatrick mission to Kathmandu
1802–3	East India Company's envoy Captain Knox in Kathmandu
1806 April	Assassination of Rana Bahadur Shah and beginning of Bhimsen Thapa's predominance
1809–10	Sikh ruler Ranjit Singh halts Gorkhali expansion in the west
1814–16	Anglo-Gorkha War
1837 July	Dismissal of Bhimsen Thapa
1840	Appointment of 'British ministry'
1842	'National Movement' of courtiers and army press King Rajendra to grant powers to his junior queen
1846 September	Jang Bahadur Rana becomes prime minister after Kot Massacre
1850	Jang Bahadur Rana's visit to Europe
1855–56	Third Nepal–Tibet War
1856	Jang Bahadur Rana becomes maharaja of Kaski and Lamjung
1857–8	Nepal assists British in suppression of Indian Mutiny
1877	Death of Jang Bahadur Rana
1885 November	Shamsher Ranas seize power
1904	Chandra Shamsher Rana assists the Younghusband expedition to Tibet
1914–18	Around 100,000 Nepalese involved in support of Britain in First World War
1919	Opening of Trichandra College in Kathmandu
1923	Britain recognises Nepal's complete independence
1924 November	Chandra Shamsher Rana's speech calling for abolition of slavery
1934 January	Major earthquake destroys many buildings in Kathmandu Valley
March	Removal of C-Class Ranas from the Roll of Succession

1939–45	Mobilisation of Nepal's resources in support of Britain in Second World War
1941 January	Execution of 'Four martyrs'
November	Abdication of Juddha and accession of Maharaja Padma Shamsher Rana
1947 January	Formation of Nepali National Congress
August	India becomes independent
November	Tripartite agreement gives India twelve and UK eight of existing Gurkha battalions
1948 January	Padma Shamsher Rana promulgates constitution
April	Following Padma Shamsher Rana's resignation, Mohan Shamsher Rana becomes prime minister and maharaja
August	Formation of Nepali Democratic Congress
1950 April	Merger of Nepali National Congress and Nepal Democratic Congress to form Nepali Congress
November	King Tribhuvan's flight to the Indian embassy
1951 February	Formal end of Rana regime and establishment of coalition government (now celebrated annually as Democracy Day) under restored King Tribhuvan
April	Bir Gorkha Dal revolt in Kathmandu
November	M. P. Koirala forms Congress government after collapse of coalition
1952 January	Raksha Dal mutiny, leading to banning of Communist Party
1953 June	Second M. P. Koirala government
1955 March	Death of King Tribhuvan in Switzerland
1956 January	Tanka Prasad Acharya appointed prime minister with cabinet of Praja Parishad and independent ministers
July	K. I. Singh becomes prime minister with cabinet of United Democratic Party members plus royal nominees
November	K. I. Singh government dismissed
1958 February	Mahendra announces appointment of Constitution Drafting Commission, government without a prime minister, and a nominated Advisory Assembly
1959 February	Promulgation of constitution
February–April	Voting in general election
May	B. P. Koirala becomes prime minister

1960 December	Mahendra removes Congress government and imposes direct royal rule
1962 November	Subarna Shamsher Rana calls off Congress armed resistance to Mahendra after outbreak of war between China and India
December	Promulgation of Nepal's new constitution
1963 April	New Civil Code (Muluki Ain)
1964	Land Reform Act
1965 January	Secret agreement for Nepal to use other sources for arms only if India unable to meet its requirements
1968 May	Subarna Shamsher Rana pledges 'loyal co-operation' with King Mahendra
October	Release of B. P. Koirala and Ganesh Man Singh from prison
1969 June	Kirtinidhi Bista, prime minister, denounces defence agreements with India
1972 January	Death of King Mahendra and accession of King Birendra
August	Congress launches armed raid from India on Haripur (Sarlahi district)
1973	Suppression of Jhapeli communist group's Naxalite-style campaign of violence
1974	Three-month army operation to clear out Khampas using northern Nepal as base for raids into Tibet
March	Biratnagar bomb attempt on Birendra's life
1975 February	Birendra makes Zone of Peace Proposal
June	Indira Gandhi declares emergency rule in India
1976 December	B. P. Koirala and Ganesh Man Singh return to Kathmandu from India and are immediately arrested
1979 May	Birendra announces referendum on future of Panchayat system
June	Surya Bahadur Thapa becomes prime minister
1980 May	Referendum decides in favour of reformed Panchayat system rather than return to multi-party democracy
December	Third amendment to constitution provides for direct election of Rastriya Panchayat
1985 May	Congress launch civil disobedience campaign
June	Bomb explosions in Kathmandu

1986 May		Start of Gorkha National Liberation Front agitation in Darjeeling
	May	Second general election under the reformed Panchayat system
1987 December		End of Gorkha National Liberation Front campaign in Darjeeling
1989 March		India imposes semi-blockade of Nepal
	November	Janata Party wins Indian elections, Rajiv Gandhi replaced by V. P. Singh
1990 February		Start of 'People's Movement'
	March	Start of nightly 'light-outs'
	March	Patan 'uprising' begins
	April	Dismissal of Marichman Singh Shrestha's government, appointment of Lokendra Bahadur Chand as prime minister and Darbar Marg shootings
	April	King meets opposition leaders and lifts ban on political parties
	April	Dissolution of Rastriya Panchayat and Krishna Prasad Bhattarai appointed prime minister
	November/ December	People claiming to be refugees from Bhutan set up makeshift camps in Jhapa
	November	Promulgation of constitution
	November	CPN (Unity Centre) established
1991 January		Merger of CPN (M) and CPN (ML) to form Communist Party of Nepal (Unified Marxist-Leninist)
	January	Establishment of United People's Front as electoral vehicle for the far-left Unity Centre
	May	General election and formation of Girija Prashad Koiral's Congress government
	December	Girija Koirala's cabinet reshuffle intensifies conflict within Congress
1992		Recognition of Nepali as one of India's national languages
	February	Thapa and Chand factions amalgamate to form United National Democratic Party
	April	Police shooting of left-wing demonstrators in Kathmandu
1993 May		Death of Madan Bhandari and Jivraj Ashrit in jeep accident at Dasdhunga

1994 May		United People's Front splits into Baburam Bhattarai and Nirajan Vaidya factions
	July	Girija Koirala requests dissolution of parliament
	November	Man Mohan Adhikari appointed prime minister following elections giving CPN (UML) a plurality
1995 March		Prachanda's faction of Unity Centre renames itself CPN (Maoist)
	September	Central committee of CPN (Maoist) adopts 'Plan for the historic initiation of the People's War'
	September	UML government leaves office after parliament passes a no-confidence motion
	September	Sher Bahadur Deuba becomes prime minister heading Congress-National Democratic Party-Sadbhavana coalition
	November	Police launch Operation Romeo against Maoist supporters in Rolpa
1996 February		Commencement of 'People's War'
	May	Girija Koirala is elected president of Nepali Congress
	September	Joint meeting of both Houses of parliament approves the Mahakali treaty by a two-thirds' majority
	December	New trade and transit treaty with India
1997 March		Deuba fails to gain vote of confidence
	March	Swearing-in of NDP-UML-Sadbhavana coalition under Lokendra Bahadur Chand
	October	Chand government loses no-confidence vote
	October	Surya Bahadur Thapa becomes prime minister heading NDP-Congress-Sadbhavana coalition
1998 January		Formal split of NDP into separate Chand and Thapa parties
	March	Dissidents formally split from UML to form the CPN (Marxist-Leninist)
	April	Thapa resigns in accordance with original agreement with Congress
	April	Girija Koirala sworn in as prime minister of a Congress minority government
	May	Beginning of Kilo Sierra 2 police operation against the Maoist insurgents
	August	CPN (ML) ministers join Koirala government

	December	CPN (ML) ministers resign from government
	December	Formation of new Congress-UML-Sadbhavana-Independent cabinet
1999	April	Death of Man Mohan Adhikari
	May	Elections held in two main phases
	May	Krishna Prasad Bhattarai appointed prime minister
	September	Seven policeman killed and an inspector taken prisoner at post in Rukum
	December	Bhattarai sets up commission under Deuba to make recommendations on Maoist problem
	December	Thapa and Chand factions of the National Democratic Party announce they will re-unite
2000	February	Police burn down houses in Rukum following death of nineteen police in bomb explosion
	May	Girija Koirala replaces Krishna Prasad Bhattarai as prime minister
	July	Government declares *kamaiyas* (bonded labourers) free
	August	Death of musician Praveen Gurung in collision with vehicle allegedly driven by an inebriated Prince Paras
	September	Maoists attack Dunai, district headquarters of Dolpo, killing fourteen policemen and destroying government buildings
	December	Five die in police firing in Kathmandu in rioting over alleged anti-Nepalese remarks by Indian film star Hritik Roshan
2001	January	Birendra approves ordinances setting up Armed Police Force and system of regional governors
	February	Adoption of 'Prachanda Path' as party doctrine at Maoists' second national conference which also elected Prachanda as party chairman
	April	Maoists kill seventy policemen in attacks at Rukumkot (Rukum) and Naumule (Dailekh); government announces plans for Integrated Security and Development Programme involving key role for army
	June	Crown Prince Dipendra shoots dead king, queen and seven other members of royal family before apparently committing suicide

	June	Raj Parishad proclaims Dipendra (now on life support) king and Gyanendra regent
	June	Death of Dipendra and accession of King Gyanendra
	June	Koirala's resignation after army's failure to engage with rebels holding captured policemen
	June	Sher Bahadur Deuba appointed prime minister and declares ceasefire
	August	Leaders of constitutional leftist parties meet Prachanda at Siliguri in West Bengal
	August	Talks begin between government and rebels
	November	Prachanda announces withdrawal from negotiations over government's refusal to concede demand for constituent assembly
	November	Rebels break ceasefire with attacks on police and (for the first time) an army barracks in Dang
	November	Declaration of state of emergency throughout country and full mobilisation of army against rebels
2002	February	Bamdev Gautam and most CPN (ML) members rejoin UML
	February	Rebel attacks on Mangalsen, district headquarters of Acham, and on nearby airfield kill around 150 soldiers and police as well as the local chief district officer
	May	Deuba obtains dissolution of parliament after clashing with Koirala over extension of state of emergency
	June	Formal split in Congress
	July	Unity Centre and Masal merge and their electoral vehicles (United People's Front and National People's Front) combine to form People's Front, Nepal
	September	Forty-nine police killed in attack on post in Sindhuli
	September	Rebels overrun Sandhikharka, district headquarters of Arghakhanchi, killing sixty security personnel
	October	Following discussions amongst political parties, Deuba formally requests king to approve postponement of the elections until November 2003

Acknowledgements

Since the contents of this book reflect many years of involvement with Nepal, very many people contributed to the final product and I must apologise for not being able to mention everyone by name. I can, however, express special thanks to a few whose help was particularly valuable. As they have done for over twenty years, Abhi Subedi and his family provided me with a home base on visits to Kathmandu and with constant help and encouragement, whilst Nirmal Tuladhar and his colleagues at Tribhuvan University were always generous with their time and suggestions. Rishikesh Shaha, another old friend and collaborator, alas died before the book was finished but it benefited from conversations with him over many years. David Gellner, who first got me involved in the project, offered constructive comments on the entire draft, whilst Prayag Raj Sharma, Harka Gurung, Chaitanya Mishra, Michael Hutt, Mark Temple and Abhi Subedi helped similarly with individual chapters. Krishna Hachhethu helped with specific queries as well as sharing his deep knowledge of contemporary Nepalese politics in general discussions. I am also grateful for assistance from Lok Raj Baral, Rhoderick Chalmers, John Cross, Kanak Mani Dixit, Will Douglas, Krishna Khanal, Dhruba Kumar, Randy LaPolla, Pancha Maharjan, Triratna Manandhar, Don Messerschmidt, Steven Mikesell, Pratyoush Onta, Greta Rana, P. J. Shah, Hari Sharma, Indira Shrestha, Deepak Tamang, Deepak Thapa and Mark Turin. Needless to say, none of those mentioned is in any way responsible for shortcomings in the book, particularly as there are many points on which we have agreed to disagree.

I would not have been able to get the illustrations together without help from Kanak Dixit and his staff at Himal, Kiyoko Ogura, Marie Lecomte-Tilouine, Padma Shrestha and Chiran Chitrakar, whilst Marigold Acland and her colleagues at Cambridge University Press coped bravely with a whole book arriving late and in bits and pieces! I should also thank the

Nepalese politicians who have kindly given me interviews over the years, including in particular Sher Bahadur Deuba, Dipak Gyawali, Girija Prasad Koirala, Chandra Prakash Mainali, Madhav Kumar Nepal, Ram Krishna Poudel, Minendra Rijal and Surya Bahadur Thapa. Last but not least, I am grateful to my wife, Rita, for constant support, despite the domestic disruption writing always brings.

Notes on romanisation and terminology

When using Nepali words in the text, I have generally followed the principles explained in my Nepal volume in the World Bibliographical Series (Whelpton 1990: xxiii–iv). The standard Indological system of transcription has been taken as a base, but diacritics have been omitted and some modifications made to come closer into line with anglicisations well established in non-technical writing, and also to reflect the actual pronunciation of Nepali as perceived by speakers of English. The main points to note are:

- 'Ch' has been used for both of the consonants respectively transcribed as 'c' and 'ch' in the Indological system or as 'ch' and 'chh' in another common style of romanisation; the difference is roughly that between the sounds of 'ch' in the English words 'exchange' and 'change'.

- 'S' is used for the dental sibilant and 'sh' for both the palatal and retroflex sibilants; the three sounds were clearly distinguished in Sanskrit but are all now pronounced by most Nepalese as a single sound somewhere between the 's' in English 'sip' and the 'sh' in 'ship'.

- Indological 'v' is represented by 'b' or 'w', according to current pronunciation, and the voiced retroflex consonant similarly transcribed as 'r' rather than 'd' when this is nearer to the actual sound (e.g. 'Pahari' rather than 'Pahadi'). I have, however, retained the original 'v' in a few words taken directly from Sanskrit, notably Vajracharya and *vamshavali*.

- Both the first and second vowels of the Devanagari script are transcribed as 'a', even though the first sound is normally pronounced either like the English 'o' in 'son' or the vowel in 'sock' whilst the second is nearer to 'a' in 'father'. Many Nepalese when romanising their own names still follow the nineteenth-century English convention of employing 'u' for the first sound, so the spellings 'Jang' and 'Shamsher' used here are often replaced by 'Jung' and 'Shumshere'. I have tried to follow individuals' own preference when they are mentioned as the writer of a book or as an informant rather than as historical characters.

Nepali terms used in the main text have been romanised on the above principle, italicised on first occurrence and defined in the Glossary (pp. 259–67).

With some misgivings, I have also decided to continue using 'Nepalese' as an adjective of nationality and reserve 'Nepali' for the language alone. I realise that this usage will strike many as old-fashioned but still feel it is appropriate to have different words for language and nation in a country as multi-lingual as Nepal. I have also retained the established English spelling 'Gurkha' when referring to Nepalese troops serving in the British army, but the more correct 'Gorkha' as an ethnic label and for Nepalese in the post-1947 Indian army.

Abbreviations

CIAA	Commission for the Investigation of the Abuse of Authority
CPN (M)	Communist Party of Nepal (Marxist)
CPN (Maoist)	Communist Party of Nepal (Maoist)
CPN (ML)	Communist Party of Nepal (Marxist-Leninist)
CPN (UML)	See UML
GAESO	Gorkha Army Ex-Servicemen's Organisation
ILO	International Labour Organization
IMF	International Monetary Fund
IRD	Integrated Rural Development
NDP	National Democratic Party
NESP	New Education System Plan
NFC	Nepal Food Corporation
NWPP	Nepal Workers' and Peasants' Party
RNAC	Royal Nepal Airlines Corporation
SAARC	South Asian Association for Regional Co-operation
SATA	Swiss Association for Technical Assistance
SLC	School Leaving Certificate
Tam.	Tamang
ULF	United Left Front
UML	Communist Party of Nepal (Unified Marxist-Leninist)
UMN	United Mission to Nepal
UNCTAD	United Nations Conference on Trade and Development
UNPM	United National People's Movement
UPF	United People's Front

Introduction

Despite its geo-strategically important position in the Himalayas between India and China and its popularity as an exotic tourist destination, Nepal has not normally loomed large in the consciousness of the average educated person in the English-speaking world. This changes briefly when the spotlight of media attention falls on the country, as during the 'People's Movement' for democracy in 1990 or with the massacre of the royal family and the intensification of the Maoist insurgency in 2001. Sudden and violent political change has indeed been a recurrent part of the country's history but should not distract attention from less dramatic, long-term processes affecting conditions of life for the majority of its people. These remain even today primarily dependent on subsistence agriculture, though they also rely increasingly on supplementary income from other activities.

Nepal as a state emerged in its present form only in the late eighteenth century when the small hill kingdom of Gorkha, some eighty miles west of Kathmandu, brought much of the Himalayan foothills and an adjoining strip of the North Indian plain under its control, and the kingdom's Shah dynasty moved its court to the Kathmandu Valley. From 1846 to 1951, though the Shahs remained on the throne, effective political power was in the hands of the Rana family, who as hereditary prime ministers were in a roughly analogous position to the Japanese shoguns before the Meiji restoration. The Rana system was eventually brought down by an alliance between the monarchy and modernising intellectuals, with decisive backing from newly independent India, and a policy of seclusion from the outside world that the country had followed throughout most of its modern history was finally abandoned. After experiments with parliamentary democracy in the 1950s, party politics were banned and power centralised in the royal palace from 1960 until the mass protests of 1990 brought about a return to the multi-party system and rule by elected governments. However, the failure of the new system to provide stable government at the centre was compounded by the growth of 'Maoist' insurgency from 1996 onwards, and deep-seated economic and social problems remain to be solved.

In order to understand a country's present, what matters is often not just the past as such, but rather the way in which that past is now understood and interpreted. Nepalese naturally differ among themselves in their interpretations, these differences often reflecting current political controversies. As in many parts of the world, however, the dominant view, enshrined in school textbooks, sees the creation of the modern state as the political unification of a people and a territory which in some sense already belonged together. A key theme of subsequent history is then the determination of the nation as a whole to preserve its unity and independence, with individual political leaders being viewed as heroes or villains to the extent that they embodied or frustrated this national will. The choice of the word 'unification' rather than 'conquest' to describe the expansion of Gorkhali power is one example of this approach, as is the eagerness of some scholars to claim the Butwal *Ramopithecus*, a primate that ranged what is now the Nepalese Tarai 11 million years ago, as a direct ancestor of early man in Nepal.

Another manifestation of this nationalist approach is a wish to date as far back as possible the beginnings of the political connection between the Kathmandu Valley, to which the name 'Nepal' originally referred,[1] and the much wider territory covered by the modern state. It is thus frequently claimed that the Licchavi dynasty which ruled in the Valley in the early centuries AD also controlled the hills up to or even beyond Nepal's current borders. This is in fact highly unlikely, but it is true that the Kathmandu Valley, with its urban civilisation and situation on a major trading route made it the only political unit of major importance in the hills between Assam and Kashmir. It is Kathmandu that looms largest in references to the area in ancient Indian and Chinese sources, and events there also tend to dominate modern histories of the country. Any history of Nepal has to be 'Kathmandu-centric' to some degree, but it is important to focus also on what was happening elsewhere, including the Tarai plains in the south where half the total population now live.

Underlying the history of both hills and plains is the complex relationship between human beings and their physical environment. The middle hills offered early settlers a refuge from the enervating heat and the greater risk of infection on the plains, factors which later led the British in India to flock to their 'hill stations'. More recently, population pressure in the hills and improved technology have made the Tarai plains more attractive. The linked problems of overpopulation and environmental degradation should not be seen simply as a product of 'modernity' undermining a supposed unchanging 'traditional' state in which people lived a simple life in harmony with nature. In fact, human pressure on the environment began long before Nepal 'opened up' in the 1950s, much of the deforestation in the hills, for example, dating back to the period of Gorkhali expansion around 1800. In addition, rapid erosion and loss of topsoil, often portrayed as a recent development, are natural consequences of the geology of the mountains and predate the arrival of any human inhabitants. Population growth began to accelerate some time before 1950 and is often attributed to the lowering of the death-rate with the reduction of internal conflict and the first effects of modern medicine. Others, however, argue that the high birth-rate is itself a natural reaction to poverty resulting from oppressive social and economic structures and from the accelerating incorporation of the hills into the subcontinental and global economy. The present situation is, in fact, the result of multiple factors and the hunt for a single cause is a misguided one.

Another key theme running through Nepalese history is the country's status as a cultural contact zone: the kingdom may have tried to close its borders to Europeans for one and a half centuries but over the millennia peoples have arrived from many different regions. Here again reality is more complex than is often realised. Focusing on a straightforward dichotomy between southern, Hindu influences and northern, Buddhist ones belies the country's great ethnic/linguistic variety, with at least seventy mutually incomprehensible languages or dialects among a population numbering only 23 million. Seeing religion in terms of a clear divide also ignores the fact that Hinduism and Buddhism grew out of a shared cultural and religious background and that of the vitality of tribal religions and shamanic traditions which are only lightly influenced by either great tradition.

Another oversimplification, which plays a role in current 'ethnic' controversies, is to regard the 'Mongol' groups, with linguistic links to Central and Eastern Asia, as 'indigenous', and the speakers of Nepali and other Indic languages as recent immigrants. Migration and the assimilation of migrants into existing populations have been going on for thousands of years, and, while the 'Mongol' stratum is on average the older one, some of the groups with cultural links to the north entered what is now Nepal later than those with affinities to the south. Above all, it has to be remembered that the language and culture of particular groups have been shaped by influences both from the north and the south. The prime example is the Newars of the Kathmandu Valley, who speak a Tibeto-Burman language, but whose urban civilisation in many ways reflects that of Hindu India before the Muslim conquests.

Just as Nepal straddles the boundary between the cultures of the 'Sinosphere' and the 'Indosphere', the modern kingdom has since its foundation had to survive as a buffer state between the much larger states of China and India. Until about the middle of the nineteenth century, the power that the Qing emperors could exert in the Himalayas was roughly equivalent to that of the British East India Company, and Nepal thus had leeway for playing one side off against the other. With the consolidation of British control over the whole of India and the growing enfeeblement of China, this stance was replaced for a century by Nepal's alignment with its southern neighbour. There was a limited reversion to earlier tactics after the establishment of the People's Republic of China in 1949 and its assertion of authority over Tibet. However, the scope for this was and is limited both because contact on a people-to-people basis is much greater with India and, even more, because it is on India that land-locked Nepal is primarily dependent economically.

A fourth important motif in the history of modern Nepal is the development among its people of a sense of common identity. Without accepting the more extreme claims of nationalist historians, it can certainly be argued that, among at least some sections of the population, this started even before the reception, largely through British India, of Western conceptions of the nation-state. The building blocks were a sense of belonging to the hills rather than the Indian plains; shared cultural characteristics, including a particular brand of Hinduism and what is now known as the Nepali language; and loyalty to the state and to the dynasty that had founded it. These feelings could in the beginning be fully shared only by those most closely (and most advantageously) associated with Gorkha and its ruling elite, and they excluded in particular the people of the Tarai. They nevertheless did form a core that others could later join.

How complete and satisfactory this process of nation-building has been is another contentious issue in present-day Nepal. Even the most radical opponents of the present Nepalese state share with the establishment a sense of 'Nepaleseness' based on separateness from India, just as Irish, Portuguese or Ukrainian nationalism rests to a considerable degree on *not* being English, Spanish or Russian. There is much less agreement on the value of the positive factors listed above, and some, including today's Maoist rebels, argue they should be abandoned in favour of a secular republic affording equal recognition to the country's many languages and cultures. Such controversies shape the way in which history is viewed, as ethnic activists and others seek to highlight the coercive elements in the foundation and building of the state and to challenge the 'establishment' view emphasising the role of consensus and of peaceful assimilation to the dominant culture.

The study of the past is for many a worthwhile activity in its own right. However, particularly for the general reader, for whom this series is chiefly intended, there is a hope of gaining from a country's history a deeper understanding of its present and of its future potential. I have tried to keep this broader objective in mind and to make allowances for the kinds of conflict of perspective that I have just outlined. I am aware, though, that all writers, foreigners as much as Nepalese themselves, must remain to some extent prisoners of their own particular biases. I can therefore only ask for a critical assessment both of this volume and of the more detailed works to which I hope readers will later turn.

CHAPTER I

Environment, state and society in the central Himalayas to 1743

THE PHYSICAL ARENA

The history of the Himalayas began with the slow collision of what is now the Indian subcontinent with Central Asia. About 70 million years ago, this forced rock strata upwards to form the mountains along Tibet's southern rim, which are still today the watershed between the Ganges and Tsangpo/Brahmaputra river systems.[1] Between 16 and 10 million years ago, further movements produced to the south the main Himalayan range and, to their south, the middle hills – a confusion of interrupted ridges and spurs, which in Nepal still form the cultural and political heart of the country. At around the same time the Tibetan mountains rose further and then, between 800,000 and 500,000 years ago, the main Himalayan peaks were again uplifted to tower far above them. Subsequent movements produced the Mahabharat hills along the southern edge of the middle hills and the Siwalik (or Chure) range slightly further south along the edge of the Gangetic plain. This shifting of the earth's crust continues today and different sections of the Himalayas are still rising at rates of between 5 millimetres and 1 centimetre per year.

The rise of the Mahabharats and the Siwaliks temporarily dammed some of the rivers flowing south towards the Ganges, forming lakes in the valleys between the two ranges and also in the Kathmandu Valley. The Kathmandu lake may have dried up only 100,000 years ago, by which time its shores were almost certainly inhabited. The mythical account of the draining of the Valley by Manjushri (Buddhist version) or Pradyumna (Hindu version), like the similar myths encountered all along the Himalayas, could just conceivably represent an oral tradition dating back more than 3000 generations. It is, though, more likely that the myth-makers simply drew their conclusion from the lie of the land. By way of comparison, there is a Chinese folk story about a land link between Taiwan and the mainland, which were in fact joined until around 8000 BC, but no folk memory of

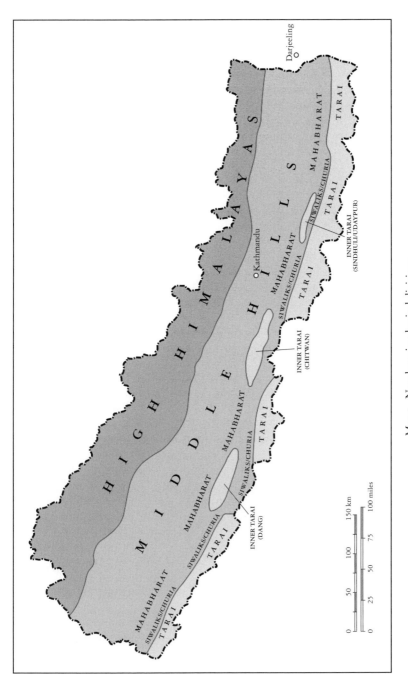

Map 1. Nepal: main physical divisions.

the land bridge between Britain and mainland Europe, which existed until about 7000 BC.

The movement of the earth had other, more lasting consequences. Further north, as the main Himalayan range rose, the force of the rivers was sufficient for them to maintain their course, cutting deeper and deeper down to form the world's most spectacular gorges. Through these flow the headwaters of Nepal's three main river systems: from west to east, the Karnali, the Gandaki and the Kosi. Young mountains are easily eroded so loss of topsoil and its deposition further south formed the deep, rich alluvium of the Ganges plain, covering the bedrock to a depth of almost two miles. A ten- to thirty-mile-wide strip of this plain is now included within Nepal's southern borders and is known as the Tarai (low, marshy ground). Together with the valleys of the inner Tarai between the Churia and Mahabharat ranges, this area now grows most of the country's food and contains almost half of its population. Along the western section of its northern border, Nepal also includes a slice of the arid land in the rainshadow of the main Himalayan peaks.

PEOPLES AND MIGRATIONS

As well as producing wide variation in local climate and soil conditions, the rugged terrain has also worked to preserve cultural differences. Something of the resulting variety is summarised in table 1.1, which shows groups within the population normally regarded as ethnic as well as the castes into which some of these groups are subdivided. Significantly, the distinction between an ethnic group and a caste is not really recognised in colloquial Nepali, which uses *jat* (perhaps best translated as 'descent group') for both.

The Parbatiyas ('people of the mountains'), whose culture has always dominated the Nepalese state, were the original speakers of what is now known as Nepali. This is one of the Indo-Aryan languages, whose speakers make up the great majority of the population of central and northern India as well as Pakistan and Bangladesh. Nepali is about as similar to Hindi, the national language of India, as is Spanish to Italian. There is a particularly close relationship between the more formal, literary styles, as both languages borrow technical terms directly from Sanskrit, the classical language of India.

The Parbatiyas' linguistic ancestors were the Khasas, a people who had entered the subcontinent from the north-west, migrating into the hills either directly from the steppelands of western Eurasia or via the Iranian plateau. The Khasas probably first penetrated the Himalayas west of Nepal

Table 1.1 *Major ethnic and caste divisions*

(1) **Parbatiyas** (Nepali-speaking) (40.3%)

Twice-born:	**Brahmans**	12.9%
	Thakuris	1.6%
	Chetris (formerly **Khasas**)	16.1%
Renouncers:	Dashnami Sanyasis and Kanphata Yogis	1.0%
Untouchables:	Kamis (metal-workers)	5.2%
	Damais (tailors)	2.0%
	Sarkis (cobblers)	1.5%

(2) **Newars** (Newar- or Nepali-speaking) (5.6%)[a]

Entitled to full religious initiation:[b]

Brahmans	0.1%	Vajracharyas/Shakyas	0.6%
Shresthas	1.1%	Uray (Tuladhars etc.)	0.4%
Other pure castes:	**Maharjans (Jyapus)**	2.3%	
	Ekthariyas and other small groups	0.7%	
Impure castes:	Khadgis (Kasais), Dyahlas (Podes) etc.	0.4%	

(3) Other hill or mountain ethnic groups ('tribes')
(speaking other Tibeto-Burman languages or Nepali) (20.9%)

Magars	7.2%	**Limbus**	1.6%	Bhotiyas	0.1%
Tamangs	5.5%	**Sherpas**	0.6%	Thakalis	0.1%
Rais	2.8%	Chepangs	0.2%	Thamis	0.1%
Gurungs	2.4%	Sunuwars	0.2%		

(4) **Madheshis** (speaking north Indian dialects, including Awadhi, Bhojpuri and Maithili) (32.0%)

(a) Castes (16.1%)

Twice-born:	**Brahmans**	1.0%
	Rajputs	0.3%
	Kayasthas **(Kshatriyas)**	0.3%
	Rajbhats	0.2%
	Baniyas (Vaishyas)	0.5%
Other pure castes:	**Yadavs**/Ahirs (herdsmen)	4.1%
	Kushawahas (vegetable-growers)	1.1%
	Kurmis (cultivators)	0.9%
	Mallahs (fishermen)	0.6%
	Kewats (fishermen)	0.5%
	Kumhars (potters)	0.3%
	Halwais (confectioners)	0.2%
Impure, but touchable:	Kalawars (brewers/merchants)	0.9%
	Dhobis (washermen)	0.4%
	Telis (oil-pressers)	0.4%

(*cont.*)

Table 1.1 *(cont.)*

Untouchable:	Chamars (leather-workers)	1.1%
	Dushadhs (basket-makers)	0.5%
	Khatawes (labourers)	0.4%
	Musahars (labourers)	0.8%
(b) Ethnic groups (9.0 %):		
Inner Tarai:	Kumals	0.4%
	Majhis	0.3%
	Danuwars	0.3%
	Darais	0.1%
Tarai proper:	**Tharus**	6.5%
	Dhanukas	0.7%
	Rajbamshis	0.4%
	Gangais	0.1%
	Dhimals	0.1%
(c) **Muslims** (3.3%)		
(d) **Marwaris** (0.2%)		
(e) Sikhs (0.1%)		

Notes and sources: Based on data in the 1991 census (Nepal, Central Bureau of Statistics 1993: II, part VII, tab. 25) and analyses by Harka Gurung (Gurung 1994: tab. 1; Salter and Gurung 1996: tab. 1) and Mark Gaborieau (1978). The largest and/or most important groups are shown in bold. The table excludes the 1.0 per cent of the population who were native to the hills but not placed in any specific category in the census. The subtotal of 32.0 per cent for Madheshis (section 4) includes 3.6 per cent of the population who were recorded as Tarai natives but were similarly left unclassified. There are other small discrepancies in subtotal because of roundings and because groups constituting less than 0.1 per cent of the population have been omitted.
[a] Harka Gurung treats the Newars as a single group. Figures for the main subdivisions are taken from Gaborieau 1978: 198–206.
[b] Shown in parallel columns because there are separate blocks of Hindu (l.) and Buddhist (r.) upper castes, neither of which recognises the other's superior status. See also p. 31.

around 1000 BC and moved through the hills to reach the Karnali basin early in the first millennium AD, displacing or assimilating the existing population. In the centuries after AD 1000, they were joined by a small number of Rajputs, ruling clans from Rajasthan in western India, who fled into the hills to escape the Muslim invaders. The Rajputs were the descendants of the Gurjaras, who had risen to power in India just before the arrival of the Muslims and may have in fact originally come from the hill country. By late medieval times, the ruling families in the hills of central and western Nepal, known as Thakuris, were claiming descent from these Rajput refugees, usually from the dynasty controlling Mewar, whose fortress at Chittaur fell to Muslim besiegers in 1303 and again in 1568.

Although a considerable amount of immigration from the plains did occur, in many cases Khasa rulers and also perhaps members of Tibeto-Burman groups dominant in a particular area had simply provided themselves with a suitably prestigious ancestry, as happened frequently throughout South Asia. Rajput blood, real or imagined, was to remain an important status symbol and this may even have been a factor in Crown Prince Dipendra's murder of his family in 2001: Queen Aishwarya is said by some to have thought the woman he wanted to marry was not a true Rajput.

The rulers' suspect genealogies were generally composed by Brahman priests who also claimed plains origins. Brahman immigration did occur, but many present-day Nepalese Brahman surnames point rather to local origin. Genuine medieval migrants also include the Churautes, a North Indian caste whose members entered the foothills between the fourteenth and eighteenth centuries after converting to Islam. Quite possibly the Doms, as the Untouchable hill castes are known in western Nepal and in the Indian Himalayas across the border, are also later arrivals, rather than the descendants of a conquered, pre-Khasa population.

Many, though not all, of the other ethnic groups in the Nepal hills were there before the Khasas, but it is difficult to date their arrival. In some cases it may be very early, given the archaeological evidence discussed below. Recent genetic research suggests that in general the bearers of new cultures and languages tend to assimilate rather than totally displace earlier populations, and so Nepalese from many different ethnic groups will be at least partly descended from those earliest inhabitants. If we simply look for groups who have preserved their own distinct culture on Nepalese soil for the longest time, the obvious candidates must be among the very small numbers who still live as hunter-gatherers on the margins of an overwhelmingly agricultural society. One such people, the Kusundas, a handful of whom survive in the Mahabharat hills, have borrowed many words from their Tibeto-Burman-speaking neighbours, but the core of their language may still represent the oldest linguistic stratum in Nepal. Most scholars regard Kusunda as a linguistic isolate like Basque in Europe, unrelated to any other known language, but it is possibly a distant relation of languages now spoken in Papua New Guinea and the Andaman Islands.[2] Another hunter-gatherer group, the better-known Rautes, now speak a recognisably Tibeto-Burman language but are probably also the continuation of a distinct pre-Tibeto-Burman population. The Tharus of the Tarai are now agriculturalists and their speech has almost totally converged with local Indo-Aryan dialects, even though language activists often claim to speak 'Tharu'. Nevertheless their speech does show traces of a pre-Tibeto-Burman language.

Other possible forerunners of Tibeto-Burman in Nepal are Munda, the western branch of the Austroasiatic family, and Dravidian, the family to which the major languages of South India belong. Munda and Dravidian are now represented in Nepal only by the small and dwindling number of persons in the eastern Tarai speaking Sant(h)ali/Satar and Kurukh (also known as Dhangar or Jhangar) respectively, but there is evidence that related languages were once spoken widely in northern India. Most Austroasiatic languages (including the best-known, Vietnamese) are nowadays found in South-east Asia, so Munda-speaking peoples presumably spread towards the west from north-eastern India. Dravidian languages, which show evidence of contact with ancient Mesopotamian languages, probably spread into South Asia from the north-west.

Tibeto-Burman-speaking peoples are the largest linguistic grouping in the Nepalese hills after the Parbatiyas. Tibeto-Burman forms one branch of the Sino-Tibetan family which probably originated in western China. Members of this branch who speak Tibetan dialects are known in Nepal as Bhotiyas (from the Nepali word for Tibet), and they clearly reached their present homes over the high passes directly from the north. One such group, the Sherpas of the Solukhumbu region beneath Everest, possesses written records of their migration in 1531–3. The Sherpas' own oral traditions suggest that they displaced the Rais, who still occupy the hills further south. In any case Solukhumbu had already been inhabited for many centuries: 2000-year-old cereal pollen has been discovered there, as well as evidence that much of the region's present-day open grassland was cleared of forest cover at least 400 to 800 years ago.

Earlier arrivals from Tibet were the Tamangs, the largest ethnic group in the hills surrounding the Kathmandu Valley; the Gurungs, mainly found in Lamjung, Kaski and Gorkha districts; and the Thakalis who live along the Kali Gandaki Valley south of Jomosom. The languages of these peoples are clearly closely related to one another and, while not actually varieties of Tibetan, are closer to it than are most other Nepalese Tibeto-Burman languages. This similarity later helped many individual Tamangs 'pass' as Gurungs, an advantage as the latter group enjoyed greater prestige and was considered fit for military employment. All three peoples were probably once a single ethnic group and the split has been dated on rather speculative linguistic grounds to the fourth century AD. One recent theory is that the common ancestors of this group and the Tibetans had much earlier travelled eastwards along the north side of the Himalayas from Kashmir, where the 'northern neolithic' culture which developed from 3000 BC onwards had some similarities with the northern Chinese neolithic.

According to an account drawing on Gurung oral tradition, their ancestors settled about 2000 years ago in Mustang and crossed to the south side of the Himalayas around AD 500.[3] This would coincide with a general expansion of speakers of Tibetan at about this time. Kohla Sombre, a ruined village remembered as the site of the first Gurung settlement on the south side of Annapurna was probably inhabited for between 70 and 150 years in the twelfth and thirteenth centuries. The buildings seemingly had flat roofs, the standard design in arid areas to the north of the Himalayan peaks.

With other Tibeto-Burman peoples the picture is less clear. They may have come from either the east or, less likely, the west. Those found in eastern Nepal, where the Tibeto-Burman proportion is highest, are collectively known as 'Kiranti'. They include the well-known Rais and Limbus as well as smaller groups such as the Sunuwars and Chepangs, and their own myths show their acknowledgement of a common origin. 'Kiranti' derives from the Sanskrit 'Kirata', the name applied in the classical Indian texts to the Tibeto-Burman hill peoples generally. The *vamshavalis* (chronicles) of the Kathmandu Valley claim that Kiratas ruled there before the Indianised Licchavis came to power early in the first millennium AD.

Kiranti legends suggest that eastern Nepal was mainly populated by a series of expansions from Assam, and that the different groups moved west along the Tarai before penetrating the Arun Valley and other routes into the hills. There are similarities in culture between the two regions and also strong resemblances between Kiranti languages and the Rong languages found in Yunnan and Burma. There could thus have been a migration (or series of migrations) from south-west China through the Tsangpo/Brahmaputra gorge into Assam with some of the migrants then moving on into Nepal. Although it is much less likely that the Kiranti or other Tibeto-Burman speakers originally came from the west, the flow of people does seem to have turned eastwards at one time. The evidence of river names suggests that both Rai and Magar dialects were once spoken in areas of western Nepal that are now exclusively Nepali-speaking; there are also oral traditions among some Rai groups of migration from the Karnali basin. Eastward movement may have occurred under pressure from the advancing Khasas, or for climatic reasons: although there are wide microregional variations, rainfall generally increases towards the south-east and, in periods of drought, it would have been the logical direction to move.

Many ethnic groups in the hills could actually have been formed by the fusion of groups entering the area from different directions. The Rais are particularly heterogeneous and the term 'Rai' itself seems to have been applied by Nepali-speakers to Kiranti groups that could not fit into a more specific category. In the mid-western hills, origin myths of the northern (or Kham) Magars, the ethnic group who formed much of the support base for Nepal's Maoists, tell of a merger between one clan originating locally and others from 'Mongolia'. Multiple origin is even more obvious for the Magars as a whole. The Kham Magar language itself is very different from that of most southern Magars, while other Magar groups speak dialects very close to Gurung. The term 'Magar' was perhaps once simply a prestigious title that was adopted by numerous otherwise unconnected groups.

Although the Newars of the Kathmandu Valley speak a Tibeto-Burman language, they are usually treated separately from the various hill groups because of their long tradition of urbanisation and because, like the Parbatiyas, they have a caste system. Linguists argue about whether their language is more closely related to Kiranti or to Gurung-Tamang-Thakali and, while most scholars see Newar society as a continuation of that of the Kiratas who once dominated the Valley, the Newars, too, are an amalgamation of different peoples. The largest Newar caste, the Maharjan agriculturalists, nowadays regard themselves as indigenous, but many other castes have traditions of migration, some of which will be genuine. The word 'Newar' itself is related to the Newar 'Nepa' and the Sanskrit 'Nepala', which originally designated just the Kathmandu Valley.[4] The Newars were thus simply the 'people of the Valley', wherever they had originally come from.

The final major population category of the country is the Madheshis – the people of the plains. The term is reserved for those whose ancestors have long lived in the Tarai and who share language and culture with those living south of the Indian border, thus excluding the hill Nepalese who have settled in large numbers in the Tarai in recent decades. Although the Madheshis are often regarded by the hillmen as a single group, the Tarai has traditionally been home to caste Hindus, to a substantial Muslim minority (especially in the western districts) and to various ethnic groups ('tribes'). The largest of the latter, the Tharus, are of particularly diverse origin and probably had no sense of collective identity until very recently. They were regarded as a single group by outsiders because of their association with the Tarai jungles and particularly because of their immunity to the *aul*, a virulent form of malaria prevalent there until the 1950s and often preventing year-round settlement by other groups.

The Indo-Aryan dialects spoken by the Madheshis were brought into North India from the north-west. The main wave of migration down the Ganges Valley commenced probably towards the end of the second millennium BC, and one of the principal routes lay along the base of the hills on the northern edge of the Tarai, probably because it was easier to clear forest for agriculture there than nearer the Ganges itself. For caste Hindus, and now also for most of the 'tribals', the Tarai forms a dialect continuum with speech changing gradually from one village to the next, and no sharp divisions between one language and another. However, it is usual to recognise three main varieties: from west to east, Awadhi, Bhojpuri and Maithili, the last of which has the largest number of speakers in Nepal after Nepali itself.

The Tarai became less important later on as the focus moved nearer to the Ganges itself. There is a widespread oral tradition among both Hindus and Muslims living there today that their ancestors moved into the area only about 200 years ago, which was around the time of the Gorkhali conquest of the Kathmandu Valley. However, the region was certainly affected by the waves of Muslim invaders from AD 1000 onwards. States based in the plains came under Muslim control while, at least from the fifteenth century onwards, hill rajas with land holdings in the plains were required to pay tribute. Muslims who settled as cultivators were, however, overwhelmingly the descendants of Hindu converts rather than Turks, Afghans or Arabs.

HUNTERS, HERDERS AND FARMERS

The earliest evidence of human activity in Nepal is provided by 'hand-axes' (really a kind of stone scraper) found in the valleys of the Inner Tarai, between the Siwalik and Mahabharat ranges. These are at least 100,000 years old and were used by *Homo erectus*, the predecessor of the Neanderthals and of modern man. These prehistoric hunter-gatherers presumably lived on the shores of the lakes formed as the hills were uplifted. A similar environment must have existed around the lake which once filled much of the Kathmandu Valley. Fossils discovered there include those of an alligator and a hippopotamus.

From early on, Nepal was a meeting point for different traditions. The earliest tools discovered in the Kathmandu Valley, dating from around 30,000 years ago, show Central Asian features, and tools of similar age from the western Tarai resemble Indian ones. A Mesolithic site in the Rato Khola valley in Mahottari (eastern Tarai), dating from 5000 BC or earlier, has some similarities with the Hoabinhian culture of Vietnam. Neolithic tools found in different parts of the country and dating from the second millennium BC generally resemble Assamese types but in the Dang Valley in the western inner Tarai they follow a different, North Indian pattern. It is impossible to identify the carriers of particular neolithic cultures, but it is tempting to speculate that Assamese influence could be the result of Munda-speaking farmers moving further afield as food production boosted their numbers. A similar process could have brought Dravidians or others into the Tarai from the north-west.

Tool discoveries so far suggest the introduction of agriculture had occurred in some parts of Nepal by 2000 BC. The herding of animals, the other component of the Neolithic Revolution, will probably have been introduced at about the same time, and the earliest remembered dynasties in the Kathmandu Valley are supposed to have been buffalo- and cow-herders. Both crop planting and animal husbandry might have started even before the third millennium BC in view of their early introduction in neighbouring regions: for example, barley and rice were probably being grown in northern India before 6000 BC.

The earliest Nepalese farmers burnt and cut away the forest to clear an area for planting, then moved on to a different site so that soil fertility was not exhausted. In many areas slash-and-burn agriculture was still widespread until well into the nineteenth century. It was often combined with hunting and herding and the Gurungs appear from their own oral traditions to have been basically wandering shepherds until about the seventeenth century. Intensive, sedentary cultivation, with a central place for wet-rice cultivation, was first introduced in areas of the Tarai and then in the Kathmandu Valley. Within the Himalayan foothills it had established itself by the twelfth–fourteenth centuries AD in the Karnali basin, where the main slopes were probably denuded of forest cover by the eighteenth century. Wet-rice spread with the Parbatiyas, and in the eastern hills it may have been established only in the seventeenth century, probably not becoming of major importance until around 200 years ago. In areas of the hills where the Parbatiyas settled, paddy was planted on fertile, low-lying valley bottoms while the higher slopes were generally planted with non-irrigated crops, particularly millet and (on a large scale from the eighteenth century onwards) maize.[5] Further north, in areas more 'Tibetan' in culture, the mix was most typically barley, wheat and buckwheat.

In the Kathmandu Valley the early-established staple crops included rice, wheat, garlic, onions, radishes and pulses. New World crops such as chillies, potatoes and maize were introduced in the seventeenth or eighteenth centuries from India, where they had been brought by European traders. Innovations were thus adopted but could meet with initial suspicion. This was the case with the arrival of unfamiliar maize seed at Bhaktapur, then an independent city-state within the Valley, in the early seventeenth century. According to a nineteenth-century *vamshavali* the new grain was sent back

1. The Gurung village of Ghandrung beneath Annapurna. Maize, an important crop in the hills since the eighteenth century, is drying on the platforms in the foreground.

out of fear it might cause a famine. In the nineteenth century, maize was regarded by upper-caste Newars as food for animals, but it was often eaten by the lower castes.

The main techniques of agricultural production employed in the Tarai and in the more fertile parts of the hills had evolved on the Ganges plain around the middle of the first millennium BC. At about this time iron implements began to be used extensively for forest clearance and particularly for ploughshares. This enabled the heavier soils to be exploited more efficiently, while the introduction of new varieties of rice and of improvements in transplanting techniques allowed substantial growth in population. Maximum productivity could be achieved in the most favourable areas by growing two or three crops in a single year in one field, a practice known in India even in Vedic times (c. 1500–800 BC). In the hills, low population levels meant that multiple-cropping was not necessary and it did not become general there until the late twentieth century. The more intensive method was, however, probably adopted early on in the Kathmandu Valley, where there was a greater density of settlement, although population growth was restrained by natural calamities.

The Newar Maharjans, who were the principal cultivators of the Kathmandu Valley, did not generally adopt the plough but continued to rely chiefly on their traditional hoe-like *ku*. This was generally more effective than the Indian scratch plough for breaking up heavy clay soil before planting, and it is mainly for this reason that the plough was not used in most parts of the Valley. However, Maharjans themselves now generally claim that they avoid ploughing because it is sinful to use the bullock in this way, and in places such as the Banepa Valley where it *would* be advantageous to use the plough, they refrain from doing so.

STATE FORMATION IN THE ANCIENT AND MEDIEVAL PERIODS

The remoter parts of the subcontinent, including much of present-day Nepal, remained organised on a lineage basis, either completely outside or only loosely connected to a state, throughout the ancient and medieval periods. However, in the middle of the first millennium BC, the Ganges Valley, and in particular the region of Magadha (Bihar), saw the emergence of kingdoms whose rulers did not claim kinship with their subjects and who extracted taxation on a regular basis. After a long struggle, the Magadhan monarchs succeeded in subduing tribal confederacies in the Nepalese Tarai, among which the Licchavis and the Shakyas are the best known. It was against this background that Siddhartha Gautama Buddha (born c. 400 BC), a Shakya, established the religion which bears his name.

By early in the first millennium AD, a state on the new North Indian model had emerged in Nepal, controlling the Valley and probably also the hills between the Trisuli in the west and the Sun Kosi in the east. The rulers called themselves Licchavi but it is uncertain whether their claim to descent from the Licchavis of the plains is genuine. Even assuming that it is, we do not know whether the ruling family was accompanied in their migration from the plains by any substantial number of followers. There is no doubt, however, of the cultural links with the Vaisali region: there are similarities between pottery found at Dumakhal in the Valley and at Basarh, the ancient Vaisali. In addition, ancient place names suggest a link with the Kolis and Vrijis, members of the confederation of peoples in the Tarai to which the original Licchavis belonged.

The rulers' public pronouncements, which form the major part of the surviving inscriptions of the period, also faithfully reflect Indian developments. The earliest substantial inscription, that of Manadeva at Changu Narayan dating from AD 465, describes how the king persuaded his mother not to end her own life when his father died. This is probably the first reference to *sati* (widow-burning) in any South Asian inscription. The earliest in India is a monument at Sagar (Madhya Pradesh) erected in AD 510. For good or ill, the Licchavi state was abreast, or even slightly ahead, of trends in the south, and the matrimonial links of later rulers with prominent North Indian families suggest that those in the south accepted the Licchavis as their equals.

The Valley's strategic importance and its flourishing commerce, which greatly impressed Chinese visitors in the seventh century, rested on its location on a major trans-Himalayan route. With the establishment of a united Tibetan kingdom under Srong-tsen-Gampo (reigned c. 627–49), the Banepa–Kuti and Rasuwa–Kirong routes into Tibet became important links between India and China. Although some historians doubt the existence of Bhritkuti, the Nepali princess who Tibetan sources claim married Srong-tsen-Gampo, there was certainly a strong political connection. When in around 624 the legitimate Licchavi ruler was ousted by the rival Gupta family, he fled to Tibet and regained the throne with Tibetan military assistance. Nepal probably then became a Tibetan dependency until a revolt at the beginning of the next century.[6] In 647, after a Chinese envoy had been maltreated by an Indian ruler, he obtained help from both Nepal and Tibet to launch a punitive expedition.

During the eighth century, central control over the Valley apparently weakened and the Licchavi line ended. From the late tenth to the middle of the eleventh century *dvairajya* (simultaneous rule by two individuals) was common, as it had been at times during the Licchavi period. This Sanskrit term could refer either to an actual division of territory or to joint rule by the two kings over the whole kingdom, the latter arrangement sometimes being referred to in Nepal by the special term *ubayarajya*. However, the monarchy remained the central institution throughout the medieval period, which is conventionally regarded as starting with the establishment of the Nepal Era in 879. It is uncertain why it was decided to start reckoning the years from this new starting point, but the Nepal Era has now become a symbol of Newar cultural identity and each new year is marked with a

2. A statue of Garuda, the mythical man-bird who carried the god Vishnu. The face may be that of Manadeva, the Licchavi ruler whose inscription of 465 AD begins the recorded history of the Kathmandu Valley.

motorcycle rally around the Kathmandu Valley. The Valley's main centres, Kathmandu, Patan and Bhaktapur, emerged as urban settlements through the amalgamation of existing villages in the early medieval centuries. In 1200, a new king, Ari Malla, was the first to adopt the suffix 'Malla', an honorific title which was probably initially used by the Pallava dynasty of southern India. The 600 years to Prithvi Narayan's conquest of the Valley in 1768–9 are consequently referred to as the 'Malla period'.

Throughout the Licchavi and medieval period, the kings had to reckon with powerful subordinates who might become a threat to royal power. In Licchavi times these were principally the *samantas*, a term which originally meant a neighbouring ruler but then came to be used for a subordinate one, normally a ruler in a peripheral region that had been brought under the king's control. The title then seems to have been extended to powerful courtiers even if they had never ruled a separate territory of their own. Amsuvarman, who became co-ruler with a Licchavi king at the end of the sixth century and finally sole ruler, is first referred to in inscriptions as the *mahasamanta* (great *samanta*). The *samantas* are commemorated in modern Nepali by the word for 'feudalism' (*samantabad*), but during the medieval period the title dropped out of use and nobles outside the main cities were most commonly known as *bharos*, a title first recorded at the beginning of the eleventh century. At the top of the social order in Kathmandu and Patan, though seemingly not Bhaktapur, were the *pradhans* or (*maha*)*patras*. It has been argued that both country and city nobles were a court aristocracy owing their position to royal favour rather than the independent local power base that some of the *samantas* had possessed. This was probably not true of the *pradhans*: in particular at Patan they were immensely influential and acting as kingmakers as early as 1099. They may have been successors to the headmen of the smaller settlements that had been merged to form the cities. Whatever their origins, the *bharos* also could be a powerful force. They were certainly a numerous class: 1700 of them assembled to swear fealty to Jayasthiti Malla in 1383.

From 1255, politics were dominated by the rivalry of two important *bharo* families associated respectively with the Tripura Palace in Bhaktapur and with the Banepa region (Bhonta). Strife between them was accompanied by attacks from outside. For half a century from 1288 the Valley was frequently raided by the Nepali-speaking Khasas from the Karnali basin and Maithili-speaking Doyas from the Tarai. There was finally a short but highly destructive incursion by Shams ud-din Ilyas, Muslim ruler of Bengal, in 1349. In 1311 the Bhonta family had actually called in the Doyas as a means of putting pressure on their Tripura rivals, and there may have been other occasions when the raiders acted in collusion with a faction within the Valley. The pattern foreshadowed what was to happen during Prithvi Narayan's siege of the Valley in the eighteenth century, and, to a lesser extent, during the Maoist 'People's War' in the twentieth.

Although the Doyas seemed at this point to have been Bhonta's allies, a few years later Rudra Malla, head of the Tripura family and de facto ruler of the Valley, arranged the marriage of his sister, Devaladevi, to the Doya ruler, Harisimha. In 1336, threatened by the forces of the Delhi Sultanate, Harisimha fled into the hills where he died before reaching the Valley. Devaladevi assumed leadership of Tripura and married her granddaughter to Jayasthiti Malla, probably a Maithil nobleman. Jayasthiti Malla's acknowledgement as ruler of the Valley in 1382 restored strong central control, but, following the death of his grandson Yaksha in 1482, an arrangement for his sons and nephews to rule collectively broke down and Kathmandu, Patan and Bhaktapur eventually emerged as independent city-states.

Within the Valley states, politics in the later medieval period was as intrigue-ridden as before and frequently entangled with inter-state relations given the proximity of the three cities to each other and the family ties between rulers. Power was frequently in the hands of queen regents or ministers. The most famous of the latter was Lakshminarayan Joshi of Kathmandu, who at the climax of his career came close to dominating the whole Valley. According to his enemies (whose version of events is preserved in the surviving sources), Joshi poisoned King Parthivendra (ruled 1680–7), seduced his queen and arranged at least two other murders before his own assassination in 1690.

Although the wealth and sophistication of the Valley was unrivalled in the hills, it was nevertheless part of a wider network of states. The Khasas, whose raids into the Valley have already been noted, had established an empire which at its greatest extent covered some 142,000 square kilometres, compared to the 200,000 that would be included in the later Gorkhali empire. Centred in the Karnali basin, it also included south-eastern Tibet and parts of Kumaon. Because Khasa rulers adopted the Malla title in imitation of its use in the Valley, their state is sometimes referred to as the Malla empire, although they were not related to the Newar Malla kings. The Khasa state's economy rested on the development of wet-rice cultivation in the main river valleys. It has been argued that this was possible on a large scale only because the Khasa rulers were strong enough to conscript labour for the construction of irrigation facilities. The state's role here was certainly important but in some cases the cultivators probably organised this among themselves without government intervention.

After the Khasa empire fragmented around the beginning of the fifteenth century, a network of statelets emerged in the western and central hills. There are slight variations in the lists in the various sources but those in the Karnali basin were conventionally known as the *baisi* ('twenty-two') and in the Gandaki basin as the *chaubisi* ('twenty-four'). While some of the new rulers were genuine refugees from the plains, others were really of Khasa or Magar origin, though claims and counterclaims make it impossible to be sure of the true origins of any particular family. The Sen rulers of Palpa and Makwanpur are referred to as Magars in documents from the Kathmandu Valley and from Sikkim. The Shahs of Gorkha were also sometimes described as Magars and the names Kancha and Micha, which occur in the genealogy linking the dynasty to the brother of a Chittaur ruler perhaps support this. The ruler of Baldeng (near present-day Butwal), overthrown by Palpa and other *chaubisi* states around 1700, was also supposedly a Magar.

Genuine Rajput newcomers were not necessarily simply fleeing Muslim wrath. The traditional dates for the foundation of many Rajput states both in Nepal and India are around the end of the fifteenth century – the kingdom of Palpa, for example, is said to have been established in 1493. This period saw a general agrarian expansion in South Asia as a whole, together with a progressive monetisation of the economy. Against this background, individuals failing to find a niche in plains areas immediately south of Nepal may have decided to carve out lordships for themselves in the foothills. The founder of Palpa's Sen dynasty may be an example of this: according to one version of the story, he moved north from Allahabad into the Tarai and then into the hills rather than directly from Rajasthan.

Newcomers from the plains sometimes established themselves by outright conquest but often more by a process of infiltration, offering their services to one section of the existing population in quarrels with another. Drabya Shah, younger brother of the king of the *chaubisi* state of Lamjung and ancestor of Nepal's ruling dynasty, took control of Gorkha in 1559 by the violent removal of the existing chieftain, who was either a Khasa or a member of one of the Tibeto-Burman groups. In contrast, further west in Musikot, there was probably a split between Magar lineages, one of which turned to the newcomers for military assistance.

The kingdom of Palpa, the largest of the states in the central hills, broke up on the death of Mukunda Sen in 1553. One of his sons received

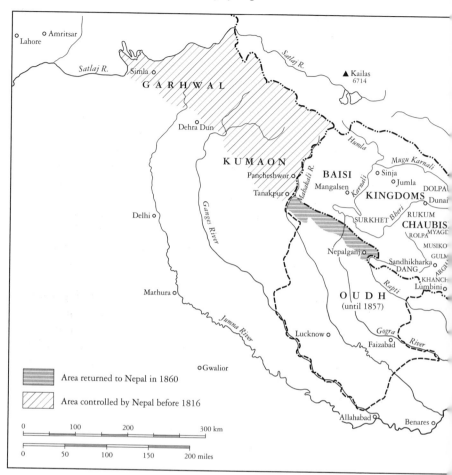

Map 2. Nepal and neighbouring regions.

Makwanpur to the south of the Kathmandu Valley, and then seized control of Vijaypur, a kingdom centred near Dharan. Although he was thus master of the entire eastern Tarai, by the middle of the eighteenth century 'greater Makwanpur' had again fragmented into four states. In Vijaypur, Sen power depended on Maithil Brahman administrators but even more on support from the Limbus of the eastern hills. The Limbus provided military man-power and also a hereditary chief minister, while remaining autonomous in their own lands. Vijaypur clashed from time to time with neighbouring

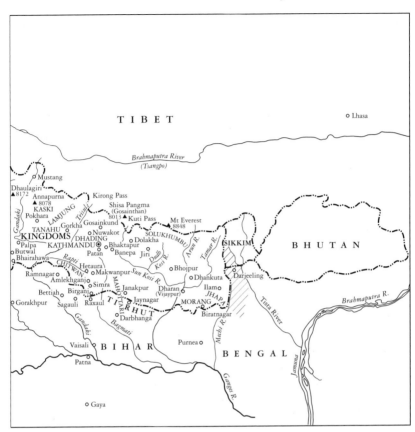

Map 2. (cont.)

Sikkim, where a Tibetan prince (the first Chogyal) had established himself in 1640. The boundary between the two states was not a clear line even in the Tarai and the situation was still more fluid in the hills. Sikkim's rulers claimed sovereignty as far west as the Arun, and Bhotiya *gowas* (chiefs) collected taxes in some areas on their behalf.

Like Gorkha, Makwanpur and Vijaypur intermittently allied or clashed with the kingdoms of the Kathmandu Valley. Alignments were continually shifting, though the hill states did make some attempt to help the Sens to resist pressure from the Mughal rulers of the plains in the late seventeenth century.

THE CONTROL OF RESOURCES: LAND, TRADE AND MANPOWER

Even at the hunter-gatherer stage, there must have been competition for resources both in the hills and in the Tarai. In a pre-agricultural society, one square kilometre was needed to support one person, so those who had established themselves in an area did not welcome the arrival of others, who would decrease their available land. As first shifting cultivation and then sedentary agriculture were introduced, land was still seen as belonging to particular peoples or clans, but individuals acquired some claim over plots they had cleared though they were unable to sell it to people outside their group. Lineage heads or chieftains had some general control over a group's territory and, in the case of the Kiratas who preceded the Licchavis in the Kathmandu Valley, this developed into something approaching a state structure. This is shown by apparent references in the Licchavi inscriptions to a Kirata taxation system replaced by the new rulers. However, over the hills as a whole, the power of chieftains or headmen was probably much less than in recent centuries when they were recognised by the state as holding land on their community's behalf.

As kingdoms were established, the older system was gradually superseded by the concept of the king as ultimate owner of the land, entitled to claim a share of the crop from the cultivator. The king's share varied in size but, as in South Asia as a whole from ancient times, in the medieval centuries in the Kathmandu Valley it was probably around 50 per cent. The king's entitlement from a given plot could be assigned temporarily in lieu of salary to the holder of a particular post, or permanently for the maintenance of a religious institution or for the support of those with special religious status: Brahmans, Buddhist monks or other ascetics. At least in the Kathmandu Valley in the late medieval period, the king's claim could also be transferred to ordinary individuals in return for cash payment. Although residual state rights probably made transfers less than absolute, there are records of sales and mortgages in the Valley dating back to the tenth century. These show that transfers of land were normally from the lower castes to higher ones and also that religious institutions frequently acted as money-lenders.

Large-scale land assignments, which often carried with them some rights of administration over the local cultivators, sometimes weakened central authority; such transfers may have been one of the causes of the disintegration of the Khasa empire in the western hills. However, where government was tenuous, grants may actually have strengthened the state by extending the cultivated and regulated area. Land grants to Buddhist monasteries or Jain ascetics in ancient India were often made for this reason. In Nepal grants by the Licchavis to the Pashupatas, the Shaivite sect linked to the emergence of Pashupatinath as the Valley's central shrine, and by the *baisi* and *chaubisi* states to the Kanphata Yogi sect played a similar role.

In the hills, both those receiving royal grants and others moving into new territory on their own were predominantly Parbatiyas, and there was potential conflict with earlier Tibeto-Burman inhabitants. In the early stages, however, this was mitigated because the new settlers were often moving into different ecological niches than those occupied by the indigenous population. Magars, Gurungs and others dependent on herding and on shifting cultivation would probably have preferred to exploit the higher slopes rather than the valley bottoms most suitable for paddy. The present pattern found over much of the hills, with Tibeto-Burman groups predominating at higher altitude and Parbatiyas at lower ones, was not necessarily the result of the latter pushing the former off the more fertile land.[7] As land was normally still plentiful at this stage, the newcomers were sometimes actually welcomed, as they brought with them new skills, such as writing, which the earlier inhabitants valued.

Trade was an important supplement to agriculture from early on and the exchange of southern grain for northern salt was a feature of the local economy in many areas. Long-distance trade was part of the economic base of the Khasa empire but was particularly important for the Kathmandu Valley, whose position at the junction of two important routes into Tibet has already been mentioned. The Valley was a natural entrepôt for trade between Tibet and India since merchants from the south could only cross the Tarai in the cold season when the *aul*, a virulent form of malaria, had abated, but then needed to wait for warmer weather before crossing the mountain passes to the north. In Licchavi times or even earlier, Nepal was famous in North India as the source of a particular type of woollen blanket,[8] while in AD 783 it was mentioned in an Arab treatise as a source of musk. Yak-tails, horses and metal utensils were other important exports to India, while medicinal plants and luxury goods such as silk cloth from China and handicrafts were also traded.

A Chinese visitor in the seventh century AD claimed that the Valley contained few agriculturalists but many merchants. While this is obviously an exaggeration, it must also reflect the scale of mercantile activity along the major routes. The town of Banepa, which lies just beyond the rim of the Valley on the present-day road to Tibet through the Kuti Pass, derives its name from the Sanskrit *Vanikpura* (City of Merchants), while 'Bhonta', the name of the surrounding region, comes from *Bhota* (Tibet). Trade was probably one key to the influence of the 'Bhonta house' which vied for power in the fourteenth century and also for the Ramavardhana family. The latter maintained their independence in Bhonta for some time from Jayasthiti Malla and his successors, even convincing the government of China, with which they exchanged embassies several times between 1384 and 1427, that they were the real rulers of the Nepal Valley. In the later Malla period, though political instability meant that Nepal lost out to Kashmir as a source of woollen goods, the scale and variety of trade probably increased with the quickening of economic activity in India referred to above. An Armenian merchant who spent three months in the Valley in 1686 recorded 174 trade items and estimated that Indian merchants trading with Nepal and Tibet gained a return of 70–130 per cent on their investments.

The sums at stake were important factors in political calculations. When in the 1630s the expansion of Gorkha under King Rama Shah up to the pass at Kuti threatened Kathmandu's trade along that route, King Lakshminarayan and his son Pratap Malla fought two campaigns against Tibet. By 1650 Kathmandu had achieved privileged status for its own citizens in Lhasa, the right to mint Tibet's coinage from silver the Tibetans themselves would supply and an agreement that all Tibet's trade with India would be channelled through the Kathmandu Valley. This jostling for position had alarmed Patan, which therefore sought closer relations with Gorkha and the neighbouring *chaubisi* state of Tanahu. Merchants from Patan were allowed to establish themselves at Gorkha and the use of Patan's coinage became widespread in the hills to the west of the Valley.

To control of revenue from crops or from trade, one must add direct power over human beings. From ancient times in South Asia governments regularly conscripted their subjects for particular projects, whether irrigation works that might benefit the whole community, porterage or the construction of a palace for the ruler. In the hills around the Kathmandu Valley, before the abolition of the system after the end of the Rana regime in 1951, this burden fell particularly upon Tamangs, and this state of affairs probably existed from very early on. Labour of this kind was on an occasional basis but slavery was also a feature of all the Himalayan kingdoms. After the establishment of Gorkhali rule in the eighteenth century, the western hills were a major source of slaves and, as with the Tamangs, the pattern had probably established itself very early.

SOCIAL STRUCTURE

Religion played a key role in social organisation throughout the Himalayas. At the simplest level these were 'tribal' animistic beliefs, but they were increasingly overlaid by the influence of Hinduism and Buddhism. The different systems were not seen as mutually exclusive at grassroots level: contemporary records from Licchavi times onwards show rulers making donations to both Buddhist monks and Brahmans. However, the powerful and wealthy tended to favour one side or another, and the religious specialists definitely saw themselves as competing for patronage. Stories in the *vamshavalis* of a *shankaracharya* (head of a South Indian Shaivite sect) violently suppressing Buddhism on a visit to Nepal are doubtless exaggerated but do reflect a very real tension.

Although there were many *viharas* (Buddhist monasteries) in the Valley in Licchavi times, the kings appear to have been primarily devotees of Hinduism, with particular emphasis on Shiva, worshipped as Pashupatinath ('Lord of the Beasts') in what is still Nepal's most important shrine. The importance of Buddhism increased in the post-Licchavi centuries, possibly because of a decline in the power of the monarchy, but also probably because of the influence of the strongly Buddhist Pala dynasty in Bengal. At this time Nepal served as a channel of communication between Tibet and centres of Buddhist learning in northern India, in particular the university city of Nalanda. Nepalese Buddhists also played an important role in the rebuilding of Tibetan Buddhism in the tenth century after the collapse of the Tibetan empire had weakened it there. Buddhism continued in a stronger position within the Valley until the end of the thirteenth century.

By this time, however, a process of decline had already begun. The major cause was probably the renewed prestige of Hindu kingship in the wake of the South Indian Chalukya dynasty's forays into the north. As well as direct South Indian cultural influence on the Valley, this development led to the replacement of the Buddhist Palas by the Hindu Sen dynasty in Bengal and, most importantly, Nanyadeva's establishment in 1097 of the kingdom of Tirhut in the Maithili-speaking region. Nanyadeva's invasion of the hills in 1111 was a failure and the subsequent raids by the Maithils (known in the Valley as Doyas) were short-lived affairs, but their ideology was more successful. The accession in 1382 of Jayasthiti Malla, whose Maithil connections have already been noted, marked the culmination of a thorough re-Hinduisation of the state. Buddhism in the Kathmandu Valley found itself under continuing pressure, while the religious connection with South India was maintained: South Indian priests were brought in by Yaksha Malla in the fifteenth century to take charge of the shrine of Pashupatinath. The majority of ordinary Newars remained predominantly Buddhist in orientation, but in political terms the religion was in a strongly subordinate position.

During the medieval centuries, Newar Buddhism also saw major changes in its organisation. Celibacy by Buddhist monks was gradually abandoned, although 'monasteries' survived as institutions, providing homes to members of the Vajracharya and Shakya castes, descendants of the monks who made the transition to householders in the medieval period. The change, largely complete by the middle of the thirteenth century, was perhaps connected primarily with the adoption of the Vajryana (Diamond Way) school of Buddhism, which involved the use of sex (even if only at a symbolic level) at its highest ritual level. Non-celibate religious practitioners had become increasingly important throughout the Vajryana area (mainly North India, the Himalayas and Tibet) but it was only in the Kathmandu Valley that celibacy disappeared completely. Whatever the causes underlying it, this change, together with the adoption of new canonical texts in the fifteenth century, established Newar Buddhism as a unique form of the religion. Vajracharyas and Shakyas served as priests for the Buddhist laity and continued to regard themselves as monks, holding ordination ceremonies for each succeeding generation.

In the western hills, the Khasa empire had been primarily Buddhist in orientation, but there was also state patronage of Hinduism. The *baisi* and *chaubisi* states were, in contrast, strongly Hindu, whatever the relative contribution of immigration from the south or acculturation. Hindu settlers, particularly Brahmans, might help an adventurer claiming Rajput status to establish military control and also provide him with religious legitimation. A similar function was probably played by ascetics of the Kanphata Yogi sect, who are associated with the early history of many of the hill kingships. Particularly in the north, however, and among groups least integrated into the new state structures, Buddhism remained an important element of the religious mix, with Tibetan lamaism a strong influence, while in the Khasa heartland the egalitarian cult of the god Masta remained as a counter-weight to Brahmanism.

In all the Hindu kingdoms, caste played a vital role. In the Kathmandu Valley the nineteenth-century *vamshavalis* generally credit King Jayasthiti Malla with organising Newar society into castes in the fourteenth century. There is no contemporary evidence for this, however, and the story may have originated simply because *sthiti* in Nepali can mean 'system' or 'arrangements'. The composers of the *vamshavali* probably chose to highlight the king's role simply to make Newar institutions seem worthy of respect in the eyes of the Gorkhali conquerors.

Nevertheless, the Newar caste system did assume its present shape during the medieval period, and it was the existence of the 'ex-monks' that produced its 'double-headed' structure (see table 1.1). The Vajracharyas and Shakyas formed the head of the Buddhist hierarchy with the Uray, the Buddhist lay patrons, who were most typically involved in trade, beneath them. On the Hindu side, the Brahmans had formal precedence with Kshatriyas, including the royal family and the various groups now known as Shresthas, coming next. Below this level the Buddhist/Hindu distinction was not really relevant and there was a single hierarchy of occupational castes. This was headed by the largest group, the Jyapus or Maharjans, followed by groups such as the Khadgis (butchers), from whom the upper castes could not accept water, and finally outright Untouchables such as the Pode (sweeper) caste.

In the hills to the west the bulk of the Khasas acquired upper-caste ('twice-born') status, ranking below beneath the supposedly Rajput ruling elite, who called themselves Thakuris. Like the Thakuris, they were regarded as Kshatriyas, the warrior/ruler class within the classical, four-fold *varna* hierarchy. They adopted this as their caste name and the Chetri caste (Nepali *chetri* from Sanskrit *kshatriya*) are today 16 per cent of Nepal's total population. Their key position was strengthened because the offspring of a Chetri father and a mother from one of the Tibeto-Burman-speaking hill tribes or the children of a Brahman father and Chetri mother themselves became Chetris. Early descriptions of this process by European observers made the Brahmans the agents of the transformation but, while the Brahmans did play a vital role as legitimators of the system, it was the Thakuri rulers who made the crucial decision. The elimination or emasculation of royal power in India itself by British colonialism has obscured the vital role of the king in sustaining and regulating a caste system.

The division between 'plains Kshatriyas' (the Thakuris) and 'hill Kshatriyas' (the Chetris) is also found west of the present-day Nepalese border in Kumaon and Garhwal. However, in comparison with the situation in what was to become Nepal, the subordination of the Khasas to the immigrants from the plains was always much stronger in the North-west Indian Himalayan districts. It has been suggested that the Khasas in Nepal were more able to hold their own because of the strong position they had held under the Malla empire and also because in Nepal, but not in Kumaon and Garhwal, they were supported by a relatively large Magar and Gurung population.

When the whole system was codified in the nineteenth century, Magars, Gurungs and some other Tibeto-Burman groups were allocated a position clearly below the high, twice-born castes but were not regarded as ritually unclean. A Brahman, Thakuri or Chetri could accept water or food other than boiled rice from their hands, and, most crucially, a high-caste male could have sexual relations with them. They thus ranked above the Nepali-speaking occupational castes, who formed the base of the hierarchy. This had certainly been the position of the bulk of Magars and Gurungs in the medieval period, but until the eighteenth century the situation was complicated by a fairly fluid boundary between Magars and Khasas. The former might also receive Kshatriya status and this happened on such a scale that a British officer who visited Nepal in 1793 could refer to the 'Khus and Mungur tribes of the Chetree class'.[9] Consequently, many of the same clan names, such as 'Thapa', are equally common among both Chetris and Magars.

Despite being Nepali-speakers like the upper Parbatiya castes, the artisan castes were mostly Untouchables, ranking below the Tibeto-Burman groups in the hierarchy. Chief among these groups were the Kamis (blacksmiths), Sarkis (cobblers) and Damais (tailors) who probably amounted to around 20 per cent of the total Parbatiya population. The existence of the high caste/Untouchable divide within Parbatiya society arguably dictated the incorporation of the Tibeto-Burman groups in their intermediate position. A non-caste people coming into contact with high-caste Hindus and Untouchables could associate with the former only if they joined them in avoiding physical contact with the latter.

The eastward drift of the Parbatiyas, whether high caste or low, continued. The Khasa raids in the thirteenth and fourteenth centuries had not led to any extensive settlement in the Kathmandu Valley, any invaders who had remained there appear to have been assimilated into the existing population. From the sixteenth century onwards, however, there appears to have been a growing Parbatiya presence in the Valley. In 1580/1, land-transfer documents preserved in the Rudravarna Mahavira (ex-monastery) begin to employ the Nepali/Hindi forms of numerals rather than Sanskrit or Newar, which suggests these were in frequent use. In the seventeenth century an increasing number of inscriptions in the Valley began to have sections in Nepali. By the end of the century Khasas and Magars were becoming an important factor in the court politics of the three kingdoms, particularly when physical force was employed. In 1703 an agreement between Patan and Bhaktapur provided that if either party broke its terms they might be plundered with impunity by the 'Khas and Magar Omraos' (chiefs, headmen).[10]

There is no sign that these trends were seen as a real danger by the Newar population, presumably because the Khasas seemed just one more group to fit into the elaborate set of divisions already established in the Valley.

Those with any contact with the royal courts were in any case used to their employment of Maithili as the preferred literary language and to the presence of specialists from the plains. There was, however, some tension when Muslims were first settled in Kathmandu under King Ratna Malla in the fifteenth century and also after Capuchin friars established a Catholic mission in 1715. These newcomers were more difficult to fit into the existing scheme of things, but the king of Bhaktapur did actually at one point offer some of his subjects to the Capuchins to be converted.

While not subject to the indignities suffered by the Untouchables, the bulk of the population in the different kingdoms had little influence over the conduct of the political elite. There are, however, examples of crowd action in the Valley cities affecting the course of events. In 1697 the young King Bhupalendra was brought back by the people of Kathmandu when he had withdrawn from the city after a quarrel; a few years earlier the citizens of Bhaktapur had forced King Jitamitra to dismiss a trusted minister. The role of the crowd became important at certain critical moments, usually when rivalry within the elite had reached a particularly high level.

A tradition of localism and of ritual confrontation between different areas in the Valley probably facilitated citizens' participation in quarrels between the rulers. Ritualism served, however, to limit the destructiveness of inter-state warfare, as can be seen from the comments of Fr Desideri, who visited the Valley in 1721:

When two armies meet they launch every sort of abuse at one another, and if few shots are fired, and no one is hurt, the attacked army retires to a fortress, of which there are many, resembling our country dovecots. But if a man is killed or wounded, the army which has suffered begs for peace, and sends a dishevelled and half-clothed woman who weeps, beats her breast and implores mercy, the cession of such carnage, and such shedding of human blood.[11]

Serious fighting was increasingly left to mercenaries from the hills or the Tarai, who were first employed in Kathmandu in the reign of Ratna Malla (1482–1521).

Competition between the Valley states often took non-military forms and is perhaps best understood in terms of the notion of a 'theatre state'.[12] Kathmandu, Patan and Bhaktapur vied with one another in the splendour of their architecture and of their festivals, religious performances that one nineteenth-century observer estimated took up about a third of the time of the cities' inhabitants. Pratap Malla of Kathmandu, a successful practitioner of *Realpolitik* in his policy towards Tibet, was also one of the Valley's most theatrical characters. He himself participated in dance performances for the gods, staged within the royal palace but probably with large sections of the population admitted as spectators. In an inscription on a 1673 statue of Vishnu within the Hanuman Dhoka palace, the king himself explains how he had been possessed by the god after impersonating him in ritual performance and been told to construct the statue as a form of exorcism. Pratap Malla was also the builder of Rani Pokhari ('Queen's Pond') and set the trend for Valley rulers to erect statues of themselves on a pillar facing a temple of Taleju, the Mallas' patron goddess.

Both inside and outside the Valley, kings also competed as exemplars of traditional Hindu kingship, as men of letters who wrote some of the plays they themselves performed in and also as consumers of the new trends in luxury set by the Mughal rulers to the south. Although the Mughals were non-Hindus, they were the greatest power in South Asia and so association with them brought prestige. The stories of Mahendra Malla of Kathmandu obtaining permission to mint coins from the emperor in Delhi and of Rama Shah of Gorkha similarly receiving a new formal title must be understood in this sense, whether or not they are strictly historical.

To an observer in the early eighteenth century, it must have seemed that the performance of the Himalayan state could continue much as it had done before, with only minor fluctuations in the cast of mini-states which occupied the hills. The accession of a new king in Gorkha in 1743 was, however, to lead to fundamental change.

CHAPTER 2

Unification and sanskritisation, 1743–1885

THE GORKHALI CONQUESTS: EXPANSION AND AFTERMATH

The single image most strongly associated with the history of modern Nepal is surely that of Prithvi Narayan Shah of Gorkha, girded for battle, a look of determination in his eyes and his right hand pointing skywards. This is his pose in the statue that stands outside the Government Secretariat in Kathmandu (illus. 3, p. 36) and in countless printed representations. Historians are rightly wary of making 'great men' the central focus of their analysis but in the case of Prithvi Narayan one individual did play a crucial role. Gorkha's rulers had long been intent upon expansion and Prithvi Narayan's father Narbhupal Shah had tried unsuccessfully to seize from Kathmandu the town of Nuwakot, which overlooked the Trisuli River which formed Gorkha's eastern boundary. It was Prithvi, however, who possessed both the ability and the determination to realise that ambition. From his accession in 1743, he fought continuously for control of the Kathmandu Valley, entering Kathmandu itself on 25 September 1768 and finally capturing Bhaktapur the following November. Between then and his death in 1775 he occupied all of eastern Nepal and much of modern Sikkim.

Prithvi's success rested partly on sound logistical preparations but even more on his political skills and a shrewd combination of conciliation and intimidation. He motivated his rank-and-file troops by offering them their own land assignments rather than relying on his officers raising and paying soldiers themselves. Most crucially, he took advantage of the rivalries between and within the Valley cities, where a sense of common 'Newarness', in so far as it existed at all, was not of great political importance. Non-Newar involvement in the Valley was nothing new, and Khasas had played an important role since the beginning of the seventeenth century. Gorkha itself had been a factor in intra-Valley politics for many years, and the Malla kings initially imagined that they could continue safely to make use of the Gorkhalis against each other, as they had made use of the Doyas in

3. Statue of Prithvi Narayan Shah, the creator of modern Nepal, outside the Singha Durbar (Government Secretariat) in Kathmandu.

previous centuries. Consequently, apart from a brief period of united resistance in 1757, Kathmandu, Patan and Bhaktapur strove to reach separate accommodations with the Gorkhalis.

On top of the lack of unity between the city-states, Jaya Prakash Malla was also engaged in a constant battle to maintain his own control over Kathmandu. He had always been unpopular with his Khasa officers, and in 1746 his execution of one of them for failing to recapture Nuwakot led to the dead man's brother's defection to Prithvi Narayan Shah. Afterwards Jaya Prakash relied more on soldiers from the Tarai and from the far western hills. Help from India was provided in 1763 by Mir Kasim of Bengal, angered at Prithvi's conquest of his vassal, the king of Makwanpur, while the British East India Company, alarmed at the disruption to their trade with the Valley, intervened in 1767. However, these small expeditionary forces were easily defeated by the Gorkhalis. The real wonder is perhaps that Jaya Prakash Malla managed to keep up the fight for so long rather than that the Mallas finally succumbed.

Prithvi's establishment of his new kingdom formed part of a pattern of state-building and expansion across a wide area of Asia. New regional powers were emerging, in particular the East India Company, which gained control of Bengal in 1757. To the north, China had completed the conquest of Sinkiang in 1759, just nine years after strengthening its supervisory role in Tibet. In his political testament, the *Dibya Upadesh*, dictated a few months before his death, Prithvi famously described his kingdom as 'a yam between two rocks' and recommended a defensive stance against both China and the British. His particular apprehension of the southern threat probably stemmed mainly from the abortive British attempt to assist the Mallas. Many Nepalese today believe that the British had a central place in Prithvi's thinking from much earlier and that the Gorkhali conquests were primarily designed to forestall the advance of colonialism into the Himalayas. There is no real evidence to support this view, which in any case ignores the fact that from the classical Hindu perspective a Hindu ruler's wars of expansion were viewed as legitimate in their own right. They did not need to be presented as defensive moves against possible aggression from elsewhere.

Both early British sources and the writings of the Capuchin missionaries stress Prithvi's ruthlessness, whereas mainstream Nepalese historians have often tried to discredit accounts of Gorkhali cruelty as biased. The British had initially seen the Gorkhalis as barbarians from the hills threatening their Newar trading partners, while the Capuchins, who had once enjoyed cordial relations with Prithvi, were later barred from the kingdom in the

4. The old palace of the Shah dynasty at Gorkha, eighty miles west of Kathmandu.

belief that they had encouraged British intervention. Both parties thus had reason to dislike the king, but it is still unlikely that the Capuchins in particular would have fabricated what they present as eyewitness accounts of atrocities.[1] Most notorious was the order to cut off the lips and noses of the inhabitants of Kirtipur after its surrender in 1766, a story corroborated in at least two Nepali sources.[2] Prithvi Narayan also enforced his blockade of the Valley by hanging at the roadside anyone caught trying to smuggle in supplies. It can be said in Prithvi's defence, however, that Jaya Prakash Malla had also often acted ruthlessly and that applying current human rights standards would turn many nations' heroes into war criminals: England's Henry V, who massacred prisoners at Agincourt, is just one example.

While the Gorkhalis' ultimate goal was probably conquest of the range as far west as Kashmir, Prithvi was anxious not to provoke major powers outside the hills. In 1771 he obtained from the Mughal emperor, who had been deprived of real authority by the British in 1764, the title *bahadur shamsher jung.* This nominal acknowledgement of Mughal superiority had no effect on Prithvi's freedom of action but, in contemporary eyes, strengthened his legitimacy. At the same time Prithvi also advocated a policy of economic self-sufficiency, and the encouragement of local rather than Indian merchants.

The *gosain* (Indian ascetic) merchants, whom Prithvi had cultivated during his campaign against the Valley states, were expelled and British attempts to establish trading relations and access to Tibet were rebuffed. This approach is in accord with present-day resentment of Indian economic dominance and has earned Prithvi some appreciation from the Nepalese left, even though in other respects they regard him as a feudal oppressor.

The accession to the throne of Prithvi's son Pratap Singh in January 1775 marked the beginning of serious factionalism within the court. After Pratap Shah's death in 1777 his widow, regent for the infant King Rana Bahadur, contested for power with Pratap's brother, Bahadur Shah, until he himself assumed the regency on the queen's death in 1785. By then the precedent of losers in the power struggle paying with their lives had been set: Pratap's influential Newar concubine had been compelled to commit *sati* and in 1778 the queen regent's minister and alleged lover had been executed.

Under Bahadur Shah, the Gorkhalis annexed not only the hill states of the Gandaki and Karnali basin but also Kumaon and Garhwal, now part of the Indian state of Uttaranchal (until 2000 part of Uttar Pradesh). The westward drive had to be halted when an aggressive policy towards Tibet over trade and border issues triggered a Chinese invasion. Crossing the border pass at Kirong in 1792, the Chinese advanced down the Trisuli Valley towards Nuwakot. They withdrew after Nepal had agreed to surrender the recent gains negotiated with Tibet and to send five-yearly tribute missions to Beijing. The defeat was not, however, a crushing one, as the submission to the emperor was again nominal, and Nepalese troops had inflicted a reverse on the Chinese in the final engagement of the campaign.[3]

In autumn 1791, when the Chinese attack was already anticipated, Bahadur Shah had concluded a trade treaty with the British, despite continuing misgivings among the *bharadars* (courtiers). Faced with appeals for help from both Beijing and Kathmandu, the governor-general delayed action as long as possible, dispatching Colonel William Kirkpatrick to Kathmandu in 1793, some months after the Chinese withdrawal. Finding that his presence was proving a political embarrassment to Bahadur Shah, Kirkpatrick soon retreated to India. Association with the *firangis* had indeed helped weaken the regent and the following year King Rana Bahadur Shah took the government into his own hands. After Bahadur Shah had unsuccessfully solicited Chinese help to regain his position, he was imprisoned until his death (natural or otherwise) in 1797 at the age of thirty-nine.

In 1799, Rana Bahadur abdicated in favour of Girvana Yuddha, his two-year-old son by an illicit union with Kantivati, a Maithil Brahman widow. His intention was to dedicate himself to religious devotions to save the life

5. Betrawati on the Trisuli River below Nuwakot. This was the furthest point reached by
the Chinese invasion force in 1792.

of the mother, who had contracted smallpox, and also to ensure that the
boy was not pushed aside despite his irregular birth. Rana Bahadur secured
signatures of almost all the *bharadars* on a document recognising the boy
as king, but shortly afterwards Kantivati died. Rana Bahadur reacted with
violence against the Brahmans and against the temples of the gods, who he
thought had betrayed him. He also attempted to reassert control over the
government, but this was resisted by his son's ministers. He was compelled
in 1800 to seek refuge in Benares in East India Company territory. On
one interpretation of Rana Bahadur's subsequent actions, he now deliberately gave his Nepalese opponents the false impression that he was seeking
British support, thus frightening them into reaching an agreement with the

6. Bhimsen Thapa, the statesman who dominated Nepalese politics in the early decades of the nineteenth century. Painted by Dirgha Man Chitrakar.

East India Company themselves and then exploiting anti-British feelings within Nepal to undermine them. In fact, some of his own proposals to the company were themselves an alarmed reaction to news of an agreement already reached with his opponents. Rana Bahadur did nevertheless skilfully promote dissension within the government in Kathmandu, and the commercial treaty it had concluded with the British in 1801 proved unworkable. Captain Knox, the British resident appointed under the agreement, withdrew after less than a year and the ex-king returned home in triumph in 1804. He executed Dalmodar Pande, his leading domestic opponent, but in 1806 he was himself assassinated by his half-brother, Sher Bahadur, son of Pratap Shah's Newar concubine.

At this point, Bhimsen Thapa, a young *bharadar* who had accompanied Rana Bahadur to Benares, seized control, sending ninety-three men and women to their deaths. These included several of Rana Bahadur's wives, burned on their husband's funeral pyre to ensure the regency went to a junior queen, Tripura Sundari, Bhimsen's own political collaborator. Although his power was not always unchallenged, Bhimsen was to remain the central figure on the political stage for the next thirty years.

Westward expansion continued until the Gorkhali forces were checked on the Satlaj in the winter of 1809–10 by Ranjit Singh, ruler of the Panjab. The Gorkhali commander also prudently accepted British demands to withdraw from the possessions on the Panjab plains of hill chieftains he had conquered. War with the East India Company had only been postponed until 1814 when, at Bhimsen's insistence, the Nepalese rejected a fresh ultimatum to withdraw from two disputed areas on the frontier further east, at Butwal and Syuraj.

The issue was in fact a highly complex one. The ruler of the hill state of Palpa had held the territory by a grant of revenue rights from the plains kingdom of Oudh but, since such rights also carried judicial and administrative jurisdiction, confusion could easily arise. There were similar problems all along the Tarai, often made worse because local land-holding families might try to ensure their own rights by obtaining grants for the same area from different rulers and proclaim themselves the subject of whichever state suited their current convenience. The British wanted a clear and unambiguous frontier and had difficulties with the fluid, overlapping systems of control that characterised the Tarai. However, the Gorkhalis seemed at times to appeal to the same logic. 'How can one government exist inside another?' asked King Rana Bahadur in a 1783 letter to Warren Hastings.[4] In practice, both governments used arguments in one sector of the frontier that were inconsistent with what they were arguing elsewhere.

Though outnumbered and unpopular with their newly acquired subjects in the far west, the Gorkhalis had the advantage of better knowledge of the ground and inflicted several reverses on the East India Company's forces. However in 1815, General Ochterloney compelled the Gorkhali commander, Amar Singh Thapa, to evacuate the hills west of the Mahakali River. Negotiations for a general settlement produced a draft which was initialled at Sagauli in Bihar in December 1815 and required Nepal to give up all territories west and east of its present-day borders, to surrender the entire Tarai and to accept a permanent British representative (or 'resident') in Kathmandu. The Nepalese government initially balked at these terms, but agreed to ratify them in March 1816 after Ochterloney occupied the Makwanpur Valley only thirty miles from the capital.

Bhimsen Thapa managed to retain his hold on power, aided by the continuance of Lalita Tripura Sundari's regency: another infant, Rajendra, succeeded to the throne after the deaths of King Girvana Yuddha and his queen towards the end of 1816. Although there was speculation about foul play, the residency, which was in a position to receive messages from Bhimsen's opponents, believed that both deaths were natural. With considerable skill, Bhimsen managed within one year to negotiate an improvement in the peace terms. Rather than pay pensions to the Nepalese *bharadars* who had held land assignments in the Tarai, the British agreed to return to Nepal the central and eastern Tarai, though not the far western section (i.e. the present-day districts of Kanchanpur, Kailali, Banke and Bardiya), which had already been gifted to the kingdom of Oudh.

Realising the need to co-operate with the British but also the depth of anti-British feeling within the country, Bhimsen for many years successfully played both ends against the middle. He scrupulously obeyed the terms of the 1816 agreement and encouraged the British to see him as their guarantee of peace. He also maintained a large standing army and presented himself to his own countrymen as their bulwark against further British intervention. There was no general opening-up of the country for Indian traders, and access to the British resident in Kathmandu was carefully controlled. The residents, and the East India Company itself, were prepared to accept this situation until Brian Hodgson took over as resident at the end of 1832, only a few months after Bhimsen's position within the country had been weakened by the death of Lalita Tripura Sundari.

Hodgson, who had by then been in Nepal in a junior capacity for many years, believed that Nepal's stance was a long-term threat to peace and should be changed by encouraging the growth of commerce and by employing the country's 'surplus military manpower' in the East India Company's forces; the British had been employing 'Gurkha' troops (a misspelling of 'Gorkha') since Ochterloney organised a corps of deserters to assist him against Amar Singh Thapa in 1815, but Nepal did not allow recruitment on its own territory. Hodgson now convinced himself relations would improve if in the hands of King Rajendra rather than Bhimsen, who depended on the goodwill of the army. He therefore sympathised strongly with Bhimsen's opponents and, when Bhimsen himself sought to buttress his position by moving closer to the British, Hodgson rebuffed him. Bhimsen's final fall came more suddenly than expected when he was arrested in 1837 on suspicion of involvement in the sudden death of the king's infant son; the child had allegedly drunk poison intended for his mother, Senior

Queen Samrajya Lakshmi, who was a backer of Ranjang Pande, Bhimsen's leading foe.

The change did not bring the improvement Hodgson had hoped for, since both King Rajendra and Ranjang's faction were ready to capitalise on anti-British feeling at home and in other independent Indian states. Hodgson was alarmed and in summer 1838 he transferred his sympathies to the Poudyal brothers, Brahmans whose family had long been rivals with that of Ranjang's own Brahman ally. After Bhimsen's death in prison in 1839, Ranjang's group's quest for revenge and financial exactions began causing alarm among many of the *bharadars*. Then, in February 1840, after the news of the outbreak of the Opium War between Britain and China had reached Kathmandu, Ranjang was appointed sole *mukhtiyar* (minister). Tensions increased further when Nepalese troops occupied 200 square miles of British territory in the Tarai, and a brief army mutiny seemed at one point to threaten the residency itself.

As well as successfully demanding a Nepalese withdrawal, the governor-general, Lord Auckland, now authorised Hodgson to press the king to appoint new advisers friendly to the British. With substantial forces committed in Afghanistan, Auckland was not in a position to fight a full-scale campaign against Nepal. However, the movement of troops closer to the border and Hodgson's manoeuvrings secured the appointment at the end of 1840 of a 'British ministry' composed of the resident's Nepalese allies. Then in 1842, there was a major change in British policy. A new governor-general, Lord Ellenborough, ordered a disengagement of the residency from involvement in Nepal's internal politics. Hodgson accomplished this smoothly enough, but court politics were now increasingly disturbed by the erratic behaviour of Crown Prince Surendra, including acts of cruelty against leading *bharadars*. Surendra's disturbed mental state prefigured the much greater violence displayed by his descendant Crown Prince Dipendra in 2001. It was possible, however, that he was initially encouraged by his father as a way of intimidating the *bharadars* without the king's having to take responsibility for it himself.

The immediate outcome of all this was the 'National Movement of 1842', as Hodgson enthusiastically styled it. This was a concerted effort by most of the nobility with backing from the army to make King Rajendra restrain Surendra, whose mother had died the previous year, and grant authority to the junior queen, Rajya Lakshmi. Although this seemed at first to have succeeded, there was no clear redistribution of power and later in the year the king and queen agreed to the return to Nepal of Bhimsen's nephew, Mathbar Singh Thapa. Mathbar was finally appointed minister in December, a few days after Hodgson's final departure from Nepal.

In terms of long-term British policy towards Nepal, Hodgson's role in 1840–2 had been rather an aberration. The authorities in Calcutta wanted a friendly regime in Kathmandu but were unwilling to take on onerous responsibilities to ensure this. Hodgson had been explicitly instructed in the 1830s not to become involved in Nepal's internal politics, and Ellenborough's change of tack, though arguably made too abruptly, was simply a reversion to an earlier policy. However, the fact that the British had for two years given overt backing to one faction meant that Nepalese politicians did not believe later protestations of neutrality. This reinforced the tendency for rival groups either to seek British support, to denounce their opponents for seeking it or, better, to pursue both options simultaneously. It has also led many Nepalese looking at their own history to see the hand of the British residency in almost all major developments from 1840 through to the end of the Rana period. The effect of this legacy was immediately apparent in the tactics of Mathbar Singh. He was deeply suspicious of Hodgson because of the resident's failure to save Bhimsen Thapa in 1839, but made great efforts to cultivate his successor, Henry Lawrence. As Lawrence himself suspected, Mathbar also told other Nepalese that he enjoyed the resident's backing: his propaganda of this time is reflected in a nineteenth-century Nepalese chronicle that claims it was Mathbar who persuaded the British to send Lawrence to Kathmandu in the first place. In fact the residency was a spectator rather than a participant as Mathbar, who had initially been inclined to back the queen, instead threw his weight behind Surendra. King and queen both now combined against him, and Mathbar was assassinated as he entered the royal palace in May 1845.

The shot that killed Mathbar was fired by his own nephew, Jang Bahadur Kunwar, acting, as he later claimed, under duress. The Kunwars were an old Gorkhali family and Jang's great-grandfather had been a successful commander under Prithvi Narayan. Since the turn of the century the family had usually been associated with Bhimsen Thapa, and Jang's mother was Mathbar's sister. Jang himself was known as a daring army officer, as a victim of Surendra's cruelty and also as a man who enjoyed Mathbar's patronage. As a reward for his sudden change of sides, Jang was included in a 'coalition ministry' appointed in September 1845 under a compromise between king and queen. Nominally headed by Fateh Jang Chautara, the coalition's most powerful member was actually the queen's confidante and rumoured lover, Gagan Singh.

THE ESTABLISHMENT OF THE RANA REGIME

On the night of 14 September 1846, Gagan was shot dead while at prayer in his own home. The murder was most probably the result of a conspiracy in which King Rajendra, Fateh Jang and Jang Bahadur Kunwar were all involved. Immediately, the queen summoned all civil and military officials to the Kot, the arsenal situated next to the royal palace, and demanded that the culprit be found. Shooting broke out, probably ordered by someone in Jang's party in the belief that he or they were in danger, though it is also possible that the whole episode was pre-planned. In any case, Jang's soldiers then entered the building from the courtyard and a massacre of his opponents ensued. During the carnage the queen appointed him 'prime minister' – since Mathbar's time the Nepalese had preferred the English loan-word to the Arabic *mukhtiyar*. Thirty leading *bharadars* died, including Fateh Jang himself. The families and followers of the dead, some 6000 in all, were expelled from the country and Jang then proceeded to place his own relatives and followers in all positions of importance.

The queen had believed that Jang would be her instrument to dispose of Surendra and replace him as heir to the throne with a son of her own. Jang decided instead that he would himself make use of Surendra, and killed or captured a number of the queen's followers who, he alleged, had been plotting his own assassination. He then persuaded both the king and Surendra to agree to the queen's banishment. King Rajendra, who had withdrawn from the Kot before events reached their climax and then confirmed Jang's appointment, suddenly decided to accompany his wife to Benares. He made an abortive attempt to regain power in 1847 but he and his followers were arrested soon after crossing the frontier; he was then kept under virtual house arrest for the remainder of his life. King Surendra was now completely under Jang's control, though more out of fear than gratitude.

Jang was eager to establish good relations with the British, particularly as he needed them to restrain the activities of his opponents in exile in India. Contrary to the belief still prevalent in Nepal today that the British were involved in Jang's seizure of power, he was in fact initially regarded by them with great suspicion. He was, however, able to overcome this and in 1850 visited London, thus breaking the taboo on crossing the *kalo pani* ('black water' or ocean) traditionally observed by high-caste Hindus. First-hand experience of Britain's military and industrial strength ensured that he took the British side during the Indian Mutiny of 1857, personally leading a large force to take part in the capture of Lucknow from the rebels. In return, the

British restored to Nepal the western Tarai, taken in 1816, and conferred an honorary knighthood on Jang himself.

Although prepared to co-operate closely in matters of peace and war, Jang remained suspicious of British intentions. He maintained the 'closed-door' policy of previous Nepalese governments, refusing to allow European traders into the country, rejecting a proposal for a road connecting Kathmandu to India and allowing the British resident and his staff access only to strictly limited areas. He also tried to hinder the recruitment by the British of Nepalese to serve in the Gurkha regiments of the Indian army.

With his southern flank secured, in 1855–6 Jang attempted to expand at the expense of Tibet, with whom Nepal was in dispute over the treatment of Nepalese traders. China's internal troubles meant that, in contrast to the last time Nepal had tried a 'forward policy', Tibet could expect no effective help from Beijing. However, the 1855 invasion soon led to a protracted and prohibitively expensive stalemate, and the war was ended by negotiating terms that gave only marginal concessions to Nepal.

Jang was anxious to put his family's dominant status on an enduring basis. In 1849 he secured a royal decree recognising the Kunwars as Rajputs, and thus as the equals in caste status of the royal family. This opened the way for a series of marital alliances between the Ranas (as the family was now called for the first time) and the Shah dynasty. Jang's sons and daughters were married to King Surendra's children, while Jang himself married both a sister and a niece of Fateh Jang, the minister who had died in the Kot Massacre. Intermarriage between the two families continued until the end of the Rana regime and beyond.

A further move in Jang's strategy was his surprise resignation in 1856 in favour of Bam Bahadur, the eldest of his six full brothers. A few days later a royal decree was issued conferring on Jang the title of maharaja of Kaski and Lamjung, two formerly independent principalities in central Nepal with which the Shah dynasty and Jang's own ancestors had both been closely associated. The document gave the new maharaja ('great king') complete authority within his own domain and also broad supervisory powers over both the maharajadhiraj ('great king of kings' – the title of the king of Nepal) and the prime minister. Jang's intention was evidently that the position of maharaja and its prerogatives should be inherited by his own direct descendants while the premiership was passed on by agnate succession, going in turn to each of his brothers and then to his sons and nephews. In this way he apparently hoped to secure his brothers' continued loyalty, while also founding a dynasty of his own.

7. Jang Bahadur Rana (seated) with his brother Jagat Shamsher (left) and son Babar
(standing behind him) in camp in 1871.

Jang's ultimate aim may well have been to move up from maharaja to
maharajadhiraj, and supplant the Shah dynasty completely, but in this he
was thwarted by the British, who refused to recognise any authority in
Nepal other than that deriving from the king and the prime minister. Jang
was thus frustrated in his attempt to continue to manage British–Nepalese
relations after his resignation. Presumably for this reason he resumed the
post of prime minister in 1857, after the death of Bam Bahadur, when the
start of the Indian Mutiny crisis made it vital for him to gather the reins of
control fully into his own hands.

Jang's plan for the office of maharaja to pass to his own eldest son was
not fulfilled. When he died, on a hunting expedition in 1877, his surviving
brothers acted quickly to ensure that the eldest among them, Ranoddip,
was invested simultaneously as both prime minister and maharaja. Jang's
sons believed themselves cheated and subsequently became involved in a
conspiracy against the new maharaja. The plot was foiled and Jang's oldest
son, Jagat Jang, was removed from the Roll of Succession to the premiership.
Nevertheless, after the death of Dhir Shamsher, Jang's youngest brother,
his sons became apprehensive that Ranoddip, under the influence of his

second wife, would restore Jagat Jang to favour and make him his heir. This would have put their own lives in danger, since Jagat Jang was known to be eager for revenge against the Shamshers.

In 1885, Bir Shamser, Dhir Shamsher's oldest son, together with the rest of his brothers, decided to forestall the restoration of Jagat Jang with a coup of their own, which involved the cold-blooded killing of their uncle Ranoddip and of Jagat Jang himself. Other members of Jang Bahadur's family escaped to take refuge with the British residency; safe passage to India was subsequently negotiated for them. The exiles, with covert support from the maharaja of Darbhanga, later attempted to launch an armed attack against the new rulers, but they were completely unsuccessful and several were then put under supervision by the authorities in India. Nepal was now firmly in the hands of the Shamsher Ranas.

STATE AND SOCIETY

Despite the difference of scale, the political system established by Prithvi Narayan's conquests was a continuation of that of Gorkha and the other hill states west of the Valley. Hindu kingship was central but institutions and cultural practices in many ways followed the example of Mughal India, as was now the case in South Asia generally. Mughal administration could, very loosely, be termed 'feudal' but the most appropriate term is perhaps 'patrimonial', meaning that the state was organised as an extension of the ruler's household. Three features of the system of particular importance in Nepal both before and after 1768 were: the need for personal attendance on the king, the *pajani* under which all appointments were subject to annual review, and frequent changes in the location of an individual's *jagir*, the land assigned to a state servant in lieu of salary. Though the system of payment by land assignment has long been discontinued, the word *jagir* continues in use in modern Nepali as the term for a salaried government post.

Traditionally, the king's chief minister was a member of a collateral branch of the royal family or *chautara*, a title reflecting the intimate nature of government in the pre-unification states. The word derives from the name of the stone platforms found throughout the hills where porters could easily set down the loads from their back or villagers could gather for discussion. At Gorkha other posts in the administration went traditionally to members of Khas–Chetri and Brahman families who were believed to have helped Drabya Shah found his kingdom in 1559. During the wars of expansion and the accompanying factional struggles, however, other families gained influence. Success as a military commander, or at least popularity with the army, was a major factor and here the Khas–Chetris had an advantage. They were the major military force, even though Magars and Gurungs provided around half of the ordinary soldiers and, initially, also some of the senior officers. The military rank and file normally had little influence, but Prithvi Narayan's policy of providing them with their own land assignments raised their status and Bhimsen's concentration of the main units in Kathmandu after 1816 gave them a potential political role. During the instability of the 1840s they verged on becoming an independent force, but in the end always followed their patrons among the *bharadari* elite.

Although Brahmans formed a major part of the East India Company's Bengal Army, hill Brahmans were normally not employed as soldiers. They did, however, possess influence as providers of legitimation for the ruler, as interpreters of the traditional Hindu law codes (*dharmashastras*), as astrologers and as *gurus* both to members of the royal family and to other Thakuri or Chetri families. In addition, the connections of the three *rajguru* ('royal guru') families with the plains, and especially to Benares, gave them an edge over most other *bharadars* in connections to the world beyond the hills. They were therefore important as negotiators with the British; the Poudyal family were especially prominent during the period of active British intervention in Nepalese politics in 1840–2. Vijay Raj Pande, who was already the *dharmadhikar* (chief religious judge) in 1846 became a close ally of Jang Bahadur's and was rewarded with appointment as chief *rajguru*.

The political system as a whole depended on a strong individual at the centre for everything to work. The inability of Prithvi Narayan's successors to play this role resulted in instability until first Bhimsen Thapa and then Jang Bahadur Rana were able to fill the gap. The Rana regime is often portrayed in Nepal today as an interlude of autocracy between the supposedly people-oriented rule of the Shah dynasty before 1846 and the advent of democracy under royal sponsorship in 1950/1. This version owes its origin to the collaboration between the monarchy and the activists of the Nepali Congress Party which brought down the Rana system. However, for the bulk of the population, 1846 did not represent a radical break with the past, but was rather the institutionalisation of one family's dominance at the expense of the Shahs and other leading families within the traditional elite. The Ranas did strengthen central control, but this was a tendency already operating under Bhimsen and changes such as the strengthening of caste barriers (see p. 59) or the weakening of local autonomy were already well under way. The shift from tactical co-operation with the British to full-hearted identification of the ruling family's interests with those of the British Raj came in 1885 rather than 1846.

As had always been the case in both the hills and the Tarai, the state's economic base was the taxation of agricultural production. There were other sources, such as customs duties, payment in return for monopoly supply contracts which both Bhimsen Thapa and Jang Bahadur awarded to trusted adherents and, later on, the supply of timber for the construction of Indian railways. However, revenue from land provided around three-quarters of the government's income in the middle of the nineteenth century and must have been even more important earlier. The proceeds could go directly to the government, whether through its own employees or by the allocation of tax-farming contracts. Alternatively, as explained in the previous chapter, the state's rights on particular plots could be assigned temporarily as *jagir* to one of its own employees or permanently to individuals or to religious institutions. Assignments under the latter two systems were known in Nepali as *birta* or *guthi*; the second type is still recognised under Nepalese law today. In cases where a pre-unification ruler had reached an early accommodation with the Gorkhalis, he continued to collect some or all of the revenue from his own previous domain and submit a proportion to Kathmandu annually, an arrangement which persisted until 1961.

Whatever the system, locally based individuals (for example, village headmen or *mukhiyas*) were normally at the bottom of the pyramid and their connection with the state tended to buttress their authority compared with the situation before unification. The Limbu chieftains, known by the Nepali/Mughal term *subba*, were one example, becoming more like local landowners than simply the representative of their clan. In the case of a smaller Kiranti group, the Jirels of Dolakha district, one clan probably boosted its status at the cost of the others, being recognised in 1795 as owners of the entire Jiri Valley, though they later lost control of much of the land to Parbatiya settlers. In many cases throughout Nepal the wealthiest individuals at local levels are very often still those whose ancestors obtained revenue-collection rights during the eighteenth and nineteenth centuries.

Jang Bahadur sought to strengthen control of the revenue-collection machinery, continuing a trend already noticeable in the 1830s away from the appointment of contractors and towards greater reliance on the government's own salaried agents. In the Tarai he introduced a new category of official known as *jimidars* to take charge of each *mauja*, as the smallest revenue-collection unit was known. They did not evolve into a class of 'improving landlords', as Jang may originally have wanted. They did, however, eventually become a network of locally based individuals closely tied to the Ranas themselves, depressing the status of the older-established *chaudhuris* and also of the individual peasants who had formerly dealt directly with them.

As was seen in the previous chapter, land grants to Brahmans or to religious institutions were a means of boosting a Hindu ruler's legitimacy and thus particularly attractive when that legitimacy was in question. It was probably for this reason that Hindu ascetic communities were able to obtain extensive grants in Janakpur in the second half of the eighteenth century, when states in the region worried about their survival as Gorkha relentlessly expanded. Similarly, shortly after coming to power, Jang Bahadur announced that he would restore *birta* grants to Brahmans that had been rescinded at the beginning of the century by Rana Bahadur in a drive to build up Nepal's military strength. Jang let the project drop once he felt himself securely in power, but it was revived after 1877 by his more pious brother and successor, Ranoddip.

Religious practitioners were also patronised because they could supply an organisational framework in areas where the state was relatively weak. This had long been the case both in South Asia and in many other parts of the world. In the last decades of the eighteenth century, in much of northern India monastic orders of *bairagis* and *gosains*, ascetics devoted to Vishnu and Shiva respectively, had become a major military force as well as prominent entrepreneurs. In Nepal, as well as land grants to the Vaishnavite communities in Janakpur and the Chaughera Yogi Shaivite monastery in the Dang Valley, individual *gosains* were assigned land in different parts of the Tarai. While a strong egalitarian trend developed within the Indian Vaishnavite communities and was a factor in later movements for the 'upliftment' of lower castes, the ascetics in Nepal were content to work within the hierarchical structures of the Hindu state.

In the middle of the nineteenth century the normal revenue demand, whether going into the state treasury or assigned to a *jagirdar* or other grantee, was on average about one-third of the crop in the western hills and Tarai and one-half in the eastern hills. However, where the lower rate prevailed, the person liable for the payment would frequently choose to sub-let at least part of the land, so that the amount paid by the actual cultivator was usually around half the main crop throughout the country. In many parts of the country, land was in surplus and did not acquire a capital value until towards the end of the period covered by this chapter. There was therefore always the danger that peasants might abandon the land and move elsewhere, or that revenue-collectors in the Tarai would abscond across the border with their entire takings. The latter was a particular worry of Jang Bahadur's during his early years in power: one of the issues he tried unsuccessfully to discuss with the British authorities in London in 1850 was the extension of extradition arrangements to cover this situation.

Governments had to conciliate intermediaries between themselves and the peasantry but also not let them acquire too much leeway. The principle was laid down in identical wording in government orders of 1781 and 1807: 'The money of the people must either remain with them or be paid to us; it cannot be appropriated by cunning people.'[5] Jang Bahadur was, at least in theory, particularly concerned to check unreasonable exactions, writing to his brother Bam Bahadur from London in 1850 that 'God put us where we are to protect the common people.'[6] Statements of good intention were sometimes given practical effect. A British traveller returning from Kathmandu in 1851 was told by his guide that he had moved into Nepal from East India Company territory after hearing of Jang's punishment of one oppressive official. In 1883 Ranoddip Singh blocked a proposed tax increase in Rautahat in the eastern Tarai after just eighteen peasants had submitted a petition against it. However, strict supervision of every official or revenue-contractor's conduct was impossible, especially when letters regularly took a month to reach the western border from Kathmandu. The actual burden imposed on the taxpayer must have varied greatly in different locations and at different times.

In addition to the revenue demand, the state could requisition the labour of its subjects. In some cases, peasants were given permanent responsibility for specific tasks like the carrying of government mail and supplies along the foot trails and were allocated small, rent-free plots of land in return. For others, the labour requirement was less, but it was in addition to normal taxation. There was a particularly heavy burden on the Tamang communities in the hills around Kathmandu, including tending the state cattle herds and carrying farm produce to the royal palace. The system remained in operation until 1952 and the recollections of older Tamangs recently gathered and published are probably representative for the earlier period also.[7] Slavery and bonded labour were also commonplace, particularly in the western hills from where people were frequently sold as slaves to India.[8] At the beginning of the nineteenth century, the authorities were worried that even Brahmans and Chetris were being reduced to slave status, and in 1803 an order was issued banning high-caste enslavement throughout the empire. Later in the century, a number of other groups similarly had their liability to enslavement removed, but, as in the case of the Magars of the mid-western hills, they might have to pay an additional tax for the privilege. For many of the lower castes, enslavement remained a possibility until its abolition in 1921, while bonded labour was only finally ended in 2001.

Although it was not sudden or dramatic, the early Rana period did see the beginning of a significant change in the state's relation to the land.

Under Jang Bahadur's Muluki Ain (Civil Code) of 1854, cultivators on land other than *birta* holdings could not be evicted simply for refusing to pay an increased rent. Following elaborate land surveys in 1854 to 1868, the 1870 edition of the Ain allowed for the person paying tax on any plot of land to be registered as its holder. Although actual practice did not always follow the letter of the law, these legal changes paved the way for the development in the eastern hills of a de facto market in land, which was already saleable in the western hills and the Tarai. The process was accelerated by the decline in the supply of new land that could easily be cleared for cultivation and also by the government's leaving largely unchanged the revenue rates fixed in 1854–68.

The Ranas could easily forego any increases in the percentage of total agricultural production paid in taxation because total production was itself expanding. From Prithvi Narayan's time onwards, the state had always sought to encourage such expansion through tax concessions but had still faced continuous revenue problems. Financing military expansion in the early years had created a vicious cycle as the conquest of new land required more soldiers, and more soldiers then needed more land to support them. The problem continued with squabbles over a shrunken resource base in the post-Sagauli period. However, the Ranas secured a steady rise in state revenue, which rose from around 1.4 million rupees in 1850 to perhaps 12 million in 1900, a substantial rise even allowing for inflation.[9] Pressure was relieved initially by a short-term reduction in the competition for *jagir* assignments at the top with the expulsion of Jang's political opponents, but then by the continuing expansion of the area under cultivation. Particularly important was the return to Nepal in 1860 of the western Tarai districts, which were initially very sparsely populated. A substantial proportion of the new area was appropriated as *birta* (permanent, tax-free holdings) by the Ranas themselves but the state coffers still profited substantially.

The majority of the cultivators brought into the Tarai by the *jimidars* were from India since the plains were an alien environment to most of the hill people, and the heat and endemic malaria made them particularly unwilling to remain there during the hot weather. Attracting peasants was easier because of the harsh conditions in the British territory to the south, where, in contrast to Nepal, landlords could evict tenants at will. The problem was admitted by British officials themselves in the 1850s and 1860s and was in ironic contrast with William Kirkpatrick's confident prediction at the end of the nineteenth century that the blessings of the East India Company's Permanent Settlement would soon have Nepalese peasants flocking into India.

Once political stability was restored, the nineteenth-century Nepalese state was quite effective in meeting the traditional objectives of maintaining law and order and collecting revenue. Its success was achieved, however, only by encouraging production within the limits of existing techniques. Although Jang Bahadur did at one point toy with the idea of importing British irrigation equipment and he and later maharajas experimented on a small scale with plantation agriculture, there was no sustained attempt to improve agricultural productivity. At the same time, resource depletion was already occurring. Much of the deforestation in the hills which is sometimes attributed to population pressure in the twentieth century is actually a result of land clearance during Gorkha's period of expansion. Copper deposits in the Gulmi–Baglung area and iron in Sindhupalchok had enabled Nepal from about 1790 to manufacture almost all its own munitions, but the low level of mining technology meant that many mines soon had to be abandoned and by the 1860s iron and copper were being imported from India. At the same time Nepal was also slowly beginning to be more dependent on India not just for luxury products for the Kathmandu elite but for more items of everyday use.

QUESTIONS OF IDENTITY

A key question for historians, and also a live issue in present-day politics, is how far the territories brought under Gorkhali control achieved a sense of common identity and how far they remained simply conquered territory. It must be said in any case that belonging to the same state did normally not provide people with their primary identity. Family, clan, village and perhaps also caste or ethnic group, as these categories are now understood, were all more important. When people did think of themselves as subjects of a single king or a single state, it was not 'Nepal' they thought of. This word retained its original meaning of the Kathmandu Valley and did not begin to replace 'Gorkha' or 'Gorkhali' in official use until early in the twentieth century.

There was nevertheless a basis on which some sense of unity could develop. Most obvious was the sense of being 'Paharis', people of the hills: during Prithvi Narayan's 1743 journey to Benares he was told by the king of another *chaubisi* state that on the plains only their common status as hillmen mattered.[10] Among the Paharis, the Parbatiyas were linked together both by language and by a brand of Hinduism somewhat less rigid than that on the plains. The Nepalese hills also differed from Kumaon and Garhwal in the higher standing enjoyed by 'indigenous' Brahmans and

Chetris. It is questionable, however, if this was a psychological reality for the Untouchable Parbatiya castes, who suffered greater exclusion than most Tibeto-Burmans.

Hindu monarchy itself could be regarded as another bond. In the *Dibya Upadesh*, Prithvi Narayan had envisaged his kingdom as a land for Hindus, contrasting with *Mughlana* (India), the land polluted by the rule of the Mughals and their British successors. It was the king's responsibility to sustain the Hindu moral order for his subjects throughout his realm. Until the middle of the nineteenth century the king's realm in this religious sense was probably not seen as including the entire area that he physically controlled but as a smaller, ritually significant core territory. For the Shah kings as successors to the Newar monarchies, this area was primarily the Kathmandu Valley. It was, however, still necessary that the king try to enforce certain Hindu values throughout all of his possessions, in particular the banning of cow-slaughter, and the distinction between realm (*desa*) and possessions (*muluk*) was narrowed further with the promulgation of the Muluki Ain in 1854. The main significance of the code was to commit the state to the enforcement of a uniform caste-based moral order throughout the country. The country's borders, which had already lost their former fluidity with the Treaty of Sagauli in 1816, now became of increased psychological importance.

At least for those closely associated with it, the state itself was another focus of identity. Among the Parbatiya elite there was from early on a concept of the *dhunga* (literally 'stone') or state as something separate from the person of the reigning monarch; this was reinforced by the idea that, in extreme circumstances, the *bharadari* as a whole had the right and duty to act as a check on the king's conduct. Shared memories of a common armed struggle to build the state formed an additional bond and in principle could extend to humbler members of the army and to their families. Such a community of feeling was certainly detected by British observers, such as Brian Hodgson, who wrote of the 'eminent nationality' (i.e. national spirit) of the Nepalese.

Among this whole complex of values and cultural practices, assimilation to those of high-caste Hindus, a process known as sanskritisation, continued slowly throughout the period. Hinduism itself had always been flexible enough to accommodate local religious traditions, so those who wished for patronage from the Gorkhali state did not have to abandon their own previous belief system. At least in externals, they did, however, need to demonstrate their allegiance; one way in which this was done was through the autumn Dasain festival, which renewed the bond between king and subject: for precisely this reason, those in Nepal today who reject both monarchy and Hinduism often call for a boycott of Dasain rituals. Another example was the trend for Khasas in the western hills who had not already done so to adopt the sacred thread and become Chetris,[11] while everywhere non-Parbatiyas were more likely to take Sanskrit personal names and to invite Brahmans to perform some of their rituals. External observance did not, however, necessarily mean full internal acquiescence, particularly lower down the state-sanctioned caste hierarchy, and many remained wedded to alternative values. The cult of the Masta in the western hills, for example, still presented an egalitarian counter to the dominant Brahmanical order.

Naturally enough, identification with the new state was strongest in the central hills where the political and social structure were most similar to those of Gorkha. The Gorkhalis were a more alien presence in the Kiranti areas east of the Dudh Kosi River and west of the Bheri River, regions where one of Nepal's leading historians has described their rule as essentially colonial.[12] The Kirantis had been under nominal control of the Sen kingdoms based in the Tarai but in practice had largely been left to their own devices. Many of them rose in rebellion when the Chinese invaded in 1792. By mid-century doubts about their loyalty had lessened, and Jang Bahadur in 1847 made them eligible for recruitment into the army and in 1863 removed their liability to enslavement. However, throughout the nineteenth century, increasing tension was caused by the movement of Parbatiya settlers into their territories. The Kirantis had been allowed to keep possession of their communally owned *kipat* land and the new arrivals were initially simply their tenants. Nonetheless, the Parbatiyas' greater familiarity with the legal system and with a partially monetized economy led to their gradually gaining control of an increasing proportion of Kiranti land.

An alternative to revolt was simply to move further east along the Himalayas. There was still virgin land to be cleared for settlement and the establishment of Darjeeling as a hill station in 1839 and subsequent growth of tea estates, covering 700,000 acres by 1871, also created a huge demand for labour. One estimate is that 12 to 15 per cent of the Kiranti population in the eastern hills moved across the border between 1840 and 1860.[13] Ironically enough, in mixing here with other ethnic groups from Nepal, the emigrants' need for Nepali as a lingua franca was higher than at home; this in turn affected their own languages. A sample of the Thangmi language collected by Brian Hodgson in Darjeeling in 1847 shows more Nepali influence than is found in the Thangmi spoken today in the Dolakha and Sindhupalchok districts of Nepal itself.

In the Karnali basin and further west, the Shah dynasty's newly acquired subjects were Parbatiyas but still found it difficult to adjust to the new rulers. The state of Jumla, once the seat of the great Khasa empire, fought doggedly to preserve its independence and then, like neighbouring Acham and Doti, also rebelled in 1792. Repression and high revenue demands produced substantial out-migration. A study of tax records suggests that Jumla's population had declined from around 125,000 before annexation to under 80,000 by 1860. The higher level was not regained until the 1930s.[14] During the twenty-five years of Gorkhali rule beyond the Mahakali River, the situation was if anything worse, particularly in Kumaon. The British rule that succeeded it was far from perfect but, in contrast to Jumla, the population expanded steadily throughout the nineteenth century.

The Tarai was also in many ways a colony, although a better-managed one. The great bulk of the cultivators were always from the plains and, in the pre-Rana period, so were many of those in intermediate positions in the revenue-extraction hierarchy. However, Madheshis were never part of the inner core of the *bharadari* and when the *jimidar* system for tax collection was introduced by Jang Bahadur those appointed were predominantly from the hills.[15] The superior status of hillmen in the Nepalese state was made clear in the Muluki Ain, which ranked Parbatiya Brahmans higher than Madheshi ones. Since a common sense of separation from the plains was the main thing that hill Nepalese shared, Madheshis were naturally felt to be outsiders. Conversely, even though they might appreciate the Nepalese government's land-tenure policy, few Madheshis can have felt any strong sense of identity with the Gorkhali state.

Within the central hills, the Tamangs, known at this time as Murmis, had also rebelled in large numbers in 1792. After the Chinese withdrawal, they served the new state as porters and labourers but were not recruited as ordinary soldiers. They remained less assimilated to Parbatiya culture than many Magar communities; still today a larger proportion retain their original language than any other major Tibeto-Burman minority. They, too, felt little identity with the state, but their sense of a common Tamang identity was also still very weak. Membership of a particular clan was more important and some clan names overlapped with those of the Gurungs or Sherpas. There was no clear linguistic boundary between Gurung and Tamang while, as lamaistic Buddhists, the Tamangs were also frequently included with Tibetan dialect speakers under the rather pejorative 'Bhotiya' label. It was arguably the state's own definition of the Murmis/Tamangs as a distinct group which helped turn them in upon themselves and provided a foundation for Tamang ethnicity. They were, however, certainly aware of the divide between themselves and the *jarti,* as they referred to the high-caste Parbatiyas. A well-known Tamang myth (also current among the Sherpas) tells how the ancestor of the Brahmans tricked his brother, the first Tamang, into eating the flesh of their cow-mother and how the cow's intestine then became the Brahmans' sacred thread.

In contrast, Magars and Gurungs had long been part of the military forces of Gorkha as of other *chaubisi* states; Magars in particular could until the eighteenth century be 'promoted' to Chetri status. This seems to have happened on a reduced scale with the Gurungs: Narsingh Gurung was among the *bharadars* executed in Bhimsen Thapa's 1806 purge. Caste lines hardened not, as often supposed, with the coming of the Ranas but rather with the ending of territorial expansion. By the 1830s British observers were reporting that the officer corps was completely Parbatiya. There were still some important Magar *bharadars*, including Abhiman Singh Rana, one of the victims at the Kot but these seemed to be regarded as 'honorary Parbatiyas', and 'Magar' and 'Chetri' were normally exclusive categories. Nevertheless many Magars could still regard themselves as 'Gorkhalis'. It was significant that the abandonment of their own language by many (mostly southern) Magars for Parbatiya (Nepali) had probably been underway since before the Gorkhali conquests,[16] and that people Francis Hamilton spoke to in 1801–4 thought that the Magars would eventually become a Parbatiya caste.[17] Shortly before Jang Bahadur's death, a Magar proclaimed himself an incarnation of the god Lakhan Thapa and led a brief revolt before being captured and killed. Some sympathy with the rebel survives in local folk tradition but, interestingly, the villain in this version of the story is not Jang Bahadur but rather the local twice-born Parbatiyas who prevented Jang's order for a reprieve reaching the local authorities in time. Thus tension between Magars and their immediate neighbours did not exclude some sense of belonging to the more distant state itself.

There was finally the complex case of the Newars of the Kathmandu Valley, who after 1769 seem definitely to have accepted the new rulers: they were described by a British visitor in 1793 as 'tolerably reconciled to the chains imposed upon them by their conquerors'.[18] The predominant feeling seems to have been simply relief that the long war was over and Newar traders, who had even before Prithvi Narayan's time begun to settle on a small scale in the hills, now spread out in greater numbers.[19] In the Valley itself there is no evidence of any attempted revolt. When the Newar *mir munshi* (foreign secretary) Lakshmi Das told the British residency just after Jang's 1846 seizure of power that the Newars would rise at his command, the British rightly assumed that he was merely acting as an *agent provocateur,* testing on Jang's behalf whether the residency's professions of non-intervention were genuine.

At the same time, however, there remained a strong gulf between Gorkhali and Newar. One prominent Newar *bharadar,* Tribhuvan Pradhan, was among Bhimsen's victims in 1806; thereafter a small number of Newars were appointed to government posts or receiving lucrative contracts, but they were never at the centre of power. There was little social integration either. Prithvi Narayan Shah himself is said to have praised the charms of Newar women, and his son had an influential Newar mistress as well as an interest in the tantricism which was an important feature of Newar religion, but regular marriage between Parbatiyas and Newars was not permitted. The Parbatiyas seem to have been particularly disdainful of the *banre,* the Vajracharyas and Shakyas: Kirkpatrick records a conversation with a 'Rajpoot' (i.e. Thakuri or perhaps Chetri), who was eager to point out that none of his caste ever visited the Buddhist temple of Swaymbhunath, normally frequented by these castes and by Tibeto-Burmans from the hills.[20] This attitude served, of course, to strengthen Newar identity rather than encourage full identification with the state. The Newars did, however, have a strong sense of belonging to the Kathmandu Valley and, as kings of the Valley, the Shah dynasty could expect a degree of loyalty.

During the nineteenth century, assimilative forces in Nepalese society, strongest when the state was expanding rapidly, slowed. If Hamilton had visited Nepal in Ranoddip Singh's time he would have been unlikely to describe Parbatiya as 'rapidly extinguishing the aboriginal dialects of the mountains',[21] but change was still occurring. The power of social and economic change to transform group boundaries is illustrated by the growth of the Chantel people in the mining districts of Baglung and Myagdi in the central hills. The core of the ethnic group was probably a single clan speaking a dialect closely related to Thakali.[22] They seem to have entered the area around 1800 and, after they had acquired the exclusive right to copper mining in the district, another eleven or twelve clans formed, as outsiders (probably Magars and low-caste Parbatiyas) joined the group. The pace of change was slower for most Nepalese but would begin to quicken over the following century.

CHAPTER 3

Nepal under the Shamsher Ranas, 1885–1951

The Shamsher Ranas ruled Nepal for sixty-six years from 1885. It was a period that saw the beginnings of the takeoff in population growth and, consequently, increasing pressure on land in the hills. These years also brought the tightening of the economic bonds between the Nepalese and Indian economies and the slowly increasing exposure of Nepal's people to new ways of thinking from India and the world beyond. These were, however, long-term processes and, particularly in the earlier part of the period, they did not make a strong impact on political developments. Here the important factors were the jockeying for power within the Rana family itself and also the regime's relationship with British India. Co-operation with the British had been the norm since even before Jang Bahadur's takeover, but it was strengthened by the accession to power of a new generation of Ranas. All had been educated to some level in English and, while still a little wary of British intentions, they did not feel the deep suspicion of *firangis* which Jang had shared with all Nepalese statesmen before him. The new attitude was also helped by a major change in British policy in India after the Mutiny crisis of 1857. Whereas before they had seemed intent on elbowing aside traditional rulers and substituting their own direct administration, greater caution now ruled, and the British were anxious to sustain rather than supplant what remained of traditional political structures. With the rise of the Indian nationalist movement around the turn of the century, this more conservative stance was further reinforced because such rulers – whether the Indian 'princes' or the Ranas in Nepal – seemed natural allies against radical demands for political change.

FROM BIR TO BHIM: THE HIGH TIDE OF RANA RULE

The system of agnate succession continued after 1885, and the joint position of maharaja and prime minister was held in turn by five of Dhir Shamsher's sons and then by two of his grandchildren. Following the practice already adopted by Jang Bahadur, the principal offices of state were held by the Ranas next in line to succeed the maharaja and thus at the head of 'the Roll'. The most senior of these was the commander-in-chief, whose role was in fact the supervision of the *civil* administration. Below him in the hierarchy was the western commanding general, the man who had actual day-to-day control of the army and was popularly known as the *jangi lat* (war lord); next came the eastern, southern and northern commanding generals. All the Ranas continued to acknowledge the theoretically higher status of the king, who was known as Shri Panch Sarkar (Five-Times Illustrious Ruler), while the maharaja was merely Shri Tin Sarkar (Three-Times Illustrious Ruler).

Even if Maharaja Bir Shamsher, eldest of Dhir's sons, had shared earlier rulers' deep suspicion of the British, close co-operation would still have been inevitable. During his early years in power, Jang Bahadur's sons attempted to launch armed raids from India, and Bir had to ensure he gave the British no reason to assist them. The British had decided just before the Shamsher takeover to increase the number of Gurkha regiments from five to ten; Bir helped them to achieve this by allowing serving soldiers to recruit when they were home on leave and also by legal changes which made it easier for a man who enlisted to retain control of land in Nepal. By 1890 the British were satisfied they were getting full co-operation.

Despite at least two conspiracies against him involving several of his brothers, Bir ruled Nepal until his death from natural causes in April 1901. He is commemorated today in the name of the border town of Birganj, which forms the principal gateway to Nepal for travellers coming by land from India. An existing small settlement was expanded and renamed to mark Bir's appointment by the British in 1897 as Knight Grand Commander of the Star of India.

Bir was succeeded by Dev Shamsher, who combined extravagant tastes (even by Rana standards) with genuinely liberal leanings. He proposed to establish a network of vernacular schools and also attempted to emancipate female slaves in the Kathmandu Valley and in the maharaja's own special domain of Kaski and Lamjung. He held an unprecedented public meeting in the main hall of his own residence to invite suggestions for reform, and, to provide a continuing forum for people to express their grievances, he founded Nepal's first newspaper, the *Gorkhapatra*. Dev's liberalism did not, perhaps, extend as far as is sometimes suggested today, for he specifically excluded the powers and privileges of the maharaja himself from discussion in his people's assembly. Nevertheless, these moves greatly alarmed his more conservative brothers and they combined to force his abdication after only

8. Chandra Shamsher Rana, maharaja from 1901 to 1929.

four months in office. He was sent into internal exile and later moved to India. Most of his initiatives were abandoned but the *Gorkhapatra* survived, though as a kind of official gazette rather than a channel for complaints, and today it remains the government's Nepali-language newspaper.

The man who took over, Chandra Shamsher, maharaja from 1901 to 1929, was a skilful administrator, and also a veteran intriguer. Although he had probably been involved in at least two plots against Bir, he had managed to avoid the blame when these failed. He was the only one of the brothers to study in Calcutta University and he was also unusual for the austerity of his personal lifestyle: he was both teetotal and monogamous.

Respected rather than loved, it is said that he rarely smiled but that when he did it was an ominous sign for the person he was talking to. Chandra's two most visible legacies in Kathmandu are Trichandra College, set up in 1919, and his palace, the Singha Darbar, which now houses the government's main secretariat in Kathmandu. Chandra also formally abolished slavery and *sati* in Nepal as well as systematising the administration, which had previously depended heavily on the maharaja personally making even very minor decisions.

Close co-operation with the British was for Chandra very much a strategic choice rather than one of compulsion. Before moving against Dhir, he had hinted at his intention in a letter to a former British resident, and it has often been assumed that he sounded out the viceroy, Lord Curzon, on the plan when hunting with him in the Nepalese Tarai. Chandra subsequently became an enthusiastic partner in Curzon's 'forward policy' in Tibet, actually taking the initiative himself to warn the British of the need to forestall Russian interference. When the Younghusband expedition was sent into Tibet in 1904, Nepal provided logistical help, and the Nepalese representative in Lhasa was of great value to the British both as a source of information and as a mediator between them and the Chinese authorities.

During the First World War, Chandra assisted in obtaining 55,000 recruits for the Gurkha regiments of the Indian army, and also sent some 18,000 of Nepal's own troops into India to take up garrison duties. Including Nepalese in other units such as the military police in Burma, around 100,000 were involved in the war effort, with at least 10,000 killed and another 14,000 wounded or missing.[1] While the claim by one Nepalese historian that in relation to its population (then around 5 million) Nepal's losses were greater than those of any other country[2] is thus clearly untrue, the contribution was a significant one.

In recompense Chandra would have most preferred the return of some or all of the territory lost under the Treaty of Sagauli, but this was considered politically impossible, and he received instead an annual subsidy of 1 million rupees. Subsequent maharajas continued to press for a land grant but, although they might gain sympathy from the British representative in Kathmandu, the authorities in India and in Britain valued the hold over Rana behaviour that an annual subsidy gave them.

The 1923 treaty between Britain and Nepal explicitly recognising Nepal's complete independence was also partly a reward for wartime co-operation. Here, though, the British may have had the additional motive of securing the loyalty of Gurkha troops used to quell disturbances in India: if Nepal were completely separate from India, such troops were less likely to feel that they had something in common with Indian nationalists. Even before 1923 the Nepalese themselves had never admitted that they were not completely independent and Britain, too, had at one time fully accepted the Nepalese position. However, by the late nineteenth century, British Indian officials had begun arguing that Nepal's status was somewhere between that of fully independent Afghanistan and the 'princely' or 'native states' within India subject to the British Crown.

Chandra died in 1929, leaving to his brother Bhim plans for war with Tibet over the arrest of a man of mixed Nepalese and Tibetan descent. Under the 1856 treaty, such individuals were supposed to be subject only to Nepalese jurisdiction. Hostilities were, however, averted through British mediation. Bhim's lasting mark on Nepalese life was the institution of a weekly holiday on Saturday and the fixing of working hours on other days as 10 a.m. to 5 p.m., an arrangement only recently superseded by a five-day week for civil servants in 1999.

FROM JUDDHA TO MOHAN: THE LAST YEARS OF THE OLD REGIME

Bhim's short administration had been marked by tension between rival groups of Ranas. The Shamsher brothers had fathered many sons by their various wives and concubines, swelling the numbers on the Roll of Succession to the premiership. Legitimate sons resented having to take their turns for the highest office behind their illegitimate half-brothers and cousins. In 1920 Chandra had attempted to tackle this problem by a threefold classification of the family: A-Class Ranas, whose mothers were of equal caste status to the father and were married with full religious rites; B-Class, whose mothers, although still high-caste (Thakuri or Chetri), had been married by a simpler ceremony (this was often employed where a couple had had a relationship before the marriage); and C-Class, who were illegitimate and normally the sons of lower-caste mothers. Chandra decreed that in future only A-Class Ranas would be added to the Roll, but he did not remove anyone already on it, and the illegitimate sons of Bir Shamsher included by their father in 1885–1901 thus retained their right to the premiership. Bhim then undid Chandra's work by adding his own C-Class sons and grandsons to the list.

Bhim's successor, Juddha, the last of Dhir's sons, faced a major disaster on 15 January 1934 when a large part of Nepal, and of neighbouring areas in India, was devastated by a severe earthquake. Around 7000 died across the country, and there was large-scale damage to buildings. The calmness displayed by most of the population and the energetic reaction of senior Ranas greatly impressed the British legation, as the residency was now styled. Juddha himself was hunting in the Tarai at the time of the quake and did not reach Kathmandu until three weeks later, but then organised relief work and rebuilding successfully without the need to accept any foreign help. Especially appreciated was the setting aside of 10 million rupees for loans to private citizens and subsequent waiving of the requirement of repayment; the impact of this gesture may be gauged from the fact that many individuals simply refused to take advantage of the offer, believing that it was sinful to take the king's money. Major monuments such as the clock tower of Trichandra College and the minaret erected by Bhimsen Thapa were reconstructed, but the destruction of part of Kathmandu's crowded city centre was turned to advantage and Juddha Sadak (Juddha Street) was driven through the area. New Road, as it came to be called, remains today the main focus of much of the city's commercial and social life.

The earthquake was followed two months later by a political upheaval. When Juddha became premier he had as his commander-in-chief and successor-designate Rudra, illegitimate son of Bir, while lower down the Roll the presence of other C-Class individuals depressed the position of the legitimate sons of Chandra and of Juddha himself. Tension between the two groups increased, and on 18 March 1934 Rudra and the other C-Class Ranas on the Roll were summoned to the Singha Darbar for a meeting of the state council, only to find the building ringed with troops. A few minutes later Juddha himself entered with a pistol in each hand and ordered their removal from the Roll. Almost all were sent to live outside Kathmandu, and several, including Rudra, were appointed as district governors.

Juddha undertook the purge with some reluctance, for he and his nephew Rudra were of virtually the same age and had been brought up together. Apart from concern for the interests of his own sons, Juddha's motive was probably fear that unless he resolved the quarrel between A- and C-Classes he could himself meet the same fate as Ranoddip Singh, whose assassination in 1885 had been the result of the rivalry between Jang and the Shamsher Ranas. The actual timing was apparently determined by the argument that it would be considerate to oust the C-Class before they had had the trouble and expense of rebuilding their houses after the earthquake.

Threats from outside the family were now beginning to emerge as well. Since the end of the First World War, anti-Rana agitation had developed among Nepalese living in India. Within Nepal, too, there were anti-Rana stirrings, though these were largely confined to a minuscule minority educated in India or at Trichandra College in Kathmandu. In 1931, during Bhim's time, a small group of would-be revolutionaries (Prachanda Gorkha) had been broken up and the members imprisoned. In the mid-1930s an embryo political party, the Nepal Praja Parishad (Nepal People's Council), was secretly formed and its members had managed to make contact with King Tribhuvan. Tribhuvan, who had become king in 1911 at the age of five, had long resented his status as a powerless tool of the Ranas and was also involved in at least one other clandestine movement, ominously known as the Raktapat Mandal (Bloodshed Committee).

On the outbreak of war in 1939, Nepal declared support for Britain immediately, just as in 1914. Unlike many other members of the Rana family, Juddha was personally convinced even after the defeats of 1940 that the British and their allies would eventually win and committed Nepal to their cause. Gurkha troops, whether enlisted in the Indian army or serving in Nepal's own forces, again played an invaluable role.[3] Three Nepalese battalions actually fought as part of the Fourteenth Army in Burma under General Slim and perhaps another 200,000 Nepalese served with British Indian Gurkha units or in the Indian military police. There was no formal conscription, but, as in the First World War, some recruits did join under pressure from the authorities. However, just as the Congress Party in India had refused to back the war, so dissidents in Nepal saw no need to postpone their demands. In 1940, Tanka Prasad Acharya, the son of a revenue-collector who had been unfairly dismissed by Chandra, was elected president of the Praja Parishad. Sympathisers in India published propaganda on its behalf and then in September, using a smuggled duplicator, the members themselves were able to print and distribute in Kathmandu leaflets calling for people to rise up against the government.

The identities of those involved were betrayed to the authorities and in January 1941 three leading members, and one sympathiser who was only marginally connected with the Parishad, were executed: they are commemorated today by Sahid (Martyrs') Gate in Kathmandu. Tanka Prasad and three other colleagues escaped with their lives only because as Brahmans they were exempt from the death penalty under Nepalese law. Tanka Prasad in fact survived to become prime minister himself for a short period in the 1950s and remained active in public life until his death in 1992. The executions, as forecast by the British minister when he advised against them, increased public resentment against the maharaja, and it is possible that Chandra's sons urged a hard line precisely in the hope that it would indeed make Juddha more unpopular.

The king's connection with the Praja Parishad was also uncovered, either because incriminating documents were found in the house of one of the activists executed or because the activist himself implicated him. Juddha and his associates considered pressing Tribhuvan into abdicating in favour of his son, Crown Prince Mahendra. However, Mahendra refused to play the role projected for him and it was politically dangerous for Juddha to use visible coercion on the royal family: powerless though he might be, the king was still seen by his subjects as the ultimate source of legitimacy.

For the remainder of the war the internal situation in Nepal remained quiet, but anti-British activists fled into the Tarai after the crushing of the Indian National Congress's Quit India movement in 1942. Nepal was at first reluctant to co-operate fully with the British in extraditing them but did so after local people in Saptari stormed a jail to release Jaya Prakash Narayan and others. Of 490 wanted Congressmen, 465 were eventually captured and handed over. In 1945 the British refused Juddha's request to replace the annual subsidy with land which would be ceded to Nepal. However, they offered to double the subsidy to 2 million rupees and also, as independent India could not be expected to continue the old arrangement, they proposed conversion of part of this nominal sum into a single lump payment to Nepal.

In November 1945, believing that he had not much longer to live, Juddha resigned his office and went into religious retreat in the Indian Himalayas. His successor, Padma, the son of Bhim Shamsher, was faced with a difficult test. The British were preparing to relinquish their Indian empire, and the Indian nationalists who would replace them had strong ideological sympathies, and sometimes personal ties, with the Ranas' Nepalese opponents. In October 1946 the All India Nepali National Congress, with a largely student membership, was set up at Benares. This group merged in January 1947 with the Calcutta-based Gorkha Congress and with another Benares organisation, the Nepal Sangh, to form the Nepali National Congress. Tanka Prasad Acharya was chosen as president but, as he was still in prison in Kathmandu, this was merely a symbolic gesture: the real leader was B. P. Koirala, son of an old opponent of Chandra Shamsher. Under B. P. as acting president, the party promoted a strike in the jute mill at Biratnagar, the Koiralas' home town, situated just across the border from India. B. P. Koirala was arrested, but further demonstrations took place in Kathmandu, and the campaign continued until May 1947, when Padma Shamsher announced that a programme of reforms would be brought forward.

Padma's inaugural speech, in which he referred to himself as a 'servant of the people', had in fact already given an indication that he favoured a conciliatory approach. However, in addition to being less wealthy than most leading Ranas, he was from the start a comparatively isolated figure. His brothers and nephews had been among the C-Class Ranas purged in 1934, and it was his A-Class cousins who held the senior positions on the Roll of Succession and who were therefore the key powers in the administration. Among these cousins, Chandra Shamsher's three eldest sons, Mohan (now commander-in-chief), Babar and Keshar, were particularly reluctant to make concessions to the opposition. Some of Padma's advisers, including one of his C-Class nephews whom he had recalled to Kathmandu, urged him to take steps against his cousins before they could move against him, but although he initially agreed to this scheme his nerve later failed him and the plan was abandoned. Details of this abortive purge were nevertheless learned by the intended victims and this rendered Padma's own position all the more precarious.

In January 1948, five months after India had become independent, Padma announced his plans for a new constitution, involving an elected assembly. Although his new body was to have strictly limited powers, the offer was welcomed by the Nepali National Congress as a reasonable start. The following month, however, apparently convinced that his life might be in danger from Rana hard-liners, Padma crossed into India pleading 'medical reasons', and in April he wrote a formal letter of resignation. The commander-in-chief, Mohan Shamsher, duly became the next prime minister and maharaja. Power thus returned to Chandra's family.

The new regime did not formally abandon Padma's reform programme, but cracked down on opposition activity, banning both the Congress and subsequently a new Kathmandu-based organisation, the Praja Panchayat, which was campaigning for implementation of the new constitution. A parliament of sorts, packed with Rana supporters, met in 1950 but its sittings were suspended after a short period.

Mohan's strategy was to preserve the internal status quo while seeking to buttress his position externally. In 1945 Britain had been the only country with an official representative at Kathmandu, but under Padma overtures had already been made to the United States and France; Mohan now announced that Nepal wished to establish diplomatic relations with any country willing to reciprocate. The most important priority was, of course, to reach an understanding with newly independent India, and Mohan found Nehru's government less intractable than might have been feared. However much India might have liked to see a more democratic government in Nepal, it was also eager for stability on its northern border at a time when the Communists were on the verge of winning the civil

9. Mohan Shamsher Rana rides through Kathmandu on an elephant to mark his
inauguration as prime minister and maharaja in 1948.

war in China and of re-establishing that country as a major power. The
Nepalese government allowed the use of Gorkha troops to help maintain
order in northern India in 1949 while Indian forces moved against the
ruler of the former princely state of Hyderabad, who had been resisting
the demand that he merge his territory with India. In the following year
Mohan was able to conclude security and commercial agreements with
New Delhi.

Mohan's Nepalese opponents were far from placated, however, and he
foolishly strengthened their ranks by confiscating the assets within Nepal of
some of the C-Class Ranas. Two of these, Subarna and Mahavir Shamsher,
grandsons of Bhim and nephews of Padma, reacted by funding the establishment of the Nepali Democratic Congress in Calcutta, with the aim of
beginning an armed struggle against the Rana regime. In spring 1950 this
organisation merged with the Nepali National Congress to form a unified
party, known simply as the Nepali Congress. The new party claimed to
employ non-violent methods, but it secretly commissioned B. P. Koirala
and Subarna Shamsher to organise a fighting force. Among the recruits
were both students and former Gurkha soldiers of the British Indian army,
particularly a number who had been captured by the Japanese and then
joined Sarat Chandra Bose's 'Indian National Army' to fight alongside
the Japanese against the British. The Indian government appears to have

given tacit approval but wanted to retain 'deniability' by insisting that they obtained weapons from outside India. Arms were secured from Burma with the help of leaders of the Indian Socialist Party and ferried into India by an aircraft of Mahavir's Himalayan Airways company.

Plans were made for the abduction of King Tribhuvan from the palace and for a revolt within the Nepalese army, but the conspiracy was uncovered by the Rana authorities and arrests were made in Kathmandu. The king's position was now extremely precarious, and he decided he must escape from Rana custody. On the morning of 6 November 1950, he and most of his family left the palace, ostensibly for a hunting expedition. The princes drove their cars themselves and the accompanying Rana aides were thus unable to prevent them suddenly turning aside from their official route and entering the gates of the Indian embassy. Although attempts were to be made to disguise the fact, the Indians had been secretly warned of what was to happen, and the gates were immediately locked behind them.

The king's youngest grandson, three-year-old Prince Gyanendra, had been left behind in the palace, presumably to ensure the future of the dynasty in case anything should happen to the rest of the family. On 7 November, Mohan had the child proclaimed king in Tribhuvan's place. After negotiations with the embassy he permitted Tribhuvan and the remainder of the family to be flown to India from the military airstrip at Kathmandu.

With Tribhuvan safely on Indian soil, the Nepali Congress volunteers launched a series of armed attacks across the border and succeeded in capturing the town of Birganj. The Indian government planned to rely on diplomacy to negotiate a compromise settlement between the Ranas and King Tribhuvan, and in late November clamped down on the fighters, in particular denying them the use of the Indian railway system to transport men and materials. This gave Mohan's regime some respite, and Birganj was recaptured by Nepalese troops.

By the end of the month, however, the Indians had found the Ranas unwilling to make the required concessions, and from about 20 December they therefore covertly relaxed their control of Nepali Congress activity. Rebel forces took control of Biratnagar and penetrated deep into the eastern hills to capture Dhankuta, Bhojpur, Terhatum and other district centres. In the first week of January 1951 there was a mass surrender of government troops on the Kosi River, while in the hills west of Kathmandu the key garrison at Tansen, where Rudra Shamsher was district governor, defected to the rebel side.

Away from the battlefield Mohan's diplomacy also proved unequal to the occasion, despite the advantage of support from the British government, which still regarded the Ranas as valuable allies and cannot have been pleased by the Nepali Congress leaders' avowed hostility to the continuing recruitment of Gurkhas into the British army. The British in fact wanted to recognise the new king and appeared to have US support in this. They wished to avoid a breach with India if possible and sought at first to persuade Nehru not to insist on Tribhuvan's return, but were probably on the verge of recognising Gyanendra unilaterally when they received news that a Rana delegation would travel to Delhi. They now accepted an Indian suggestion to delay any announcement and were also influenced by the massive anti-Rana demonstration that greeted a British fact-finding mission on its arrival at Kathmandu airport at the beginning of December.[4] Nevertheless the British still hoped to keep Mohan's regime in power and in discussions in Kathmandu endorsed a strategy of announcing a constituent assembly and fully representative government as long-term aims and also setting up a regency council for Gyanendra.

Mohan, however, failed to implement this plan in full, and the Indians continued to press for proposals they had put to Nepal on 8 December: Tribhuvan's return and the setting-up of a cabinet including both Rana and Nepali Congress representatives. The regime was now faced with a deteriorating military situation and were unwilling to confront India, instead only putting forward further reform proposals for discussion. A contributing factor was probably that many of the leading Ranas, who had invested much of their personal fortunes in India during British rule, were anxious that their assets might be seized. By 2 January Rana representatives in Delhi were indicating that Tribhuvan might after all be acceptable and on the 8th Mohan formally agreed to accept both Tribhuvan as king and a coalition cabinet made up of Ranas and 'representatives of the people'.

This did not go far enough for the Nepali Congress, which had wanted to fight on until it achieved a complete victory. The Nehru government, however, feared that, if the Rana regime completely collapsed, their opponents might not be able to put anything in its place, and some at least in the Nepali Congress were unsure of their ability to control their armed followers.[5] The Congress leadership therefore accepted what had been signed and on 15 February, after further negotiations on points of detail, Tribhuvan returned in triumph to Kathmandu and the extraordinary power granted to the Rana prime ministers by the royal decrees of 1846–57 were formally revoked. Although Mohan remained prime minister until November, at the head of a cabinet that included B. P. Koirala and other Congress leaders, it was the king who now held the ultimate authority in fact as well as in theory.

10. Bishweshwar Prasad Koirala ('B. P.'), bare-headed and wearing a Nehru jacket, with King Tribhuvan (centre) during the anti-Rana struggle.

ECONOMY, PEOPLE AND GOVERNMENT

The final collapse of the Rana regime had resulted not from a widely based popular movement but rather from divisions within the political elite and from the policy adopted by newly independent India. Nevertheless, the Shamsher years had seen changes that had a profound effect on the lives of people throughout the country. Foremost among these was the beginning of the dramatic acceleration in population growth that remains a key challenge today. Precise statistics are not available, since formal censuses began only in 1911, and even then the data generated were not fully reliable. The figures do, however, show a moderate upward trend through the early years of the century, accelerating sharply in the 1940s. The effects of modern medicines might possibly have been a factor towards the end of the period, but these were never widely enough available in the hills before 1950 to make a great difference. Changing in cropping patterns such as the introduction of the potato or increased maize cultivation may also have contributed. However, the basic explanation seems rather to have been the removal of Malthusian checks which had previously been restraining population growth. In the early, pre-unification years, high birth-rates had been matched by high levels of infant mortality, perhaps producing a rise in population of around 0.5 per cent in a normal year. This growth rate could be reduced or even reversed as a result of a natural or manmade disaster, such as military conflict, or the demands for higher revenues from the populace during and after the unification campaigns.[6] Relatively stable conditions during the latter half of the nineteenth century and the scope for agrarian expansion provided by the far western Tarai allowed the upward trend to resume and perhaps slightly accelerate. A combination of factors provided the capital needed to bring more land under cultivation. Money could be earned working in India, the central government's revenue demand was decreasing as a proportion of total production and there were also increased opportunities to export agricultural surplus to an expanding market economy in India.

The decline in revenue demand was particularly marked after 1910 when Chandra Shamsher fixed rents in cash terms, which were then left virtually unchanged for many years. Previously, rents had been paid in cash, but rose with inflation since they were calculated each year on the basis of the price the government's nominal share of the crop would fetch. The new method in some cases reduced the demand from 20–25 per cent to under 1 per cent of total produce, but this was not necessarily to the advantage of the actual cultivator. The registered tenant was now often able to sub-let the land and, after paying the reduced government land tax, take a landlord's share of the larger surplus being left in the village.

Rising population was initially accompanied by some increase in disposable income. In the Sherpa country beneath Mt Everest, for example, paid work in India helped make it possible for the community to establish Buddhist monasteries and support monks for the first time. However, pressure on resources over most of the country was becoming too great. Already by the start of the Shamsher period the expense involved was usually high enough to give land previously cleared a capital value; eventually the point was reached at which new land was completely unavailable. Around Ilam in the south-eastern hills, this stage had apparently already been reached by the 1890s; in much of the central hills the crucial date was probably some time between the two world wars. As land became scarcer, it had to be used more efficiently. The old pattern of communally orientated pastoralism, supplemented by slash-and-burn agriculture, which had been retained especially by some of the non-Parbatiya groups in the hills, now almost everywhere gave way to intensive use of privately owned land.

There were also significant changes in the structure of land holdings. The *jagir* system, under which government servants received the right to the revenue from particular plots of land, was gradually replaced under

Chandra with a uniform system of cash salaries. Though the word remains in use in Nepali in the meaning of 'salaried (government) post', *jagir* in the old sense had virtually disappeared by 1950. Around 60 per cent of agricultural land was now under *raikar* tenure, with the owner (nominally still a 'tenant') paying 'rent' directly to the government, while another third was *birta,* with rent going to the *birtawala* (usually a Rana), who paid either no revenue or only a nominal amount to the government. In 1906 Chandra had extended from *raikar* land to *birta* the tenant's security against dispossession when another would-be cultivator offered a higher rent. Unfortunately, this legal protection was not always effective and, in any case, as with the freeze on rent levels in 1910, the benefit did not necessarily go to the actual cultivator. The nominal tenant could simply sub-let the land and make a living on the difference between the rent he paid and the rent he received.

Two other categories of tenure which survived until the end of the Rana regime were *guthi* (2.3 per cent of total land) and *kipat* (4.6 per cent). *Guthi* land was held revenue-free by religious institutions, which in practice might mean just an ordinary family who had formally gifted land to a shrine but then appointed themselves the shrine's guardians. Under *kipat* tenure, which survived from pre-unification times among some of the Tibeto-Burman hill groups, land could not be alienated to anyone outside the clan, who were the ultimate, collective owners. This system declined steadily during the Rana years and had disappeared completely from the Rai areas west of the Arun River in the 1940s. Further east, however, the Limbus, a more cohesive grouping, succeeded in retaining the old order. Legislation in 1886 had provided for Limbu *kipat* lands leased out to non-Limbu cultivators to be automatically converted to *raikar* tenure and thus (in practice) to be sold freely. But in 1901 such conversions were ended. Henceforth Limbu *kipat* lands might be mortgaged to an outsider but could be regained at any time by repayment of the loan. With the increasing demand for land, Limbus had the option of repaying the original mortgage by obtaining a higher one from another bidder. While the Limbu *subbas* lost some authority and were no longer government agents for tax collection from non-Limbu settlers in their area, the Limbu community as a whole enjoyed a certain degree of security.

Large-scale population movements continued throughout the Shamsher period. Land was still being cleared for settlement on the Tarai but those who moved in to work it were normally from across the Indian border. Many hillmen, especially from the Tibeto-Burman-speaking communities, moved eastwards along the Himalayas, now driven by land hunger rather than the simple wish to escape the government's exactions. British-ruled Darjeeling had already had a Nepalese majority in 1872 while by 1891 Nepalese immigrants were 65 per cent of the population of Sikkim. From around the time of the 1864–5 Anglo-Bhutan war until the 1930s, migrants also settled in southern Bhutan, opening up areas unattractive to the Lepchas of the north. Many others sought short- or long-term employment in India to supplement agricultural incomes. Even when land had been more plentiful, such temporary absence had been part of the subsistence strategy of many highland communities, and the usual intention was still to return to one's village. The end result could, however, be permanent migration and around one-third of those who served in British Indian Gurkha regiments in the First World War did not return to Nepal, most often settling in the hill areas of north-western or north-eastern India where they had previously been stationed. The outflow in the war years for both military and non-military employment was in fact so great that there was a shortage of agricultural labour within Nepal and of recruits for Nepal's own army. Chandra even had to ask the British to bar Nepalese from working in tea gardens and similar civilian occupations. However, annual recruitment for the Brigade of Gurkhas reverted after 1918 to 1800 and the effects of both world wars produced mere blips in long-term population growth.

Like migration, external trade was long established, but patterns changed radically with economic development in India and especially the extension from 1885 to 1898 of the railway system to the Nepal border opposite Nepalganj, Biratnagar, Janakpur and finally Birganj. There were now greater opportunities for export of grain and other produce to India, and, taking advantage of the Indian railway system's own demand for wooden sleepers, Bir Shamsher established a saw mill in the Tarai to process Nepalese timber. However, it was also easier for Indian imports to penetrate the hills. Indian salt, for example, began slowly to replace the Tibetan salt which had for centuries been obtained through local salt–grain exchange networks. After the beginning of petroleum production in India in the 1880s, kerosene for lamps and cooking became another increasingly important commodity import.

New trading patterns spelled the end for Kathmandu's centuries-old role as an entrepôt for trade across the Himalayas. The process began when the British established control over Sikkim in 1860, and began to develop the route into Tibet via the Chumbi Valley. After the completion of the Calcutta–Darjeeling railway in 1881, Lhasa could be reached in three weeks from Calcutta, about half the time of the journey via Kathmandu. The final blow was the Younghusband expedition of 1904, which forced Tibet to permit unrestricted trade. Nevertheless, localised commerce between Nepal and Tibet remained important, particularly the salt–grain exchange, and disputes over this, and also over the extra-territorial privileges of the Newar community in Lhasa, brought the two countries to the brink of hostilities in the 1890s and again in the 1930s.

More important for the Nepalese economy as a whole was the growing share of the country's internal market captured by imported manufactures. The political elite had long been dressed in imported cloth, but its use gradually spread among the general population. Similarly, utensils used in agriculture and household tasks became more likely to have been made outside the country. This trend was reinforced as production at many of Nepal's own copper and iron mines became uneconomical. There is conflicting evidence on how early and how fast the changes developed. Import penetration must have been swiftest around bazaar towns: at one such centre west of Gorkha, Newar merchants were already in the middle of the nineteenth century importing British fabric on a large scale and using the profits to branch out into money-lending. As early as 1861 the British resident could write that the products of Nepal's own artisans were 'annually deteriorating'.[7] However, in 1879 another resident argued that there was little scope for increasing trade between India and Nepal because the great majority of the population remained largely self-sufficient.[8] It is possible that Nepalese artisans held their own against British competition until after the First World War and that it was a flood of Japanese goods allowed into the country duty-free under the provisions of the 1923 treaty that transformed the situation.

However far back the displacement of Nepal's own craftsmen had begun, it was certainly in the inter-war years that the Rana regime became aware of this process as a serious problem. From the time of Jang Bahadur onwards, the government had tended to see trade as a source of government revenue and also as a means for individual Ranas to make money, often as partners to Newar merchants granted monopoly rights for the import of particular goods. This attitude did not disappear but now some efforts were made to promote domestic production. Partly inspired by the Indian nationalists' emphasis on 'homespun' cloth, Chandra and Juddha encouraged cottage industry, setting up training schemes and also helping with the supply of raw materials. In addition, Juddha sponsored larger-scale enterprise, including the establishment with local and Indian private capital of a jute mill at Biratnagar in the eastern Tarai in 1936. Processing plants for matches, cigarettes, rice and vegetable oil were established in the same area soon afterwards.

Although the Second World War ensured high demand for some products, particularly jute sacking, the overall impact on the economy of all these
initiatives was marginal. In some cases, lack of determination and consis-
tency may have been to blame. In Bandipur, for example, local Newar
merchants set up a small textile operation in 1943 but this had to close
when the government ended the supply of subsidised Indian yarn, perhaps
under pressure from the British Indian authorities.[9] But even if the Ranas
had been more willing to risk angering their powerful neighbour, Nepal's
long frontier with India posed a crucial problem. First, it was then (as now)
impossible to keep complete control of the movement of goods across it,
so that Juddha's prohibition on the import of any commodity which could
be produced in Nepal was a dead letter from the start. Secondly, since
raw materials needed for manufacturing had normally to be brought in
across Indian territory, no policy for industrial development could succeed
without Indian support. This was difficult to secure because, under the
pressure of Indian nationalism, the British administration was increasingly
concerned with the protection of India's own industry and already in 1924
was worrying that Indian tariffs might be circumvented by Japanese goods
imported through Nepal. In 1937 it turned down Juddha's request that the
Nepalese imports allowed a waiver on customs duty at Calcutta be allowed
to go directly to factories in the Tarai rather than be sent to Kathmandu
for British residency inspection. A 1938 proposal that India itself impose
duties on its own exports to Nepal was also rebuffed. A treaty regulating
commerce was finally reached in 1950, when Mohan Shamsher's bargaining
position had been weakened by the anti-Rana movement. It allowed for free
trade between the two countries but robbed Nepalese industrialists of any
chance of competing in the Indian market by requiring Nepal to impose
on imports from abroad duties equivalent to those imposed by India itself.

In addition to limited steps towards industrialisation, the Shamshers also
began the development of modern infrastructure. In 1889, Bir Shamsher
established the Bir Hospital, which is still Kathmandu's leading medical
institution; he also employed a British engineer to install a piped water
system in the capital. Water was brought to taps inside Rana palaces and to
public taps for the general population, and villagers believed that drinking
from these 'Bir taps' was a cure for diarrhoea. Chandra Shamsher's most
expensive project was his Singha Darbar palace, but he was also responsible
for a number of suspension bridges on major trails in the hills, for the
ropeway from Bhimphedi on the edge of the Tarai to the Valley opened in
1926, and for bringing electricity to Kathmandu. Chandra toyed with the
idea of building a road from the plains, but, as had been the case with Jang

Bahadur before him, he abandoned the scheme in the face of opposition from the traditionally minded around him. The few cars running on the Valley's roads in the inter-war years had been disassembled and carried over the foothills by porters in the traditional way. Communications between Kathmandu and the rest of the country were, however, improved indirectly by railway expansion in India. Instead of travelling across the grain of the land, one could now descend one river valley to the plains, travel west or east by train and then ascend another valley. In this way the journey from Kathmandu to Morang (the area around Biratnagar) was shortened from ten to four days. Finally, the air age dawned in 1942 when the British resident hastily prepared an airstrip at Simra north of Birganj to re-establish communications with Calcutta after their disruption by the Quit India campaign. Subsequently an Indian military airport, now Tribhuvan International Airport, was established to the east of Kathmandu.

Critics have frequently pointed out that the Ranas' attempts to promote economic change were limited by their concern with their own survival. This is borne out by the words of Mohan Shamsher's son Singha, who argued in the early 1930s for promoting 'a gradual rise in the prosperity of the people with the help of government grants and subsidies', but stressed that 'we cannot possibly take steps which in any way may be subversive of our autocratic authority'.[10] The agnate succession system was also a particular disincentive to large-scale public expenditure. The wish to provide for their own offspring led each maharaja to pocket as much as possible rather than leaving funds to pass to the control of the brother or nephew who would succeed him. Nevertheless, a start of sorts had been made, and experience since 1951 suggests that the intractability of the problems rather than the nature of a particular regime may have been the most important factor retarding progress.

NEW GODS AND OLD

The ideological foundation for the anti-Rana movement was provided by new Western ideas of democracy and often also socialism, normally transmitted through India. These ideas were combined, however, with older, traditional values stressing fraternity and equality, values that formed one strand within Hinduism (as within most religions), despite the central place afforded to hierarchy within it. An early influence was the ideas of the Arya Samaj, an Indian movement advocating a 'Protestant' version of Hinduism which had been founded in Bombay in the early nineteenth century. Its teachings were spread in Kathmandu and Pokhara in 1893 by a

Newar scholar, Madhav Raj Joshi. Possibly the doctrine found some rein-
forcement in the ideas of the Josmani Sants, an ascetic sect that had been
active in Nepal for many years and that, like the Samajis, rejected many of
the hierarchical aspects of Hindu orthodoxy. Bir Shamsher, eager to reduce
prejudice against a favoured low-caste wife, was sympathetic to Joshi but
he was eventually imprisoned under Chandra and subsequently went to
Darjeeling. Two sons returned in 1920 to continue his work but were then
themselves expelled. Another son, Shukra Raj Shastri, was subsequently
imprisoned for giving an unauthorised public lecture on the *Bhagavadgita*,
the god Krishna's homily on right action, which is one of Hinduism's most
important devotional texts. He was later executed because of the involvement of some of his followers in the Nepal Praja Parishad conspiracy.

It was in India that Nepalese were most likely to encounter new ideas,
whether religious or political. Ordinary hillmen who found temporary
employment in the plains or who returned to their villages after service
in the Indian army must have had their outlook changed, but this did
not yet translate itself into political action. More significant was the effect
on members of better-off families who travelled to India for education.
Particularly in the case of Brahmans, they were continuing a long tradition,
but whereas before the objective had often been the study of Sanskrit or of
Persian and of the culture that went with them, English education was now
the goal.[11] Also exposed to new influences were those Nepalese, often from
humbler backgrounds, who actually settled in India. In some cases they
clung fast to traditional ways and would even refer disputes on caste status to
the Nepalese government, much to the alarm of British officials.[12] Yet these
emigrants often developed both awareness of their own status and needs
within Indian society and a concern over Nepal's continued backwardness.
Political consciousness could develop among the communities established
by ex-servicemen and their families near army barracks and resulted in
the founding in 1924 of the All India Gorkha League at Dehradun and
the publication of the paper *Tarun Gorkha* (Young Gorkha), later renamed
Gorkha Sansar (Gorkha World). The league remained staunchly committed
to the Indian nationalist cause, even though it came to co-operate with the
Ranas during the 1930s.

The Nepalese community in Darjeeling was not in the forefront of
the anti-Rana movement, but developments there foreshadowed and also
helped determine long-term changes within Nepal itself. Christian missionary activity began in the area in 1842, with a permanent mission, run
by the Church of Scotland, established in 1870; however, it produced only
a small number of converts and was never allowed to establish a hoped-for

bridgehead in Nepal itself. Nevertheless, those who did adopt Christianity were particularly likely to abandon their original ethnic mother-tongue in favour of Nepali, while, as elsewhere in South Asia, the missionaries' educational work had an effect on non-believers. The status of the Nepali language was also boosted by the work of Darjeeling intellectuals, who fought successfully in the 1920s for its use as a medium of instruction in government schools. Among them was Surya Bikram Gyawali who pioneered a nationalist historiography which stressed the achievements of the Gorkhalis in the foundation and expansion of the state and was to become the orthodoxy taught in an expanding school system after 1951.

Even before such the efforts of such well-known figures, a broad Nepali-speaking community united by access to the printed word had begun to emerge. Benares, a major destination for Nepalese students, was also the first major centre for the publication of printed books in Nepali. Official statistics record the production of 298,257 copies of 218 publications between 1896 and 1920 and the actual total must have been much larger.[13] Devotional literature, especially Bhanubhakta's poem *Ramayana* of the middle of nineteenth century, was most popular but love poetry and tales of military heroism also sold well. Literacy honed on such material might be put to other uses later on.

The leadership roles in the 1950–1 revolt were played by men who had spent some or all of their formative years in India. The most important of these was Bishweshwar Prasad ('B. P.') Koirala. He and his elder half-brother, Matrika Prasad, had been schooled in India after their father offended Chandra Shamsher. B. P. grew up moving constantly between the worlds of Hindi, Nepali and English. He was also profoundly affected by the political atmosphere around him, becoming sympathetic to Gandhism and also to the socialist wing of the Indian Congress Party and participating in the struggle for Indian independence. While always aware of his Nepalese identity, he naturally tended to identify also with India, and political opponents in Nepal were able to make a lot of capital out of this. Particularly embarrassing in later years was his statement at the inaugural session of the Nepali National Congress that because of racial, religious and economic links 'Nepal and India are not two countries' and that 'the political difference you find is basically the game of selfish diplomats and politicians'.[14]

In addition to an affinity for India, many of the leaders of the anti-Rana movement shared membership of the elite group of perhaps 200 families which monopolised government employment under the Ranas. B. P. Koirala's father was restored to favour as soon as Bhim Shamsher succeeded

his brother in 1931. He was arrested and imprisoned in 1943 for sheltering Indian nationalist fugitives, but until then had remained unmolested
even when he bluntly told Juddha not to follow the usual Rana practice of
wasting public revenue on palatial residences for his sons. Chandra, too,
had evidently regarded him with respect, sending him medicine and books
while he was in exile. Similarly, Ganesh Man Singh, who was arrested for
anti-Rana activity in Kathmandu and fled to India after breaking out of jail,
belonged to the family of Marichman Singh, a trusted senior civil servant.[15]
This elite status perhaps explained why émigrés' attempts to bring over serving Gurkha soldiers to their side in India were largely unsuccessful. Many
from the Tibeto-Burman hill communities may well have regarded their
quarrel with the Ranas as a squabble between their overlords which did not
directly concern them.[16]

Although dovetailing with new aspirations, older values were also significant. 'National feeling' on lines already displayed in the nineteenth century
was the starting point for another member of the Nepalese community in
Benares, Devi Prasad Devkota. He had been dismissed from the Foreign
Office by Chandra after arguing that Nepal was violating its 1856 treaty
obligations to Tibet by supporting Younghusband's 1904 expedition. Caste
ideology sat less easily with democratic norms than did traditional patrio-
tism, but it was evident in the pamphlets put out by the Raktapat Mandal, a
dissident group active in Kathmandu during the Second World War. These
echoed the language of Russian anarchism and boasted of contacts with the
Soviet and Japanese governments, yet indicted Juddha from a clearly Brahmanical standpoint: 'you will not be blessed with peace and tranquillity in
this Hindu Raj as long as . . . administration . . . is in the hand of this igno-
ble outcaste with whom, according to the laws of our Shastras, we should
not even drink and dine . . . one who captures the budding, beautiful,
innocent Brahman damsels to be his concubines'.[17] The hold of Hindu
orthodoxy affected even the Praja Parishad leader Tanka Prasad Acharya,
who, politically, combined a quasi-Marxist outlook with an admiration for
the British parliamentary system. He and other Brahmans imprisoned with
him turned vegetarian for fear that meat meant for them might be mixed
with the buffalo meat eaten by their Newar comrades.[18]

Another older strand working against Rana rule was the resentment of
other groups against Parbatiya domination. The Ranas themselves told the
British that the Praja Parishad was essentially a Newar creation. In fact the
principal dissidents acted as Nepalese rather than as members of particular
castes or ethnic groups, but specifically Newar discontent did play some
part. When Dharma Bhakta, one of the Praja Parishad's 'four martyrs', first

recruited fellow Newar Ganesh Man Singh, he thought it wiser to tell him that the plot was directed against the Parbatiyas generally. Tanka Prasad Acharya later found that some of his Newar fellow prisoners clearly did still feel themselves a conquered people and hoped for support from the Japanese against both the British and the Parbatiyas. It was, however, among the Limbus of the eastern hills that ethnic particularism was strongest. Plans for a declaration of independence in 1950/1 were never fully implemented but there was violence against Brahmans, some of whom had to take temporary refuge in the Tarai. A Brahman friend of the author's, who was five years old at the time, remembers charred pages floating through the air from a burning library in Terhathum and bands of Limbus raising the cry 'Shri Char Sarkarko Jay' – 'Victory to the Four-times Illustrious Ruler(s)'. By this they meant the Limbus themselves as opposed to the 'Five-Times Illustrious' King Tribhuvan and 'Three-Times Illustrious' Mohan Shamsher Rana.[19]

Finally, although there were few areas where true mass risings occurred, increasing peasant discontent probably made it easier for anti-Rana forces from across the border to hold and seize strong points. Congress agitation had some effect in Tamang areas north of the Valley,[20] while K. I. Singh attracted considerable support in the western Tarai. In fact, local grievances of many kinds contributed to the end result, even though force applied from outside the country was the most decisive factor.

In their ultimately fruitless struggle against growing opposition, the Shamshers had sought first to prevent the education system from undermining their authority. Chandra Shamsher supposedly told King George V that the British were faced with the challenge of Indian nationalism because they had made the mistake of educating Indians. Chandra actually closed down many of the thirty or so schools that Dev had set up during his brief period in power. These schools provided a basic education in Nepali, and one historian has seen this as a sign of Dev's non-elitist attitude.[21] It is also possible, though, that Dev thought the vernacular politically safer than education in English. In the late 1940s, when it was proposed under another relatively liberal Rana, Padma Shamsher, to set up vernacular schools on the lines of Mahatma Gandhi's 'basic schools' in India, many in Kathmandu saw it as an attempt to keep people in their place. Chandra (in his later years) and also Juddha had encouraged Gandhian-style training but Chandra had in addition allowed the development of a small number of English-medium secondary schools. His main objective in the 1919 foundation of Trichandra College, which was affiliated to Calcutta University, was to allow Nepalese students to take Indian university exams without being exposed to the increasingly radical atmosphere on Indian campuses.

The Shamshers did allow some scope for intellectual expression, but the literary magazine *Sharada*, established in 1938, remained subject to strict censorship.

As a more positive ideological defence, the Ranas sought to sustain values that had underpinned the Nepalese state since its creation. In the first place, the Shamshers projected themselves as the guardians of the Hindu social order enshrined in Nepal's legal system. This entailed strict religious observance, special reverence for Brahmans and cows, and also systematic discrimination against those at the bottom of the hierarchy. If, for example, a member of a 'pure' caste came into contact with an Untouchable while carrying home sweets from a shop, he was entitled to insist that the other man refund him the price of the now polluted purchase. The Ranas felt able to incorporate some Gandhian ideas into this framework but not, of course, Gandhi's commitment to egalitarianism. While their stance angered the more radical, it did buttress their legitimacy among the traditionally minded within Nepal and also attracted support from Hindus in India. Though the principle of the formal equality of all citizens was acknowledged after 1950/1, the Shah kings continued to use Hinduism as a means of legitimation, as seen in King Gyanendra's well-publicised visit in 2003 to major shrines in Nepal and India. And here lay the fundamental problem for the Rana regime: it was the king, not the maharaja, who was traditionally regarded as an incarnation of Vishnu, so that, once the monarchy came out against the Ranas, the Hindu card was no longer theirs to play.

As the Newar kings had once sought to stand tall on the stage of the Kathmandu Valley, the Ranas aimed for prestige among South Asian royalty. As well as Hindu credentials, this also required recognition from the dominant power on the subcontinent, the British. An obsession with matters like British decorations conferred on the maharaja or the precise status of the British resident/envoy stemmed from the desire to have their own superior status as rulers of a fully independent state acknowledged. It has even been suggested that Bir Shamsher's infrastructure projects were intended primarily to impress the British rather than actually to improve the living conditions of ordinary Nepalese.[22] Similarly, Chandra's emancipation of Nepal's slaves improved his own international standing, but very few of the 60,000 freed slaves accepted the offer of land in the unhealthy environment of Amlekhganj ('Emancipationville') in the Tarai and the majority remained in de facto dependence on their former masters.[23] Nevertheless, foreign opinion was not the Ranas' only consideration. The idea that a ruler should care for his people was already part of Hindu political thought, even if often disregarded in practice.

The Shamshers also sought to project themselves and their regime as natural champions of the Parbatiyas and particularly of the Thakuri–Chetri caste to which they themselves belonged. This was probably a major reason behind the 1905 decision to allow only Nepali-language documents to be allowed as evidence in court[24] and also behind their attempt to portray opposition as Newar-inspired. Pride in the conquest of the Newar kingdoms was still reflected in the national anthem which referred before 1967 to the maintenance of *Gorkhali* rule over Nepal. The Magars and Gurungs, who had been associated with the Gorkhali state since long before 1769, could also claim the label 'Gorkhali' but they, too, had to be kept in their place. It was acceptable for them to join Britain's Indian army, but the Shamshers were unhappy if individual soldiers were singled out for special privileges. A British Gurkha officer, Santabir Gurung, who had been honoured by the British for his long hours standing vigil over the body of Edward VII, was in 1913 denied readmission to his country and caste, despite the displeasure this caused to the new British monarch, George V. In a similar spirit, there was a ban from 1926 to 1936 against Gurkhas travelling to Britain under the King's Orderly scheme allowing officers of the Indian army to be attached to the royal household.

Yet at the same time the Shamshers did try to foster a common Nepalese identity, centred, of course, around themselves. The official adoption by the 1930s of the name 'Nepal' for the whole kingdom and of 'Nepali' for its principal language, replacing 'Gorkha' and 'Gorkhali' was probably part of this strategy, even though it seems also to have been a response to demands by Gorkhali-language activists in India, and was opposed by some Newar-language activists, also India-based, who used the name *Nepal Bhasha* (language of Nepal) for Newar. Official insistence on a single Nepalese identity, including use of Nepali, for all citizens and resistance to this by ethnic activists was to continue after Rana rule itself came to an end.

CHAPTER 4

The monarchy in ascendance: domestic politics and foreign relations, 1951–1991

The political dynamic of the forty years following the overthrow of the Rana regime was principally the result of interaction among three forces: the monarchy, around which traditional elements, including much of the Rana family itself, were to regroup; the political parties, whose support bases were initially quite narrow; and the Indian government, ideologically sympathetic to the Nepali Congress Party, but still seeing Nepal primarily in terms of border security. During the 1950s, as has again been the case in Nepal since autumn 2002, the royal palace remained the effective centre of government, especially after King Mahendra's accession in 1955, but political parties functioned freely and everyone, including the king, at least paid lip-service to multi-party democracy. When parliamentary elections were finally held in 1959, the centre of gravity shifted briefly to the elected government but in the following year Mahendra aborted the democratic experiment and took full control of the state into his own hands. Royal dominance, clothed in the rhetoric of 'partyless Panchayat democracy', remained secure until Mahendra's death in 1972, buttressed by the king's ability to balance adroitly between India and China. However, his son, Birendra, who initially tried to retain the old system, faced a more difficult task. Rapid change in Nepalese society, including in particular the regime's own success in expanding education, coupled with failure to increase opportunities in line with expectations, produced growing tension. In addition, international room for manoeuvre was reduced when India confirmed its dominance in South Asia by its victory over Pakistan in 1971. Following disturbances in 1979, Birendra called a referendum on the constitution, which, thanks to the regime's grip on village Nepal, endorsed the Panchayat system. However, the results showed clearly that urban Nepal was committed to the party system and, when a dispute with India and the reverberations of the collapse of autocracies in Eastern Europe sparked protests in 1990, Birendra gave way and allowed the restoration of the multi-party system. Elections in 1991 were won by the Nepali Congress

Party, which thus regained the position Birendra's father had deprived it of a generation previously.

THE FIRST MULTI-PARTY EXPERIMENT: 1951–1960

The Congress–Rana coalition was beset with difficulties from the start. There were continuing disturbances in several parts of the country as well as tension between the two partners themselves. Immediately upon assuming office in February 1951, the government had to invite Indian troops into the Bhairawa region of the Tarai to arrest K. I. Singh, a Congress fighter who had refused to lay down his arms after the Delhi agreement. The Indians were called in again in April to suppress a peasant revolt in another part of the Tarai and in July to recapture Singh after his escape from Bhairawa jail. In Kathmandu, hard-liners among the Ranas set up a group known as the Gorkha Dal and on 11 April, amidst rumours that a coup was being planned, B. P. Koirala ordered the arrest of its secretary-general, Bharat Shamsher Rana. The rumours were in fact probably untrue but Bharat's infuriated supporters stormed the jail to release him and then attacked B. P. Koirala's house. They retreated only when B. P. himself shot dead one of the ringleaders. Fortunately Bharat decided at this point to slip away rather than follow his supporters' advice to seize power, and the army was kept loyal to the government by Chandra's son Keshar.

Many of B. P.'s attackers had been palace guards of Bharat's grandfather, Babar, another of Chandra's sons, and he was now forced out of the cabinet. The prime minister, Mohan Shamsher, had been at least nominally associated with the Gorkha Dal, and the crisis within the government was only resolved by talks brokered by the Indians in Delhi. The soldiers who had been quartered at the prime minister's Singha Darbar palace were moved to the royal palace and Congress now had an excuse to retain their militia, reorganising some of it as part of the local police force. These developments encouraged the army to look to the king and the police to the political party in power, a pattern which was to re-emerge in the 1990s. Another legacy of the Gorkha Dal affair was the Public Security Act, brought in as coup rumours were circulating, which provided for detention without trial for up to twelve months. Finally, Bharat Shamsher and his father Mrigendra switched to constitutional methods of opposition, setting up in 1952 a new political party, the Gorkha Parishad. Their core following was old dependants of the Ranas, but the Parishad could nevertheless reach beyond this circle: Ranadhir Subba, the party president, was a Christian who had been active in Darjeeling politics in the 1940s.

The coalition government also faced opposition from other quarters. Dilli Raman Regmi's Nepali National Congress had split from B. P. Koirala's party in summer 1947 after Regmi, appointed as acting president during Koirala's imprisonment in Kathmandu, had refused to relinquish the post on Koirala's release. When Koirala's faction merged with the Nepali Democratic Congress to form the Nepali Congress in 1951, Regmi's group had retained the old name and opposed Congress's resort to violent tactics. The arrival of Regmi and his associates in Kathmandu in January, while Tribhuvan and the Congress leadership were still in India, had aroused suspicion of collusion with Mohan Shamsher and, while this was probably unfounded, the Nepali National Congress remained strong critics of their parent party. Also agitating against the government were the old Praja Parishad and the Communist Party of Nepal, which in July 1950 together formed a United Front to oppose Indian influence. Following Regmi's arrest and imprisonment in September for contempt of court in criticising the newly appointed chief justice, Regmi's own party and the United Front organised a protest strike in the Valley. This resulted in turn in the arrest of Praja Parishad leader Tanka Prasad Acharya and others under the Public Security Act.

Opposition grievances were increased the following month when Tribhuvan announced nominations to a 35-member advisory assembly. Although the decision to set up this body had been made in talks between the Rana and Congress sides in May, those now named were either Congress supporters or independents, with no representation either of the Ranas or of the other political groups. Tensions continued and on 11 November students demonstrating against the government surrounded the police headquarters at Hanuman Dhoka in the centre of the old city. In the kind of incident which was to be repeated many times over the succeeding years, a demonstrator allegedly tried to snatch one policeman's weapon and the police opened fire, killing one of the crowd. B. P. Koirala, as home minister, was in charge of the police and, when Mohan Shamsher implicitly criticised their action in a radio address, Koirala and his Congress colleagues took it as a breach of collective responsibility and submitted their own resignations.

Under the Interim Government Act, passed in April at the same time as the Public Security Act, the coalition government had held power in the king's name; its collapse left the initiative in Tribhuvan's hands. Tribhuvan had himself pledged to arrange elections to a constituent assembly to decide on long-term arrangements, but in practice a different pattern was now established. The royal palace was the primary seat of power, with India wielding considerable influence in the wings and party politicians alternating between outright opposition and eagerness to obtain office through royal favour.

Tribhuvan invited Congress to form a single-party government, but he was unwilling to accept as prime minister B. P. Koirala, the most popular leader among party workers. Instead he insisted on appointing B. P.'s elder half-brother, Matrika Prasad Koirala, who had become party president in 1950 as part of the deal worked out when the original Nepali National Congress merged with the Nepal Democratic Congress. Tribhuvan reportedly threatened that if Congress did not accept his proposal he would himself rule directly with the help of his brother-in-law, Keshar Shamsher Rana, son of Chandra. Tribhuvan's stance was partly the result of Indian mistrust of B. P., but also important was Matrika Prasad's background as a one-time member of the Rana bureaucracy as well as his greater willingness to accept royal authority.

Since B. P. had the support of the party's Central Working Committee, Matrika Prasad's appointment set the scene for what was to become another constant in political life – the tussle for power between the party organisation and the members of the party actually in government. B. P. argued that the government should take instructions from the party rather than acting independently; at one stage the veteran Indian politician Jaya Prakash Narayan had to be brought in to arbitrate. To a large extent, the issue arose from personal rivalry, but there were also real differences of philosophy: M. P. saw himself as responsible to the king and as lacking any mandate for radical measures, but B. P. argued that the party should rely on its own 'revolutionary legality' and start straightaway on land reform. In an attempt to reach an accommodation, Matrika agreed to B. P.'s becoming president at the party's May 1952 convention, but the wrangling continued and Matrika and his cabinet colleagues were expelled from Congress in July 1952.

In addition to the intra-party rivalry, the new government was faced in January 1952 by a revolt in the ranks of the party's militia, the Raksha Dal. They released from prison both K. I. Singh and two leaders of a Kiranti secessionist organisation. Singh then fled with a few followers to Tibet, declining the offer of leadership of the revolt, and the authorities managed to reassert control without the intervention of Indian troops, which both the prime minister and the Indian ambassador had at one point believed necessary. The government then disbanded the Kiranti sections of the Raksha Dal and police force and, on India's suggestion, also banned the Communist Party, which had been sympathetic to the revolt. Another consequence was the dispatch of an Indian military mission charged with upgrading Nepal's own army.

Despite already being able to influence Nepal in many ways, the Indian government was still impatient with the factional rivalries and drift in the administration and in summer 1952 Jawaharlal Nehru, the Indian prime minister, suggested that the king dispense with the Congress government and rule himself with the help of a council of advisers. Tribhuvan made the change in August 1952 but an element of continuity was provided by the inclusion among the councillors of Keshar Shamsher, who had been defence minister in the M. P. Koirala cabinet. Keshar's key role in the early 1950s underlined the fact that the Shahs and the Ranas were in some ways two branches of an integrated aristocracy and that 1951 had simply seen the senior and junior partners exchange roles.

Out of office, M. P. Koirala remained at loggerheads with his brother and in April 1953 he set up his own Rastriya Praja Party (National People's (or Democratic) Party). Tribhuvan soon grew impatient with direct responsibility for the administration and, now that Matrika seemed to have a viable political base, Tribhuvan reappointed him as prime minister in June 1953. The government was strengthened in August when the Leftist Nepali Congress, one of two splinter groups which had left B. P.'s party in 1952, merged with the Rastriya Praja Party. Then, in February 1954, Tanka Prasad Acharya's Praja Parishad and Regmi's Nepali National Congress agreed to join a coalition with the governing party. The Nepal Jana Congress, the second of the groups that had split from B. P.'s party in 1952, also became a coalition partner. These alignments very obviously reflected power politics rather than ideology, since both the Praja Parishad and the Leftist Nepali Congress, which previously prided themselves on their radical credentials, were now joining forces with the more conservative of the Koirala brothers. Unsurprisingly, relations between the partners were often strained and the prime minister also had to contend with opposition from within his own party. He finally tendered his resignation in January 1955, after Nepal's second nominated advisory assembly, packed with his own party members, had nevertheless rejected his budget proposals. Crown Prince Mahendra, acting as regent while his father was in Switzerland for medical treatment, accepted the resignation in March a few days before news of Tribhuvan's death reached Nepal.

The old king's four years of stewardship of Nepal had not been entirely unfruitful. The Tribhuvan Rajpath, the tortuously twisting road linking Kathmandu with the plains, was constructed rapidly by the Indian army and largely completed by 1955. Another, more controversial Indian project, the construction of a dam and irrigation works on the Kosi River in eastern Nepal, was launched in 1954. There was also the establishment of a system of local panchayats (administrative committees) in 1953. However, the post-Rana regime was unable to make progress on the constitutional front or even to establish a stable interim administration, and the rapid social and economic progress eagerly hoped for in 1951 had not materialised. The resulting frustration, as well as the jostling for power between parties which had yet to demonstrate mass support, further strengthened the atmosphere of continuing instability.

While still regent for his ailing father, Mahendra had appeared sympathetic to the Congress Party's demand for early elections to a constituent assembly, but he soon demonstrated an eagerness to keep control in his own hands and an adroitness in playing off one party against another. Tribhuvan had been prodded into a more interventionist role by India but Mahendra required no encouragement. He initially governed with the help of a second council of royal advisers until January 1956, and then, after the parties had refused to allow him to pick their representatives in a multi-party government, he appointed Tanka Prasad Acharya as prime minister with a cabinet including both members of Acharya's own Praja Parishad and a number of royal favourites. Following on the opening of diplomatic relations with China, the choice of a politician well known for his anti-Indian views underlined Mahendra's determination to reduce the dependence on India that had become the norm under his father. Mahendra was also able to use Acharya to begin backing away from Tribhuvan's 1951 promise of a constituent assembly. In a speech in June, Acharya floated the idea that the elections Mahendra was now promising for October 1957 might simply be for a parliament. This implied that the monarchy would 'gift' a constitution to the people rather than the monarchy's own future being determined by elected representatives. Acharya himself insisted in later years that his intention had been that parliament, not the king, would be sovereign and argued that Indian manipulation of a constituent assembly might have threatened Nepal's independence.[1] At the time, Acharya's proposal was bitterly contested both by Congress and by many of his own supporters.

Also probably initiated by the king in order to increase his own room for manoeuvre, but more in line with Acharya's own political convictions, was the rescinding in April 1956 of the ban imposed on the Communist Party in 1952. A condition of the ban's removal was apparently a secret pledge by party leaders not to oppose the monarchy, and the compromise was resisted by those within the party who would rather have continued organising on a clandestine basis. The party had in fact been fairly successful in this way, and the nominally independent candidates whom it backed had won the

1953 elections for a Kathmandu local authority, aided by popular discontent over a surge in the price of imports since 1951.

From the start of his administration, Acharya had faced problems within his own party. On the collapse of M. P. Koirala's government the year before, two dissident Congress groups, which had combined with Koirala when he was in power, had joined Acharya's Praja Parishad. The leader of one of these groups, Bhadrakali Mishra, was an unlikely ally for the anti-Indian Acharya as he had originally been included as a Congress minister in the 1951 government only on Indian insistence. Nevertheless, Mishra became president of the Praja Parishad and in summer 1957, amidst street demonstrations over food shortages, he and his executive committee made the impossible demand that Acharya should dismiss the royal nominees in his cabinet, thus precipitating the government's resignation in July.

A few days later, Mahendra turned to a new organisation, the United Democratic Party, whose setting-up he himself had probably funded. The party's leader was K. I. Singh, who had tried to fight on in the mid-western Tarai after Congress accepted the 1951 ceasefire and who had gone into self-imposed exile in Tibet after his release from jail by the Raksha Dal mutineers in 1952. On return to Nepal in autumn 1955, the erstwhile anti-Indian firebrand had reversed his line and begun warning of danger from China. By appointing him in place of the supposedly pro-Chinese Acharya, Mahendra was able to maintain a balance between Nepal's two large neighbours, a tactic which was to become his trademark. Singh's radical, Robin Hood image also made him a useful card for the monarchy to play against more centrist politicians, and even Tribhuvan had been thinking of making use of him before his jailbreak: this kind of royal manipulation was to be continued over many years and helps explain why some Nepalese believed that the palace was supporting the Maoists in the early years of the 'People's War' that began in 1996.

The Singh government was a short-lived one, marked by controversy over his announcement that the October 1957 elections were to be indefinitely postponed and also over an attempt to impose Nepali as the medium of instruction in Tarai schools, where Hindi had previously been widely used. Above all, there were tensions resulting from Singh's own abrasive character, which had stymied earlier attempts to form a coalition with other factions. Listening to the radio on 14 November 1957, Singh learned to his surprise that Mahendra had accepted an offer to resign apparently made only as a ploy to obtain greater influence over civil service appointments.

Just after the formation of Singh's government, Congress had joined the Praja Parishad and the Nepali National Congress in an alliance called the United Democratic Front. In December 1957 they began a *satyagraha* (civil disobedience campaign) to force the holding of elections within six months. They were opposed by Singh's United Democratic Party and by the Rana-orientated Gorkha Dal as well as by some smaller groups, which collectively proposed a date of 12 February 1959. Finally, Mahendra suggested 18 February 1959, the anniversary of Tribhuvan's 1951 return from Delhi, and Congress and the others accepted this. With the exception of the Communists, all parties also accepted Mahendra's announcement in February 1958 that the elections would be for a parliament and that a council of representatives from different parties would be appointed to supervise the administration in the meantime. Congress's decision to abandon the struggle for a constituent assembly was probably influenced by the limited support gained by the *satyagraha* and by the Democratic Front's poor showing in Kathmandu municipal elections held in mid-January. In any case, the constituent assembly question had been put to rest for a generation.

The Council of Ministers, which included representatives of the main parties as well as two royal nominees, was established in May, and remained in office until after the elections. The constitution was nominally prepared by a Drafting Commission including party politicians, but in practice was drafted in accordance with Mahendra's wishes by the British constitutional lawyer, Sir Ivor Jennings, who had already lent his expertise to other new Asian democracies. The document was finally promulgated on 12 February 1959, only six days before the start of voting. It provided for a bicameral legislature, with a directly elected Lower House (the Pratinidhi Sabha, or House of Representatives) of 109 members and an Upper House (Mahasabha or Senate) of 36 members, half to be elected by the House of Representatives and half appointed by the king. The constitution stated explicitly that executive authority rested with the king, and 'shall be exercised by him either directly or through ministers or other officers subordinate to him'. The king was also entitled under articles 55 and 56 to declare a state of emergency, enabling him to override all organs of government except for the Supreme Court. Perhaps it is wrong to put too much emphasis on these provisions, since the crucial factor was not so much the technical wording of the constitution but the fact that public servants, and in particular the army, continued to look to the king rather than any party politician. However, the wording did ensure that if the king chose to impose his will on other actors he could claim his actions were perfectly legal.

The struggle for power among political parties had until 1959 been largely dependent on the ability to attract royal and/or Indian support and to marshal significant numbers of demonstrators on the streets of Kathmandu. As the time to test their popularity nationwide approached, at least three of the competing parties, though all in theory advocated radical land reforms, offered clearly contrasting policies on other issues. On the far left, the Communists, not yet embarrassed by the Sino-Soviet split, were strong opponents of Gurkha recruitment into the British army and advocated abolition of the 'unequal' 1950 treaty with India and opposition to 'American infiltration'. The Nepali Congress could be classified as centre-left, having in 1955 adopted a clearly democratic socialist line, similar to Nehru's in India. It advocated state development of heavy industry but with assistance from foreign, preferably Indian, capital. Finally, the Gorkha Parishad shared the Communists' aversion to India but adopted a right-wing stance, strongly supportive of monarchy and of the role of private enterprise and foreign investment throughout the economy.

Six other parties contested the polls. K. I. Singh's United Democratic Party was strongly monarchist and, like the Gorkha Parishad, drew its support more from the Thakuri and Chetri castes than from the educated Brahmans who formed the backbone of both Congress and the Communist Party. Singh also took a strongly pro-Hindu line, as did the Prajatantrik Mahasabha, set up in 1957 with money from two of Rudra Shamsher's C-Class Rana family and also rumoured to have palace support. There was in addition Vedananda Jha's regionalist Tarai Congress, Dilli Raman Regmi's Nepali National Congress and two rival Praja Parishads, as factions led by Tanka Prasad Acharya and Bhadrakali Mishra had split in 1958.

The Nepalese electorate was composed largely of illiterate peasant-farmers, for whom the actual content of manifestos was even less important than for voters in industrialised countries. Thus Congress easily won all eight parliamentary seats in eastern Nepal despite their commitment to abolish the Limbus' traditional *kipat* rights and the Gorkha Parishad's promise to preserve these. What counted was the ability of the parties to forge linkages with influential individuals and factions at local level. Networks of activists were crucial here, and these must have been much smaller than the inflated figures claimed by the two major parties: 800,000 for the Gorkha Parishad in 1953 and 600,000 for Congress in 1956 out of a total population of about 9 million. The Parishad's figure was probably merely fanciful, and Congress's total the result of their policy of allowing anyone to become and remain a member for a one-time payment of one rupee. However, Congress did at least have an effective, nationwide machine with the nature of the support they attracted differing from area to area. In the eastern Tarai, the Koirala family's standing in Biratnagar was important: the Koirala brothers' father Krishna Prasad had played a role in establishing the town as a major centre almost on a par with that of Stamford Ruffles in Singapore. In some areas, as for example among the Tamangs north and west of the Kathmandu Valley, the party championed tenant grievances, but elsewhere they also attracted a strong following among landlords. Within the hills, they retained the support of those ex-servicemen who had fought for them in 1950–1, although they had lost many members in the western Tarai because of bringing in the Indian army against K. I. Singh and his fellow diehard revolutionaries in 1951. Most importantly, perhaps, Congress attracted many who simply regarded the party as the strongest political force and so wished to align themselves with it.

A shortage of staff and the difficulties of communication in the hills meant that polling had to be continued over several weeks. Voters were expected to walk anything up to twenty-eight miles to cast their ballot, but despite this a turnout of 43 per cent was achieved. The final result, declared in May, was a decisive win for Congress, which received 37 per cent of the votes cast, giving them 75 seats in the 108-member House of Representatives (see table 4.1 for details).

As had been forecast by a British diplomat in 1955,[2] the losers were quick to accuse the victors of malpractice, and some of the smaller parties went to court in an unsuccessful attempt to get the results annulled. In some cases questionable means had certainly been used. Tamangs in one village claim today that they paid a bribe of 3000 rupees in 1954 'to Matrika Prasad Koirala and the Congress Party' to obtain an increase in the price they were paid for paper they had to produce under the still-existing compulsory labour scheme.[3] The accusation cannot be correct in all its details, since in 1954 Matrika Koirala was leader of the Rastriya Praja Party, not the Nepali Congress, but incidents of this type must have occurred and certainly money was accepted from individuals and organisations and possibly also from foreign sources. However, there is no reason to doubt that Congress won principally because a plurality of influential people at local level thought the party represented their best hope for the future.

B. P. Koirala was finally invited by the king to form a government on 27 May, after a delay which suggested to many, including B. P. himself, that Mahendra wanted another Congress politician as premier. Despite the inauspicious start, his relationship with Mahendra appeared at first quite harmonious and the government was able to initiate three major reforms. First was the abolition without compensation of the *birta* system of tax-free long-holdings of which the Ranas and their closest favourites had been the chief beneficiaries. This measure did not have much effect on the actual cultivators, since an intermediate class of landlords had already developed

Table 4.1 *1959 election results*

Party	Seats contested	Seats won	% of total seats	% of total vote
Nepali Congress	108	74	67.9	37.2
Gorkha Parishad	86	19	17.4	17.3
United Democratic Party	86	5	4.6	9.9
Nepal Communist Party	47	4	3.7	7.2
Praja Parishad (Acharya)	46	2	1.8	2.9
Praja Parishad (Mishra)	36	1	0.9	3.3
Nepal Tarai Congress	21	0	0.0	2.1
Nepali National Congress	20	0	0.0	0.7
Prajatantrik Mahasabha	68	0	0.0	3.3
Independents	268	4	3.7	16.7

Source: Gupta 1993: 146.
Notes: Full results for each constituency are set out in Devkota 1979: 99–111. Congress in fact originally won seventy-five seats, but lost the immediate by-election caused by Subarna Shamsher Rana's resigning one of two seats he had successfully contested.

on the *birta* estates (see pp. 74–5), but it did show that Congress was willing to make a start with land reform. A second major step was the abolition of the *rajyauta* system under which some of the formerly independent rajas of central and western Nepal had kept control of their territories in return for a fixed annual tribute to the central government. Finally, Congress extended measures already begun for nationalisation (this time with compensation) of the country's forests, some of which had previously been the personal property of the king's own brothers.

In foreign policy, Congress had the advantage of relatively close ties with India, but B. P. trod carefully to avoid entanglement in growing tension between India and China in the wake of the revolt in Tibet and the Dalai Lama's flight to India in March 1959. Shortly after taking office, the government announced a 100 per cent increase in defence expenditure to secure the northern border and agreed to the continued presence of Indian military monitors at points along it. However, after China had taken a conciliatory line towards Nepal in the intervening months, the Nepalese delegation abstained at the UN in autumn 1959 on a resolution censuring China's conduct, and B. P. subsequently rejected the idea of a defence pact between India and Nepal. At the same time he remained willing to make veiled criticism of Chinese policy and the government took a firm line against Chinese claims to control of Mt Everest, perhaps even deliberately playing up the issue to counter public preoccupation with an alleged threat from India. They also obtained an apology and compensation after Chinese troops fired on a Nepalese border patrol in June 1960. In the midst of these political difficulties, the government concluded an agreement with India for the development of the Gandaki River, despite criticism at home that the terms infringed Nepalese sovereignty. Less controversial was a new trade agreement which in principle allowed Nepal independent control of its foreign currency and also freedom to determine its own tariff structure. Another plus was a pledge from China to follow India and the United States in offering Nepal development aid.

While not amounting to the immediate transformation of society that all parties' rhetoric had promised, the Congress reform programme was radical enough to alarm individuals likely to be affected by it, in particular former adherents of the Ranas. A first major demonstration against taxation proposals was held in December 1959 and the Jana Hita Sangha (Public Welfare Association), set up in April 1960, staged strikes in support of their call for royal intervention. The National Democratic Front, an alliance formed in June 1959 between the Praja Parishad (Acharya), United Democratic Party and Prajatantrik Mahasabha, organised frequent demonstrations in Kathmandu. They accused the government of corruption, of 'Congressification' (packing the administration with the party's own supporters) and of weakness in dealings with India and then with China – all charges which were to become standard ones again when parliamentary politics were revived in 1991. The Front was sometimes joined in its activities by the Communists, though not, of course, when China was the target.

B. P. had the stature to dominate his party more thoroughly than any subsequent Congress leader, and was re-elected as party president by an overwhelming majority at the party's May 1960 conference. Nevertheless, there was internal opposition from a group of twenty-seven disgruntled MPs as well as constant sniping from his elder brother. Matrika had rejoined Congress in 1956 but now was openly backing the National Democratic Front's anti-government campaign and inveighing in particular against B. P.'s being simultaneously prime minister and party president – a combination which B. P. had himself objected to when Matrika had held both in 1951–2. Perhaps most serious was the disaffection of two cabinet ministers: Tulsi Giri, a B. P. protégé, resigned from the government in August 1960 while Bishwabandhu Thapa remained in post until the royal takeover, supplying the palace with details of his colleague's deliberations.

In some ways the main opposition party, the Gorkha Parishad, was less of a threat to the government than were its other opponents. Party leader

Bharat Shamsher, in contrast to the leaders of the smaller parties, accepted the general elections as free and fair, and in parliament he and his colleagues' rhetoric became quite radical in tone, thus removing the ideological contrast previously found between the Parishad's conservatism and B. P.'s democratic socialism. There was also a volte-face in foreign affairs: in a speech in January 1960, Bharat abandoned his previous anti-Indian posture and demanded an alliance with India to guard against a possible threat from China, thus going further even than the allegedly pro-Indian Congress government.

However, some of his colleagues in the party at national level were unhappy with his change of stance, while in Nuwakot and Gorkha to the west of the Valley, which were represented in parliament by Gorkha Parishad members, there were serious clashes between activists of the two parties, probably resulting from Congress cadres' attempts to undermine the Parishad's local predominance. Whereas two years previously pro-Congress farmers in the Tarai district of Rautahat had clashed with poor peasants backed by the Communists, here Congress organised poorer sections of the community against landlords and money-lenders. There was also an ethnic edge to the dispute as at least some of those who fled their homes were members of the Parbatiya high castes driven out by aggrieved Tamangs regardless of whether they had personally appropriated Tamang land. When King Mahendra returned to Nepal after a world tour in 1960, it was these refugees who met him and appealed for help, and the king cited failure to maintain law and order, as well as corruption and 'encouragement of anti-national elements', when he removed the Congress government at the end of the year.

Concern over public order was in fact probably a pretext rather than a principal motivation for Mahendra, since he himself had funded at least one conservative Hindu organisation, Naraharinath Yogi's Karmavir Mandal, which encouraged the *rajyauta* chiefs to resist abolition of their fiefdoms and was also involved in disturbances in Gorkha in October 1960. Mahendra had really hoped to retain effective control of the government all along and had probably agreed to the 1959 elections only because he believed that they would lead to a hung parliament which he could easily manipulate. Faced with a Congress majority in parliament and a strong-willed prime minister, he hoped initially to use the Gorkha Parishad and party dissidents to unseat the government and, when it was clear this would not happen, he finally used his emergency powers and control of the army to arrest B. P. Koirala and his colleagues at a public meeting on 15 December. It would, however, be unfair to see this as purely a matter of personal ambition for, just like B. P., the king genuinely believed in his own unique ability to guide the country. In the words of one Indian analyst, for King Mahendra, 'Nepal was an idea and none but he could realise what it was destined to be.'[4]

The royal takeover was achieved without initial opposition. There had been speculation since August that the king would intervene and two months later Mahendra himself had actually told Subarna Shamsher of his intention, but the cabinet had decided that trying to forestall the king by organising a party militia would only precipitate his move against them. There were no protests on the streets of Kathmandu and many of the educated elite swung behind Mahendra, including fifty-five of the Congress Party's own seventy-four MPs.

Subarna Shamsher, who had been on a private visit to Calcutta, was the one minister to escape arrest, but seemed at first reluctant to act. He was urged to do so by others, including most importantly the Indian prime minister, Jawaharlal Nehru, who, as in 1950, saw autocracy in Nepal as not just wrong in principle but also likely to lead to instability on a sensitive frontier. Pressure for action was increased towards the end of 1961 when the Gorkha Parishad leader, Bharat Shamsher, arrived in India and merged his own group with Congress. There had been isolated incidents earlier but from autumn 1961 onwards Congress began a more serious military effort. A guerrilla force around 3000 strong, formed with the help of activists who had fled into India, launched raids across the border. The beginning of the campaign coincided roughly with Mahendra's October signing of an agreement with the Chinese for the construction of a road from Kathmandu to the Nepal–Tibet border. This was regarded by the Indians as a security threat, and it is possible either that they gave the green light to Congress in response to the road agreement, or, indeed, that Mahendra accepted the Chinese proposal because of increased Indian support for his opponents.

The insurgents never attempted to hold territory and total casualties were small compared with the 'People's War' launched a generation later: on government figures, seventy-seven insurgents, thirty-one members of the security forces and twenty-two civilians were killed over one year. The pressure was nevertheless already enough to make Mahendra consider compromise during summer 1962; his situation became much more critical when India imposed an unofficial economic blockade towards the end of September 1962. The king was rescued by the outbreak of war between India and China the following month. India now needed Mahendra's co-operation and, on Nehru's request, Subarna called off the armed campaign.

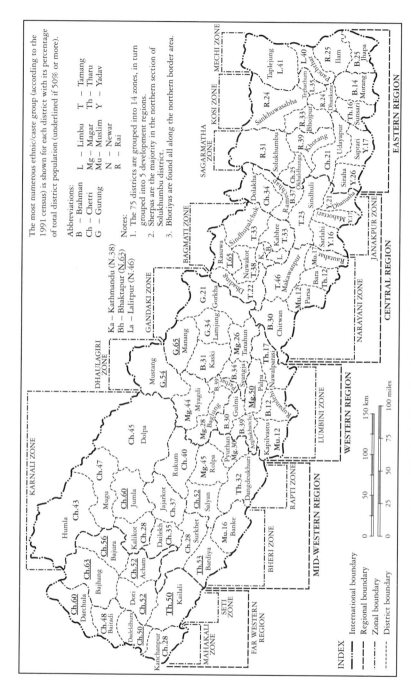

The most numerous ethnic/caste group (according to the 1991 census) is shown for each district with its percentage of total district population (underlined if 50% or more).

Abbreviations:

B – Brahman	L – Limbu	T – Tamang	
Ch – Chetri	Mg – Magar	Th – Tharu	
G – Gurung	Mu – Muslim	Y – Yadav	
	N – Newar		
	R – Rai		

Notes:
1. The 75 districts are grouped into 14 zones, in turn grouped into 5 development regions.
2. Sherpas are the majority in the northern section of Solukhumbu district.
3. Bhotiyas are found all along the northern border area.

Ka – Kathmandu (N.38)
Bh – Bhaktapur (N.63)
La – Lalitpur (N.46)

KARNALI ZONE

DHAULAGIRI ZONE

GANDAKI ZONE

BAGMATI ZONE

SAGARMATHA ZONE

KOSI ZONE

MECHI ZONE

JANAKPUR ZONE

NARAYANI ZONE

LUMBINI ZONE

RAPTI ZONE

BHERI ZONE

SETI ZONE

MAHAKALI ZONE

EASTERN REGION

CENTRAL REGION

WESTERN REGION

MID-WESTERN REGION

FAR WESTERN REGION

INDEX
·——·——· International boundary
----- Regional boundary
·—·—·— Zonal boundary
------- District boundary

0   25   50   75   100 miles
0   50   100   150 km

Map 3. Nepal: administrative divisions and ethnic/caste composition.

Mahendra was thus free to concentrate on building a system without political parties: 'Panchayat democracy' as enshrined in his 1962 constitution. The system was modelled to some extent on forms of indirect or 'guided' democracy then existing in Pakistan, Egypt, Indonesia and Yugoslavia but had also been foreshadowed in Maharaja Padma Shamsher's abortive 1948 constitution. It provided for directly elected village or town councils (panchayats), their members forming an electoral college to choose district-level representatives. These latter in turn selected from among themselves the majority of members of the national legislature or Rastriya Panchayat, the remainder being either representatives of government-sponsored 'class organisations' or royal nominees. These class organisations were supposed to represent broad sectors of the population – for example, 'Peasants', 'Youth' or 'Workers' – but in practice were often little more than a nominated central committee. The Rastriya Panchayat's powers were limited and the whole arrangement was designed to allow an element of popular representation while the king ruled unhindered by the pressures of parliamentary democracy.

Until the introduction of direct elections to the Rastriya Panchayat under Mahendra's son Birendra in 1980, the system remained the same in its essentials. There were, however, amendments to the constitution in 1967 and 1975. The first of these largely involved technicalities but also incorporated into the constitution the ban on political parties that had been in place since January 1961. The 1975 amendment, partly a response to unrest after Birendra's accession in 1972, widened the number of district representatives who could vote for candidates to the Rastriya Panchayat and removed the original ban on public reporting of Rastriya Panchayat proceedings. However, perhaps emboldened by Indira Gandhi's suspension of democratic liberties in India the same year, Birendra also tried to strengthen central control by giving a government-appointed committee Politburo-like powers to vet candidates and to nominate members to the councils at different levels. In addition, he abolished the representation in the Rastriya Panchayat of the class organisations, thus ending the regular embarrassment of anti-establishment candidates being elected by the Graduates' Constituency.

After the rapprochement of autumn 1962, India accepted the reality of royal rule in Nepal, and Indian development aid, which had not been cut off even in the aftermath of Mahendra's takeover, remained significant. Relations continued to have their ups and downs, however, with recurrent tensions over tariff arrangements and Nepal's transit rights across Indian territory for imports and exports involving third countries (see ch. 5). There

Table 4.2 *Composition of the Rastriya Panchayat*
under the 1962 constitution

Elected by district panchayat members	90
Peasants' Organisation	4
Youth Organisation	4
Women's Organisation	3
Ex-Servicemen's Organisation	2
Workers' Organisation	2
Graduates' Constituency	4
Nominated by the king	16
TOTAL	125

were also differences over security issues. Although Nepal remained opposed to any formal alliance, some degree of co-operation was maintained on defence issues; in January 1965 Mahendra even concluded a secret agreement not to purchase military equipment from other countries if this could be provided by India. However, in 1969, his government asked for the ending of the stationing of Indian monitors on its northern border and the prime minister, Kirtinidhi Bista, gave an interview implying that the semi-alliance established by the 1950 Treaty of Friendship was no longer relevant and explicitly renouncing the 1965 agreement. The central problem was that Indian governments still wanted some acknowledgement, however indirect, that Nepal was in their sphere of influence, something neither Mahendra nor Birendra was willing to give. While not wanting an open breach with India, they wished to maximise their freedom of action and were also aware that being seen to stand up to Indian pressure boosted their popularity at home.

Nepal's room for manoeuvre was reduced at the end of 1971, only weeks before Mahendra's death, when India's swift defeat of the Pakistani army allowed East Pakistan to secede and form Bangladesh. Particularly because China offered nothing more than verbal support to Pakistan, the reality of Indian predominance in South Asia was clearly underlined. Even more alarming from Nepal's point of view was the absorption into India in 1974 of the kingdom of Sikkim, which had previously been independent, though it accepted Indian regulation of its foreign relations. This change of status was facilitated by leaders of the ethnic Nepalese majority in Sikkim, who saw it as a means to emancipate themselves from control of the Lepcha monarchy. However, within Nepal it was seen as naked expansionism, and demonstrators in Kathmandu vented their anger on Indian buildings and vehicles. The following year, in a farewell address to guests attending his coronation, King Birendra tried to assert Nepal's strategic equidistance from India and China by calling for Nepal's recognition as a 'zone of peace'. This vague formulation was accepted by most countries with which Nepal maintained diplomatic relations, but not by India, which saw Birendra's move as an attempt to repudiate the 1950 agreement by stealth. The whole exercise merely introduced an extra irritant into India–Nepal relations.

The setting-up in 1983 of the South Asian Association for Regional Co-operation (SAARC), which linked India and Nepal with Pakistan, Bangladesh, Sri Lanka and the Maldives, did not strengthen Nepal's bargaining power since India insisted that bilateral matters could not be discussed in the forum. The new organisation did, however, raise Nepal's international profile since Kathmandu was chosen as the site for the SAARC secretariat.

Aside from differences with its southern neighbour, the royal regime's foreign policy was generally a success story. There were very brief periods of tension with China over the activities of Chinese diplomats in Kathmandu at the height of the Cultural Revolution in 1967 and also, according to rumour, over the raids into Tibet by Kampa guerrillas based in northern Nepal. These had been supported both by India and (before Nixon's opening to China) by the CIA, and the Kampas were not disarmed until a three-month campaign by Nepalese troops in 1974. In general, however, Nepal enjoyed friendly relations both with other countries in South Asia and with those outside it, and was able to obtain large quantities of economic aid both from individual donors and from multi-national organisations. There was an element of rivalry in the aid programmes, particularly between India and China and between India and the United States, but this, of course, served to increase the total amount of help Nepal received. Whether this assistance was used to the best long-term advantage of the Nepalese people is, however, a pertinent question that will be examined in the next chapter.

Domestically, there were small-scale acts of resistance by party activists and also local disturbances, often centring on agrarian disputes, but no really serious challenge to the regime until 1979. This reflected the fact that the party system had not put down firm roots in Nepal, perhaps mainly because the educated middle class was still such a small proportion of the total population. The monarchy was in any case promising development as well as continuity with the past and some major reform measures were indeed introduced (see chs. 5 and 6 for a fuller discussion). Ironically, Mahendra began by following the Congress blueprint: *birta* and *rajyauta* abolition had been legislated for in 1959–60 but were actually implemented after the royal takeover. The 1964 Land Reform Act was also similar in some ways to B. P.'s own proposals. Thus, the Panchayat regime should not be seen as simply a triumph for reactionary social classes. The monarchy was careful not to antagonise major vested interests, and power structures at village level largely retained their traditional shape, but some of the largest landowners saw their influence reduced and the position of tenants in the Kathmandu Valley was markedly improved. At least in the early days of the system, there were reasons for many at least to give it the benefit of the doubt.

The impressive façade of royal rule nevertheless concealed important weaknesses. Most important for the nation's long-term future, though not yet a pressing difficulty, was the failure to resolve the underlying economic problems. More immediately apparent was the factiousness among *panchas*, as those active politically within the system were known: government propaganda stressed the need for co-operation in place of the old quarrels between parties, but unity of purpose was easier to advocate than to achieve. It also became increasingly apparent that, while the educated classes as a whole accepted and adjusted to royal rule as a reality, the elaborate Panchayat ideology discussed in chapter 6 had very few really committed adherents. Pre-1960 intellectual alignments still asserted themselves, and it was significant that from 1967 onwards the files at the Rastriya Panchayat employed the labels 'leftist' or 'rightist' to describe the beliefs of individual members. The very success of the regime's drive to expand access to education meant that the number of potential dissidents would increase, especially once the aid-driven expansion of the bureaucracy ceased to be able to offer educated youngsters employment commensurate with their expectations.

Dissent among those who had previously collaborated closely with the king began early. Rishikesh Shaha, who had served as foreign minister and as finance minister in the early 1960s and who had also been one of the main architects of the 1962 constitution, emerged in 1967 at the head of a group of legislators calling for the Rastriya Panchayat to be directly elected and to have a say in the choice of prime minister. In 1969 Shaha criticised the prime minister for denouncing defence co-operation with India without first consulting the legislature. He was imprisoned for a time and, in contrast to the limited support he had received two years previously, sixty-four MPs signed a petition calling for his release. After King Birendra succeeded his father in 1972, Surya Bahadur Thapa, a former chairman of the Council of Ministers, called for reform on the lines Shaha had earlier suggested. He, too, was imprisoned as a result.

Those who had been opposed to the Panchayat system from the start pursued varying strategies. In 1968, Subarna Shamsher as leader of the Congress Party in exile issued a statement offering King Mahendra 'loyal co-operation'. B. P. Koirala, who was at this time still in prison in Kathmandu, was upset at this seeming surrender and refused to make a similar declaration. However, Mahendra now released him anyway, calculating that he would not in practice oppose Subarna's new line. Once at liberty B. P. made speeches critical of the king and, after a warning from Surya Bahadur Thapa that he was in danger of rearrest, he went into voluntary exile in India early in 1969. Apparently in the hope of managing a reconciliation, Mahendra ordered work to begin on drafting amendments to liberalise the constitution, but he died before this was finalised; Birendra, confronted both with Surya Bahadur Thapa's opposition in the Rastriya Panchayat and student strikes across the country, preferred initially to retain his father's old system unaltered. Against this background, B. P. opted for military action, even though, in contrast to both 1950 and 1961, the campaign would not have the covert backing of India. Incidents such as the hijacking of an aircraft to a remote Bihar airstrip in 1973 and a bungled attempt on Birendra's life in Biratnagar the following March were of little military significance but may have contributed to Birendra's decision in December 1974 to set up a constitutional reform commission.

Although the eventual amendment of the constitution in 1975 was actually a tightening rather than a liberalisation of the system, B. P. still returned to Nepal with his old comrade-in-arms Ganesh Man Singh in December 1976; both were arrested on arrival. B. P. claimed publicly that he wished to contribute to national solidarity against a danger to Nepal's independence, presumably a reference to India's annexation of Sikkim two years previously. However, the real reason may have been that India provided a less congenial environment after Indira Gandhi's imposition of emergency rule in 1975. Legal proceedings went ahead slowly, interrupted by two trips abroad for cancer treatment at the government's expense. At the end of one of these B. P. met Subarna Shamsher on his deathbed in Calcutta in October 1977 and received charge of the party organisation from him, but Subarna's former followers were soon unhappy with his leadership and by summer 1978 they were effectively functioning as a rival party under Bakhan Singh Gurung. In autumn 1978, B. P. was finally acquitted on all charges in Nepal. Birendra may genuinely have wanted a reconciliation with his father's old foe, but leniency may have stemmed also from realisation that the Janata Party which replaced Indira Gandhi in March 1977 would be less tolerant of repression in Nepal.

While Congress by the end of the 1970s had for practical purposes become two parties, the Communists had split into at least seven factions. Each claimed to be the true continuation of the party founded in 1949, but they were divided both on tactics towards the royal regime and the Nepali Congress, and by their stance regarding the Sino-Soviet split. The firmly pro-Soviet group led by Keshar Jang Rayamajhi had been prepared to accept the royal regime and work with it ever since, as secretary-general of the undivided party in 1960, he had welcomed Mahendra's takeover. The more radical majority among the cadres had quickly broken with Rayamajhi but then themselves had splintered further. Pushpa Lal Shrestha, still today honoured by most Communists as the founding father of their movement in Nepal, was sympathetic to Beijing, but unwilling to break completely with Moscow and had also consistently advocated tactical unity with Congress. Even closer to Beijing and more suspicious both of Congress and of India were the followers of Man Mohan Adhikari. Another relatively moderate faction was led by Narayan Man Bijukche (Comrade Rohit), who had been a collaborator of Pushpa Lal's but had broken with him over the latter's backing for Indian intervention in the 1971 Bangladesh independence war. Rohit's support was largely confined to Bhaktapur, but his group had had considerable success there organising the tenant farmers and in infiltrating Panchayat institutions.

Most important for the future were two more radical groups. The Communist Party of Nepal (Marxist-Leninist) was established in 1978 by former members of the extremist Jhapeli group. In the early 1970s this faction had followed the example of the Naxalites across the border in India and begun a campaign of assassination of 'class enemies' in the villages of Jhapa district in the far eastern Tarai. Prompt action by the security forces ended their campaign while the number of victims was still in single figures, and the group reverted to clandestine but non-violent agitation. More influential than the Marxist-Leninists in the 1970s but, like them, Maoist in ideology was the Fourth Convention. This group, set up by Mohan Bikram Singh in 1974, also laid particular stress on the old demand for a constituent assembly.

While many Communist activists operated underground, liable to arrest and imprisonment if their identities became known, the regime generally during these years regarded the Nepali Congress rather than the leftists as the main threat. At times the government tried to use Communist factions as a foil against B. P. and his supporters. Congress sympathisers were more likely to be purged from professions such as teaching, while there is some evidence that officials occasionally even channelled money to radical groups such as the Marxist-Leninists. Once again, those who followed Nepalese politics were given reason to be on the lookout for strange bedfellows.

Despite the official ban on party politics, student union elections provided an arena within which it could still thrive. The contests were most usually between pro-Beijing Communists and Congress supporters, the latter normally calling themselves 'Democrats'. Pro-Panchayat students also competed but normally came a poor third. Until its abolition in 1975, the Rastriya Panchayat's graduate constituency was similarly an arena for opposition. It gave Rishikesh Shaha a platform in the late 1960s, and Ramraja Prasad Singh, who won the 1971 election, was eventually expelled from the legislature for his criticism of the Panchayat system. The administration and the courts' tolerance for activities of this kind varied from time to time, partly as a result of the attitudes of different individuals within the system but also depending on tactical judgements made by the palace. As memoirs such as those of Durga Pokhrel, now president of the Women's Commission, make clear, those who publicly opposed the system were at times treated with great brutality. Across educated society as a whole, however, there seemed to be an understanding that criticism of the system could be safely expressed in private as long as its open expression was curtailed. The frankness with which Nepalese expressed their complaints to one another and to foreigners was proof that at least there was not the pervasive fear of informers prevalent in truly totalitarian societies.

THE SYSTEM UNDER CHALLENGE: 1979–1988

The catalyst for the protests that brought the first major change to the system was the hanging in February 1979 of two Congress fighters who had been sentenced to death some time previously for the 1974 attempt on Birendra's life and for leading an armed incursion in 1975. The palace – whether that meant the king himself or some of his key advisers – seems to have decided that after the leniency shown to B. P. Koirala a counterbalancing display of firmness was required. The immediate effect, however, was to increase discontent among students, who were already unhappy over recent changes to the education system (see ch. 6). On 6 April 1979 students marched on the Pakistan embassy, ostensibly protesting the execution of Pakistan's former prime minister Zulfikar Ali Bhutto but with the Nepalese executions also in mind. Police heavy-handedness against the demonstrators led to escalating protests in the Kathmandu Valley and in some Tarai towns. The government opened negotiations with a student action committee dominated by Congress and the relatively moderate Rayamajhi and

Pushpa Lal Communist factions. They reached an agreement by conceding most of their demands for the tertiary education sector. These included automatic university entrance for all who had passed the School Leaving Certificate exam, abolition of the pro-Panchayat student organisation, the Rastrabadi Swatantra Bidyarthi Mandal (Independent Nationalist Student Association) and establishment of an independent union at national level. However, the more radical leftists in the Marxist-Leninist and the Fourth Convention groups denounced this as a sellout and organised further demonstrations in Kathmandu, culminating in the setting on fire of government newspaper offices on 23 May. With the police already fully stretched, the army had to be called out on to the streets.

The security situation was still under control: the level of violence had remained low by contemporary Indian standards and in comparison to what was to follow some years later in Nepal itself. However, it was still the largest internal challenge ever mounted to the Panchayat regime, and Birendra may also have worried about the possibility of Indian intervention as well as the recent fate of the shah of Iran. Following all-night consultations in the palace, and possibly against the advice of other members of the royal family, Birendra announced over Radio Nepal the following morning that a national referendum would be held to choose between retention of the Panchayat system 'with suitable reforms' or adoption of multi-party democracy. It was made clear in December 1979 that 'reform' would include the election of the Rastriya Panchayat by universal suffrage, as had been advocated by Rishikesh Shaha, Surya Bahadur Thapa and others for many years. Appropriately enough, Thapa himself was brought in as prime minister to boost the Panchayat side's chances in the referendum.

Although B. P. Koirala declared that he expected the referendum to be fair, many in Congress, including even the moderate Bakhan Singh Gurung group, agreed with the leftist factions that some sort of interim government should be put in place first. Birendra did in fact suspend the Back to the Village National Campaign central committee, the body whose supervision of the Panchayat system had caused great resentment even among the *panchas* themselves, but other institutions remained in operation. Nevertheless, most opposition groups did in practice campaign for the multi-party option, although the Marxist-Leninists and the Fourth Convention remained theoretically committed to a boycott. Their campaign was also helped by some of those working within the system: a number of prominent *panchas* deserted the Panchayat camp, as did some entire local panchayats.

During the campaign leading up to the referendum on 2 May 1980, the opposition was able to make its case at public meetings, but Radio

Nepal put only the Panchayat case and the king's own neutrality was purely nominal. In addition, Thapa made full use of the government's resources to affect the outcome, allegedly allowing lucrative logging concessions to businessmen in return for 'donations' and also encouraging people from the hills to occupy government land in the Tarai on the understanding that they would vote the right way. Given also that in many areas of the country the village elites were still fully committed to the royal system, the result is quite explicable without assuming, as did many in the multi-party camp, that wholesale rigging took place. The high turnout figures and low percentage of spoiled ballots in remote northern constituencies suggest that in some cases malpractice occurred, but victory for the Panchayat side by 2.4 million to 2 million votes was probably a reasonably accurate representation of public opinion. In any case, the size of the multi-party vote (actually a majority in all the main urban centres) indicated that pressure for a return to parliamentary democracy would grow in future. King Birendra himself reportedly told one Panchayat stalwart, the future prime minister Lokendra Bahadur Chand, that he should be ready to compete in a multi-party system in ten or twenty years' time.

Under the third amendment to the constitution, enacted at the end of 1980, the Rastriya Panchayat was expanded slightly to 140 members, 112 of whom were to be directly elected and 28 nominated by the king. Candidates were required to take an oath of loyalty to the Panchayat system and also to be members of one of the government's class organisations. The government was to be responsible to the legislature, but it could select an individual as prime minister only if 60 per cent of the members supported him. Otherwise the House had to submit three names from which the king would make his choice. The whole system was also to be subject to supervision by a Panchayat Policy and Evaluation Committee, whose remit seemed ominously similar to that of the defunct Back to the Village National Campaign central committee.

B. P. Koirala, who had been almost alone among opposition figures in accepting the referendum verdict, wanted to participate in the first general elections under the new system but was overruled by others in his faction. The largest leftist groups also stayed out. Some other factions did, however, put up candidates, though, under the partyless constitution, these individuals were nominally independents. In the polls held in May 1981 with a 52 per cent turnout, two candidates backed by Bakhan Singh Gurung's moderate Congress faction and three leftists were successful. One of the latter won the Bhaktapur seat for Rohit's Nepal Workers' and Peasants' Party, which had already managed to entrench itself in local government.

Five years later, the Marxist-Leninists, who had overtaken Mohan Bikram Singh's faction as the largest Communist grouping, decided to participate, and four of their party members plus one sympathiser were elected. The Rohit group retained Bhaktapur and a member of the Rayamajhi group and two independent leftists were also elected, one of these, the Newar cultural activist Padma Ratna Tuladhar, winning one of the prestigious Kathmandu seats. B. P.'s wing of Congress still boycotted the national election but successfully put up a candidate for *pradhan pancha* (mayor) of Kathmandu, only to have him thrown out of office a few months later for refusing to take part in celebrations of the anniversary of the Panchayat system. In addition to this small-scale but increasing party penetration of the Rastriya Panchayat, direct elections meant that candidates for Tarai seats no longer needed to secure the votes of hill district representatives in their *anchal* (zone). This enabled more members of the Tarai middle-ranking castes, in particular the Yadavs, to secure election.

Overall, the palace still determined the selection of the prime minister, orchestrating the nomination of Surya Bahadur Thapa immediately after the election as well as his replacement by Lokendra Bahadur Chand in 1983. However, on the latter occasion, Thapa refused to resign when privately requested to do so by the king. Instead he insisted on remaining in office until removed by a vote of no confidence. Afterwards he continued a public campaign against the *bhumigat giroh* (underground gang), an extra-constitutional group who he alleged had worked for his removal. It was in fact widely believed that Rastriya Panchayat members originally well disposed to Thapa had been instructed to turn against him by the king's brothers Gyanendra and Dhirendra. Somewhat in the manner employed by George III of Great Britain in the eighteenth century, the palace was getting its way through the use of patronage and manipulation rather than by directly overruling the legislature. However, also as in the British case, there was clearly the possibility of something like a two-party system evolving within the legislature, based on the division between the 'ins' and the 'outs'.

In the meantime, B. P. Koirala had just before his death in 1982 arranged for leadership of Congress to pass to a troika of his old comrades. These were Ganesh Man Singh, Krishna Prasad Bhattarai and B. P.'s younger brother, Girija, all of whom had been active in the party since before 1950. Girija was less senior than the other two but had been party secretary-general since 1976 and had built up support among party activists outside Kathmandu. In 1985, despite Girija's misgivings, the three decided to launch a *satyagraha* (civil disobedience campaign) for the restoration of full rights for political parties. A parallel agitation was organised by a number of Communist groups. The campaign was launched in May but was suspended the following month after four bombs went off in Kathmandu, killing three staff at the Hotel de l'Annapurna, which was owned by the king's sister, as well as an MP at the Singha Durbar complex to the south-east. Ramraja Prasad Singh, a former Congress-aligned Rastriya Panchayat member now leading an extreme anti-royalist group from exile in India, claimed responsibility, but there were also unsubstantiated rumours that the king's brothers might actually have been involved and then paid Singh to take the blame.

Aside from direct action campaigns of this sort, Congress and those other political parties who did not opt to stay underground were able to meet, debate and recruit members but always under the pretence that they were not actually political parties. The location of their offices was public knowledge, but no sign could be erected and reports of their activities in the media always noted 'outlawed' (*pratibandhit* in Nepali) in brackets after the party's name. Journalists were subject to intermittent harassment, but outright bans on newspapers were normally evaded by reopening under another name. There was also a growing number of 'civil society' organisations that were not party-political but took some interest in political developments. What angered educated public opinion in the 1980s was not so much outright political repression as a growing resentment of political and economic drift and of increasing corruption which was believed to reach into the royal palace itself. Matters came to a dramatic head in 1987 when Bharat Gurung, former aide-de-camp to Prince Dhirendra, was convicted, along with other senior figures, of drug-smuggling and of the attempted murder of an investigative journalist the previous summer. The case coincided with a rift in the royal family as Prince Dhirendra wanted to divorce his wife, a sister of Queen Aishwarya; the affair ended with his renouncing his royal title and setting up home in the UK with his British partner. Aishwarya herself was not immune from scandal: there were suspicions that she was misusing her role as patron of the National Social Service Co-ordination Council to divert money for her own purposes.

All this was accompanied by growing malaise within the *panchas*' own ranks, particularly after Marichman Singh Shrestha's appointment as prime minister following the 1986 election and then the refusal to allow a vote of no confidence to be held against him. Singh was the first Newar to be the king's chief minister since Prithvi Narayan Shah's conquest of the Newar kingdoms two hundred years earlier, but his own family had lived for some generations outside the Valley and he had no popular support in Kathmandu to balance his lack of a strong following among *panchas* nationwide.

On top of domestic discontent, Birendra had also to contend with adverse trends within the South Asian region. From 1986 to 1988, a violent campaign was conducted by some of the Nepali-speaking majority in Darjeeling to have their district removed from control by the government of West Bengal in Calcutta and made into a separate state of 'Gorkhaland' within the Indian Union. The leaders of the agitation eventually settled for limited autonomy while still remaining part of West Bengal, and the central government had seemed at times almost to welcome the movement as a tool to be used against the Communist Party of India (Marxist) administration in Calcutta. However, the whole episode raised suspicion in Indian minds that some Nepalese still nursed the dream of a 'Greater Nepal' reaching all along the Eastern Himalayas. This was so even though the Gorkhaland activists themselves stressed that they wanted recognition as a community within India, not closer links with Nepal itself. The violence also probably served to harden attitudes among the Drukpa highlanders controlling the Bhutan state against the large Nepali-speaking community in the south of their country.

There were also expulsions of Nepalese settlers from several states in India's troubled north-east. This had started as early as 1967 when members of indigenous ethnic groups drove out 8000 people from Mizoram, but a new wave of 'ethnic cleansing' began in 1979 in Assam. Here a nativist student movement was initially (like the Gorkhaland agitation) directed against Bengalis, but Nepalese were subsequently also forced out. The situation was complicated: it was often unclear whether individuals held full Indian citizenship through long residence in India or whether they were Nepalese citizens taking advantage of the 1950 agreement which allowed citizens of India or Nepal to live and work freely in the other country. Either way, the expulsions were unlawful, but the Indian government, faced with ethnic unrest throughout the region, was reluctant to defend the settlers' rights.

While many Nepalese depended on access to the Indian labour market, the provision of the 1950 treaty permitting this was unpopular with many others because of the large numbers of Indians taking advantage of it to find work in Nepal. There was in fact a vague provision in the treaty for special arrangements to be made if numbers coming into Nepal were too high and Marichman Shrestha's government in 1987 announced unilaterally that Indians would in future have to apply for work permits in the three districts of the Kathmandu Valley. This move soured relations with India, which was also alarmed by the decision the following year to import a small quantity of weapons from China.

Despite all these difficulties, most observers at the beginning of 1989 would still have expected the Panchayat system to endure a few more years. Its sudden collapse was precipitated in the first place by India's decision in March of that year to impose a semi-blockade of Nepal. This came after King Birendra's government had failed to accept an Indian demand to revert to a single treaty covering both trade and transit arrangements instead of the separate treaties which the Janata government had agreed to sign in 1978. As in 1962, the Indian government did not formally announce its measures but simply found 'administrative reasons' to restrict the movement of goods. The real Indian concern was not just with economic questions but also with the work permit and Chinese arms issues. New Delhi now evidently felt that Nepal should be pressured into returning to what had been agreed with the last Rana maharaja in 1950. The resulting shortages, particularly of kerosene, imposed considerable hardship on Nepal and at first the general public tended to blame India alone. However, discontent with their own government soon mounted, especially after the failure to reach an agreement after the more sympathetic V. P. Singh replaced Rajiv Gandhi as prime minister in November 1989.

At the same time, the dramatic changes in Eastern Europe encouraged hopes among Nepalese activists generally; there were also shifts in the thinking of some of the Communist factions. Especially important was the Marxist-Leninists' conference in August 1989, at which the party formally abandoned Maoism and accepted alliance with Congress to struggle for a parliamentary system as a short-term goal. Against this background, it was announced at the Nepali Congress's conference at Ganesh Man Singh's Kathmandu home in January 1990 that a Movement for the Restoration of Democracy would be launched on 18 February, the anniversary of the establishment of the post-Rana interim government. Congress were joined in organising the campaign by the United Left Front (ULF), an alliance of seven Communist groups formed earlier in January and chaired by one of the leaders of the Communist Party of Nepal (Marxist), Sahana Pradhan. The Marxists were the product of a merger in 1987 involving the followers of Sahana's late husband, Pushpa Lal Shrestha, and those of Man Mohan Adhikari, who was married to Sahana's sister. Other groups in the ULF included Rohit's Nepalese Workers' and Peasants' Party, the Fourth Convention and, most importantly, the Marxist-Leninists. The Marxist-Leninists had replaced the Fourth Convention as the major force on the left partly because of splits in the latter. The Fourth Convention's founder, Mohan Bikram Singh, had lost control of the organisation in 1983 and had set up a new party, Masal, which then split in turn, with the dissidents under Pushpa Kumar Dahal (Prachanda) adopting the confusingly similar name of 'Mashal'.[5] Masal and Mashal were unwilling to join the ULF but, with other, smaller groups, set up the United National People's Movement (UNPM) and announced they would carry out protests of their own.

Despite the lack of a common strategy, all the factions would at least confront the government simultaneously. There was also some open assistance from across the border: the presence at the Congress conference of Indian politicians, notably the Janata Party's Chandra Shekhar, enabled the government to accuse the opposition groups of facilitating foreign interference in Nepal. For once, though, playing the anti-India card was of little use to the Panchayat establishment.

The movement began with demonstrations by party supporters, among whom students were predominant. Clashes with police led to a number of deaths and thousands of arrests in Kathmandu and elsewhere in the country. The nationally known leaders of the political parties were either taken into custody or placed under house arrest. Lower-level leaders were able to maintain a degree of co-ordination, relying particularly on reports of their activities and their calls for action carried by the BBC Hindi Service and All India Radio, but by mid-March the movement appeared to be flagging. However, anger over the killing of a student at Mechi campus in south-east Nepal brought fresh energy to student protests in Kathmandu; a call to the public to extinguish their lights at set times each night proved even more significant. Starting from 29 March, these 'light-outs' enabled large numbers of people to register their protest in safety, while darkened streets emboldened an activist minority to confront the police. Protests from professional groups and human rights activists, and from among *panchas* themselves, as well as expressions of concern by foreign aid donors, on whom the country was highly dependent, were also heightening the pressure on the government.

The turning point came on 31 March, when anger over police firing led the inhabitants of Patan to set up a Public Safety Committee, confine the police to the old palace on the central square and block all access roads with ditches. An important factor here (and also in Bhaktapur) was that the city centre was almost entirely Newar with a tight network of kinship and caste connections helping ensure that police violence against local demonstrators would be taken as a challenge to the community as a whole. Demonstrations continued elsewhere in the Valley towns and then, on 6 April 1990, King Birendra made a dramatic broadcast to the nation. He announced the dismissal of Prime Minister Marichman Singh and the appointment of Lokendra Bahadur Chand, who, it was later learned, had agreed to take the job only after three other ex-prime ministers had turned it down. The king also promised discussions with the opposition and the setting-up of a constitutional reform commission. These concessions were made just after India had submitted the draft of a new treaty reaffirming the security relationship set up by the 1950 agreement. The Indian proposal might have been timed to tempt the king into acceptance in the hope of obtaining Indian support while he stood firm against domestic opposition. It would have been politically almost impossible for Birendra to accept such an offer or for the Indians to keep the bargain implicit in it. Not surprisingly, he preferred to make concessions at home.

However, the royal offer was now not enough to satisfy public opinion. Later in the day around 200,000 people took to the streets in Kathmandu demanding an immediate end to the ban on political parties. A smaller number marched towards the royal palace, some shouting slogans directly against the king. Apparently fearing that the palace itself would come under attack and having failed to stop the crowd with tear gas, senior police or military officials ordered marksmen to open fire. Although the reports of fifty deaths in Kathmandu that day were exaggerated (later investigation could confirm only sixty-three over the whole period of the movement), the incident had a decisive effect. The Valley towns were placed under curfew, but the government also approached the party leaders and allowed them to consult together.

On 8 April, after a meeting at Ganesh Man Singh's bedside, Congress leaders Krishna Prasad Bhattarai and Girija Koirala, together with Sahana Pradhan and the CPN (Marxist-Leninist)'s Radha Krishna Mainali went to the palace for direct negotiations with the king. They agreed to accept, for the moment, a simple ending of the ban on political parties; this was announced over state media late that evening. Bhattarai told an interviewer that the movement was now over and there were joyous celebrations in the streets on the 9th. However, Lokendra Bahadur Chand still hoped to get the political parties simply to join his existing cabinet. Further pressure from crowds on the streets was necessary before the complete abolition of Panchayat institutions (which the leftists would have preferred to insist upon on the 8th) and Chand's own resignation were achieved on 16 April. Ganesh Man Singh was offered the premiership but declined on grounds of health, and on the 19th Bhattarai was appointed to the post with a cabinet of three ministers each from Congress and the ULF, two independents and two royalists. The interim government was invested with the legislative powers of the dissolved Rastriya Panchayat and was tasked to run the government until elections in the following spring.

The next few days saw some alleged instances of violence by *mandales*, as the strong-arm supporters of the Panchayat regime were known. There were also lynchings of police personnel. Law and order continued to be a problem in different parts of the country, made worse by the demoralisation and sometimes outright disaffection of the police force. There was also industrial unrest, with particularly serious strikes by civil servants. The situation was further exacerbated by price rises instead of the relief people had expected. Against this background, Congress in particular was unwilling to press charges against people implicated in the suppression of the People's Movement, and no action was taken on an inquiry commission's recommendations to prosecute named individuals. Amidst all of this, Bhattarai managed to keep the coalition together, but arguably only by postponing hard decisions.

In an attempt to claw back lost ground, Birendra bypassed the ministers and appointed a constitutional reform commission on his own. He eventually had to back down, and a commission with representatives of Congress, the ULF and the king was tasked with writing an entirely new constitution. This was finally promulgated in November after an abortive attempt by the palace to increase significantly the powers the document left with the king. There was to be a bicameral system (as in 1959) with a 205-member Lower House – the House of Representatives (Pratinidhi Sabha) – elected under the first-past-the-post system. The king would be constitutionally obliged to appoint as prime minister the leader of the party – or combination of parties – with an absolute majority in the Pratinidhi Sabha and, in the case of a hung parliament, to appoint the leader of the largest single party.

The decision to set up the Drafting Commission had itself been controversial, since many on the left would have preferred to leave the task to the elected constituent assembly, as had been envisaged originally in 1951. Consistent with the line which the undivided Fourth Convention had taken in the 1970s, Masal and Mashal were particularly adamant on this point, but both Congress and the more moderate leftist parties believed that it was necessary to get a constitution in place quickly, and this could most easily be done by an appointed committee. Within the commission, the party representatives together had a majority, but discussions were affected by the Communists correctly anticipating that Congress would probably win the forthcoming elections. As a result, although the constitution stipulated that the king must normally act on the recommendation of his ministers, provisions for the declaration of a state of emergency and for dissolving the House of Representatives on the prime minister's recommendation were worded so as to leave some discretion in the king's hands. The Communists took a more radical line in opposing Congress's wish to entrench basic features of the constitution, such as the principles of multi-party democracy and constitutional monarchy. The leftists wished to leave the door open for possible abolition of the monarchy at a later date and also for the replacement of 'bourgeois democracy'. Eventually Congress got its way on these points, and also on declaring Nepal a Hindu rather than a secular state. However, partly because its own lawyer representatives sided with the ULF on the issue, it conceded that major treaties would require ratification by a two-thirds' majority in parliament.

The drafters of the constitution also went some way to meet demands for recognition of the role of languages other than Nepali, put forward by ethnic activists and supported particularly by the radical left. The final document declared Nepal a 'multi-ethnic, multi-lingual' kingdom and, while giving Nepali the pre-eminent position as 'language of the nation' (*rastrabhasha*), recognised minority languages as 'national languages' (*rastriya bhasha*) and gave communities the right to operate primary schools in their own language. However, no obligation was placed on the government to fund such education.

While the country prepared for elections there was a continuing influx of former *panchas* into the Congress Party. To some extent this could be seen as a return home, since so many of those who had backed Congress forty years earlier had afterwards co-operated with the royal regime. However, it made it more difficult for the party to oppose the old establishment, dismayed some of Congress's old guard and finally gave the left a ready-made propaganda weapon. The more moderate Communist groups which had ministers in the government would nevertheless have preferred to go into the election in alliance with Congress, but this possibility was finally rejected at Congress's January 1991 national conference.[6] Even had the two sides of the interim government agreed to co-operate in principle, reaching a detailed agreement on which party would put up candidates for which constituencies would have been extremely difficult.

This certainly proved to be the case among the leftist factions themselves. The Marxist-Leninists and the Marxists did achieve a full merger in January to form the Communist Party of Nepal (Unified Marxist-Leninist). However a full electoral alliance with the other, smaller parties proved impossible. In areas where a particular group was clearly extremely strong,

11. Leftists play the anti-Indian card with this banner from the 1991 election campaign depicting the three Congress leaders, Girija Koirala, Ganesh Man Singh and Krishna Prasad Bhattarai as monkeys controlled by the veteran Indian politician Chandrashekhar. The Indian is ordering them, 'Dance and say "The rivers are common."' The reference is to a phrase used by Bhattarai and criticised as representing a surrender of control over Nepal's water resources.

others sometimes agreed to withdraw, but the UML's insistence that it be allocated 180 of the 205 seats proved unacceptable to the rest.

All parties' election platforms generally promised economic progress and a more equitable society, but beyond this there were marked differences of approach. Whereas the Communists expounded their ideology at length, Congress preferred to emphasise their commitment to 'democracy' and their record of struggle to achieve it. To the right of Congress were the ex-Panchayat loyalists, now grouped in rival National Democratic Parties led by Lokendra Bahadur Chand and Surya Bahadur Thapa. Both joined the Communists in attacking Congress for making too many concessions to India during the interim government period. Krishna Prasad Bhattarai was particularly criticised for using the expression 'common rivers' to describe stream that flowed from the Himalayas through Nepal and then entered the Indian plains (see illus. 11, above). Issues of ethnicity, caste and religion, which had been the subject of the bulk of submissions to the Constitution Drafting Commission, were also to the fore. Challenging Parbatiya dominance was the raison d'être of the Tarai-regionalist Sadbhavana Party and also of the Rastriya Janamukti Party, which sought to appeal to the Tibeto-Burman-speaking ethnic groups in the hills. Affirmative action to improve the lot of the non-Parbatiyas was also generally supported by the left, though the leftist parties themselves were, like Congress, led mostly by Parbatiya Brahmans.

While the UML was still ambivalent about parliamentary democracy and the monarchy, the most radical of the competitors in the election, the United People's Front, declared it was participating only to 'expose' the system. The UPF was basically a front organisation for the Unity Centre, an underground party formed in November 1990 by a merger between Nirmal Lama's Fourth Convention and Prachanda's Mashal. Lama's and Prachanda's groups had both originally been part of the Fourth Convention founded by Mohan Bikram Singh in 1974, but Singh himself, now heading a rump group of followers in Masal, stayed aloof and called for a boycott of the elections.

Many voters were certainly unaware of the finer points distinguishing all the different parties, but an opinion survey before polling day indicated that a majority could at least distinguish between the more traditionally orientated parties and the more radical ones. In particular, over much of the country there was a perception of Congress as the party of the 'haves' and of the various Communist groups as representing the 'have-nots'. This was especially so in the more developed eastern region of the country.

The campaign was vigorously fought, with students successfully demanding a month's leave from the university to return to their home areas to take part. There were also accusations of corruption. A leader of one minor leftist faction, for example, alleged that the UML was fomenting strikes and then accepting payment from employers to get the workers back. There certainly were donations from businesses and also some coercion. The candidates of the two National Democratic Parties were frequently prevented from campaigning freely by activists of other parties, while Girija Koirala was barred from campaigning in Mohan Bikram Singh's Pyuthan base. The tendency for a party's supporters to behave more like a private army than agents of peaceful persuasion was already making itself felt. Nevertheless there was relatively little bloodshed: twelve deaths in the course of the campaign was shocking by the standards of Western Europe or North America, but it was a low total by South Asian ones.

The election results were roughly in line with the admittedly limited sampling of opinions beforehand. Congress won comfortably on a 65 per cent poll but, despite attracting a larger percentage of the vote than they had done in 1959, they did not achieve such an overwhelming victory in terms of seats (see table 4.3). Congress had been particularly successful in the less developed western hills, where Chand's National Democratic Party had been expected to do well. Presumably, many of the NDP's potential supporters

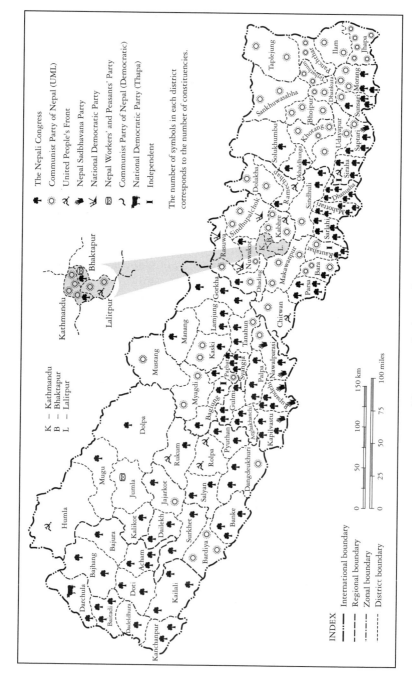

Map 4. 1991 election results.

Table 4.3 *1991 election results*

Party	Seats contested	Seats won	% of total seats	% of total votes
Nepali Congress	204	110	53.7	37.8
Communist Party of Nepal (Unified Marxist-Leninist)	177	69	33.7	28.0
National Democratic Party (Chand)	154	3	1.5	6.6
National Democratic Party (Thapa)	162	1	0.5	5.4
United People's Front	69	9	4.4	4.8
Nepal Sadbhavana Party	75	6	2.9	4.1
Communist Party of Nepal (Democratic)	75	2	1.0	2.4
Nepal Workers' and Peasants' Party	30	2	1.0	1.3
Independents	193	3	1.5	4.2

Note: Another nineteen parties contested the election but failed to win seats.

had decided Congress would offer better protection. In contrast, the UML established itself as the main opposition force, relying on its strength in the more developed eastern region and also in the Kathmandu Valley. Here the party president, Madan Bhandari, whose name had been unknown before the end of the *janandolan*, defeated veteran Congress leader Krishna Prasad Bhattarai. Consequently it was not Bhattarai but Girija Prasad Koirala who became prime minister, following in the footsteps of his two elder brothers. He and his party now faced the enormous challenge of at last meeting the expectations of the previous spring.

CHAPTER 5

The quest for 'development': economy and environment, 1951–1991

POPULATION MOVEMENTS

Particularly in their final years, the Ranas had acknowledged an obligation to raise the living standards of the ordinary Nepalese people and, after 1951, this objective became central to the rhetoric of successive governments. The actual efforts made over the next forty years did have some success, particularly in raising life expectancy and the literacy rate. There were also real improvements in many villages, including the provision of running water and latrines. Most dramatically, there was a great expansion in the facilities available to residents of the Kathmandu Valley. To a large extent, however, all this was overshadowed by the relentless rise in population. This trend had already begun to emerge towards the end of the Rana years but now began to accelerate sharply. The 8.4 million Nepalese at the time of the 1954 census had become 18.5 million by 1991. By world standards, they were an overwhelmingly poor population and, because there had been no breakthrough in agricultural productivity, the rise in numbers threatened to make matters even worse. By the 1980s Nepal had turned from a net exporter to a net importer of food grains and the continuing fragmentation of holdings made it more and more difficult for ordinary peasant families to feed themselves. The result was rising indebtedness as well as an increase in temporary and permanent emigration. The fundamental problem was not only a growing shortage of cultivable land but also of easy access to the forests which were the source both of firewood and of fodder for livestock.

Conventional wisdom from the 1960s onwards saw the shrinking Himalayan forests as the cause of soil erosion, which in turn increased the silt load carried by rivers to the Gangetic plain and raised the danger of flooding. This ignored the fact that a high degree of soil erosion was normal in geologically young mountain ranges, even without any human habitation at all, and also that traditional terracing in the hills was often a more effective barrier against erosion than virgin forest. The extent of deforestation was also rather less than often supposed, and the prophecies of the country turning into a mountain desert by the end of the twentieth century proved unfounded. There was nonetheless a thinning-out of forests in the hill areas, while the Tarai, where land could most easily be reclaimed for agriculture, lost 25 per cent of its forest cover in just fourteen years from 1964–5. Over the country as a whole around 50,000 hectares of 'crown cover' (land directly sheltered by tree branches) were being lost each year by the end of the Panchayat era, a serious depletion of resources even if not yet an environmental disaster.

Like soil erosion, migration in search of a better livelihood was nothing new for Nepal: many communities in the hills had long combined long-distance trade and spells of work on the plains with subsistence agriculture in their home villages. In the late 1950s, for example, an American survey in one hill area found that almost 87 per cent of the male population looked for seasonal employment away from their homes, while over the country as a whole in the 1960s perhaps a quarter of the population were continually on the move. The numbers involved, and in particular the total of those relocating permanently, continued to rise and by 1991 over a million people had left the mountains or hills to set up new homes in the Tarai.[1] The bulk of them acted on their own rather than as part of official government resettlement programmes. In the 1950s and 1960s the great majority of migrants moved into the central and eastern Tarai. From the 1970s onwards, though these areas still remained the major destination, the western Tarai, where more land was available for clearance, became increasingly important. By the 1980s, only 45 per cent of Nepal's population lived in the hills, compared with 60 per cent twenty years earlier.

The concentration of resources and economic opportunities in the Kathmandu Valley, and, to a lesser extent, in the Tarai towns, acted as a magnet for some, but most migration was from one rural area to another. Only 12 per cent of Nepalese lived in urban areas in 1991, though a large number living along the major highways could be classified as semi-urban dwellers. The Kathmandu Valley's population rose from around 400,000 in 1952 to 1,200,000 forty years later but this was more or less in line with the overall national trend, and the growth of other urban centres, especially Pokhara and Biratnagar, meant that Kathmandu city's own share of the total urban population decreased from 36 per cent in 1961 to 25 per cent in 1978.

Many who left their hill villages went in search of work in India, whether on a seasonal basis or for extended periods. In 1991, some 1.5 million Nepalese were believed to be in India, in addition to several more million people of Nepalese descent who had moved across the border earlier. Some

12. A Parbatiya family in their new home in Parsa district in the Tarai north of Birganj. Hundreds of thousands made a similar move from the hills to the Tarai from the 1950s onwards.

settled in areas of the Himalayas which were already Nepali-speaking but the majority moved elsewhere, often finding work as security guards, a role for which the Gurkhas' military tradition was supposed to make them particularly suitable. Emigration was made easier by the 1950 treaty which allowed Nepalese citizens full freedom to live and work in India but, as seen in chapter 4, this right was sometimes challenged by indigenous-rights activists in the north-east. The continuing stream of new arrivals was also seen as a threat by those born in India of Nepalese stock, who felt that they themselves were classed together with the newcomers by other Indians rather than being accepted as full Indian citizens.

The 1950 agreement allowed similar rights for Indians in Nepal, and there was a steady counter-flow across the border. Often Indians moved to specialised niches in the small but growing urban economy, working, for example, as electricians, plasterers or itinerant vegetable and fruit sellers. Employers, especially if they were themselves Indians, generally preferred to bring in trained Indian workers rather than train Nepalese ones themselves. Even where technical skills were not an issue, the Indians were often more adapted to routine industrial work, enjoyed less legal protection and were also thought less likely to steal industrial secrets and set up in competition on their own. A disputed number of Indians moved into the Tarai, where, before large-scale migration from the Nepalese hills began in the late 1950s, the great majority of the inhabitants were already Indian in language and culture. Against this background, and since few had birth certificates or other proof of their status, it was difficult to tell who was or was not a 'genuine' Nepalese. An apparent reduction in Nepal's foreign-born population from 337,620 in 1961 to 234,039 in 1981 may simply have meant that many were 'passing' as citizens without having gone through the cumbersome naturalisation process laid down in Nepalese law. It was in fact widely believed that many non-Nepalese had been included on the electoral roll for the 1980 referendum on the future of the Panchayat system. Two years later, the Tarai's foreign-born population was estimated to be growing at around 4.2 per cent each year with about half of the newcomers going to urban centres. The total would be considerably larger if seasonal and temporary workers were also included.

Also important throughout this period was the exodus from all South Asian countries to other regions. The number of Nepalese involved was, of course, small compared with the country's larger neighbours, but by the 1980s it had become a growing trend. The Middle East was the principal destination but Japan and Korea were also increasingly popular. An unknown but significant proportion went as illegal immigrants.

PLANNED DEVELOPMENT AND FOREIGN AID

The government's commitment to economic transformation was given formal shape by the setting-up of the National Planning Commission in 1955, a move already foreshadowed by Mohan Shamsher's 1949 Economic Planning Committee. From 1956 onwards, Nepalese governments drew up a succession of 'five-year plans', combining details of the government's own projected expenditure on development projects, general guidelines for the private sector and targets that the economy as a whole was expected to meet. The original concept derived from the Soviet Union's industrialisation drive, but Nepal naturally followed the Indian adaptation for an economy not under full state control. In the early years, infrastructure, in particular road-building, was given the highest priority, but there was also an emphasis on increasing agricultural production in the Tarai through the promotion of high-yielding varieties and the expansion of irrigation. In addition, the second plan (1960–5), prepared under the short-lived Congress government, increased the budget allocation for industry from 7.5 per cent to 17 per cent.

From the early 1970s onwards, after King Birendra came to the throne, more attention was given to agriculture in the hills, to resource conservation and to regional planning. The country was divided into five development regions – Eastern, Central (including the Kathmandu Valley), Western (including Pokhara), Mid-Western and Far Western – each of which combined high-mountain, hill and Tarai districts. It was hoped to counterbalance the concentration of resources in the Kathmandu Valley and (to a lesser extent) the eastern Tarai, by promoting the growth of small towns in the other regions. However, the limited degree of urban development achieved tended to benefit only the local merchant classes, without any general rise in living standards. The development regions remained a fairly weak tier in the administrative structure, and decentralisation to the more important district level was not very successful. Although the 1982 Decentralisation Act nominally gave district panchayats control over government technical staff running development projects, they continued in practice to look to their parent department in Kathmandu. Some argued that the seventy-five development districts themselves, established in the 1960s, were in any case not ideal units for planning purposes because boundaries between them tended to run not along the ridges separating river valleys but along the rivers themselves. The districts were therefore not usually natural economic or cultural units.

Another 1970s innovation, and one which Birendra had been closely involved in even before his 1972 accession, was the New Education System Plan. This brought most schools and colleges into an integrated national structure under government control. It also attempted to solve a problem common to many Third World countries of a school and college system geared to prepare students for high-level administrative positions rather than to turning out the middle-level technical personnel in greatest demand. The attempt to reorientate education on more vocational lines, and also to raise the minimum qualifications needed to enter the tertiary system, was, however, extremely unpopular with students, who derided it as *shiksa niyojana* (literally 'education limitation', a phrase coined by analogy with *pariwar niyojana* or family planning!). The experiment collapsed in the 1979 crisis, but until then one partial success had been the National Development Service. Under this, students studying at master's level (in fact roughly equivalent to first (bachelor's) degree level in the UK or USA) had to spend an academic year living and working in a village before being allowed to complete their course. The programme was ended by the government itself in order to prevent radical students from influencing voters in the referendum on the future of the Panchayat system.

In general the economy failed to meet the growth targets laid down by the Planning Commission, GDP growing by an average of only 2.5 per cent per year during the 1960s and 2.1 per cent in the 1970s, by which time population growth was running at 2.5 per cent. When, during the sixth plan period (1980–5), the average annual growth rate did actually exceed the projected 4.3 per cent, it was accompanied by a balance-of-payments crisis. Imports in 1984–5 were running at four times the level in 1975–6 and, after 1982–3, the shortfall was no longer covered by foreign grants or loans. The country's currency reserves were rapidly depleted and the rupee was devalued in 1985. The root of the problem was partly the demand from the small but growing middle class for consumer goods, but the country had also been the victim of success in a drive to lessen its dependence on India. Some progress in import substitution (including commodities such as beer and soap) had not really helped the exchange position because of the need to import raw materials and equipment.

Against this background, Nepal had to negotiate a structural adjustment loan from the World Bank in the mid-1980s, the conditions attached including not only moves towards balancing the budget and reducing the trade deficit but also action on poverty reduction. Birendra himself in a 1985 speech called for bringing the entire population to a reasonable income level 'in accordance with Asian standards' by the end of the century. In a supplement to the sixth plan issued in 1987, this was formalised into a programme for meeting 'basic needs'. This phrase, which implied targeting the poor specifically rather than concentrating simply on boosting overall production, had first been used in an International Labour Organisation conference in 1976 and the concept had begun to influence Nepalese development thinking even before it was urged upon the country by the ILO itself. The drive was the centrepiece of economic strategy in the final years of the Panchayat regime but, as with earlier programmes, achievement fell far short of expectations. In 1991 it was estimated that 7 to 9 million of the country's 19 million people were unable to obtain their minimum daily calorific requirements. Two years later the UN's Human Development Report, based on a combination of economic indicators plus other factors such as literacy level, placed Nepal in 152nd position of 173 countries surveyed.

The meagre results of the 'basic needs' programme was blamed by some on a failure to elaborate and then implement the very broad objectives the government had set itself. Others held that, as with much of Nepal's overall development effort, the key problem was the success of the elite at village level in steering benefits in their own direction. Those *panchas* or civil servants who were genuinely concerned with meeting the government's avowed objectives were allegedly frustrated by their inability to mobilise resources from the wealthier (often high-caste) households and by resentment from poorer families at being made to work on local development projects the benefits of which went to others.[2] It could, however, be argued that economic development in any country generally does benefit local elites and that the administration should have been able to design programmes which did so in a way that also benefited the wider community.

The failure to break the grip of poverty over most of the country occurred despite extensive development aid received from 1950 onwards. By the end of the century this had amounted to around US $5.2 billion, which, in proportion to its population, was much more per capita than other South Asian states had received. Foreign funds, either as grants or 'soft' loans, regularly made up more than half of the government's 'development budget', which included both the capital cost of new projects and some recurrent expenditure. This dependence peaked in the late 1980s, when the aid component reached around 80 per cent (equivalent to 40 per cent of all government spending or 14 per cent of annual GNP). Grants from individual countries tended to be more common in the 1950s and 1960s, when geopolitical rivalries in the region were at their height. Thereafter, loans and the role of international agencies such as the Asian Development Bank, United Nations Development Programme and the World Bank became more important. Debt service as a percentage of GDP increased from less than 0.1 per cent in 1974–5 to almost 1 per cent in 1987–8 and total outstanding debt from 346 million rupees to almost 21 billion rupees (approximately US $400 million),[3] though this was still a relatively low level by Third World standards.

The foreign aid era opened formally just after the Ranas had accepted the 'Delhi compromise'. On 23 January 1951 Nepal signed an agreement to accept assistance under the United States's 'Point Four' programme and received a first token payment of US $2000. American aid was primarily aimed to strengthen countries and governments that might be vulnerable to communist influence; the model was the highly successful Marshall

Plan which had put Western Europe back on its feet after the Second World War. The hope was that, as in Europe, a relatively small injection of funds and expertise would trigger self-sustaining economic progress. Early American efforts were quite successful in assisting the expansion of the national education system and establishing a teacher-training college. Another effective contribution was support for the setting-up in 1959 of the Nepal Industrial Development Corporation, which shortly afterwards established the country's first industrial estate at Balaju on the northern outskirts of Kathmandu.

However, promoting wider change in Nepal's traditional agrarian society proved more difficult than aiding recovery in countries that already possessed highly educated workforces and had functioned as industrialised societies for many decades. In agricultural extension work, the focus of much of their early efforts, the Americans were up against factors such as a land-tenure system that provided the cultivator with no incentive to increase production and local trainees for extension work who lacked enthusiasm for the task. Frustration over the government's failure to institute reforms led the United States to scale back its agricultural assistance programme in 1962.

Foreign technical advisers felt they faced the dilemma of reducing efficiency if they remained in a purely advisory role or stoking resentment if they tried to take control themselves. The Americans opted initially for the first alternative but then in 1954–8 tried to work through a system of 'co-operatives', in which they nominally worked as equal partners with the Nepalese but were in fact in control. A 1958–63 programme for the construction of suspension bridges was again largely meant to be carried out by the Nepalese themselves with the Americans simply providing materials along with supervision and training in the initial stages. The original target was seventy bridges over two years but in fact only one had been completed after five.[4] A project to install radio communications links, also begun in 1958, was more successful, but there were problems training local technicians to maintain it.

Whatever the division of responsibilities, the system was still vulnerable to disruption from the frequent changes of administration during the 1950s and again in the purge that followed Mahendra's 1960 takeover. Americans complained that attempts to urge reform within the administrative system itself met with Nepalese resistance, especially as their suggestions included the posting of advisers in the heart of government departments. The advisers were in any case also themselves responsible for some badly executed projects including initial anti-malaria efforts that used inadequate amounts of insecticide over too wide an area and trials of new plant varieties conducted without proper controls.

The American programme was also hampered by the tensions with other powers which had triggered the whole venture. In 1958, funds were temporarily diverted from the suspension bridge programme to start up Nepal's national airline – Royal Nepal Airlines Corporation (RNAC) – with a fleet of three DC3s, following King Mahendra's return from a visit to Moscow and revelation that the Soviets had offered help with civil aviation. The most serious problem in the early years, however, was friction with India, despite the fact that both countries shared the same basic objective of minimising Chinese influence in Nepal. Rivalry in the field of village development became so intense that the Americans in 1958 initiated a three-year phased withdrawal from this sector. In 1961–2, however, during the Indo-Nepalese tension that followed Mahendra's removal of the elected government, Nepal asked the Indians to discontinue their involvement, and the Americans then had the field to themselves. An attempt by the United States and India to collaborate in road-building also came to an end in 1962. In five years no fully usable road had been completed and the project's heavy equipment was later taken over by the Chinese to build the road from Kathmandu to the Tibetan border.

While many of those in the American aid programme retained faith in technical 'quick fixes' to development problems, others began to stress more the importance of will and determination on the Nepalese side: hence the United States Operations Mission director's public campaign from May 1961 for land and taxation reform and a cutback in American involvement in the agricultural sector when the reforms did not materialise. American aid continued for some time as a major component in the development budget, amounting to 46 per cent of all individual-country aid in 1960–6, but the rapprochement with China in the early 1970s reduced the strategic importance of the Himalayan region to the United States, and its contribution declined to 10 per cent in 1980–90. The United States nevertheless remains an important stakeholder in the Nepal Aid Group set up under the World Bank in 1976 to co-ordinate aid from Western countries and Japan and from UN agencies. Scholarships for Nepalese students to study in the United States, under the Fulbright and other schemes, also remained an important contribution.

Despite India's intimate involvement in the events of 1950–1, it only began a full-scale programme of development aid after an appeal for assistance by prime minister M. P. Koirala in January 1952. The first two major projects, construction of the Tribhuvan Rajpath (Highway) linking

13. A street scene in Birganj in the early 1970s. The town was named in honour of Bir, the first of the Shamsher maharajas. Its importance grew further after 1950 with the construction of a road linking the town to Kathmandu and some industrial development.

Nepal with the Indian border at Birganj and of an international airport in Kathmandu, were begun in 1953 and the costs were initially regarded as loans though they were later converted into outright grants. The village development programme begun in 1956 was in response to American involvement in the same sector. India had seen even the initial US establishment of diplomatic relations with Nepal in 1947 as a threat to its own influence in the country, and hoped that the United States and the Soviet Union would agree to provide financing for development projects but agree to let Indian personnel carry them out. This would have both served India's strategic interests and conserved resources needed for its own development, but, not surprisingly, neither of the two major powers was willing to accept the arrangement. Indian involvement in village development continued, and was boosted under the 1959–60 Congress government, but terminated by King Mahendra shortly afterwards.

To avoid the problems associated with the American 'co-operatives', in which Nepalese and foreign advisers theoretically had equal authority, the Indians set up a system of 'joint boards', with Nepalese formally in charge but with Indian approval needed every three months for the release of further funding. In practice, the Indians retained control in their own hands, and there was naturally resentment over this 'big brotherly' approach, so that Mahendra's ending of the joint board system in 1962 must have pleased many Nepalese. The failure of Indian efforts to win the goodwill hoped for was also ensured by the impression that India worked with urgency only on projects directly serving its own strategic interests. Thus the Tribhuvan Rajpath was rapidly completed, but the Trisuli dam and hydro-electric power plant, which were unambiguously under full Indian control, were completed only in 1971, nine years behind schedule.

The most controversial part of the Indian programme involved the use for irrigation and power generation of water from the country's major rivers, all of which flowed into India. This involved division of benefits between the two countries, and Nepalese nationalists strongly opposed the Indian insistence on Nepal's share being related to what it could presently utilise rather than to its long-term potential needs. The Kosi agreement of 1954 caused outrage in opposition circles in Kathmandu because, in return for allowing India to construct a dam on Nepalese territory that would principally benefit India itself, Nepal would receive only enough water to irrigate 33,000 acres, together with a 9000 kW power plant. Although India later agreed to construct a canal that would allow the irrigation of an additional 180,000 acres, the arrangement was still widely regarded as a sellout. Similar controversy greeted the 1959 deal reached by the Nepali Congress government for the Gandaki scheme. This would allow India to irrigate up to 5 million acres while Nepal would receive water for up to 343,000 acres and a 10,000 kW power station. Nepal's reluctance to 'surrender' any more rivers to India helped ensure that in 1990 plans for schemes on the Karnali and other western rivers had still not got beyond the feasibility-study stage.

India declined an invitation to join the Nepal Aid Group in 1976 but continued assistance, principally in road construction, irrigation and water supply projects. As a percentage of total individual aid, its contribution had declined to only 6.5 per cent in 1990 but, as in the case of the United States, this was mainly the result of growth in the number of donors rather than of a reduction in absolute terms.

China's purpose in becoming an aid donor was to win some influence but (except during the 1962 war) to do this without unduly provoking India. This second point was made explicit by Zhou Enlai when explaining to B. P. Koirala in 1960 why the help being offered was rather less than India's. Chinese assistance had begun four years earlier, during the government led by the pro-Chinese Tanka Prasad Acharya. There was an initial gift of US $4.2 million in cash and $8.4 million in credits for Chinese goods. The credits were not actually used because no other foreign power would provide technicians to construct a factory from Chinese aid, and Nepal lacked the money to meet local construction costs itself. The cash was used partly to fund Nepal's contribution to American aid projects and partly in an abortive attempt in 1957 to prop up the Nepalese rupee. Subsequently China constructed a shoe factory and then, in the 1980s, a paper mill and a sugar factory. There was also assistance in road-building, including principally the road to the Tibetan border at Kodari, which was more of political and strategic than economic value, and the more useful Prithvi Rajmarg linking Kathmandu and Pokhara. A Chinese offer to construct part of the East–West Highway, a short distance from the Indian border, was turned down at Indian and US insistence in 1964. But China was able to make highly visible contributions to the Kathmandu Valley in the form of a ring-road and a trolleybus system connecting Kathmandu with Bhaktapur, nine miles to the east. Chinese aid was nevertheless never on a level with American or Indian contributions: it reached a maximum of 28 per cent of individual aid in 1977 and declined afterwards. In the last two years of the Panchayat regime there was apparently no aid at all. However, Chinese firms had bid successfully for various projects within Nepal and when, in contrast to the 1960s, they were actually allowed to work in the Tarai, it contributed to the crisis in Indo-Nepalese relations that triggered the collapse of royal autocracy.

The Soviet Union's aid programme commenced in 1959, the year after King Mahendra's Moscow visit. Major projects, financed by loans that Nepal was in theory supposed eventually to repay, included the Birganj Sugar and Agricultural Tools Factories, the Janakpur Cigarette Factory and a hospital in Kathmandu. All of these were completed in the 1960s and then operated as government enterprises. As part of the initial aid package, the Soviets had agreed to carry out a survey for the East–West Highway through the Tarai at a time when both India and the United States thought the project would not be cost-effective. Different sections of the road were

eventually built by different countries, with the Soviet Union responsible
for the sector between Simra (north of Birganj) and Janakpur. Soviet aid
reached a maximum of 23.6 per cent of individual assistance in 1962 but
ceased completely for five years after the completion of the road project in
1972. Aid resumed in 1978 but was never again more than about 3 per cent
of the total. The Soviets retained an interest in containing both US and
Chinese influence in the region but, from the 1970s onwards, they were
content to stand behind India, with whom they now had a very close
security relationship.

One valuable component of the Soviet programme, and the only one
still operating when the Soviet Union itself was dissolved in 1991, was
the provision of scholarships to Nepalese students for higher education,
especially in medicine and engineering. From 1970 onwards, sixty to sixty-
five students were accepted annually and, by 1990, over 2000 Nepalese had
been trained under the scheme. Students normally had to spend longer
in the host country than did those on scholarships to the United States
or India, since at least a year's full-time language study was needed before
entering Russian-medium universities.

Nepal also received aid from a large number of other countries, including, from the 1950s, the UK, Australia, New Zealand and Israel. The Swiss
were involved from the 1950s onwards in small-scale but relatively successful projects, setting up plants for the production of cheese from yak milk
and also building suspension bridges and running a demonstration farm
in Jiri in Dolakha district. Israel offered assistance to the Nepali Congress
government and provided help with the setting-up of the Nepal Construction Company as well as in the design of a programme for the resettlement
of hill farmers in the Tarai.

Aid from smaller countries grew steeply from the 1970s onwards, eventually dwarfing aid from the major powers and Nepal's neighbours. In the
1980s, Japan was the largest single donor, followed by the Federal Republic
of Germany. The Japanese programme, begun soon after an embassy was
established in Kathmandu in 1968, helped with rural water-supply schemes,
medical services, agricultural development, loans for hydro-electric and
other infrastructure projects and forest conservation. The Scandinavian
countries also emerged as major donors, starting in the mid-1960s with
Norwegian support for hydro-electric development at Butwal. There was
an increasing contribution from Britain, including the controversial project
of building a 'Nepalese Eton' at Buddhanilkante north of Kathmandu as
well as other help in the educational sector. The British programme also
placed particular emphasis on the resettlement of returned Gurkha soldiers:

agricultural research stations, which also served as the base for extension workers introducing new crops and techniques, were established at Lumle near Pokhara and at Pakrabas in eastern Nepal, in the centre of major recruiting areas. This was partly in compensation for the reduction in size of the Brigade of Gurkhas, which, in its post-imperial incarnation, could be regarded as a rather strange form of foreign aid. By 1990 its strength was down to around 7400 from a total of 10,000 in 1947, and a cutback to only 2500 was planned. However, around 21,000 retired servicemen were drawing pensions, which, although small by British standards, still made an appreciable contribution to the Nepalese economy.

By 1987, the Nepal Aid Group had expanded to include sixteen individual countries and six international organisations.[5] International agencies had been involved from at least as early as 1952, when the Commonwealth's Colombo Scholarship Scheme was extended to include Nepal and, later in the decade, the World Health Organization malaria-eradication programme in the Tarai had paved the way for mass migration into the region from the hills. It was only in the 1980s, however, that aid from such agencies started regularly to exceed aid from individual countries. The number of organisations involved on the Nepalese side was also increasing as donors now began to prefer co-operation with Nepalese non-governmental organisations rather than with government departments. The NGOs, usually private consultancies rather than advocacy organisations on the Western model, were registered and regulated by the government's National Social Services Co-ordination Council, of which Queen Aishwarya was patron, but generally operated more flexibly than the civil service. International NGOs were also playing an important role, though this, too, was not an entirely new development. Catholic religious orders had been running schools in Kathmandu since the early 1950s and the United Mission to Nepal (UMN), a coalition of Protestant church groups, had started providing medical services in the same decade, later expanding its activities to include a hydro-electric plant and industrial training centre at Butwal in the central Tarai. Despite the plethora of organisations now involved in aid at different levels, it was, of course, the major international bodies, in particular the World Bank and IMF, which had the greatest influence over the government's general development policy and therefore had to share responsibility for development failure.

An influential study of aid in the 1950s and early 1960s argued that it was largely ineffective because of the donors' failure to realise that ordinary Nepalese were not eager for change and that the political elite were not committed to bringing about change.[6] Many Nepalese saw this kind of culturalist argument as unfair and, even supposing popular attitudes had been as fatalistic as some supposed, by the end of the Panchayat era, the extension of education and rise in political consciousness meant this was certainly no longer the case. However, commitment at higher levels was still questionable. The monarchy was dependent on conservative support against radical members of the intelligentsia and the administrative machinery was still relatively weak over much of the country, making it difficult for either Mahendra or Birendra to impose a 'revolution from above'. Landholders generally preferred to exploit the rising scarcity value of land rather than increase its productivity or become industrial entrepreneurs, and much of the bureaucracy remained focused primarily on seeking and exercising patronage. As a result, the Nepalese system tended simply to absorb the extra resources aid made available rather than use it as a tool for the transformation of the country.

This fundamental reality was exacerbated by flaws within the aid process itself. In the early days, the Nepalese government encouraged rivalry between donors rather than a more integrated approach, believing that this was the best way to maximise both total receipts and its own freedom of action.[7] The difficulty was lessened by the creation of the Nepal Aid Group, though this was partly offset by the growing number of organisations involved. More seriously, the aid bureaucracies often focused simply on spending their budget rather than ensuring that projects met local needs and were sustainable over the long term. This tendency was strengthened by the interest of national governments in seeing that aid money flowed back in the form of contracts to companies at home. There was also the resentment that could be created by the gulf between the salary levels of most expatriate advisers and their Nepalese counterparts. The problem was reduced when the aid-giver was itself a developing country like India or China, or when developed countries made use of low-paid labour from the US Peace Corps, Britain's Voluntary Service Overseas, the Deutsche Entwicklungs Dienst or the Japanese Overseas Co-operation Volunteers. However, both the Chinese and the Indians could in practice be as high-handed as anyone else, and volunteers worked at only relatively low levels in aid-financed projects. Finally, aid projects, even when successful in a particular area, were not replicable on a large enough scale to make a great difference at national level.

Aid's actual role was often just to keep the government machine running. In 1956, the budget was rescued by a US $4.2 million cash injection from China; American funds played a similar role after a desperate appeal from Subarna Shamsher in 1959. Until the 1970s, aid also underwrote a sufficiently rapid expansion of the government bureaucracy to allow most educated youngsters to find jobs. It is not safe, however, to argue from this that turning off the aid tap and allowing educated unemployment to rise earlier would have resulted in positive change. It might well have simply brought forward the general collapse that is threatening thirty years later.

DEVELOPMENT ACHIEVEMENTS AND FAILURES

Although the economic record of 1951–90 may be dismissed simply as 'failed development' (part of the title of a recent book by one of the country's most prominent development economists),[8] actual results differed from sector to sector. Education expanded rapidly, especially after 1971, and by 1989–90 there were over half a million students enrolled in higher secondary or tertiary education compared with under 2000 in 1950. Around 3 million were now in primary school and the literacy rate, 5 per cent in 1952–4, had reached 40 per cent (56 per cent for males) by 1991. Modern health services were still rudimentary over much of the country, with only around 1200 doctors and 3000 nurses serving a population of 19 million, and village health posts often left in the hands of a *peon* (janitor). However, infant mortality, though still very high, was roughly halved in the thirty years to 1990, when it reached 10 per cent, and the overall death-rate was halved from 27 per 1000 in 1953–61 to 13 per 1000 in 1991. This was largely the result of the malaria-eradication campaign, vaccination and improved knowledge of sanitation and basic health care.

The most visible achievement of development efforts after 1951 was in infrastructure. The expansion of the road network was particularly dramatic: from only 276 kilometres at the end of the Rana period, this had expanded to 7330 by 1990. Although twenty-four of seventy-five district headquarters were still without a road link and had to be supplied by porters or by air, it was now possible to drive between all the main centres of population. As well as the Indian-built Tribhuvan Rajpath from Kathmandu to the Indian border, the 1950s also saw the construction by the British of a road from Biratnagar in eastern Nepal to their recruiting base at Dharan and by the Americans in the Chitwan Valley from Hetaura to Narayanghadh. In the 1960s came the Arniko Rajmarg to the Tibetan border, the Prithvi Rajmarg from Kathmandu to Pokhara, the Siddhartha Rajmarg south from Pokhara to the Indian border and the East–West Highway (Mahendra Rajmarg) through the Tarai. The last project, which involved different donors for different sections, was not fully completed until the 1970s but, considering its great length, was actually built more quickly than any of the other major roads. Mahendra's inability to transfer troops rapidly from point to point along the border during the Congress insurgency had made the project a top strategic priority. Another key part of the national network was the short stretch from Mugling on the Kathmandu–Pokhara road along the Narayani (lower Gandaki) Valley to Narayanghadh. Completed in 1982, this provided a safer route from Kathmandu to Birganj, doubling back eastwards through the Chitwan Valley to Hetaura. Although longer than the Tribhuvan Rajpath, it allowed drivers to avoid the tortuous bends of the latter's middle section and made overnight bus services feasible.

Construction of these communication arteries was clearly essential, even though they had not had the economic stimulus effect once hoped for. However, controversy attended the building of feeder roads linking smaller centres to the main network. In a rugged landscape subject to major land-slips each monsoon season, the building and maintenance of modern roads was an expensive business and its cost-effectiveness could be questioned. Even the busiest stretch of trunk road, the Tribhuvan Rajpath approaching Kathmandu, was used by only 1600 vehicles each day in 1990, and there could be as few as the twenty to thirty vehicles per day using the Swiss-built Lamasangu–Jiri road. Thus, although communities all over the hills demanded access roads, meeting such demands was often a diversion of resources from more pressing needs. One method of resolving the dilemma was greater reliance on 'green roads', which involved less modification of hill slopes and relied heavily on local labour rather than imported machin-ery. This approach remained the exception rather than the rule, but, with German technical assistance, it was successfully used in the late 1980s in Dhading, the hill district immediately west of Kathmandu, at only a fifth of the cost of conventional techniques.

Roads were complemented by three other transportation systems. In 1951 there had been two stretches of railway line in operation, crossing the border between Raxaul and Birganj and between Jaynagar and Janakpur. The network was actually cut back in the 1950s when the Birganj line's continuation north to Amlekhganj was closed after the opening of the Tribhuvan Rajpath. The usefulness of the railways was limited because they were not built on the same gauge as the Indian railway system, so goods had to be offloaded at the border. The second alternative to roads was the ropeway linking the edge of the Tarai with the Kathmandu Valley. The old Rana ropeway, opened in 1925, was replaced by a new, American-built one from Hetaura to Kathmandu in 1964, but this was not used as effectively as it might have been, partly because government mismanagement made it an unreliable method for private traders.

Thirdly, and most significantly, there was air travel. Following India's construction of Tribhuvan International Airport in the early 1950s, Indian Airlines began operating regular flights to Patna in Bihar; until 1958 they also operated Nepal's domestic flights. Royal Nepal Airlines Corporation took over in 1958 and by 1990 was carrying 600,000 passengers annually, with international flights to major South Asian cities, Europe, South-east Asia, mainland China and Hong Kong, and domestic services to forty-two airfields within the country. Many of these were no more than a grass field with a small office but, for those who could afford it, air travel brought the different parts of the country much closer together. Journeys which once involved walking for days were now reduced to one or two hours.

Improved communication systems were also reducing the effect of distance. The postal service, which had been available to just a small proportion of the population in 1951, was expanded, even though in 1990 there were still a few areas of the country not covered. The number of telephone lines increased from only 25 lines to 63,000 over the same period. Radio Nepal began broadcasts in 1951 and after medium-wave nationwide transmissions started in the 1980s they could be received by about 90 per cent of the population. Nepal Television was launched in 1985 with French technical assistance, and initially served only the Kathmandu Valley but, through transmission centres at Biratnagar, Hetaura and Pokhara, it was covering 25 per cent of the urban population by the late 1980s. Also by 1990, satellite dishes and video rental services were supplementing the cinema, which had long been important in the main urban centres in Nepal as in India.

Like transportation priorities, the harnessing of Nepal's enormous hydro-electric potential caused great controversy. Until quite late in the Panchayat period, it was assumed that power should be generated on a large scale for export to India as well as for domestic use. It was also agreed that this would involve the construction of large dams to provide a greater head of water as well as to control flooding further downstream. Arguments then centred largely on who should build the necessary infrastructure and how much control over its own natural resources Nepal would need to cede in the process. As has already been seen, the issue caused considerable friction between India and Nepal as well as providing any Nepalese government's domestic opponents with a ready-made rallying cry. These old arguments continued, but by the 1980s, as scepticism about the effectiveness of large dams increased worldwide, many both inside and outside the country began to argue that Nepal would be better off relying on smaller, run-of-the-river schemes to meet its own internal needs rather than trying to sell power on a large scale to India. Amidst all the disagreements, a number of major projects were nevertheless completed, largely to supply the needs of the urban population, and by 1990 power generation capacity had reached over 160 MW compared with only 1.1 MW in 1951.

The result of the improvement in public health was an acceleration in population growth (2.6 per cent per year during the 1970s). Attempts to curb this through the government's family planning service, established in 1965, had only limited success and the growth rate remained around 2.3 per cent in 1990. Despite the prominent display of family planning posters in towns, efforts over most of the country were hampered by lack of information, the inadequate provision of clinics and a cultural gulf that often existed between the family planning staff and the villagers. Those who did actually adopt contraception were often couples who already had four or five children.

In the vital agricultural sector, total production increased on average almost as rapidly as the population, but this was mainly because new land was brought under cultivation or winter cropping (usually wheat) introduced on fields that had previously been left fallow after the autumn harvest. Taking all main crops together, the average yield per acre actually fell between 1961–3 and 1991–3, with small increases for rice and wheat offset by a fall in the productivity of maize, which was often the choice for planting on marginal land. National figures disguised the fact that yields had generally increased in the Tarai but declined in the hills. In other South Asian countries, rice yields grew three or four times and wheat yields nine or ten times faster, so that Nepal's agriculture went from being the most productive in the region at the start of the period to least productive at its end. Some cash crops, particularly sugar cane, did considerably better, but at the end of the period these accounted for only a quarter of production (10 per cent of cropped area), and the poor overall performance left the country with an increasing food grain deficit.

Farmers themselves were under pressure because deforestation involved them in longer trips to collect firewood and also made it more difficult to provide their livestock with the necessary dry-season fodder, traditionally supplied from the forest. The latter problem might also be made more difficult if they began growing a winter crop since there would no longer be a fallow field for grazing. They could reduce the number of animals they kept but this would mean less manure for the crops and less milk or meat. One response after 1960 was an increasing preference for keeping buffaloes, sheep and goats, all of which were more efficient food producers than cattle.

Another discouragement to cultivators with a marketable surplus was the low prices farmers actually received, sometimes because of their weak bargaining power vis-à-vis grain merchants, and at other times because the government deliberately kept prices artificially low. Near the southern border, there was little the authorities could do to prevent farm produce being smuggled into India, where prices were higher. Elsewhere, however, producers might have to sell grain below the market rate, so the Nepal Food Corporation was able to keep prices down for urban dwellers. Grain which the NFC sold at concessionary prices in rural areas went mostly to those with political influence. During the period 1960 to 1982, the terms of trade between the agricultural and non-agricultural sectors improved for farmers in India but deteriorated for their Nepalese counterparts.

Another key problem was the land holding structure. In the 1950s and early 1960s, many peasants, especially in the Tarai, were paying up to 80 per cent of their main crop as rent. Landlords were generally content to collect rent rather than to actively manage and improve their land and tenants had little incentive to make improvements themselves when they would retain so little of the profits. The slogan 'land to the tiller' was therefore taken up not only by the Communists but by most other political parties and also, in a very direct and public manner, by American officials in Nepal. The latter argued not only that land reform was desirable in principle but also that its implementation would deprive the Communists of their main weapon in mobilising political support. The Americans themselves tried to promote owner-cultivation when they financed a resettlement programme in the (eastern) Rapti Valley, part of the inner Tarai which malaria eradication had recently made safe for immigration. Peasants allotted land were barred from selling it during the initial three years but many plots were sold right at the start to members of the Kathmandu elite, who then became absentee landlords. A considerable number of smallholders did remain, but, with often no source of credit other than loans from a larger landholder at exorbitant rates of interest, they easily fell into unredeemable debt and became tenants in fact if not in name. By 1963 agriculture in the area was mostly operating on traditional lines. The same pattern was repeated with the Nepal government's resettlement efforts from 1965 onwards, involving around 70,000 families and 70,000 hectares, and the much larger numbers of *sukumbasis* (squatters), who cleared forest and began cultivating the land without official authorisation.

King Mahendra's 1964 Land Reform Act, a measure that was partly the result of foreign pressure, imposed ceilings of 16.25, 2.5 and 4 hectares in the

Tarai, Kathmandu Valley and hills respectively.[9] The act also provided for the registration of tenants, who would be eligible to claim for themselves ownership of a quarter of the land they were cultivating. The legislation did succeed in breaking up some of the larger holdings, but in many cases land-holders simply transferred formal ownership to members of their extended family or to trusted servants, retaining control of it in practice. In some areas, the collection of accurate information was actually blocked by the local elite: in Jumla, for example, the Land Reform Survey data was neither processed nor published. In addition, many tenants were simply not registered as such,[10] a strategy made easier for Tarai landlords by their practice of using cultivators of Indian origin who were not entitled to benefit from the tenancy-protection provisions. In the end, even though landlords received compensation for land acquired by the government, only around 30,000 hectares were actually made available for distribution to the landless. For all these reasons, official figures for 1997, which showed that 90 per cent of land in the hills and 80 per cent of the Tarai was owner-cultivated,[11] are not fully reliable. The true figure must lie somewhere between those figures and the average of 50 per cent for Nepal as a whole, which was the accepted estimate in the 1950s.

Even where land was under genuine owner-cultivation, as was certainly the case in much of the hills, distribution was highly skewed. A 1991 World Bank study showed 5 per cent of the population owning 40 per cent of the land. At the other end of the scale, in 1986, 45 per cent of holdings in the Tarai averaged 0.9 hectares and 54 per cent of those in the middle mountains 0.18 hectares, well below what would be required to sustain an entire family throughout the year. Of course none of this would matter if those with larger holdings were rapidly increasing yields and those with uneconomic holdings could find employment at adequate wages either in the agricultural or non-agricultural sector, but neither of these conditions applies in Nepal.

The agrarian structure did alter to some extent, with tenants in the more politically aware areas gradually managing to secure better terms; by 1990, legislation protecting tenants was effective enough for some landowners to leave plots fallow rather than risk a tenant gaining permanent rights on it. However, continuing subdivision of plots meant holdings became less and less economic. The government tried to increase public investment in the agrarian sector, with the allocation as a percentage of total plan investment rising from a fifth in the fourth plan (1970–5) to over 40 per cent in the seventh (1985–90). Government-sponsored irrigation schemes covered over half a million hectares by 1990, contrasting with only 6000 in 1951. A lot was also spent on subsidising the cost of fertiliser, but the supply went mostly to larger farmers, and over 90 per cent ended up in the Kathmandu Valley or the Tarai. Considerable quantities were smuggled into India where the price was higher, but the policy did contribute to the increase in cash-crop yields, which was noticeable particularly in eastern Nepal. As well as sugar cane, production of oilseed, jute and potatoes increased substantially. These were all crops in which Nepal possessed a comparative advantage and which found a ready market in India.

Another attempt to boost agricultural productivity was through several Integrated Rural Development (IRD) projects implemented from the 1970s onwards, when the concept became fashionable in development circles. Similar in some ways to the village or block-development schemes of the 1950s and 1960s, these had by 1988 involved a number of foreign donors investing almost 1800 million rupees into a range of services in designated areas. Unfortunately, much of this investment was inappropriate and the Swiss-funded IRD project in Jiri (1974–91) came in for particular criticism because of its concentration on road construction. Elaborate studies funded by both the World Bank and the British government's Overseas Development Administration showed that roads unaccompanied by other important changes were unlikely to boost agricultural output and that the maintenance costs of many roads were too high for Nepal to bear. The economic benefits they produced were not large and in any case went mainly to a small rural elite. A 1985 external report on the Jiri project claimed that the only sustainable element was the _tuki_ system, under which local farmers themselves acted as extension agents, and that this could have been set up for a small fraction of the total project cost. A final problem was that the IRD projects tended to widen the gap between richer and poorer farmers. It has thus even been suggested that the American-sponsored (western) Rapti Development Project[12] was one of the factors paving the way for the Maoist insurgency which began in that region within a few months of the project being completed.

The one hopeful conclusion from a study of overall agricultural performance in 1950–90 is that changes were sufficient to avoid the Malthusian catastrophe that some had forecast. Production did increase more rapidly in the 1980s even though yields remained low and depletion of forests was partly offset by people planting small areas with trees near their own homes. Government and donor-provided agricultural extension services were often concentrated in areas that were already relatively well off, but by the end of the period new varieties of major crops had been accepted by a large proportion of the population across the whole country. Out-migration and remittances from labour overseas have provided a breathing space and there remains considerable scope for raising yields, particularly in the Tarai.

Nepal's record in forest management was, as with agriculture, a mixed one but the overall result was generally seen as more positive with the government's growing commitment to the concept of community forestry, which meant joint management of forests by 'user groups' of local people. This approach had had support for some time within the country and was also encouraged by a number of aid donors. It represented in part a return to the system existing in 1951, when forests had been either effectively private property or under various systems of local management, at least some of which had been set up in response to Rana directives.[13] In 1957, most forests were nationalised and brought under central control. This system was strengthened by the 1959–60 Congress government and, in Solukhumbu and elsewhere, reinforced again by the setting-up of specially protected national parks. In some areas, where locals were either unaware of the change, or the state seemed too weak to enforce its claim, the measures had no immediate effect, but elsewhere individual owners, thinking their forest at risk, often converted it rapidly to agricultural land.

Over the longer term, central management proved an unsatisfactory solution. There were conflicts between government agencies responsible for timber extraction and for conservation, and the Forestry Department was unable to enforce rules effectively, either because of inefficiency or outright corruption. Abuses were also invited by the Timber Corporation of Nepal's selling of timber to selected customers at a fifth to a third of the market rate. The situation was probably further worsened when Surya Bahadur Thapa's administration allegedly sold large numbers of felling permits to finance the Panchayat campaign in the 1980 referendum. For their part, local people were now less likely to regard the forests as a resource of their own to be conserved. In the late 1970s an attempt was made to solve the problem by involving local panchayats in forest management. When this also proved unsatisfactory, both because of lack of expertise at panchayat level and because of political mistrust, the focus was shifted to the smaller 'user groups' and to the encouragement of those 'traditional' management systems still functioning. This partial bypassing of local government was in ironic parallel with the donors' tendency, beginning from about the same time, to bypass the central government in favour of direct co-operation with NGOs.

The new system still left a number of problems. The 'user groups' might be 'captured' by members of the local elite in the same way as local government institutions. In addition, in the Tarai there remained a strong conflict between the Forestry Department's wish to retain forest areas for commercial exploitation and the attempts by the landless (or supposedly landless) migrants from the hills, known as *sukumbasis*, who squatted on forest land to clear it for cultivation. However, in many areas, direct-participation investment in forests by local people did achieve a better balance between the needs for conservation and for immediate access to forest products.

One theoretical solution to increasing pressure on the land was the provision of more off-farm employment, but obstacles to the rapid industrialisation hoped for after 1951 were numerous. As in all agrarian societies, land ownership was the preferred store of wealth and those who could afford modern consumer items were by then used to buying foreign ones. Individual Ranas had tended to invest in India as insurance against political upheaval in Nepal and, when industrial undertakings at home collapsed after a short period of profitability due to wartime shortages, it reinforced the Nepalese landed elite's wariness of investing in industry. This conservatism was hardly irrational, since without coal or extensive mineral resources of its own, Nepal was at an obvious disadvantage in competing with established Indian industry.

The capital for the factories established in the 1930s and 1940s had been largely provided by Marwari businessmen from Calcutta, normally with Rana partners as political protection. In the limited industrial development that did take place in 1951–90, the Marwaris continued to be the most successful. Originally from Rajasthan in north-western India, this community had long been prominent in South Asian economic life. In the seventeenth century, their financial services had been vital in allowing the Mughals to establish control of what is now Bangladesh.[14] Their role was in some ways similar to that of the Jews in Central and Eastern Europe or the Chinese in South-east Asia, and it could evoke similar animosity. As in Rana times, the Marwaris worked in co-operation with members of the Nepalese political elite, who accepted them not only for their undoubted business acumen but also perhaps precisely because as 'outsiders' they were seen as less of a political threat than partners longer established in Nepal.

Although less successful than the Marwaris, members of other communities were active as entrepreneurs. These included in particular the Newars, who had dominated commercial activity over much of the country since unification but were perhaps hampered in switching to new economic forms by the less flexible nature of their family businesses compared to Marwari ones. A third group, the Tibetans who arrived as refugees after 1959, emerged as pioneers in the carpet industry that became important later in the period, while the Thakalis of the northern Gandaki Valley diversified from trading into other activities including, in particular, the construction industry.

Government attempts to assist the development of private industry started with the 1951 Companies Act. This authorised the establishment of private limited companies in addition to public ones permitted under the 1936 act. A 1957 statement of industrial policy, issued under a multi-party Council of Ministers but reflecting the Gorkha Parishad's market-orientated ideology, welcomed domestic and foreign private investment. After the royal takeover, the 1961 Industrial Enterprises Act offered facilities such as a ten-year initial tax holiday, and improved tax and customs duty concessions were included in the 1981 act. In 1962 there was an agreement for co-operation with India's leading business, the (Marwari) Birla Group. Infrastructure was also provided in the form of the industrial estates at Balaju (1961) and at Hetaura (1965), while from 1966 exporting and importing was in principle made easier by an agreement allowing Nepalese goods in transit exemption from Indian customs duties.

The private sector nevertheless continued to face great problems. Many businesses depended on importing raw materials and obtaining licences for this was often difficult, however liberal the government's policy was in theory. Industrialists in the 1980s complained that unless they had special political connections they were obliged to pay much higher prices on the black market rather than go through official channels. The growing shortage of foreign exchange during this period compounded the difficulty. Bureaucratic regulation was partly intended to prevent abuses, which certainly occurred on a large scale and included purchase of materials simply for resale rather than for genuine industrial use. However, the result was punishment of the honest as well as the dishonest entrepreneur and also an increase in opportunities for corruption. In addition, companies exporting manufactured goods to India often found their market disappeared if India decided that they represented unfair competition to Indian industry (see pp. 150–1).

There were also problems with obtaining finance and labour. The stock market was poorly developed, with only thirty-nine companies listed on the stock exchange in April 1990. Loans from Nepalese banks were a less than ideal source of investment capital because of their large spread (6–10 per cent) between borrowing and lending rates, and getting loans either from them or from the Nepal Industrial Development Corporation often required bribing staff. In addition to labourers' unfamiliarity with the discipline of industrial work, skilled engineering personnel were in short supply. Only 4800 were available in 1985–90 compared to an estimated requirement of 7800. Against this background, there was a tendency for businessmen to fight shy of long-term financial commitment and to prefer switching funds quickly between short-term enterprises of different types.

The sluggish growth of private industry led to the establishment of numerous state enterprises, which grew from only eight in 1961 to sixty-four in 1988–9. This development increased opportunities for rent-seeking activities by bureaucrats and also by some with links to 'the palace'. Some of these ventures, including the Janakpur Cigarette Factory, RNAC, Nepal Oil Corporation, the Nepal Telecommunication Corporation and the Electricity Corporation, did actually operate at a profit. However, overall, the public sector enterprises operated at a loss and by 1988–9 government subsidies to them were equal to 13 per cent of the total development budget. Plans for privatisation were therefore part of a major review of industrial policy in 1985–6, which also liberalised and simplified registration formalities for the private sector. Such measures were actually an explicit condition of the World Bank and IMF loans made to Nepal at this time, but had already been foreshadowed in the 1980–5 plan, probably in response to international financial institutions' growing enthusiasm for such measures. Actual implementation was slow, and in the mid-1980s private industrialists were still complaining that the state sector was competing with them and using its easier access to foreign exchange and other special concessions to gain an unfair advantage. The Marichman Singh administration (1986–90) approached the Nepal Aid Group with a proposal for the complete or partial privatisation of twenty enterprises, but found a lack of enthusiasm among the private sector and was considering scaling back the programme just before the collapse of the Panchayat regime.

If cottage and small industry are included, about 10 per cent of the country's workforce was by then employed full- or part-time in industry. However, the registered industrial units employed only around 160,000 out of an economically active population of almost 10 million, and accounted for under 5 per cent of GNP. Such enterprises were largely confined to the Birganj-Hetaura-Kathmandu corridor, which contained three-quarters of large-scale manufacturing units, and to the eastern Tarai. Most enterprises were engaged in light industry, with the manufacture of construction materials employing 45,000 out of the 152,000 employees covered in the 1986–7 census of manufacturing establishments.[15] Also very important was agro-industry of different kinds. Over half the industrial units in the census were grain mills, although these provided only about 10 per cent of industrial employment. The processing of vegetables and fruit also clearly had great potential, especially as the Himalayan foothills had a comparative advantage over the plains in the cultivation of many species. There were unfortunately still inadequate arrangements for getting such produce to the factories before it rotted.

The most conspicuous industrial success story of the Panchayat years was, however, in carpet and garment manufacture. The Tibetan-style carpet industry in Nepal began as part of the relief effort for Tibetan refugees undertaken by the International Committee of the Red Cross in the 1960s. Later, Switzerland's national aid organisation (SATA) subsidised initial imports into Western Europe and the industry took off, assisted by the vogue in the West for Tibetan culture. Wool was initially obtained from Tibet but later supplemented by imports from Australia and New Zealand. By 1985 the industry was Nepal's principal source of foreign exchange and was employing two-thirds of the refugees themselves as well as many non-Tibetan labourers. In 1986–7 government statistics showed only 20,000 employees working in the textile, carpet and garment factories, which were mainly situated in the Kathmandu Valley. However, estimates of those involved on a part-time basis, often doing contracted-out spinning or weaving at home, ranged as high as an incredible 1 million.[16] In 1990 the actual number employed in these industries was probably somewhere between 100,00 and 250,000. There were some problems, including pollution of the Valley's rivers and concern over the use of child labour, estimated in 1990 to be 30 per cent of the workforce. The export figures were also probably inflated by the inclusion of carpets actually woven in India, smuggled into Nepal and then re-exported; at one point it was alleged that cabinet ministers were involved in a scam of this kind. In any case, increasing competition from high-quality carpets legitimately exported from India was also a danger for the long term. Nevertheless, compared with Nepal's general economic experience, the industry showed what might be achieved with the right combination of local self-help and foreign technical assistance.

The second major growth area was in the ready-made garment industry. This expanded rapidly in 1983 when Indian entrepreneurs shifted operations to Nepal and other South Asian countries in response to the United States's reduction of quotas for imports from India. Although the Indian entrepreneurs worked, as usual, with *pro forma* Nepalese partners, they brought in large numbers of Indian workers whose presence caused ethnic tension in Kathmandu and led the government to institute a requirement for work permits to increase the Nepali proportion in the workforce. A large number of Indians returned home after the US government imposed quotas on Nepal in September 1985, but the government went ahead with the work permit scheme which was one of the factors leading to the 1989 crisis in Indo-Nepalese relations. Many of the factories that had recently opened had to close because of the change in US policy; the government worsened the downturn by delaying the allocation of quota shares and also by taxing rayon imports from India needed as raw material. However, the industry later recovered, although it remained vulnerable to shifts in US trade policy. In the final year of the Panchayat regime (1989–90) the garment and carpet industries were between them contributing 81 per cent of official foreign exchange earnings and 71 per cent of exports. These figures would be lower if undeclared trade and remittances were included, and much of the foreign exchange earned from them went into import of consumer goods, which were then often illegally re-exported into India. Nevertheless the two sectors remained a vital prop to the Nepalese economy.

The importance of these export-orientated industries was underlined by the poor performance of the small-scale cottage industries, mostly producing for the domestic market. A report produced by the incoming Nepali Congress government in 1991 suggested that of 43,000 of these 70 per cent had proved failures. The cottage-industry training programme had been of doubtful value because, even if equipped with adequate skills, the home producer was often not able to compete with mass production.

A contrasting success story was the tourist industry. Nepal had long attracted many visitors from India as pilgrims to Pashupatinath and other shrines of the Kathmandu Valley, but from the 1950s it became an increasingly attractive destination for tourists from Europe and North America. Thomas Cook organised its first group tour to Nepal in 1955 and the annual number of visitors grew from 4000 per annum in 1960 to 100,000 in 1976 and 250,000 in the early 1990s. The stereotypical foreign visitors in the 1950s were members of the upper classes on a 'grand tour' but this changed in the 1960s as Kathmandu became a mecca for Western hippies or, as they preferred to call themselves, 'world travellers'. The end of the hippy era was symbolised by the deportations in the run-up to King Birendra's coronation in 1975. Although Nepal remained a destination for low-budget travellers, the average visitor tended to be better off than before and foreign exchange earnings from tourism reached US $63.5 million in 1990. The bulk of this money was spent in the Kathmandu Valley, where attractions at the end of the period included not only the historic cities but also Casino Nepal. The clientele here was mostly Indian and there were rumours of involvement in money-laundering. However, there were also a growing number of adventure tourists attracted to Nepal for activities like trekking and white-water rafting.

As with the carpet and garment industries, success came at a price. Unplanned growth meant considerable overprovision of hotels in Kathmandu, and much of the foreign exchange earned flowed out of the country to import the items tourists needed for their comfort. In the hills, and particularly along popular trekking routes such as the approach to Everest Base Camp, the 'toilet-paper trail' illustrated the danger of adventure tourism destroying what it was seeking to enjoy. An influx of trekkers could also drive up the price of items such as eggs out of the reach of many local people. A related problem was the development of national parks, which could infringe on the rights of the original inhabitants. On balance, however, tourist dollars did raise the standard of living of substantial numbers of Nepalese.

FOREIGN TRADE AND THE DIVERSIFICATION ISSUE

In 1951, despite local trade across the Tibetan border and the continued presence of a Nepalese merchant community in Lhasa, Nepal's trade links were overwhelmingly with India. Under both Mahendra and Birendra, continued access to the Indian market on favourable terms was vital, but a key goal of trade policy was also diversification: an increase in the proportion of Nepalese trade that involved third countries. The effort, undertaken for political rather than economic reasons, was, of course, complicated by the fact that trade with other countries normally had to pass through India. It was agreed in principle in 1966 that Nepalese goods in transit should be exempted from Indian customs duty and Nepalese companies allowed their own warehouse space in Calcutta. Goods made from Nepalese raw materials were also to be allowed duty-free access to the Indian market and the 1960 trade and transit treaty restored Nepal's freedom to set its own external tariffs. However, disagreement over the exact nature of the arrangements continued, and the run-up to successive renewals of agreements on trade and transit regularly produced a crisis in bilateral relations.

The root of the tension was partly that India, like Nepal, often wanted to use trade as a political weapon, but there was also a genuine conflict of economic interest. India, which already at independence had a substantial industrial sector, wished to restrict imports to protect domestic manufacturers and encourage import substitution. Nepal, too, hoped to develop its own industry, but, with no prospect of becoming as self-reliant as India strove to be, followed a more liberal policy. Consequently, businessmen operating in Nepal, who were often Indian citizens or at least of recent Indian origin, were tempted to import goods from third countries for re-export into India either illegally or under special arrangements India granted for Nepalese products. Whether or not the Nepalese government deliberately connived with this practice, its diversification policy in practice encouraged it.

In the mid-1960s Nepal introduced a system of allowing its jute manufacturers to retain 60 per cent of the hard currency they earned by exporting to third countries. The Indian government was worried by the resulting deflection of Indian jute into Nepal for re-export and accordingly imposed a surcharge on Nepalese jute products exported to India equal to the levy it charged on its own jute manufacturers. A November 1968 compromise allowed Nepal itself to impose a levy equal to 80 per cent of the Indian one and for the Nepalese goods then to enter India duty-free. However, because Nepalese production costs were higher, even with the 20 per cent concession they were unable to compete in the Indian market.

Tension with India was also caused by the 1966 Gift Parcel Scheme under which businessmen in Nepal could receive packages of consumer goods from Hong Kong or Singapore, which were then smuggled into India. The Nepalese government correctly pointed out that many of those involved were in fact Indians, but this fact did not reduce the damage which India felt was being done to its own import and foreign exchange control policies.

A more serious dispute followed the 1964 introduction of the Bonus Voucher Scheme under which a Nepalese exporter to an overseas country could keep 90 per cent of the foreign exchange earned. With these incentives, factories were set up along the Indian border to process imported stainless steel and synthetic fabrics and then re-export them. The finished products went either to a third country, thus earning the foreign currency bonus, or into India, where, thanks to the low cost of the raw material and tax concessions offered by the Nepalese government, they could be priced lower than similar items from Indian factories. As a result, Nepal's synthetic fabric output expanded in five years from 5700 to 2,305,000 yards per year.[17] However, India reacted harshly and in 1969 seized as contraband 6 million rupees' worth of fabric and stainless steel. Acrimonious negotiations pegged the amount that Nepal was allowed to export to the 1967–8 level and eventually most of the factories closed.

The diversification drive nevertheless continued. A modified version of the Bonus Voucher Scheme, the Exporters' Exchange Entitlement Scheme, operated during the 1970s but was replaced as an incentive in 1978 by a dual exchange rate. After reversion to a unified rate in 1981, exporters were rewarded by the use of direct subsidies. All these efforts did eventually bear fruit: by 1988 official statistics showed India was receiving only 38 per cent of Nepal's total exports and supplying just 30 per cent of its imports. These percentages would, however, be rather different if unrecorded trade across the border, perhaps as much as half of the total, could be taken into account. More importantly, it is likely that in many cases exports to India might have been more profitable than the new markets the government had taken such trouble to develop.

Nepal also lobbied continuously for less stringent rules on how much value had to be added in Nepal to imported raw materials before a manufactured product could qualify for duty-free entry into India. In 1978, when India's Janata government allowed Nepal's long-standing demand for separate trade and transit treaties, the Nepalese content requirement was reduced to 80 per cent and discussions for a possible reduction to 60 per cent were held from 1986 onwards. Here India was caught between its long-term strategic interest in ensuring stability in Nepal through economic development, and the immediate demands of its industrialists for protection from allegedly unfair Nepalese competition.

Although India in 1960 recognised Nepal's right to separate foreign exchange dealings, the relationship between the Nepalese and Indian currencies also remained a source of difficulty. Indian rupees had for many years circulated freely in Nepal, especially in the Tarai, but in 1961 Mahendra's government began a phased programme to make the Nepalese rupee the only legal tender in the country. This was disrupted in mid-1966 when India suddenly devalued its own currency and Nepal attempted to maintain the Nepalese rupee's existing exchange rates with non-Indian currencies. Cross-border trade was seriously affected and the following year Nepal used the devaluation of the pound sterling as a convenient excuse to devalue its own currency and restore the former relationship to the Indian rupee.

Transit arrangements remained an enormous problem. India had initially tried to insist that Nepalese imports and exports allowed duty-free passage through Indian territory be transported only by rail, arguing that otherwise the system might be abused and its own security and economic interests jeopardised. Limited use of road transport was later granted, but, despite India's accepting the arrangement in principle, Nepal was in practice able to make little use of the new transit route to Radhikapur in East Bengal agreed with the government of Pakistan in October 1962. Mahendra reacted by taking Nepal's case to the international arena and Nepal spoke vigorously in favour of the rights of landlocked states at the UNCTAD conferences in Geneva in 1964 and New Delhi in 1968. India eventually responded with a partial blockade of Nepal during the negotiations for the renewal of the 1960 trade and transit agreement and even threatened a total closure of the border. Following India's defeat of Pakistan in the Bangladesh war and Indira Gandhi's election victory, Mahendra had to accept a new treaty which retained the old transit restrictions. In 1978, after Indira Gandhi had been ousted by the Janata Party, Nepal was granted its long-standing demand for a transit treaty separate from the bilateral trade agreement, but a decade later Rajiv Gandhi's government returned to a harder line. In 1989 the transit issue was in itself only one part of a much larger problem between the two countries, but it was the virtual closure of the Indo-Nepal border that sealed the fate of the Panchayat regime.

Despite the expansion in trade with overseas countries, trade across Nepal's northern border remained much less significant than that with India. Some grain and dairy produce was sent into Tibet, though grain exports were actually banned at one point under Indian pressure, as was the re-export to Tibet of items imported from India. Concerned principally with its political control over Tibet, China had by 1966 largely achieved the replacement of private, Lhasa-based Nepalese traders by state-to-state arrangements. In 1968 it also insisted on the ending of traditional transhumance and local cross-border trade. During the 1960s and 1970s, consignments of Chinese consumer goods were sold in Nepal, but this was normally at subsidised prices and intended simply to meet the local costs of Chinese aid projects. Shipment of goods in any case still depended on the Calcutta route: the Chinese trolleybuses provided for the Valley or Nepal's own jute exports to China could be sent much more cheaply by sea than by using the overland route through Tibet.

Prospects for greater trade with China did emerge at the end of the period, with China's own opening to the outside world under Deng Xiaoping. However, moves to expand trade over the Nepal–Tibet border brought Indian objections on security grounds and this, as well as the Indian belief that Nepal was allowing more favourable access for some Chinese goods than for Indian ones, contributed to the 1989 crisis. Trade with China, or with the general international community, could be no substitute for an understanding with India, nor for remedying the structural problems of the Nepalese economy.

CHAPTER 6

Lifestyles, values, identities: changes in Nepalese society, 1951–1991

Although hopes for the rapid economic transformation of Nepal after 1951 were not realised, there were nevertheless profound and far-reaching changes in Nepalese society. The expansion of the education system and the improvements in communication between different regions of the country and between Nepal and the outside world meant that the outlook and expectations of Nepalese, and particularly young Nepalese, were very different in 1990 from what they had been forty years previously. The gap between expectations and achievements was perhaps the single most important factor that brought the Panchayat system to its knees in 1990 and then drove the system that replaced it into crisis.

TOWN AND COUNTRY

The transformation naturally went further and faster in urban centres and areas of the countryside within easy reach of them. Above all, they affected the Kathmandu Valley, which was also where development in the economic sense was most successful, but very similar changes affected other towns also, especially Pokhara in the mid-western hills and urban centres in the Tarai. Moreover, the divide between the towns and the hinterland, though real, was not an impermeable barrier and the influence of ideas that took hold in urban areas was felt in varying degrees across the whole country.

The clash between old and new in the capital after 1951 was symbolised from the beginning in the language used at the centre of power. Both the Ranas and the Shah kings had addressed their subjects as *timi* (equivalent to French *tu* or German *du*). Under the new democratic dispensation, commoners now expected *tapain*, the normal polite form between adults. Mohan Shamsher Rana found it particularly galling to have to treat the Newar minister Ganesh Man Singh in this way and got round the problem by speaking to him in English. Tribhuvan and Mahendra, though they had in effect inherited the Ranas' autocratic powers, were happy to use *tapain*

154

but King Birendra, who unlike his father and grandfather received a modern education abroad, seemed to prefer *timi*, even when speaking to Brahmans. When aware that this might cause offence he followed Mohan's strategy by using English or impersonal expressions. Tanka Prasad Acharya, the Praja Parishad veteran who served as Mahendra's prime minister in 1956–7, was particularly indignant over this and even suggested in later life that some of those around Birendra had deliberately encouraged the habit in a conspiracy to make the monarchy unpopular.[1] The cause perhaps lay rather in the need Birendra felt to retain the monarchy's old religious aura even while projecting it as the leader in the nation's search for modernity.

Royalty maintained its real power throughout the period, but in the Valley's indigenous Newar community it was not only expressions of deference but also power relations themselves that were shifting. The Maharjan peasant caste, which made up about half the Newar population, benefited from effective land reform and became more independent of the higher Newar castes – Hindu Shresthas and Buddhist Vajracharyas and Shakyas. In Bhaktapur, the Maharjans formed the support base of Narayan Man Bijukche's Nepal Workers' and Peasants' Organisation (NWPO), which assisted them in court action to obtain their rights under the new legislation. The NWPO was able to take control of the local panchayat, a highly significant development, even though some saw a sign of continuity in Bijukche's own high-caste origins.

Although the Maharjans, in contrast to the higher castes, had never regarded themselves as exclusively Buddhist or Hindu, they now became more likely to choose Hindu as a self-description. This further weakened the position of the Vajracharyas and Shakyas at the apex of the Valley's unique brand of Buddhism. With reduced income from rent, it became more difficult for these castes to carry out the elaborate rituals of Vajrayana Buddhism, and their internal solidarity also tended to weaken. A poor Shakya could no longer, as in the past, depend on the assistance of richer Shakyas as a form of social security. Finally, Vajrayana now faced increasing competition from Theravada, the more 'Protestant' form of Buddhism, which was prevalent in Sri Lanka and had undergone a revival both there and in South Asia generally in the last decades of the colonial era. Theravada monks had first established themselves in the Valley in the inter-war years, when the first stirrings of modern Newar ethnic activism took place. This was also the time when the Vajracharyas' position in Kathmandu was being undermined by a long dispute over whether they could accept cooked rice from the hands of the Uray, the highest lay Buddhist caste. Theravada's theoretical rejection of the caste system, even though not always put into

practice when the lowest castes were concerned, worked even more strongly
in its favour in the liberalised, post-1951 atmosphere.

The Hindu Newar high castes remained largely distinct from their Parbatiya counterparts but from the 1970s onwards they, and to a lesser extent
other Newars, began talking to their children in Nepali rather than Newar
to help them when they entered Nepali-medium education. At the same
time, migration into Kathmandu reduced the Newar proportion of the
Valley's population and it was now less common for non-Newars living in
the centre of the city to acquire the language. Again, practice in the royal
family seemed to symbolise a wider social trend. Tribhuvan and Mahendra
had both picked up the language from their wet-nurses and other palace
servants. They were even said to have sometimes used it between themselves
to keep their conversation secret from Indian negotiators, who might pick
up the gist of a conversation in Nepali because of its close relation to Hindi
(see ch. 1). In contrast, King Birendra never learned Newar.

These trends were, however, less significant in some areas, notably Bhaktapur, where redevelopment was constrained from the 1970s by conservation measures, and the old city centre of Patan. Here the population
remained predominantly Newar and families of the same caste generally
lived close together. The heightened sense of social solidarity that resulted
was one factor in the contribution that both cities made to the 1990 'People's
Movement'.

In Newar society as a whole, the divisions between 'clean castes' tended to
become less significant, with intermarriage increasing though still frowned
upon by traditionalists. However, the divide between these castes and the
'impure' groups at the bottom of the hierarchy remained important, and
individuals belonging to the latter would sometimes try to circumvent it
by adopting the high-caste surname 'Shrestha' when they moved to a new
location. Those who could not or would not conceal their origins became
rather more assertive, with, for example, women carrying refuse in their bas-
kets marching down the centre of the road rather than keeping to the sides
to leave a clear passage for their ritual superiors. The Untouchable sweeper
(Pode) caste in particular gained new opportunities for paid municipal
employment and with the introduction of a German-aided refuse-disposal
scheme in the early 1980s many of them were to be seen riding the mini-
tractors which now ferried waste to dumping sites.

The introduction of the new Muluki Ain in 1963 formally established the
equality before the law of all Nepalese citizens and outlawed untouchability.
The relatively impersonal nature of urban life and the increased mobility
associated with urbanisation tended even without legal changes or political

14. A view over the Kathmandu Valley from the temple of Swayambhu, an ancient Buddhist shrine which stands on a small hill to the west of Kathmandu city.

campaigns to reduce the scope for discrimination against Untouchables (or Dalits, as they increasingly preferred to be called after 1990). However, even in the Kathmandu Valley Mahendra's government appeared reluctant to give full effect to the legal change. Shortly after promulgation of the Ain, a group of Untouchables were barred by police from entering Nepal's national shrine, the temple of Pashupatinath on the Bagmati River on the eastern outskirts of Kathmandu. The official explanation was that the change in the law did not affect the right of individuals to maintain their own religious customs. It was only in September 2001, following a government declaration on temple access, that a large party of Dalits was able to enter Pashupatinath unchallenged.

The democratising and homogenising tendencies of urban living were offset to some extent by the sheer size of Kathmandu. Although small by Western metropolitan standards, the city was large enough to allow ethnic groups or castes (a distinction blurred in Nepal's case) scope for forming distinct communities and separating themselves socially, if not physically, from members of other groups. In the American phrase, it amounted to a salad-bowl pattern of society. In smaller towns this was less possible and the melting-pot metaphor was more applicable, though here, too, tradition fought a rearguard action. The smaller settlements did, however form a contrast to the villages both because of the easier blurring of boundaries and because of their readier access to government services and employment opportunities.

Arranged marriages remained the preference of most urban parents, particularly those belonging to higher-status groups, but 'love marriage', as the free choice of partner was termed, was the preference of an increasing number of their offspring. Especially from the 1980s onwards, however, the line between the two began to blur as parents might formally 'arrange' a marriage between a couple who had in fact selected each other. Individual choice could cut across caste boundaries, though, in the wider Nepalese society as among the Newars, higher-caste parents were particularly opposed to any relationship with members of 'impure' groups. As the number of Nepalese educated or working abroad, and the number of foreign visitors and residents, increased, husbands and wives from outside South Asia slowly became more common, but this, though more acceptable than marriage to a Dalit, could still meet stiff opposition. The Brahman revolutionary Tanka Prasad Acharya had wanted to arrange a marriage for his daughter before allowing her to leave for study in the Soviet Union and initially had problems accepting the Russian husband she married there. For members of lower castes, marriage to a foreigner already in Nepal provided one avenue of social mobility and, like conversion to Christianity, was often condemned by members of higher castes. Often, though, accommodation with tradition could be achieved. Anthropological studies of Newar society included discussion of the integration of foreign wives into the household's ritual structure while at least one Parbatiya family devised a completely new ceremony to confer Brahman status on a British husband.

However, for the great majority of Nepalese, even in the towns, marriage and family life followed a very conservative pattern. 'Dating' on Western lines was still in 1990 considered rather daring and 'love marriages' were generally between people who met in the course of their daily routine in the streets, in school or college or at work. Most people married a partner of the same caste who might be Nepalese or (in the case of the communities that straddled the border) from India. Domestic life remained conservative by Western standards and divorce, though legally possible, remained very rare among the higher castes. A preference for sons and the belief that a woman should serve and obey her husband remained very strong in most communities, and daughters were not entitled to a share in their father's property unless they remained unmarried. Nevertheless in the urban areas enrolment in the expanding school system became virtually universal for girls as well as boys. In the past, education for women had not been entirely unknown: Queen Lalita Tripura Sundari (see ch. 2) had written a treatise on princely duties in the early nineteenth century, women had authored Nepali-language articles and books published in India early in the twentieth, and a school for girls had opened near the old royal palace of Hanuman Dhoka in 1942. All these were exceptional cases, however, and in 1950 an English-speaking member of Kathmandu's elite would quite likely be married to a spouse who spoke no English and (in the case of Newar families) might not even be fluent in Nepali. By 1990, such a wife, even if she did not work outside the home, would usually be a university graduate herself.

Among many families, the bride was still supposed to bring with her a substantial dowry, an arrangement which was sometimes cited as justification for not normally allowing a daughter to inherit a share of paternal property as her brothers did. Unlike in India, the combination of the dowry system and families' increasing appetite for consumer goods did not generally in urban Nepal lead to the horrors of 'bride burning', but it did increase the stress on middle-class families and also reinforce the general Hindu tendency, still so prevalent in the countryside, to see a daughter as a drain on family resources.

Whatever their level of education, urban women generally continued to carry out the basic Hindu or Buddhist rituals, even if some of the more elaborate ceremonies were falling into disuse. Educated men could be less enthusiastic but this differed from community to community. Among the Newar Maharjans, for example, even as their traditional respect for the Buddhist priestly castes diminished, participation in music-making at a local temple retained an important social activity for many young men. Among all the main communities in Kathmandu major life-cycle rituals continued to be carried out in the traditional manner, and even highly secularised intellectuals often still followed the custom of wearing white for a whole year after the death of a parent. There might be friction within a household, however, on whether to observe the lesser degree of mourning traditionally required on the death of a distant relative.

With the exception of the taboo on eating beef, restrictions on eating and drinking outside mourning periods were generally abandoned. By 1990, few Brahmans in the Valley still observed the prohibition on eating onions or garlic or worried about the caste of the person who cooked or served their boiled rice. The consumption of alcohol had once been thought sinful for all high-caste Parbatiya Hindus, though it was normal among Newars or the other Tibeto-Burman hill groups (and had also long been enjoyed in private by the Rana–Shah elite). By the 1980s drinking was still not as near universal in Kathmandu as in European countries and the problems of drunkenness and alcoholism caused a significant minority to reject alcohol altogether, but moderate drinking had become generally acceptable in urban society and brewing an important part of the small industrial sector. Most middle-class households still ate mainly rice and vegetables, perhaps supplemented with a little meat, for their two main meals of the day but, as had long been the case, this was a matter of habit, and also of economy, rather than principle. Western-style food including bread, cheese and later convenience food such as instant noodles became increasingly popular with urban consumers but generally as *khaja* (snacks) rather than as a substitute for the traditional staples. In the hotels and restaurants catering for foreign visitors, cosmopolitan fare was increasingly available for those Nepalese who could afford it, but had not become quite such an integral part of local culture as Indian food in the United Kingdom.

More than the food they ate, the clothes worn by urban dwellers achieved a marriage of East and West. As in the rest of South Asia, and in strong contrast to China and Japan, female fashion resisted Westernisation and the sari or the Panjabi *salwar-kamiz* remained the preference of most women. School children, however, wore European-style uniforms and teenage girls, particularly from the wealthier families, could increasingly be seen in jeans. Middle-class men, when free to choose for themselves, increasingly preferred shirt and trousers. However, those who worked for government departments were usually required to wear the *daura-sawal*, a cotton tunic and narrow trousers, over which was worn a Western-style jacket. Civil servants (and in some cases male visitors to government offices) were also required to wear a Nepalese-style *topi* (cloth cap). The insistence on this dress code was part of the government's plan to build a distinctive Nepalese identity, and although generally accepted in the Valley and the hills it was often resented in the Tarai.

Until the 1970s, the major roads built in Kathmandu as the city expanded carried only a small number of motor vehicles and the vast majority of citizens went about their business on foot, by bicycle or on one of the overcrowded buses. In 1990 this was still probably true of about half the population but tempos – basically a motorbike engine with a driver's cab and small passenger compartment built over it – had become much more common. At the same time, the ownership of a regular motorbike, rather than a bicycle, had become widespread among the middle class. Private cars were only for those who were very wealthy by local standards, and those who could afford the vehicle would often also employ a driver.

Private transport and the tempo network made it easier for many members of the middle class to leave older accommodation near the city centre and build new family homes on converted farmland. It was normal to supervise the whole process oneself rather than buy a finished house from a developer or previous owner. Families often built a larger home than they needed for themselves, extending the building in stages as more money became available. The extra rooms could be rented out or perhaps kept for family use if sons married but remained within their parents' home. There was little effective control of such building and often no public paved road leading to the new houses. The different houses had their own plot numbers but, even where there was a recognisable street, buildings were not numbered in sequence along it. Consequently, as in the old city centre, visitors needed to rely on a physical description of their destination or on simply asking people in the neighbourhood the first time they paid a call.

The less well-off tended to live in a much humbler house of their own or, particularly if they were migrants from the countryside, in a rented room. People from outside the Valley might often be employed as servants in middle-class homes, where their accommodation and treatment varied greatly. Luckier individuals, living with and working for the same family for many years, could be treated virtually as part of the family, but the less lucky ones, especially young children, might be forced to work long hours for minimal pay and inadequate food. Conditions could be similarly harsh for the 'kitchen *kanchas*' (boys) employed in restaurants and hotels and also in many of the Valley's carpet and garment factories. Kathmandu also had a growing problem of street children, who had either run away from their homes in the hills or been abandoned by their parents. However, most people did have homes of one sort or another and, even though there were some squatter settlements in the Valley, Kathmandu had so far been spared the large-scale shanty towns that are a feature of so many Third World cities.

Outside the towns, many of the same social trends operated but did so at a slower pace and with great variations between different areas of the country. Throughout the country, however, the strengthening of the state machinery, even if it remained weak by world standards, meant that village autonomy was considerably reduced. In addition, as pressure on land resources mounted, members of communities whose village organisation was relatively egalitarian had to seek employment in a market economy where they were often at a marked disadvantage.

In general, older ways disappeared more rapidly in the eastern hills than in the economically more backward west. In Mechi zone, where the uprising against the Ranas had taken the form of an ethnic revolt against Parbatiya settlers by the indigenous Limbus, the events of 1950–1 were a very direct catalyst for change. Many Brahman families had to seek temporary refuge in the Tarai (see ch. 4, p. 83) and, although they generally returned to their villages when order was restored, the dislocation hastened the abandonment of the stricter caste taboos. Previously Brahman males who had undergone the *upanayan* ceremony and begun wearing the *janai* (sacred thread) ate their meals on a special raised area inside their house, but this practice now largely disappeared. To the dismay of older Brahmans, the younger generation in the villages, like their counterparts in the towns, also began to disregard traditional dietary restrictions.

There was a cultural convergence between the young Brahmans and their Limbu counterparts, who were both influenced by the Indian nationals of Nepalese origin brought in from Calcutta and Darjeeling to serve in the rapidly expanding education system. The Limbus gave up some of their own practices which had been particularly repugnant to orthodox Hindus, such as buffalo sacrifices and the payment of bride price. Limbus also cut back on their use of alcohol just as the Brahmans and Chetris were taking to it. One Brahman scholar, surveying changes in his native village over the twenty years after 1951, noted that, in his youth, drunken fights on market days had normally involved Limbus but were now more often between high-caste youths.[2]

However, despite the growing similarity in lifestyles, the boundary between Limbu and Brahman remained a real one. Both groups retained a strong sense of their separate identity and, particularly among the Limbus, a keen awareness of rivalry over land ownership. Youngsters socialised more together and might cheer the same school football team but intermarriage remained rare and was frowned upon by both groups. The relationship was in fact becoming more like that between many ethnic groups or religious communities in the West: they saw themselves as competitors but not as ritually distinct nor as complementary units within a natural hierarchy. This was similar to developments across the border in India, where, however, expression for it was made easier by the existence of a multi-party system. In Nepal, even under the restraints of the Panchayat system, a modern form of 'identity politics', discussed in greater detail below, was laying the groundwork for the upsurge in ethnic activism which followed the collapse of the regime in 1990.

A similar pattern was found in many parts of the country, with cultural differences eroding but the rough co-relation between caste status and economic status remaining. However, in some areas where upper-caste groups thought that their political and economic dominance might be under threat, cultural barriers actually hardened. This happened in Jumla in the western hills, where the end of Rana rule was followed by a breakdown of the system of *mit* (fictive kinship) relationships that had previously bound people across caste barriers. In some cases, high-caste Parbatiya villagers withdrew from grain exchanges with Bhotiyas (groups with strong Tibetan links) unless the latter were prepared to follow Hindu purity regulations. There was a parallel with the similar 'hardening of the caste arteries' in Kumaon after the British had taken control of the region from the Gorkhalis in 1815 (see ch. 2). The social structure here was quite similar to that in western Nepal, and the higher castes, deprived of the political protection for their superior status provided by a strongly Hindu monarchy, had become more insistent on preserving the boundaries between themselves and other groups.[3]

The western hills was perhaps the region where the status of Untouchables and of women remained the worst. Partly because of the relatively low proportion of non-Parbatiya ethnic groups in this area, the barrier between the 'clean' Parbatiya castes and the low-caste Doms remained starkest. Even in the 1990s, when the region was in the grip of a Maoist rebellion spawned in part by the caste system itself, there was strong resistance in the region to a government campaign to allow all castes admittance to Hindu shrines. Even high-caste women still often had to move out of their home when menstruating to sleep in a shelter in the yard. Dom women thus carried a crushing double burden.

Elsewhere in the villages, female disadvantages were still considerable. For the high-caste Parbatiya communities in general and other hill groups subscribing to their values, and also for many groups in the Tarai, women who had married into the household were still often seen as a source of danger and pollution. Their treatment thus contrasted dramatically with the high-status women retained as daughters and sisters in their natal home. While the monthly segregation of married women was normally not so complete as in the west of the country, young girls were still often expected to move out of the house for their first menstruation, a custom significantly referred to as *gupha basne* (staying in the cave). Although polygamy was largely outlawed by the 1963 Muluki Ain, marriages contracted before that date were not affected and men were still entitled to take a second wife if the first had not produced any offspring after ten years. In addition, the law's effectiveness was limited in the remoter parts of the country. Tension and jealousy between co-wives were therefore still often a part of women's lives.

The legal system itself could make matters worse. Following traditional Hindu jurisprudence, Nepalese inheritance law provided for a man's property to be automatically divided up between his sons on his death. As in the towns, daughters were not normally eligible for a share in the family's assets. Again reflecting the orthodox Hindu standpoint, abortion was illegal and women who had one could face lengthy periods in jail. This put any woman who became pregnant outside marriage in a particularly acute dilemma since, if she continued with the pregnancy, she risked total ostracism by her own family.

Finally, the preference for sons meant that girl children often received inadequate care and were also much less likely to receive an education than were their brothers or girls in the towns. As economic pressure on hill villages mounted, girls were also in increasing danger of being sold by their parents to middlemen who took them to brothels in India. In other cases girls themselves might be lured into accepting a promise of employment in Bombay (now officially referred to as Mumbai) or another major centre. Controversy continues over how hill girls ending up in the sex trade had been deceived by promises of legitimate employment or actually physically abducted, and how far the girls or their families knowingly accepted the arrangement out of financial necessity. The undoubted reality was that by the 1980s tens of thousands of Nepalese women were working as prostitutes in India, facing brutal and degrading treatment and also, from the late 1970s onwards, increasing risk of contracting HIV-AIDS.[4]

Women from the Tibeto-Burman hill groups, particularly the Tamang community, made up a large proportion of these victims of trafficking, but in some cases women from these same groups might be better off than those of high-caste Hindu communities. Restrictions on women's freedom of movement were generally less than among strictly Hindu Parbatiyas, and a woman was more likely to be able to choose a partner freely or to leave an unhappy marriage. In a few of the high Himalayan villages, polyandry rather than polygamy was common and women also had the option of becoming a Buddhist nun rather than marrying. Among the Sherpas of the Mt Everest region, attitudes to sexual relations were highly relaxed and a child born of an extra-marital liaison was much more likely to be simply accepted and brought up by the mother's family.

THE EXPANSION OF EDUCATION

Before the collapse of the Rana regime, Nepalese who received any formal education at all had usually either had private tutors at home or attended schools in India. In 1950, there were fewer than 330 schools in the whole country and the literacy rate was under 5 per cent. However, already in the final Rana years there were plans to improve this situation, and there was also a model at hand in the expansion of Nepali-medium education in the Darjeeling district of India. In the late 1940s the government began producing its own series of primary school readers; these were clearly influenced by the work of Parasmani Pradhan and others in Darjeeling. After 1951, as was seen in chapter 5, American aid allowed the system of state schools to expand rapidly.

The steady increase in the number of enrolments was unfortunately offset by major problems. In the first place many children recorded as starting primary school later dropped out because their parents could not afford to lose their labour power. Even when students remained in class, the quality of education delivered was often questionable. Teachers were underpaid and poorly motivated, while the schools themselves lacked proper equipment and classes could be unmanageably large. Discipline could sometimes be harsh yet in some cases was sadly lacking, as witnessed by one foreign researcher during the School Leaving Certificate (SLC) examination at a high school in Pokhara in 1974:

Examinees from various parts of western Nepal sat shoulder to shoulder in the examination rooms passing answers they received through open windows from youths outside. These well-wishers approached the examination rooms through a cordon of disinterested police supposedly stationed around the school to protect the integrity of the examination. Nervous and embarrassed proctors tried vainly to maintain an appearance of propriety despite the obvious and open cheating. A teacher informant later explained that Gurkha dropouts from the Indian army had sat as private candidates in the 1966 examination with knives and grenades, and since then no one had dared bother the students from certain schools.[5]

Cheating might not be so blatant in most schools but it was widespread; there were also cases when the school itself might decide to tamper with the results of examinations it was responsible for moderating. Yet even more significant than the numbers passing the examination fraudulently was the very low overall pass rate: failure was in fact the norm in most schools throughout the rural area.

Before 1951, apart from a few government-established institutions, most schools were private ones. After the end of Rana rule, a system of government grants to private schools became the most usual pattern. The New Education System Plan (NESP) introduced in the 1970s greatly increased government financing of education but also centralised control, removing the direct links that had previously existed in many cases between the schools and the local community. Key decisions were now in the hands of the centrally appointed district education officer and, ultimately, of the Education Department in Kathmandu.

University education in Nepal, which had begun with the founding of Trichandra College in 1918, was state-run from the beginning. After the establishment of Tribhuvan University in 1959, campuses throughout the country were affiliated to it. Students who had passed the SLC and usually a subsequent entrance examination were admitted first to the two-year Intermediate Programme (rechristened Certificate Level under the NESP) and then to a two-year course leading to the Bachelor's degree (later known as Diploma Level). The Intermediate course was roughly equivalent to sixth-form study in the UK and so the Bachelor's degree was of a lower standard than a European or North American first (or bachelor's) degree. This standard was only reached (at least in theory) by students who studied a further two years for an MA at Tribhuvan's central campus in Kirtipur. The whole system ran alongside traditionally organised, and also government-supported, Sanskrit education, for which the Mahendra Sanskrit University was set up at Dang in the western Tarai in 1986.

Tribhuvan University suffered from the same problems of underfunding, compromised examinations and staff absenteeism as the school system. In addition there was the problem of the use of English as a medium of instruction, which theoretically applied to most of its courses. As in many parts of the world, the English standard of students coming into such courses was often too low for them to cope with advanced study in that language. The problem was worsened after 1979 when, in the wake of the collapse of the NESP, the university had to accept any prospective student who had passed the SLC. Attempts to deal with the difficulty by providing remedial English classes at the start of courses were of limited effectiveness given the huge size of the classes; most university teachers continued just to lecture rather than teach more interactively. The practical solution adopted by many teachers was simply to translate into Nepali the contents of English textbooks. In any case, many students chose not to come to classes but attempted to read up on their own before examinations. Against this background, chances to study overseas were eagerly sought, though only those from wealthy families or lucky enough to win scholarships could normally manage this.

Politics were an important part of university life, and the role played by student associations aligned with the main political factions was described in chapter 4. The divisions between the students were mirrored by similar ones among the teaching staff, though purges from time to time eliminated lecturers too closely identified with the banned Congress Party. The majority of students were not political activists but they would rally behind those who were when an important grievance of their own or an issue of major national importance arose. Frequent protests coexisted strangely with old habits of deference towards teachers. When this author was himself a college lecturer at a Kathmandu campus in the early 1970s, students in his class who wished to join an impromptu protest over tuition fees requested him to dismiss the class so that they could challenge the university without directly challenging an individual lecturer's authority.

The greatest problem of the Nepalese education system was not, however, politicisation but rather the fact that it was breeding aspirations which Nepalese society could not match. Those who achieved basic literacy very often then set their sights on white-collar employment, which in Nepal at this time normally meant government service. Many were disqualified early on, since, even with widespread cheating, a large proportion of students simply failed to pass the SLC or, in the case of drop-outs, failed even to take it. The small minority who did enter higher education tended to go overwhelmingly into arts courses, thus helping to produce the shortage of skilled technical personnel mentioned in chapter 5. As also already seen, the Panchayat regime's attempt to make education more vocational in the 1970s foundered on student resistance.

The chances of succeeding at university were boosted considerably by a good private schooling. This was still often sought in India and one estimate in the early 1990s was that the money leaving the country for this purpose was equivalent to around 60 per cent of the total national budget for education. King Birendra himself was an example of this pattern, studying at St Joseph's College in Darjeeling and later at Eton and Harvard. His own son, Dipendra, first entered the British-run Buddhanilkante School in Kathmandu but then he, too, was sent to Eton. Within Nepal, high-quality English education had been provided since the early 1950s at St Xavier's for boys and St Mary's for girls; alumni from these institutions normally stood out when they entered Tribhuvan University because of their fluent English. The divide between public Nepali-medium and private English-medium education caused some social tension on campus and also disquiet among education planners. Under the New Education System Plan, it was therefore stipulated that from 1974 all institutions in Nepal below tertiary level should teach in Nepali. This did not, of course, affect education in India, and the right to teach in English was restored with the collapse of the NESP at the end of the decade. During the 1980s, in a trend which accelerated greatly after 1990, many new 'boarding schools' (meaning simply private schools claiming to teach in English) opened in the Valley along with a smaller number elsewhere in the country.

Whatever the doubts about its quality, the expansion of education greatly increased the audience for writing in Nepali and about Nepal. Particularly as the market for school textbooks broadened, Kathmandu became the major centre for publishing in Nepali rather than lagging behind Benares and Calcutta, which had primarily served the Nepalese community in India but also supplied much of the small amount of printed material circulating in Nepal itself. Educational expansion also both required and facilitated standardisation of the written language. This, though still not complete, was broadly achieved by the 1970s along lines already indicated by Parasmani Pradhan and other Darjeeling writers. Pradhan had championed a style of Nepali drawing heavily on Sanskrit loanwords, in the same way that the more formal registers of English use a high proportion of words derived from Latin and Greek. The alternative approach of keeping the written language closer to colloquial Nepali, which had been favoured by Pradhan's Darjeeling rival, Padre Ganga Prasad Pradhan, also found support in post-1950 Nepal. It was the Sanskritisers, however, who won out and established the norms for the language as used today in government documents, political speeches or literary essays.

In the first half of the twentieth century, devotional literature, and in particular Bhanubhakta's *Ramayana*, had been the most popular category of publication in Nepali. Religious works still sold well after 1950, as did stories for easy reading and poetry by many authors. The education system, however, helped establish a definitive canon of Nepali literature, including Bhanubhakta himself and then the trio of Lekhnath Paudel (1884–1965), Balkrishna Sama (1902–81) and Lakshmi Prasad Devkota (1909–59). All three wrote in more than one genre, but the Brahmans Paudel and Devkota were primarily poets and Sama ('Equal'), a dissident Rana who had adopted his surname as a democratic gesture in 1948, was best known as a playwright. Paudel's status was dramatically recognised in 1954 when, in imitation of the ceremony used to honour elderly Newars, he was placed on a wheeled vehicle like those used for religious icons and pulled through the streets of Kathmandu by fellow poets including the then prime minister, M. P. Koirala. Devkota, the Nepali poet who has attracted the most attention outside the country, served briefly as minister of education in Tanka Prasad Acharya's 1956–7 government and, on his deathbed at the temple of Pashupatinath, was the focus of attention among the political and literary elite. All three authors, like other leading intellectuals, were also honoured by enrolment in the Royal Nepal Academy set up by King Mahendra in 1957. Among more recent literary figures, those coming nearest to canonical status are perhaps the novelist and poetess Parijat (1937–93) and the poet Bhupi Sherchan (1936–89).

In contrast to the Sanskritised language that Nepalese read in their school textbooks, the spoken language developed rather differently. The influence of English was substantial and one did not need to be fluent in the language to pepper one's conversation with English loanwords. In some cases, as also across the border in India, English words had established themselves so thoroughly before 1950 that it was the literary Nepali which, at least initially, felt less familiar. From the time of Mathbar Singh Thapa in the 1840s, the executive head of government had been known as the *praim ministar* and the term remained in common use even though the radio news used *pradhan mantri*. The word *polis* (police, policeman) had taken even stronger root and the 'High Nepali' term *prahari* was virtually never used in ordinary conversation. In these cases English words were used unthinkingly; in others they might be deliberately employed to give the speaker an air of learning and sophistication.

As in India, English itself, even if fully mastered only by a small minority, played an important role. In contrast to India, it was not the language of the courts nor the one in which most written government records were kept, but it became increasingly important in those areas of the administration which had to interact most extensively with foreign-aid donors. As well as being essential for the operation of the tourist industry, English was also the medium of much academic research in both the natural and social sciences. Partly because admission to foreign researchers was granted rather more readily than in the Indian Himalayas, the country attracted many outside scholars eager to explore its ethnic diversity and cultural heritage. The paradoxical result was that Nepalese sometimes had to turn to English to access knowledge of their own country and culture as well as of the world outside Nepal.

MODERN MEDIA

Before the post-1950 expansion of the education system, fewer than five in every hundred people in Nepal could read, and so the spoken word remained overwhelmingly the most important means of communication at village level. Tales of the world outside brought by returned travellers remained an important channel, and current happenings in Kathmandu and elsewhere might find their way into the songs of the Gaine (singer) caste who played their *sarangis* (Nepalese-style fiddles) to entertain villagers, especially at major festivals.

The expansion in communications discussed in chapter 5 meant that access to information in either printed or electronic form became easier for everyone, though exposure was greatest for those living in the Valley and in Tarai towns adjacent to India. In 1990 the literacy rate for Nepal as a whole was still only 39 per cent and television could reach only a small proportion of the population. Radio was thus a crucially important window on the world: a remote village might only have one or two small radios but that was enough to deliver a message to many families. The government-controlled Radio Nepal was before 1990 the only station broadcasting from inside the country. It certainly helped to make the standard Nepali of Kathmandu familiar to those whose local dialect might be very different; it also enabled singers to become familiar to a nationwide audience. Radio Nepal also made people aware of the government's proclaimed goals and in particular with the king's activities and pronouncements. However, the government's official service was probably less effective as a moulder of opinions than it might have been. The use of a highly literary style of Nepali meant that many villagers cannot have fully understood what was being said, while for more sophisticated listeners the propagandist nature of the broadcasts was so obvious as to be frequently counter-productive. From Mahendra's takeover until 1990, news broadcasts normally had to begin with an item on the royal family and this was usually something of no real news value but a purely formal act such as sending greetings to a foreign head of state on his country's national day. The activities of the political parties opposed to the regime were either ignored or simply denounced as 'anti-national'. Such an approach could work with listeners completely cut off from other sources of information but, even for many uneducated listeners, it often served only to heighten cynicism about the whole Panchayat system. Even with its message backed up, for reasons of self-interest, by many of the rural elite, Radio Nepal was unable to stop almost half the electorate voting against the Panchayat system in 1980; it failed even more decisively in the battle for opinion in the Kathmandu Valley in 1990.

Because it could reach only the educated, the government-controlled press was an even less efficient means of controlling popular opinion. While its translations of reports from international news agencies were of some value to Nepalese who did not read English (and to Westerners trying to learn Nepali), the *Gorkhapatra* was basically a government gazette rather than a newspaper in the full sense; its English-language partner, the *Rising*

Nepal, established in 1965, served mainly to amuse and also to irritate foreign residents.

Alternative views were available from several sources. Word of mouth was important, especially given the large numbers of Nepalese who travelled to other parts of the country or to India in search of work. There was also the private press, which had expanded rapidly during the 1950s. Even before 1960 the government sometimes tried to suppress the publication of dissenting views; after 1960, policy became much more restrictive, though, as seen in chapter 4, the press functioned a little more freely after the 1980 referendum. The circulation of these newspapers was limited and in many cases confined largely to the Kathmandu Valley. Private papers tended, moreover, to be the mouthpieces of particular parties or of their owners and were little more than political pamphlets. There were also some 'investigative journalists' who offered not to print embarrassing material in return for payment. Nevertheless, it was possible for anyone seriously interested in politics to gain a much fuller picture of Nepal's real situation from these publications than from the government media.

Then there was the foreign, and particularly the Indian, media. These outlets would not normally include detailed coverage of Nepal but there were occasional critical newspaper articles; in such cases the government might attempt to block circulation or distributors might prefer not to take the risk of handling the publication. In 1973, for example, the British Council Library removed from its shelves a copy of the *Guardian Weekly* in which the Panchayat system was (quite accurately) described as window-dressing to disguise the reality of royal autocracy. This did not, of course, prevent material from being passed hand to hand, and in any case there was no way of blocking foreign radio broadcasts. The regime might be the centre of power in the country but it could not determine the cultural and intellectual environment in which educated people lived.

For those who lived in or visited the towns, the Hindi-language cinema was an important influence throughout these years. Nepal did have its own film industry and the country's first Nepali-language feature film was released in 1974. Even counting Nepali films made outside Nepal, a mere forty-eight were produced between the early 1950s and 1990;[6] by the end of the period only about a dozen full-length films were being released each year. This was a drop in the ocean compared with the output of Bollywood, the Hindi film industry centred on Bombay. Hindi films accounted for the vast majority of films shown in public cinema halls from the time Kathmandu's first, the Janasewa, opened in about 1949. After the easing of import regulations in 1978 allowed the import of VCR equipment, the cinema halls were supplemented first by 'video parlours', rooms in private houses where customers paid to view, and then by the growing number of VCRs in middle-class homes. By the end of the 1980s, the cinemas had been largely deserted by the more affluent, leaving an audience of the less well-off, particularly young males. However, Hindi movies, often in pirated versions, remained hugely popular with middle-class domestic viewers.

Unlike the 'art films' of Satyajit Ray, which focused often on the Indian poor, Hindi films generally offered an escape into a world of fantasy and glamour. They were typically melodramas punctuated with song and dance routines and showcasing the lifestyles of the Indian middle and upper classes. Sex and violence featured prominently, though, particularly in the 1950s and 1960s, physical intimacy was suggested rather than explicitly portrayed. Heroes and heroines successfully pursued affluence but also usually subscribed to the virtues of family life and of religion. Specifically religious films, dramatising the deeds of Hindu gods and goddesses, were also popular. The first film shown at a Kathmandu cinema had been *Ramabibaha* (Ram's Wedding) and the audience had thrown petals and other offerings at the screen as if the god Ram were really present in the hall.

Filmi git, songs from the soundtracks, were an important element of popular culture in their own right, and were played regularly on cassettes at weddings and other social functions in Nepal as in India, despite purists' objections to the displacement of Nepal's own traditional forms of live music-making. While Radio Nepal continued to broadcast a modernised form of Nepalese folk music, it was Hindi songs that were usually requested by listeners to British Forces Broadcasting Service programmes for Nepalese soldiers in Britain's Brigade of Gurkhas. The attraction of both the music and the films themselves was also boosted as Nepalese actresses began to make their mark in the Indian industry. At the end of the 1980s B. P. Koirala's granddaughter, Manisha Koirala, was emerging as a major star on the Bollywood screen.

Nepali films had necessarily to copy the same general format of the Hindi ones, though the rhythms of Nepali folk music were incorporated into their music. The first full-length Nepalese production *Manko Bandh* (Dam in the Mind) also presented a positive image of the Panchayat system at village level and preached the message of the government's Back to the Village campaign. The hero, younger brother of the *gaun panchayat* (village council) leader, returned willingly to his native village to construct a much-needed dam, despite the pleas of the sophisticated urban woman who had tricked him into marriage. *Manko Bandh* and subsequent Nepali-language films did well at the box office and, because great care was taken to prevent pirate versions appearing before their official release, middle-class viewers, who normally watched in the comfort of their own homes, also turned out to see them.

Nepalese cinemas showed relatively few films from outside South Asia, mainly because of limited audience demand. One 1970s film that did reach the screen in Kathmandu was the English subtitled version of the French production *Les Chemins de Katmandu* (Ways to Kathmandu) set among the city's own hippy community of young Westerners. The Hindi movie *Hari Krishna Hari Ram*, treating a similar theme and probably inspired by the French film, ran for considerably longer. In the 1980s, however, there was considerable demand for videos of English-language films, while in the early years of Nepal Television, which started in 1985, BBC programmes made up a considerable part of the schedules. Those able to afford the equipment were, of course, much more likely to have fluent English than the average cinema-goer.

IDEOLOGY AND POLITICAL CULTURE

After 1960, the three-way political contest between supporters of the regime, Congress and the left represented three differing ideological standpoints. The official ideology of 'Panchayat democracy' stressed the active leadership of the king as well as the allegedly indigenous nature of the Panchayat institutions the monarchy had established. As will be discussed below, the brand of nationalism it strove to foster was also strongly dependent upon the twin pillars of Hinduism and the Nepali language. Perhaps above all, and despite the continuing failure to boost the living standards of the rural majority, the message the system delivered through the official media was that the country was firmly on the path of *bikas* – development – leading, through 'class co-ordination' to the goal of an 'exploitationless society'. *Bikas,* in fact, took on something of the status of an established religion, with constant sermons and *mantras,* generally first delivered in the monarch's own speeches. In the early years of Birendra's reign, the leading slogan was officially translated into English as 'unleash the forces of development', though the original Nepali, *bikasko mul phutaune,* was actually a metaphor from biology rather than physics – 'plant the roots of development'.

The message of the parties was also one of democracy, nationalism and development but without the stress on the themes of religion and king-ship which had been powerfully intertwined throughout Nepal's history. The left, like the Panchayat ideologues, saw an important role for an elite vanguard to guide social transformation, though this was to be the Communist Party itself rather than the *panchas* grouped around the king. The Communists saw development as leading not through class co-ordination but through class struggle to the triumph of the proletariat. This long-term view nevertheless left room for a variety of approaches in the short term. Many Nepalese Communists, including those groups which were to emerge as the most important at the end of the Panchayat period, accepted as equally valid for Nepal Mao Zedong's analysis of pre-Second World War China as 'semi-colonial and semi-feudal'. While the Western powers were seen as the primary colonialists, it was Indian capital that was most dominant in Nepal, and so opposition to India, and to the allegedly pro-Indian Nepali Congress Party, was for many more important than opposition to the 'feudal' monarchy. Nepalese Communists also often accepted Mao's doctrine of 'new people's democracy', which envisaged a government led by the proletariat (i.e. the Communist Party itself) but including parties representing other classes. This theory had been developed by Mao specifically as justification for collaboration between the Chinese Communists and the Kuomintang in the struggle against Japan, and it could potentially be used to legitimise a degree of co-operation between Nepalese Communists and Congress. However, for the more radical leftists who became predominant in the years after 1960, 'new people's democracy' implied institutionalised predominance for the Communists, rather than a fully competitive multi-party system. They were therefore unwilling to work with Congress for a return to the pre-1959 parliamentary order until, as seen in chapter 4, the largest Communist grouping, the Marxist-Leninist Party, began its retreat from Maoism in the mid-1980s. For the most dedicated activists, the radical Communist stance meant either a wholly underground existence organising clandestine resistance to the state or the 'infiltration' of Panchayat structures to make them work for their own purposes. For others, the belief that the 'feudal' or 'bourgeois' Congress Party was as bad, or worse, than the monarchy enabled them simply to maintain a theoretical commitment to revolution while in practice accepting the status quo. This stance was, ironically, little different from that adopted by those leaders of the pre-1960 Communist Party who had accommodated themselves to the post-1960 order right from the start and been reviled as traitors by their erstwhile comrades.

It was sometimes alleged both before 1960 and after 1990 that the Nepali Congress lacked a coherent ideology and that, like the Indian Congress Party, it was in practice a coalition of interest groups united only by the desire to win elections. Nevertheless, from the mid-1950s until at least the late 1980s, the rhetoric of Congress, like that of the Communists, laid great stress on socialism and economic equality. Individual members of the party differed in the depth of their personal commitment to this goal. Some, like the party's leader and chief ideologue, B. P. Koirala, were fervent advocates of socialism along the lines propounded by Jawaharlal Nehru in India, which involved a strong role for the state and for heavy industry. A few felt a lingering attachment to the Gandhian vision of village self-reliance and a rejection of Western-style industrialisation. What particularly distinguished the party, however, was its identification with multi-party democracy as practised in developed countries or in India. This was a clear-cut issue and resulted in the pro-Congress factions on college campuses being known simply as 'Democrats'. During the Panchayat years, when association with the party brought no personal rewards, liberalism on these lines sustained the enthusiasm of many activists and also ensured a degree of sympathy with the party even among those who took no part in politics and did not actively oppose the Panchayat system. Confidence was boosted by the fall of authoritarian systems overseas, including the ending of right-wing authoritarianism in Southern Europe in the 1970s and especially the collapse of Communist regimes across Eastern Europe at the end of the 1980s. But by 1990 the very completeness of the democratic triumph meant that democratic principles were no longer sufficient to provide a party with a distinct and attractive identity.

Though both communism and democratic socialism were seen as new ideologies confronting traditional forces grouped behind the monarchy, the division between old and new thinking in Nepal was not entirely clear-cut. Sometimes it was simply a matter of one individual subscribing simultaneously to old and new views, despite their seeming inconsistency. One opinion poll survey at the time of the 1991 general election found that 20 per cent of the supporters of the radical Marxist United People's Front still believed that King Birendra was an incarnation of Vishnu. The figure rose to 30 per cent of voters of the more moderate Unified Marxist-Leninist Party and 45 per cent for Congress.

More fundamentally, however, the demands for equality and for political participation at the heart of 'progressive' politics were radically new only when considering Nepalese society in its entirety. Nepalese were already familiar with such concepts inside smaller units, normally based on real or imagined kinship. These could be an extended family, or, in some cases, members of the same clan, ethnic group or caste living in the same neighbourhood. There could be marked inequalities based on age and on gender but these were normally less resented than the inequalities of power and wealth between one descent group and another. The Nepalese, like South Asians generally, are very much aware of this contrast between the relatively egalitarian world of a kinship circle and the much less friendly world outside it. The use of kinship terms such as *dajyu* (elder brother) or *bahini* (younger sister) to address strangers represents one attempt to bridge the gap between the two spheres symbolically. New ideologies advocating equality in society seemed to many to hold out the promise of bridging the gap in reality. Little wonder, then, that the Nepali Congress manifesto for the 1959 election gave as the party's long-term goal a socialism in which the whole country would be 'like one family'.

The attraction of new ideas was also enhanced by the element in traditional religion that stressed solidarity and unity of feeling between all people. Hinduism in Nepal had, of course, been intimately linked with the dominance of 'higher' over 'lower' castes, but there are still many passages in the Hindu scriptures that can be interpreted as proclaiming the brotherhood of human beings in general: the masthead of the government's principal newspaper, the *Gorkhapatra,* still today carries a Vedic prayer for universal welfare. This 'universalist' aspect was even more central to Buddhism, even though Buddhism had often been used to legitimise a highly inegalitarian social order, and caste has played an important role in traditional Newar Buddhism. For this reason, and because in recent times Buddhism has not enjoyed the state patronage afforded to Hinduism, it was more easily married with radical social and political ideas.

Nepalese leftists with a Buddhist background made full use of the radical potentiality of their religion. In the mid-1970s, a journal published by a Communist faction carried an article asserting that the future of both Maoism and Buddhism in Nepal could be assured only by a synthesis of the two.[7] The faction concerned subsequently split, with one group denouncing 'Boddhisattva Maoism', but more moderate claims for common ground continue to be voiced. This might seem strange in view of Marx's well-known denunciation of religion as the 'opium of the people', but is more understandable when one remembers that Marxism is itself in many ways a quasi-religion.

As was seen in chapter 5, a key role in elections could depend not so much on individual voters' awareness of the different ideologies on offer as on micro-politics at village level. The pattern of rural indebtedness, as well as old habits of deference, meant that many poorer families depended on the protection of richer and better-connected ones. Rather than trying to challenge this dependence, candidates, whether in full multi-party elections or the nominally partyless ones under the Panchayat system, often concentrated on winning the backing of the influential families in their area. However, the strength of the patron–client system, like much else in Nepal, differed from area to area and could be offset by personal conviction or feelings of ethnic or caste solidarity. This was particularly likely where the constituency was a large one, as in the general elections of 1959, 1981, 1986 and 1991 and in the 1980 referendum.

The role of this local elite was probably greatest where there were no strong regional or ethnic ties providing a sense of identity between the national and the family level. In Arghakhanchi, for example, a hill district south-west of Pokhara, Magar solidarity was relatively weak and the 'village panchayats' were simply areas of countryside rather than distinct villages. The mostly Brahman families who had traditionally provided the *talukdars* (revenue-collectors) before 1950 continued to dominate the area, regularly winning elections to Panchayat bodies. This did not, however, produce the total identification with the ruling system that traditional leaders sometimes delivered elsewhere. Partly because of a heritage of religious dissidence in the region and probably also because of resentment at the loss of relative independence from the national bureaucracy, prominent local families tended to identify after 1961 with one of the banned political parties. The less powerful of the two main Brahman lineages within the district supported Congress while their more successful rivals aligned with the Communists, a stance which, as explained above, did not prevent them from enjoying some of the privileges of collaboration with the Panchayat system. In 1991, the fortunes of the two lineages were reversed when both local seats went to Congress, but the position of the prominent families as a group remained unchanged.[8]

Across the country as a whole, Panchayat elections were an arena for a struggle for influence between different factional leaders. However, many were unhappy with the kind of public conflict involved in competitive elections or in panchayats themselves making decisions by majority vote. Particularly in the early days there was a tendency to seek consensus decisions, sometimes engineered by government representatives. The Panchayat institutions were generally dominated by the established local elite, and traditionally influential people could retain a role even if formally part of the new system. In at least one village panchayat in Ilam district in the early 1960s it was normal for the council to invite prominent local people to attend their meetings and not to pass any proposal without their agreement. In the longer term, the system did make it possible for some factional leaders to force through their own policies by branding their opponents as anti-panchayat. Nevertheless, many Nepalese continued to understand politics as either a no-holds-barred struggle for outright domination or as negotiation and bargaining resulting in a universally agreed compromise. The ritualised conflict involved in elections, whether of the 'partyless' or multi-party variety, was harder to fathom.

The exchange of protection or special favours for political support could easily shade into what many would regard as corruption. The whole issue was a complex one, not only because of problems in obtaining evidence but because in Nepal, as in most traditional societies, behaviour that would now be classified as corrupt was accepted as normal. In Rana Nepal, the maharajas had made no distinction between the public purse and their private wealth and simply pocketed the surplus national revenue. There was less scope, then, for the much smaller civil service to divert funds for their own use, but in society generally there was an expectation that those with power used it to help their family and friends and that those needing help from the powerful should provide 'presents'. Such practices in traditional Nepal could possibly be viewed as 'integrative corruption', since it helped bind individuals and groups into lasting alliances. However, after 1950, social and political change, the rapid expansion of government activities and the influx of funds from abroad all combined to increase the opportunity to use public funds for private gain. Specific events, such as the government's campaign to secure a majority in the 1980 referendum or an influx of Indian businessmen expelled from Burma in the 1960s, have been seen by some as marking an acceleration in the trend. Whatever the truth in these suggestions, corruption was unquestionably becoming less and less acceptable in the eyes of those not directly benefiting from it.

ETHNICITY AND NATIONALISM

The success of the 'People's Movement' in 1990 led to a great upsurge in ethnic activism as different groups, or at least those who assumed the right to speak for them, advanced claims to a greater share in economic resources and for recognition of their own language and culture. Although it was only in the new, democratic atmosphere that such claims could be easily and explicitly put forward, their roots lay in developments during the previous fifty years. Even before 1950, ethnic boundaries had, of course, been important. For example, Tamang villagers in the hills around the Kathmandu Valley, though themselves divided by dialect and other differences, were well aware of the divide between themselves and the *jarti*, as they called the Parbatiya castes. What mattered, however, was the distinction between Tamangs and outsiders in a restricted locality, since there was no real sense of a nationwide Tamang identity. As was seen in chapter 1, the Tamangs were closely related to the Gurungs and Thakalis, and indeed western Tamang dialects were sometimes closer to Gurung than to eastern Tamang speech. Their Buddhism and ritual use of the Tibetan language was also shared with these other groups. What separated the Tamangs from the Gurungs and Thakalis was principally the ritual status ascribed to them in the caste hierarchy as codified by the Nepalese state, and their centuries-old function as conscripted labourers for the elite of the Kathmandu Valley. The Tamangs of Rasuwa district, through which ran the old trading route from Kathmandu to the Tibetan town of Kirong, acknowledged their condition during the annual pilgrimage to Gosainkund Lake:

> Neither born in Kathmandu, nor in Kyirong,
> Born in the middle ground, weak, unclothed and hungry.[9]

With the beginnings of party-political agitation and increasing levels of education, such groups could begin to build a wider collective identity. A key role in this process was played by the more educated, whose literacy enabled them to act together as a community at national level. For the Tamangs, with lower-than-average access to education, the process was a slow one, and the 1960 disturbances, in which Tamangs drove *jarti* villagers from their homes in parts of present-day Dhading and Nuwakot districts, were largely a product of local concerns and also of agitation by national political parties (see ch. 4). By this time, however, there did exist at least one Tamang cultural organisation, the Nepal Tamang Ghedung, set up in 1956 or 1957 by Santabir Lama. The organisation was banned by King Mahendra in the wake of the disturbances, but re-emerged in the 1980s and remains active today (2003) though it is probably more important among urban intellectuals than at village level.

In the hills east of the Arun River, the sense of ethnic identity among the Limbus was stronger, and there was already a tradition of political organisation at the regional level. Ethnic sentiment could therefore partly offset the clientelist system. Here too, however, the majority of peasant farmers accepted in practice the domination of the local *thulo manche* ('big people'), whatever their ethnicity, even though they might feel a sense of resentment against Brahmans as a group. It was Brahmans who made up the majority of the local elite here, but status was not entirely determined by ethnicity. While Limbus were on average less well-off, there were exceptions, including in particular men who had reached the higher ranks in foreign armies. Such men played a dual role, seen very much as members of their own community by fellow Limbus but also needing to co-operate closely with the non-Limbu elite. They could expect to be addressed as *tapain,* the normal polite form of 'you' between equals, even though Brahmans normally used *timi,* the form for inferiors or intimates, to Limbus. It was newer Limbu leaders, rather than the hereditary *subbas,* who contested local elections after the setting-up of the Panchayat system, and in the 1960s these individuals acquiesced in the abolition of the *kipat* system, which had generally been regarded as a cornerstone of Limbu identity. The *subbas* themselves, already enjoying great respect within the Limbu community, apparently felt that there was no need for them also to seek elected office, especially as the Panchayat system itself was widely seen as a tool of Brahman domination. With the elimination of their function as revenue-collectors on *kipat* land, the *subbas'* popularity as symbols of Limbu tradition actually increased, but real authority was in other hands. The old vehicle of Limbu ethnic assertiveness had lost its effectiveness, and the Limbus were slow to organise newer ones.

Before 1950, the Tharus of the Tarai had been even less of a community than the Tamangs. In the eleventh century, the Arabian traveller Al Beruni used the name for forest-dwellers in the Mithila region of the eastern Tarai, but until well into the twentieth century these Tharus were probably not even aware of the existence of the people in the Dang Valley in the western Tarai or in Chitwan who were also called Tharus. Apart from the name itself, they shared only a high degree of immunity to the virulent form of malaria prevalent throughout much of the Tarai and perhaps also an ultimate origin in one or more early migrations from East Asia (see ch. 1). The word 'Tharu' was in fact simply a label for the forest-dwellers whose arrival predated that of settlers belonging to the main North Indian Hindu castes. Because Tharus were frequently dominated by the newer arrivals, the term also came to be used for slaves in general and also simply as an insult: the nineteenth-century British resident, Brian Hodgson, was referred to by his political enemies in Nepal as a 'Tharu Musulman Firangi'. Nevertheless some Tharus were major landowners, and in the 1940s a group of them founded the Tharu Welfare Society, which was officially recognised by the government just before the collapse of the Rana regime.

After 1951, the Tharu Welfare Society expanded its activities and by 1980 its biannual conferences were attended by representatives from all of Nepal's Tarai districts and from Tharu areas across the border in India. The landowning Tharu elite had under the old system not only served as revenue-collectors for the central government but also regulated the Tharu social system. This had included the enforcement of bans on intermarriage with people from different areas and between higher- and lower-status Tharu groups in the same locality. Now, however, they took the lead in removing the old restrictions and stressing a common Tharu identity across the Tarai. It was in fact mainly the elite themselves who were in a position to marry at long distance, and there were now fewer marriages between wealthy Tharu and ordinary Tharu peasants. This reflected growing economic differentiation, in contrast to earlier years when the major land-holders were certainly wealthier than other Tharus but still shared the same general lifestyle. Thus the consolidation of a nationwide Tharu community was perhaps accompanied by a decrease in Tharu cohesion in at least some localities. At the same time there were extensive relationships between Tharu and Brahman elites at village level but little interaction between poorer Brahmans and poor Tharus. The latter, like the Limbus, still regarded the Brahmans as interlopers who had tricked them out of their land. It was nevertheless the village-level Tharu elite who were probably most concerned with the issue of Tharu status relative to other groups. By the end of the Panchayat period, the wealthiest Tharus, with connections across the country, already felt relatively secure in their position within Nepal's national elite, while the ordinary Tharu cultivator was preoccupied with day-to-day economic survival. In contrast, those in between were constantly aware of the danger that they themselves might slip back into the mass of the Tharu peasantry.

At the heart of the Nepalese state, the Newars of the Kathmandu Valley continued to identify strongly with their own immediate neighbourhood, still often seen as centred round a particular religious shrine. This identification was sustained by the continuing importance of religious or quasi-religious activity, including the temple music associations to which many of the Maharjan agricultural caste still belonged. This localism, as well as divisions into castes and between Hindu and Buddhist within Newar society, helped prevent the Newars as a whole from acting as a single political block, even though 'ethnic activism' of a sort, married initially with Buddhist revivalism, had started from the 1920s. Also important perhaps was the tendency for co-operation to take place within families and wider kin groups rather than between them – a factor said to constrain Newar entrepreneurship in contrast to that of the Marwaris (see ch. 5). Perhaps above all, there was the degree of accommodation to the Parbatiya-dominated state that had already taken place. As well as a primary position across the country in retailing, even if not in manufacturing and long-distance trade, many educated Newars also enjoyed positions within the expanding civil service.

Even without the restrictions on political agitation imposed under the Panchayat system, there were thus plenty of reasons to avoid 'rocking the boat'.

At the same time, however, a strong feeling of ethnic identity persisted among most Newars, with the exception of the Rajopadhyaya Brahmans at one extreme of the caste hierarchy and the Pode ('sweeper') caste at the other, neither of which saw themselves as members of a Newar community. These feelings were initially channelled into cultural activity rather than political demands, and organisations such as the Cwasa Pasa (Friends of the Pen) and the Newar Language Council, established at the beginning of the 1950s, encouraged writing in Newar. The Rana government's ban on publication in the language had been lifted for religious texts in 1946 and was completely removed on the fall of the Rana regime; there was also now a place for Newar programmes on newly established Radio Nepal. However, the atmosphere changed under the Panchayat system, and in 1965 broadcasts in Newar were ended. Activists now gradually moved towards making specific demands on the government, though these were still of a cultural rather than economic nature. The highest profile was probably achieved by the campaign to replace Nepal's official Vikram Era, which reckoned years from 57 BC, with the Nepal Era which started in AD 879. From 1979 onwards, Newars drew attention to this demand by holding a motorcycle rally round the three towns of the Valley each autumn on the first day of the new Nepal year.[10]

In 1979 a number of smaller Newar organisations combined to form the Manka Khalah (Co-operative Group) which pressed both for the restoration of radio broadcasts in Newar and for its use as a medium of instruction in schools. Paradoxically, this campaign was launched at a time when, as already seen, many Newars, including even some of the language activists themselves, were switching to the use of Nepali with their own children. Many other Newars, including the 50 per cent or so who were still at this time illiterate, simply took for granted their own use of the language, rather than seeing it as something endangered by social change. The election to the Rastriya Panchayat of one of the best-known activists, Padma Ratna Tuladhar, was due to his reputation as an incorruptible advocate of the ordinary citizen against the establishment and to help from leftist activists rather than to support for his views on the language issue. Language activism remained very much a minority concern, though it was a growing one.

Raising general support for their demands was an even harder task for Magar activists than for their Newar counterparts. Magars were spread out over a large swathe of the central hills rather than being concentrated in the prosperous Kathmandu Valley and many of them had long ago switched to using Nepali rather than their own original dialects. Nevertheless, the first 'Magar Association' was set up by an ex-soldier around 1955; although this soon became inactive, the organisation now known as the Nepal Magar Sangh was founded in 1971. The extensive Hinduisation of many Magar communities meant that activists had to try to recover – or perhaps rather devise – 'authentic' customs and then cajole their fellow Magars into accepting them. They made only limited progress and at the end of the 1980s most Magars probably still accepted the claim to higher status of clans that used Brahman priests and did not eat pork or buffalo. It could also be argued that, even were the activists to succeed in reversing this value system, they would still only be substituting for the old hierarchy a new one dominated by the revivalists writing Magar histories and publishing old Magar texts.

The pace of ethnic and caste mobilisation increased markedly during the 1980s, partly because of the loosening of restraints on political activity but also because the government had itself been trying to enlist both ethnic minorities and lower-caste groups in support of the Panchayat system. As well as the establishment of new organisations and publications serving individual groups, there were efforts at collaboration. 'Magurali' (standing for 'Magar-Gurung-Rai-Limbu'), an informal grouping of hill minorities, emerged even before the 1980 referendum, while the Nepal Sarvajatiya Manch (Nepal All-People's Platform) was set up in 1982. Taking their cue in part from an early article of Lenin's questioning the need for an official language, intellectuals from the Newar, Thakali, Tamang, Gurung, Rai, Limbu, Sherpa, Magar and Tharu communities in 1985 set up the Nepal Mother-Tongue Council (Nepal Matribhasa Parishad) to press for education in their own languages.[11] Representatives of the lower Parbatiya castes, who in fact suffered worse discrimination than the ethnic minorities, established the Utpidit Jatiya Utthan Manch (Oppressed People's Upliftment Platform) in 1987.

This ferment among intellectuals, however significant for future developments, was nevertheless of only marginal effect compared with the government's drive to promote a uniform national culture through the school system and the media it controlled. This goal was encapsulated in the Panchayat slogan *Ek bhasha, ek bhesh, ek desh* (One language, one style of dress, one country), a modification of the poet Balkrishna Sama's earlier formulation: *Hamro raja, hamro desh; hamro bhasha, hamro bhesha* (Our king, our country; our language, our dress).[12] Although official propaganda did not always make this explicit, the unity envisaged was to be based on the customs and values of the high-caste Parbatiya elite that had dominated the Nepalese state since its foundation. As articulated during the Panchayat years, these values centred on the monarchy and its role in creating and sustaining the state, on the Hindu religion and on the Nepali language.

The assimilationist agenda was made particularly clear in 1955 when a landmark report on education planning conceded the need to use minority languages for oral communication with students just starting primary school but advocated a switch to exclusive use of Nepali as soon as possible so that 'other languages will gradually disappear and greater national strength and unity will result'.[13] The effects of this policy as shown by census returns were not, however, clear-cut. The percentage reporting Nepali as their first language (considerably less, of course, than those simply using it as a lingua franca) rose from 49 per cent in 1952–4 to 58 per cent, but in 1991, it dipped sharply to only 50 per cent. The figures in fact probably measure emotional attachment to languages, or rather the identities they represented, rather than actual language use. In fact, even supposing respondents were attempting to be objective, they could have genuine difficulty in answering the census question accurately. What was the 'mother tongue' of a Newar child whose parents spoke to him in Nepali but to each other in Newar? Or of Gurung children who had grown up using a mixture of Gurung and Nepali with their village playmates? In this situation, it was not surprising that respondents (or the enumerators) opted for Nepali when officialdom appeared to be promoting it but claimed another language as their first one when the rhetoric of multi-culturalism mushroomed following the collapse of the Panchayat system in 1990.

The 1962 constitution's explicit declaration of Nepal as a Hindu state was new in form but in substance it was only a reaffirmation of the reality from Prithvi Narayan onwards. The country's status as 'the world's only Hindu kingdom' served to link Nepal to the dominant religion in South Asia but also to distinguish it from India, which had been under non-Hindu, colonial rule before 1947 and avowedly secular after that. There was no actual persecution of other religions: Muslims (around 3.3 per cent of the population) practised their faith without interference and Mohammed Mohasin became one of the Panchayat system's leading ideologues, while Nepali-speaking Christians who entered the country from Darjeeling were also free to worship in their own way. Buddhism was actually given official support by the 1952 institution of a public holiday to mark the Buddha's birthday and by the development of the site of his birth at Lumbini in the central Tarai. It was, however, Hindu ritualists and institutions that received most state patronage, and there was legislation criminalising attempts to convert Hindus and even denying the right of an individual Hindu to change his own religion. The ban on proselytising did not cause great offence to anyone other than the small Christian and Muslim minorities, but a growing number of educated Nepalese resented Hinduism's official status because they saw it as symbolising and also legitimising the dominant position in the power structure of the high-caste Hindus. The Brahmans and Chetri–Thakuris, who were unambiguously Hindu, and the Newars, among whose upper castes Hindus outnumbered Buddhists, were together only about a third of Nepal's total population (see tab. 1.1, pp. 9–10), but between 1951 and 1991 they normally held around 60 per cent of seats in parliament or the Rastriya Panchayat. They accounted also for 90 per cent of the section officers in the civil service in 1989 and for 81 per cent of the teaching posts in Tribhuvan University in 1990.[14]

Resentment of this upper-caste predominance was also found among less educated Nepalese, but in 1991 the population as a whole almost certainly still did not share the committed activists' vehement objection to a Hindu state as such. The 1991 census data, collected after months of campaigning by the pro-secularist lobby, showed 86.5 per cent of the population as Hindu; even in 2001 the figure was still 80.6 per cent. Activists argued that the census data was inaccurate and claimed that the non-Hindus were actually three-quarters of the population. In fact, in Nepal, as in most pre-industrial societies, religious faiths were not seen as mutually exclusive and most people happily combined elements of different traditions, something that the syncretic nature of Hinduism made particularly easy. The average Nepalese farmer might not be Hindu to the same degree as a pious Brahman but he honoured Hindu gods and was probably happy enough to accept the Hindu label for himself and for the state of which he was a citizen.

In the development of the state's nationalist ideology, as in all other aspects of Nepalese life, India loomed large. Despite the very large proportion of non-Parbatiyas who made up the Nepali-speaking community in the Darjeeling hills beyond Nepal's eastern border, it was intellectuals from that district who had laid many of the foundations for the Parbatiya-orientated nationalism the Panchayat regime promoted. Some of the most prominent figures moved back to Nepal in the 1950s to assist in the national project, including Surya Bikram Gyawali, who was both the biographer of Prithvi Narayan Shah and the man responsible for placing Bhanubhakta at the head of Nepal's literary pantheon. Ironically the consolidation of nationalism within Nepal was accompanied by an attempt by some in Darjeeling itself to deny that Nepal's culture was also their own. Subhas Gising, who led the campaign for removing the district from West Bengal's control, insisted on 'Gurkha', not 'Nepali', as a label for the community and their language. His followers even vandalised the town's statue of Bhanubhakta in protest against the cult of a 'foreign poet'. Most Darjeelingites, however, while not wishing to be united politically with Nepal, accepted that they were Nepalese in a cultural sense and it was Nepali, not 'Gurkha', that was finally recognised as one of India's national languages in 1992.

If it was important for some in Darjeeling to establish a non-Nepalese identity for themselves, the touchstone of national identity for many more in Nepal was distancing themselves from India. As was seen in earlier chapters, a common sense of separateness from the Indian plains was a potential basis for unity in the hills even before the foundation of the Nepalese state. This complicated not only Nepal's relations with the Indian state but also the position of the many people within Nepal who were of recent Indian origin. The Marwari businessmen who played such an important role in the Nepalese economy were resented as foreigners even if they had acquired Nepalese passports or (as was often the case) had actually been born in Nepal. Most crucially, millions in the Tarai felt that they were denied equal treatment by the dominant hill elite while many in the hills saw in the Taraians (as they now call themselves) an Indian fifth column within Nepal's borders. Bitterness was increased because many who were born in the Tarai but had no documentary proof of their status were denied citizenship certificates, but the rich and unscrupulous from across the border could obtain papers from corrupt chief district officers.

The Tarai issue first came to prominence in the 1950s when politicians from the region mobilised in protest against the 1957 K. I. Singh government's decision to end the use of Hindi as the medium of instruction in local schools. Hindi in the strict sense was a dialect originating in the Delhi region and, with its vocabulary enriched by loans from Sanskrit and written in the same Devanagari script as Nepali, it served as India's national language. It was not the mother tongue of significant numbers in the Tarai, where most people's speech shifted gradually from village to village, but was usually classified as a variety of Awadhi, Bhojpuri or Maithili. However, Hindi was the established lingua franca of the region, fulfilling the same role here that Nepali did among speakers of other languages in the hills. The central government's efforts to remove Hindi's public role in Nepal was therefore seen as an attack on the Tarai inhabitants' cultural identity. In contrast, hill intellectuals saw the primacy of Nepali throughout the country as vital to their own national identity. The government's proposals went ahead and Nepali textbooks replaced Hindi ones in government schools, while Hindi, like Newar, lost its place in Radio Nepal's programming in 1965. However, textbook Nepali was quite similar to textbook Hindi as both took their technical vocabulary from Sanskrit, and colloquial Hindi retained its importance for informal communication.

An even more divisive issue between hills and plain emerged in the 1980s over citizenship and immigration. Apart from the Parbatiya immigrants and perhaps also the Tharus, Tarai-dwellers wanted liberal rules for the granting of Nepalese citizenship and favoured retaining the open border with India, since they shared language and culture with those on the other side of it. Many hill Nepalese, fearful of mass immigration, favoured regulation of the border and safeguards against recent arrivals from India gaining citizenship rights in large numbers. The Nepalese government was unwilling to antagonise India by pressing directly for regulation of the border, particularly as that might jeopardise the rights of Nepalese working in India. However, citizenship certificates remained hard to obtain, and legislation on naturalisation required applicants to prove competence in both spoken and written Nepali. Matters were brought to a head when in 1984 a commission on immigration headed by Harka Gurung, a former government minister, recommended stringent border controls. The report was largely unimplemented, but left a lasting legacy in the Sadbhavana Parishad (Goodwill Council), set up in 1985 to champion Tarai interests by Gajendra Narayan Singh, a one-time Congress politician who later worked within the Panchayat system. In 1990 this was reconstituted as the Sadbhavana Party, which attracted enough support in the central and eastern Tarai to secure six seats in the 1991 elections (see ch. 4, p. 121).

Nevertheless, the significant fact is that in 1991 most people in the Tarai voted for national parties rather than for Sadbhavana. Other, smaller-scale loyalties were usually more important than any pan-Tarai solidarity. People tended to identify more strongly with a particular caste or ethnic group or with a linguistically defined subregion. Many in the Mithila region centred around Janakpur were strongly attached to the Maithili language, which had been a literary language long before Nepali and had once been the most prestigious language at the courts of the Newar kings (see ch. 1). Maithili was spoken by around 11 per cent of Nepal's population, second only to Nepali itself, and many of those who reported speaking 'Tharu' in fact spoke a virtually identical dialect (see n. 11, p. 256). Maithils were, however, divided by caste, with literary Maithili often seen as a particular possession of Maithil Brahmans and Kayasthas, and the groupings which held people's allegiance elsewhere in the Tarai were generally much smaller than the region or its major linguistic divisions. In this situation, it made more sense for voters to align with one or other of the major parties. Congress, in particular, retained a strong following in the Tarai because of the Koirala family's Biratnagar connection and their links with both Tharu and Maithil leaders.

The sheer number of different groupings was, of course, a feature of the Nepalese hills as well as of the plains, and it was unusual for any one caste or ethnic group to make up more than 50 per cent of the population in any district. This meant that ethnic and caste feeling, though important, was likely to be channelled into coalition-building with other groups rather than into powerful separatist movements. Ethnic discontents were a factor in the problems that Nepal would face after 1991, including the Maoist insurgency, but they were not to be the determining one.

CHAPTER 7

Democracy and disillusionment: Nepal since 1991

The Congress administration under Girija Prasad Koirala which succeeded the coalition government in May 1991 faced vigorous opposition from the Communist Party of Nepal (UML) and the smaller Communist parties, including the repetition on a smaller scale of the street protests that had been used against the old Panchayat administration. Controversy arose almost immediately when civil servants began a third round of agitation. Koirala took an extremely firm line and a number of government employees linked to the UML, which had sympathised with the action, lost their jobs. This was to become a running sore in relations between Congress and the main opposition party, since members among lower-ranking public employees had long been an important part of the UML's support base. The issue was soon, however, eclipsed by two others. Despite its own earlier socialist orientation, Congress adopted the neo-liberal economic policies favoured by the aid donors and the resulting price rises stoked discontent. In addition, Koirala was felt by many to have secured an insufficient share of electric power and water for Nepal in an agreement legalising India's construction of a dam on Nepalese territory at Tanakpur on the Mahakali River. Street demonstrations against these policies, in which the UPF and Masal took the lead, turned violent on 6 April 1992, the second anniversary of the Darbar Marg shootings during the *janandolan.* At least twelve people died in police firing, partly because both training and equipment were inadequate, but also possibly because individual policemen wanted revenge for the killing of some of their colleagues the previous year. The extreme left groups responded with a campaign calling for the government's resignation. The UPF had only limited support in the Valley, as was shown by its candidate in the Kathmandu mayoral election in May winning only 3.4 per cent of the vote, but the one-day strike they called the same month kept almost all traffic off the roads. As on numerous subsequent occasions, fear of attack by demonstrators throwing stones or worse was enough to enforce compliance.

The UML needed to preserve its own credibility as the main force on the left but also to maintain the image of a responsible opposition. It therefore participated in protests against the killings but demanded only the resignation of the home minister, Sher Bahadur Deuba, not that of the entire government; it abandoned the campaign after Congress agreed to an inquiry into the shootings. A year later, however, the UML itself took the lead in street protests following the deaths of party leaders Madan Bhandari and Jivraj Ashrit in May 1993. The two men had been travelling in a jeep which plunged into the Narayani River at Dasdhunga on the road from Kathmandu to Narayanghadh. A government inquiry accepted the driver's version that he had lost control of the vehicle but managed to jump clear himself. The UML and the other Communist parties, however, alleged there had been an assassination plot and demanded both a fresh inquiry and Koirala's resignation. In renewed street disturbances, police again opened fire with the loss of twenty-four lives. Extensive flooding throughout most of the country later in the summer helped lower the political temperature, and the UML again reached an agreement with Congress providing for a fresh investigation. The smaller leftist parties continued the agitation on their own for some time. No definite evidence of a conspiracy was ever found and it was all too common for vehicles to plunge off mountain roads. In 1997 a Supreme Court ruling confirmed that the deaths had been accidental and the driver, who had been imprisoned for causing death through negligence, was released the following year. Nevertheless reopening of the inquiry still figured in the UML's 1999 election manifesto, and the kidnapping and murder of the driver in 2003 would probably have rekindled the controversy had much more urgent concerns not then been facing all the political parties.

The Congress government generally enjoyed good relations with India and a new trade and transit agreement was reached in December 1991, under which the origin-of-contents rule for Nepalese exports to India was further relaxed. In addition to the perennial problem of water resources, a new difficulty was presented by the flight from southern Bhutan of many ethnic Nepalese, about 90,000 of whom had, by the end of 1992, ended up as refugees in camps in south-eastern Nepal. The Bhutanese government claimed that many of them were either not actually from Bhutan or had emigrated voluntarily. They had in fact mostly left under duress after disturbances following a campaign against the Bhutanese government's campaign of forced assimilation and restrictive legislation on citizenship.

The Bhutanese king and many of the Dzonghka-speaking Drukpa community to which he belonged were alarmed at the prospect of their Nepali-speaking population, who were now perhaps the largest ethnic group in Bhutan, taking control of the country as their fellow Nepali-speakers had done earlier in Sikkim. Although India had a treaty right to exercise 'guidance' over Bhutanese foreign policy, India put no pressure on Bhutan to take the refugees back. The Nepalese government eventually reached an agreement to classify the inhabitants of the camp into those who had genuinely been forced out and other categories but disagreement over implementation dragged on for several years and 'verification' of those in the first camp was not completed until December 2001. The Congress government was widely criticised within Nepal for failing to take a stronger line, though, given India's attitude, there was little any government could have done.

Despite foreign policy embarrassments and recurrent violence on the streets of Kathmandu, the government was in a relatively secure position in the country as a whole, and its hold on power was strengthened when it won over half the seats in local elections in summer 1992. It was nevertheless brought down by dissension within its own ranks, resulting partly from genuine unhappiness with some of Koirala's policies but mainly from disputes over patronage and, as in the 1950s, over the relationship between the party machine and the party in parliament. Within the parliamentary party itself, a clear division between pro- and anti-Koirala factions emerged at the end of 1991 when Koirala dismissed six members of his cabinet without the approval of the party's president Krishna Prasad Bhattarai and its senior leader Ganesh Man Singh. At the beginning of 1994, Bhattarai, who had been defeated by UML leader Madan Bhandari in the general election, stood in the by-election resulting from Bhandari's death. His supporters were increasingly eager for him to replace Koirala as prime minister and the Communist parties claimed that, as part of the deal ending the street protests in summer 1993, Bhattarai had actually given a verbal promise to remove Koirala. Koirala responded by dissociating himself from Bhattarai's candidature and thus contributed to his defeat by the UML candidate, Bhandari's widow.

Although Bhattarai himself ruled that no action should be taken against the 'sabotage' of his campaign, thirty-six MPs opposed to Koirala stayed away from parliament in a vote on the king's speech in May; Koirala then resigned and asked Birendra to call mid-term elections. There were more street protests, involving both opposition parties and supporters of Krishna Prasad Bhattarai and Ganesh Man Singh. Bhattarai's faction controlled the party's central working committee and also dominated its organisation in

15. Girija Prasad Koirala denouncing the king's October 2002 takeover.

the Valley, but Koirala was more popular with party members across the country and he seemed ready to provoke a final showdown. However, he shied away from this and a compromise was again reached allowing Congress to go into the elections more or less united.

The elections were held in November 1994, after an unsuccessful legal challenge to the dissolution of parliament, and although the UML's share of the total vote was less than that of Congress, they emerged as the largest party, with 88 seats of 205 in the House of Representatives to Congress's 83. This left the two senior Panchayat politicians, Lokendra Bahadur Chand and Surya Bahadur Thapa, holding the balance of power: their factions had merged in 1992 to form a single National Democratic Party (NDP), which increased their vote share from just over 10 per cent to almost 20 per cent and won twenty seats. The other major change was the failure of the United People's Front to win any seats after the more radical wing, which was to launch the 'People's War' two years later, had broken away and abandoned parliamentary politics. Coalition negotiations were inconclusive and so the UML formed a minority government with Man Mohan Adhikari as prime minister and secretary-general Madhav Kumar Nepal as his deputy.

As well as lacking a clear majority, the UML government needed to allay suspicion among aid donors and in India, so, even assuming it wanted to, it was not in a position to make a radical break with the past. It did, however, freeze the privatisation drive begun under Congress and commissioned inquiries into the issue of land reform and the problems of the *sukumbasi* or squatters on government land. The government also conducted a review of a major hydro-electric project for the Arun River in east Nepal, for which the Congress government had sought World Bank financing. The project was highly controversial both because of environmental concerns and worries about the high cost of the power it would produce; although the government finally decided to go ahead, the World Bank itself pulled out of the scheme in August 1995, just before the government fell. Lobbying by Nepalese environmentalists had been one factor behind the bank's decision.

The UML's major innovation was its Build Your Village Yourself scheme, under which village development committees, as the village panchayats were now known, received grants of 300,000 rupees for local development projects. The scheme in itself was not controversial, but other parties were strongly opposed to the UML's setting up a special monitoring mechanism involving members of different political parties at local level. To Congress in particular, this seemed a deliberate attempt to bypass the now Congress-dominated local authorities. There was also criticism that the 53,000 families eventually granted titles to land by the Landless People Problem Resolution Commission had been selected for their connections to the UML rather than on grounds of need. Accusations that the party in government was abusing them were to greet any poverty-reduction schemes, however welcome in principle they might be. The UML levied similar charges against the 'Bisheshwar with the Poor' scheme introduced by the 1999 Congress government.

In June 1995, after Congress, supported by the National Democratic Party and the Sadbhavana Party, requested a special session of the House of Representatives to bring a no-confidence motion against the government, Man Mohan Adhikari tried to pre-empt defeat by recommending another dissolution and fresh elections. The king agreed to the request but, in a reversal of the previous year's roles, Congress and its allies asked the Supreme Court to declare his move unconstitutional. The court this time ruled against the prime minister, and parliament was restored. The main

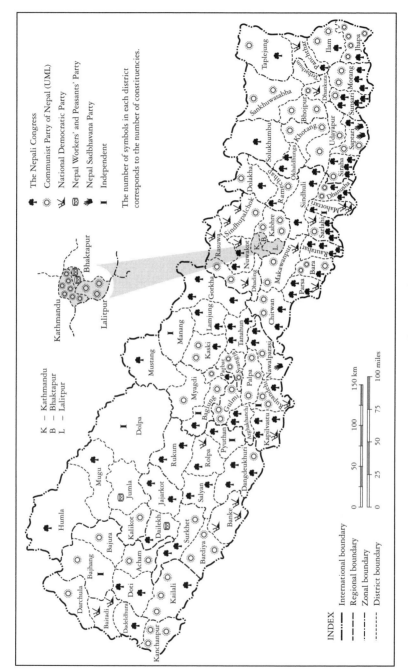

K – Kathmandu
B – Bhaktapur
L – Lalitpur

The Nepali Congress

Communist Party of Nepal (UML)

National Democratic Party

Nepal Workers' and Peasants' Party

Nepal Sadbhavana Party

Independent

The number of symbols in each district
corresponds to the number of constituencies.

Map 5. 1994 election results.

rationale was that in 1995, unlike the previous year, there was the possibility of forming a replacement government from within the current parliament. The court also ruled that the right to bring a vote of no confidence in a special session took precedence over the prime minister's right to seek a dissolution.

In September 1995, after Adhikari's government was voted out of office, Sher Bahadur Deuba, who had replaced Koirala as leader of the parliamentary Congress Party after the mid-term election, became prime minister as head of a coalition with the NDP and Sadbhavana. The government was faced from February 1996 by an escalating 'People's War' launched in the mid-western hills by the Communist Party of Nepal (Maoist) (CPN (Maoist)), as the faction that had broken away from the Unity Centre/United People's Front in 1994 was now calling itself (see p. 204), but this threat at first seemed a minor one. In January 1996, Deuba secured an agreement with India on the use of the Mahakali River, which both increased Nepal's share of benefits from the Tanakpur scheme and provided for development of a larger-scale hydro-electric and irrigation project at Pancheshwor. Despite strong opposition from the radical left and some right-wing nationalists, he managed to secure ratification of the treaty by the necessary two-thirds' majority in a joint sitting of both Houses of parliament in September. He also continued the UML's system of block grants to village development committees and its provision of grants to each MP to spend on development work in their own constituency.

Much of Deuba's attention had to be concentrated on ensuring the government's own survival. While the NDP's president, Surya Bahadur Thapa, was strongly committed to the alliance with Congress, the leader of the parliamentary party, Lokendra Bahadur Chand, was attracted by the UML's offer to join an alternative coalition under his own leadership. Chand was able to win considerable support among NDP MPs, including even ministers in Deuba's government, and no-confidence motions were brought against it in March and December 1996. These involved frantic manoeuvring by both sides to suborn the others' supporters and retain the loyalty of their own; calculations were complicated by the opportunistic behaviour of a number of independent MPs and members of minor parties. After March, Deuba expanded his cabinet to a record forty-eight members to accommodate almost every NDP MP. Ahead of the December 1996 vote, he sent several unreliable NDP ministers on a government-financed trip to Bangkok for 'medical treatment' and one Sadbhavana waverer to Singapore, thus ensuring they would not be in the House when the vote was taken. The result nevertheless showed that his government was in a minority, and he survived only because the opposition had not obtained the legal requirement of 103 votes.[1] Despite protests from his own party, Deuba now felt compelled to take back into the government the ministers who had previously resigned and voted with the opposition. However, when he himself sought a vote of confidence in March 1997, two of his own Congress MPs were persuaded to stay away from the House and the government was left without a majority.

After Deuba's resignation, Girija Koirala, who Congress hoped would be more acceptable to Lokendra Bahadur Chand, took over as leader of the parliamentary party. In the end, however, Chand rejected overtures from Congress and stuck to his earlier choice of alignment, becoming prime minister at the head of an NDP-UML-Sadbhavana coalition. Despite the NDP's formal predominance, the strongman of the government was the deputy prime minister, Bamdev Gautam of the UML. Gautam master-minded a UML victory in local elections during the summer. Maoist activity led to voting being postponed in certain areas and, in those where it went ahead, Congress candidates, who were the main target of Maoist violence, were frequently at a disadvantage. It was only after the elections were over that Bamdev Gautam tried to get through parliament a bill widening the powers of the security forces to deal with the insurgents, and critics of the UML charged that the delay had been deliberate.

The NDP was effectively split into two factions, one led by Chand and one by Surya Bahadur Thapa. Much of the time they operated as sepa-rate parties, coming together only to fight elections. Surya Bahadur Thapa was able to win back support among NDP MPs, and the government was defeated in another no-confidence vote in September 1997. Thapa then took office at the head of an NDP-Congress-Sadbhavana coalition, but in January 1998, realising the tide among his own MPs was again flowing Chand's way, he recommended that the king dissolve parliament and hold elections. On the afternoon of the same day UML members and eight rebel NDP MPs petitioned the palace for a special session of parliament which could bring a no-confidence motion against Thapa. This time, instead of accepting his prime minister's advice and allowing the opposition to make a legal challenge, King Birendra himself asked the Supreme Court for its opinion. This action caused some apprehension that the monarch might again be seeking an active role, but the royal move probably accelerated rather than altered the final outcome. After the court had ruled in a major-ity judgement that a dissolution should not be allowed, Thapa faced a no-confidence vote in February 1998. The coalition survived, as it retained the support of eleven NDP MPs and was also backed by two from the Nepal Workers' and Peasants' Party.

The fall of the Chand government had intensified tension within the UML. Bamdev Gautam, a leading opponent of M. K. Nepal's since 1994, now made common cause with C. P. Mainali, who had been a party dissident since his removal from the post of secretary-general of the pre-1991 Communist Party of Nepal (Marxist-Leninist) in 1982. Both men had opposed Nepal's decision to back ratification of the Deuba government's Mahakali treaty with India in September 1996, an issue which had bitterly divided the party. But whereas the two shared the view of the more radical left that the agreement had conceded too much to India, in terms of general ideological positioning, Gautam had sided with M. K. Nepal in his belief that the UML should adopt an essentially social democratic stance. Mainali, in contrast, had argued strongly for a more traditional communist line, nearer to Mao's original concept of 'new people's democracy', and opposed the revisionist 'multi-party people's democracy' (*bahudaliya janbad*), which had become official UML policy at the party's 1993 conference. The alliance between Mainali and Gautam rested in fact largely on a shared sense of being marginalised within the UML, and in March 1998 they broke away to form their own party. This was registered as the 'Communist Party of Nepal (Marxist-Leninist)', the name of the larger of the two groups that had merged to form the UML in 1991. They took with them Sahana Pradhan, who had chaired the United Left Front in the 1990 'People's Movement', around half the UML's MPs and also many of its activists, including a majority of those in the Kathmandu Valley. This formal split on the left, following the de facto ones in Congress and the NDP, left six major forces in the House of Representatives with seemingly no prospect of a stable coalition. In addition, Supreme Court decisions had greatly restricted the right of a prime minister to use the threat of dissolution to discipline MPs.

In accordance with an earlier understanding, though after some squabbling over the exact date, Thapa handed over the leadership of the NDP-Sadbhavana-Congress government to Congress in April 1998. Girija Koirala then formally terminated the coalition arrangement and formed a minority Congress government. Indignant at being cast aside in this manner, Thapa and his faction abstained when Koirala sought a vote of confidence. In contrast, Chand and his supporters, now organised as a separate party, joined the UML in voting for the new government. At the end of May, Koirala launched a large-scale police operation against the Maoist insurgents in the mid-western hills and, although this succeeded

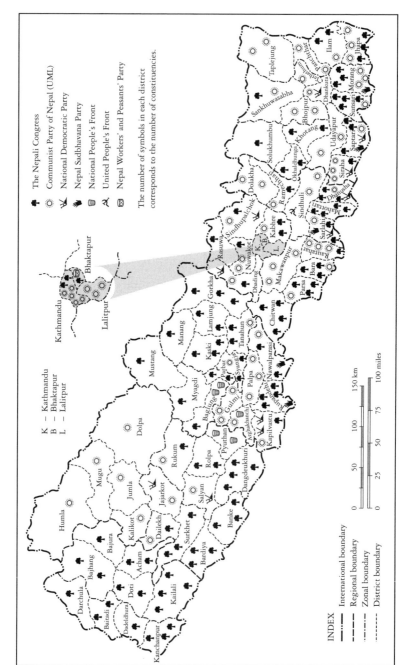

Map 6. 1999 election results.

INDEX
— · — International boundary
— — — Regional boundary
— · · — Zonal boundary
— — — District boundary

The Nepali Congress
Communist Party of Nepal (UML)
National Democratic Party
Nepal Sadbhavana Party
National People's Front
United People's Front
Nepal Workers' and Peasants' Party

The number of symbols in each district corresponds to the number of constituencies.

K – Kathmandu
B – Bhaktapur
L – Lalitpur

in inflicting heavy casualties on the Maoists, the government came under heavy criticism because of deaths among innocent civilians. In August the administration appeared to change tack, reaching an agreement with an alliance of nine left-wing groups to compensate the families of victims and not to proceed with legislation giving the security forces special powers.[2] Four days later the cabinet was expanded to include ministers from the Communist Party of Nepal (Marxist-Leninist). However, demands from the CPN (ML) for additional ministerial posts and disagreements over policy towards the Maoists led to their resignation from the cabinet in December.

Koirala reacted with an immediate request for a dissolution and, as was now customary, the opposition responded with a demand for a special session. With no need this time to consult the Supreme Court, King Birendra summoned parliament but the motion of no confidence Bamdev had planned was stymied by an agreement between Congress and the UML to form a coalition to oversee elections. This was in theory to be open to participation by other parties but in the event only Sadbhavana was actually included. Immediately after obtaining a vote of confidence on 14 January 1999, Girija Koirala applied again for a dissolution and the date for elections was then fixed for 3 May. Both the UML and the parties outside government objected strenuously to the Election Commission's plan, supported by Congress, to hold the elections in two phases on 3 and 17 May. Their argument was partly the legalistic one that this procedure violated the royal order, which referred only to 3 May, but they were chiefly concerned that the delay would increase the scope for electoral malpractice. The Election Commission's case was that, because of the threat to security from the Maoist rebels, polls could be held simultaneously throughout the country only if large numbers of temporary police were recruited, and that such police had previously been shown to be unreliable. The wrangling continued but the commission went ahead on this basis and the campaign got under way.

The campaign resulted in an outright victory for Congress, which gained 36.5 per cent of the popular vote, almost as high a percentage as in 1991, against the UML's 30.74 per cent and secured 111 seats to the UML's 71. However, the left as a whole attracted a higher number of votes than Congress and the latter's victory was really due to the 1998 split in the UML. Although the breakaway party, the Marxist-Leninists, failed to gain a single seat, they secured 6.38 per cent of the total vote. Had this gone instead to the UML candidates, the parent party would have won an additional forty-three seats and thus a comfortable overall majority.

The intensity of the power struggle within as well as between parties and, after 1994, the constant changes of government had clearly made it more difficult for administrations of any political hue to deliver the 'development' which was still the nation's avowed goal. The effects were not confined to the national level. Helped by the growth in membership of political parties – the Nepali Congress claimed 821,000 and the UML 485,000 members by the end of 1999 – decision-making structures at local level were highly polarised on party lines. Factionalism had, of course, been an important factor during the 'partyless' era, but now people who had been prominent in the Panchayat system as well as some more neutral observers argued that the tying of local factions to rival organisations outside the local area could sometimes be very disruptive. In the Jiri Valley in Dolakha district, for example, the rivalry between the two main parties contributed to a collapse in standards at the local hospital and was also blamed for the breakdown of traditional leadership by clan elders and increasing domination of outsiders with connections to major parties.[3] Although Congress did eventually enact a decentralisation measure of its own in 1998, the 1991–4 Congress government returned to central government departments control of technical staff who had been at least nominally responsible to local authorities under the 1982 Decentralisation Act. Girija Koirala was also accused of placing non-user Congress workers in charge of some of the 'user-groups' through which many villagers had been jointly managing local resources. In addition, as has already been seen, all political parties were anxious to channel grants for local development as far as possible through their own party functionaries. This ensured that they themselves were seen as the provider of largesse and also, of course, enlarged the powers of patronage in the hands of powerful party members.

None of this stopped progress completely. The improvement in key indicators seen over the previous fifty years was maintained and in some cases accelerated. Though it remained the highest in South Asia, infant mortality was reduced to around 7 per cent in 2000 from 10 per cent in 1990, while life expectancy rose from fifty-two to fifty-nine years. The road network, which had expanded from 276 to 7,330 kilometres between 1951 and 1990 had reached 15,308 kilometres by 2000. The number of telephone lines, 25 in 1951 and 63,293 at the end of the Panchayat period, stood at 255,800 by the end of the century, while the corresponding figures for hectares under irrigation were 6,200, 550,467and 716,000.[4] Literacy rose from 39 per cent to 58 per cent. Unfortunately, at the same time the main weaknesses of the pre-1990 economy were also perpetuated. Although 1993–4 did see agricultural production increase by 7.6 per cent and GDP by 7.9 per cent, this was an exceptional year and agriculture remained on the whole relatively stagnant. The twenty-year Agricultural Perspective Plan, endorsed in 1995 by both major parties, aimed to boost the long-term annual rate of increase from 3 per cent to 5 per cent, but it offered no immediate relief. At the end of the 1990s, 500,000 youngsters were coming annually on to the job market. Of these, 100,000 had completed secondary education but failed the School Leaving Certificate exam and thus had no prospect of obtaining the white-collar employment that their schooling had prepared them for.

The open political system introduced in 1990 in principle offered all those with grievances leverage to make the state more responsive to their problems. There was indeed no shortage of platforms for individuals and organisations to set out their own demands and their own vision of Nepal's future. Nevertheless there was a growing perception that the political system was failing to deliver. Among the educated, especially in the towns, there was disillusionment not only over the political infighting but also over the corruption that accompanied it. Partly, this was simply the 'democratisation' of the corruption that had marked the final Panchayat years: as an aide to a senior Congress politician admitted, 'commissions' and bribes that had gone to a relatively small circle now had to be shared out more widely. This became increasingly true with the coalition governments after 1995. In addition, as in Western democracies, fighting (and winning) elections was expensive, the difference being that money went not so much on advertising as on recruiting and maintaining as large a number of party workers as possible. Even if an individual politician could control his private acquisitiveness, he was often expected to make money for his party coffers, as Chandra Prakash Mainali later admitted he had done when minister of supply in the 1994–5 UML government.

Outside the towns, where their activities were less open to the scrutiny of a well-developed 'civil society', the electoral process itself could be corrupted. The party in power sometimes put improper pressure on the officials supervising the polls and was certainly always suspected by its opponents of so doing: it was for this reason that the UML began arguing that all-party administrations should be mandatory for the period of election campaigns. In addition, where any one party was considerably stronger than the others, activists would sometimes use their numerical superiority to take over polling stations and not allow supporters of other parties to vote freely. These practices were less common than the supporters of losing parties made out and the correspondence between opinion poll predictions and actual results showed that elections did roughly represent the state of feeling in the country. However, four months after the 1999 election, a reputable Kathmandu newspaper reported a Congress minister's admission that polls in the 1999 election had been rigged in 10 per cent of the cases, and that while he himself had rigged them in one village, his UML opponent had rigged them in another![5] Such practices contributed to an atmosphere of mistrust and to the belief that it was sensible to break the rules when one could get away with it, as the other side would certainly do so.

Since political campaigns were to some extent financed and run on criminal lines it was not surprising that regular criminals were drawn into the nexus. This had long been a problem in Indian politics, particularly in the state of Bihar bordering the eastern Tarai, and talk of the 'Biharisation' of Nepalese politics became commonplace during the 1990s. One conspicuous example of the trend was Mirja Dil Sad Beg, whose border constituency (adjoining Uttar Pradesh rather than Bihar itself) was not far from the Buddha's birthplace at Lumbini. Admitting to a criminal record, though claiming to have acted as a protector of the local community against criminals from India, Beg was elected on the Sadbhavana ticket in 1991, but by 1993 he was denouncing this Tarai regionalist party as communalist and claiming to have Congress sympathies. In 1994 he retained his constituency standing as a National Democratic Party candidate and was briefly an assistant minister when Sher Bahadur Deuba was desperately trying to shore up his administration at the beginning of 1997. Beg was shot dead in Kathmandu in June 1998, apparently on the orders of a Bombay gang leader for whose rival he was believed to have worked earlier. The crowds at his funeral confirmed that he retained a considerable following in his home area but, for most educated Nepalese, his career served only to deepen cynicism even further.

THE RISE OF THE ULTRA-LEFT

The 'People's War' launched by the CPN (Maoist) in early 1996, and from 2001 presenting the Nepalese state with its most urgent problem, could be seen in one sense as an extension of the criminal practices just outlined, with the insurgents not just trying to bend the rules of the system but to replace them altogether. At another level a principal cause of the conflict, as of so much else, was the widespread poverty that continued to afflict Nepal. However, neither explanation is a sufficient one. Also important were complex factors in the history of the country and the communist movement, as well as the fragile balance of power that had emerged from the 1990 'People's Movement'.

The area of the mid-western hills that was the Maoists' original power base had long been a site of leftist activism. During the 1950s Mohan Bikram Singh, as the Communist Party's district secretary for his home district of Pyuthan and then as a central committee member, had worked tirelessly to build up support. He was particularly successful with the village of Thawang in neighbouring Rolpa, where in the general election of 1959 all but 3 of 703 persons on the electoral roll voted Communist. During the Panchayat years, the villagers maintained their allegiance to the left, and in the 1980 referendum no votes were cast there in favour of the Panchayat system. Communist support grew in the surrounding area of north-eastern Rolpa and eastern Rukum district, fuelled by various local grievances, particularly the decline in living standards, which the inhabitants reportedly ascribed to the government's suppression of hashish production in the 1970s.[6] The people of this area were mostly Kham Magars, who spoke a very different dialect from that of the southern Magars (see p. 14) and who, unlike the latter, had largely retained their original language and religious practices rather than switching to Nepali and becoming Hinduised. This height-ened their sense of alienation from the Nepalese state and, following Mao Zedong's own example in pre-Second World War China, Mohan Bikram played the ethnic card from early on, with a special stress on minority rights in the platform of the Fourth Convention group he established in 1974. When open political activity again became possible in 1990, the area was thus an obvious one for the radicals to concentrate on.

By this time, the original Fourth Convention had splintered into three different factions. Mohan Bikram Singh's own group, the Communist Party of Nepal (Masal), maintained total opposition to parliamentary politics and boycotted the 1991 election, but his erstwhile followers, Pushpa Kumar Dahal (known as Prachanda) and Nirmal Lama, formed the United People's Front (UPF) to contest it. The UPF was simply the electoral vehicle for the Unity Centre, the underground party into which Lama and Prachanda had merged their own groups in 1990 and which another of Singh's lieutenants, Baburam Bhattarai, joined just before the 1991 polls. The nine seats the UPF won included both the constituencies in Rolpa district and one of the two in Rukum. Prachanda and Bhattarai were both Brahmans, but the UPP's Rukum MP and one of those for Rolpa were Magars while the party's other MPs included three Tamangs and one Thakali. This made the party's MPs a much more ethnically representative body than those of most other Nepalese parties.

Although the UPF members took up their seats in the House of Represen-tatives, their declared aim was merely to 'expose' the parliamentary system's inadequacy rather than to seek to join a government, and in November 1991 their party conference endorsed Prachanda's policy of achieving 'new people's democracy' through a 'People's War'. Many in other Nepalese Communist factions also proclaimed a belief in the indispensability of violent revolution yet continued to engage in more peaceful political activity, and until 1994 the UPF concentrated principally on street agitation, often in concert with other groups. The theory was that, as in 1990, enough disorder could be created on the streets of the capital to pressure the government into concessions. Within the UPF/Unity Centre, however, Nirmal Lama and his allies were coming under increasing pressure from Prachanda and Bhattarai, who probably had the greater number of activists loyal to them, and a formal split came in May 1994. In theory the dispute was over Lama's willingness to continue 'making use' of parliament and the others' wish to move towards 'People's War', but another factor may have been fear that Lama himself was becoming too popular in the united party.

Following the split, only the three MPs from Rolpa and Rukum sided with Bhattarai, the UPF's convenor, and the Election Commission accepted the claim of Lama's followers to be the legal continuation of the party. Bhattarai's group were thus no longer recognised as a 'national party' and, as well as being unable to use the old name, they had no guarantee that all their candidates would be issued with the same election symbol. In March 1995, Prachanda's wing of the Unity Centre formally renamed itself the Communist Party of Nepal (Maoist) and renounced participation in elections.

The party's intention to launch their 'People's War' was not kept secret, and in autumn 1995 as part of preparation for this an extensive propaganda and recruitment campaign was organised in Rukum and Rolpa. Since 1991, and especially after the UPF had gained control of local government in the area in 1992, there had been tension between Congress and UPF workers, and the Congress side had generally been supported by civil servants and policemen responsible to the normally Congress central government. Now more serious clashes occurred between Maoists and both Congress and NDP workers and in November a large-scale police operation was ordered by Sher Bahadur Deuba's newly installed administration. This was understandable, given the Maoists' publicly proclaimed intention to launch a rebellion, but police action was indiscriminate and brutal enough to increase local resentment against the government as well as insufficiently sustained to act as a real deterrent. On 2 February 1996, Bhattarai handed the government in Kathmandu a list of forty demands, including not only an end to police excesses but also measures such as the abrogation of major treaties with India, the declaration of a secular state and the election of a constituent assembly. The document was in effect a party manifesto, but the Maoists stated that they would take up arms if the government did not respond positively before 17 February. The ultimatum was probably intended for public relations purposes rather than in the expectation of genuine negotiations, and they launched their first attacks on police stations and government offices on the 13th, four days before it expired.

There has been much speculation on whether this slide into civil war might have been halted if Bhattarai's group had been recognised as the true UPF in 1994, if there had been no police atrocities in autumn 1995 or if Deuba's government had responded to the Maoists' ultimatum in February 1996. However, the Maoists would still have faced the problem that they were a relatively small group with little hope of competing effectively at national level unless they were content to act as a junior partner to the main force on the left, the UML. Fundamentally, they saw violence as a chance to increase their influence in remote areas where they were organisationally strong and, in the longer term, a chance to regain the leading position on the Nepalese left which the old Mohan Bikram Singh group had once held but then lost during the 1980s.

Over the next three years, the Maoists slowly extended their influence over wider areas of the countryside, concentrating particularly on Rolpa, Rukum and the districts of Jajarkot and Salyan which bordered them on the west. The task was made easier because these areas were not of crucial economic importance and were only weakly penetrated by the Nepalese state. Neither Rolpa or Rukum had any motorable roads until those to the district headquarters were competed by the army in 2002 and 2003 respectively. In the past the government had relied on a small number of local 'big men', who owed their status partly to state patronage but were also chosen partly because they were already influential. Social control was maintained by these individuals and also through the self-regulating mechanisms of village communities. In western Nepal, such people had generally worked within the Panchayat system but switched allegiance in 1990 to Congress. Their role as (relatively) large landowners and often also money-lenders meant that many of their poorer neighbours feared opposing them openly but might welcome their removal by a force from outside the village. The process was not, however, a simple one of 'class war', since one village faction or clan might align itself with a political party simply to gain support against a rival group. Thus a quarrel within a Kham Magar village which might before have been settled within the village could now end with the killing of a villager as a 'class enemy', whatever his actual economic status. Furthermore, in the Kham areas, there were no really big landlords and inequality was less than in many other parts of the far western hills.

The Maoists worked hard to put their political message across at village level and stressed in particular opposition to the caste system and to the subordination of women. This brought a response, especially from the most disadvantaged groups, but they did not, of course, need to secure mass backing to become a powerful force in a district. Once there was a significant minority of dedicated supporters, the threat of violence was enough to ensure the majority's acquiescence. In this way the insurgents had the best of both worlds. They tapped into a reservoir of frustration with the status quo but they could also rely on the old tradition of submission to authority. Concerned principally with day-to-day survival, the peasant understood that to be safe he must not anger the local Maoists just as once he could not anger the village's largest landowners. The philosophy was expressed seven years later by an inhabitant of the northern district of Jumla: 'We obeyed the Ranas and during the Panchayat we did what we were told. Democracy came and we followed. Tomorrow there may be another system and we will have to listen to them too. We can never say we won't obey.'[7]

Logistically, the Maoists relied in the first place on local resources, gradually collecting weapons from their raids on police, and financing themselves through bank robbery and extortion. When landowners were driven away, or chose to flee, those who continued to work the land now paid the Maoists the landlord's share, often at the 50 per cent rate that had long been common in the hills. In addition, the insurgents collected funds from sympathisers among the Nepalese community in India and also established links with Indian Maoist groups operating in Bihar and Andhra Pradesh. Baburam Bhattarai had been a student at Jawaharlal Nehru University in Delhi and president of the All India Nepali Students' Association, while Prachanda may possibly have once been a negotiator on behalf of Darjeeling tea workers in 1988.[8] Finally, there was moral support from RIM, an international Trotskyist grouping that Mohan Bikram Singh's Masal had helped establish in London in 1984 and to which Baburam Bhattarai had served as representative.

In responding to the insurgency, the state was hampered in several ways. First, the Nepalese police enjoyed little respect among the civilian population. Policemen were recruited centrally and thus did not normally enjoy close ties to the community in which they were stationed. As throughout

South Asia, police training was poor, pay extremely low and corruption endemic; they tended often to respond to threats by lashing out more or less at random. The Maoists, too, used outsiders to carry out actual acts of violence, but they had a reliable network of local sympathisers to act as their eyes and ears, and their coercion was more precisely targeted. As a result, many in the affected areas regarded both sides as unwelcome intruders, but the Maoists as less disruptive.

Secondly, the army, which in Nepal had been immediately employed against any armed opposition before 1990, was not directly controlled by the elected government. It was in theory under the National Defence Council, consisting of the army's own chief of staff, the prime minister and the defence minister; this was normally a two-man body since until 1999 the prime minister in Congress governments retained the defence portfolio. In practice, the army looked to the king who thus had a de facto veto upon its deployment; in this case Birendra was reluctant to let it become involved. This was partly through genuine unwillingness to use it against Nepalese citizens except as a last resort, but probably also because he himself, or those around him, saw the insurgents as a useful tool against the politicians who had forced him to yield power in 1990. Initially, the government itself was also in no hurry to use the army because it was unsure whether the soldiers could be trusted once out of barracks. All of this had most likely been factored into the Maoists' calculations in 1996.

Thirdly, political parties not in government and also educated Nepalese in general, were reluctant to see full use made of the security forces. There was genuine concern at the civilian casualties a full-scale crackdown might entail but also unwillingness among politicians to see state power enhanced if they were not themselves in control of that power. The left-wing parties in particular were in a difficult position. They were unhappy with the Maoists' tactics, especially in the case of the UML, whose cadres were sometimes victims of Maoist violence. However, there was broad sympathy with the Maoists' long-term aims and, since at village level political workers might see themselves as 'leftists' rather than as belonging exclusively to one particular faction, there was also the danger that other parties' activists might find themselves targeted in any anti-Maoist drive. As a result, except when the party was itself in government with the NDP in 1997, the UML joined the rest of the left in calling for negotiations and protesting alleged police brutality.

Over the first two years of the Maoist insurgency there were intermittent declarations by both the government and the rebels that they were willing to negotiate, but no talks were actually arranged and violence continued at a fluctuating level. The Maoists called for a boycott of the summer 1997 local elections and tried to enforce it by intimidation and assassinations, especially of Congress candidates. In the four districts forming the Maoists' main stronghold, polls were postponed until the autumn and even then no proper contest could be held in many village development committees. By early 1998 the rebels had set up their own 'People's Committees' in some VDCs with representatives of other political parties allowed (or required) to take part, but with those the Maoists deemed 'feudals' excluded. When Girija Koirala returned to power in April he at first made another failed attempt at negotiation and then in May launched the Kilo Sierra 2 police operation, which caused heavy casualties among the Maoists but also among non-combatants. A report by a Nepalese NGO claimed that from February 1996 to December 1998 409 deaths had been caused by the security forces (334 in 1998 alone) and 129 by the Maoists (75 in 1998).[9] The Nepalese press was now generally accepting a total of 800 deaths.

In a general atmosphere of violence and intimidation, it was difficult to know how much popular support the rebels really had. However, in autumn 1998 a government intelligence report was said to have forecast that should the Maoists agree to contest elections they would probably get twenty to twenty-five seats. In March 1999 another report claimed that they had the allegiance of around 25 per cent of the electorate in Gorkha, Baburam Bhattarai's home district. In the event, the Maoists again called for a boycott of the May 1999 general election but made little attempt to disrupt it, perhaps because they wished to build up their strength after losses suffered the previous summer. By the end of the year the police estimated that the Maoists had 5000–6000 full-time cadres with another 8000 sympathisers supporting them. Three-quarters of Nepal's seventy-five districts had been infiltrated and twenty-one were 'strongly affected'.

A DEEPENING CRISIS: 1999–2003

When Krishna Prasad Bhattarai, who had headed the 1990–1 interim government, became prime minister again in May 1999, Congress held a clear parliamentary majority and his position was not shaken by the row with an opposition again alleging fraud at the polls. However, he faced a graver threat from his own party president, Girija Koirala, who had agreed to Bhattarai getting the premiership only as a manoeuvre to keep the party united for the general election. Infighting recommenced almost immediately, and in March 2000, Koirala's supporters, who were a majority of the parliamentary party, forced K. P. Bhattarai out, allowing Koirala himself to take control of the government once again.

Koirala gave as one of his reasons for supplanting his old colleague his failure to improve the security situation. In the summer of 1999 some senior police officers had begun saying privately that they were now unable to cope, and after the election the police began abandoning smaller police stations in Rukum, Rolpa and Jajarkot. It was at this point that deployment of the army would have ensued immediately in most countries, and, following an attack on a police post in Rukum in September in which seven policemen were killed and a deputy superintendent taken prisoner, Bhattarai appeared to be considering this. However, the palace and even Girija Koirala appeared unready for such a step; the army itself was suggesting that an all-party consensus would be required first. In January, after nine policemen died when another post was overrun, Bhattarai announced that a special Armed Police Force would be set up to combat the insurgents. At the same time he was eager if possible to open negotiations, and in December 1999 Sher Bahadur Deuba was placed in charge of a special commission for this purpose. Prachanda did respond positively to this in February, but there was again a failure to agree detailed arrangements.

Koirala's new government appeared no more successful than Krishna Bhattarai's. Despite preliminary contacts made first by Deuba and then by veteran leftist Padma Ratna Tuladhar and an anonymous Western intermediary, full negotiations did not get under way. The Maoists stepped up their extortion schemes and began targeting in particular the country's private schools, whose abolition was one of the forty demands they had presented in February 1996. By the end of 2000, one teacher claimed that 90 per cent of such schools in the Valley were paying regular 'protection' money. In areas where the Maoists were strong, they had already for some time been demanding cuts from the salaries of government schoolteachers and also preventing the teaching of Sanskrit and the singing of the national anthem, which expressed loyalty to the king. They now also began setting up 'people's governments' at district level: the first two were inaugurated in Rukum and Rolpa in December 1999. In addition, a cult of personality around Prachanda seemed to be developing: in February 2001, the Maoists' second national conference declared him party chairman and also formally made 'Prachanda Path' its official doctrine.

The most dramatic development, however, was the temporary seizure by the insurgents in September 2000 of Dunai, headquarters of the remote Himalayan district of Dolpa, which borders Rukum to the north. The Maoists killed fourteen policemen and made off with 50 million rupees

16. The ruins of the police station at Rukumkot, which was overrun by insurgents
in April 2001.

from the bank. The money was far in excess of Dunai's normal needs and
the Maoists had delayed their attack for three days until the plane bringing
the cash from Nepalganj in the Tarai had arrived, so there was suspicion of
collusion by bank or government employees. Controversy centred, however, on the local army garrison's failure to come to intervene during the
fighting or to send reinforcements earlier. The home minister publicly
denounced the lack of co-operation but was subsequently compelled to
resign.

In parallel with continuing attempts at negotiation, army companies
were now deployed in all district headquarters, and Girija went ahead with
plans to set up the Armed Police Force mooted by Bhattarai the previous
year. Following attacks on two regular police posts at the beginning of April
2001 that killed seventy policemen, the government announced plans for
an Integrated Security and Development Programme, which would involve
the army taking responsibility both for law and order and for development
projects in selected districts. The plan was agreed by the king only with
some reluctance, and it was rejected by most of the opposition parties, while
the army chief made a speech suggesting they were ready to carry it out

only if backed by a strong national consensus. Koirala was in the meantime under considerable pressure from Deuba's supporters within his own party, while opposition parties had been boycotting parliament since February and protesting in the streets to demand his resignation over alleged corruption in the leasing of an aircraft from Lauda Air for the RNAC. Koirala was on the verge of resignation in May when the central anti-corruption body, the Commission for the Investigation of the Abuse of Authority (CIAA), requested an explanation of his conduct, but he was persuaded by his inner circle to hang on.

It was at this point that a bizarre tragedy put Nepal at the centre of world attention for a few days. On the evening of 1 June, members of the royal family assembled at the Tribhuvan Sadan, a small complex of buildings just inside the west gate of the Narayanhiti Palace, for their regular monthly gathering. Towards 8.30 p.m. Crown Prince Dipendra, who had been drinking whisky, appeared intoxicated and was helped to his room by Paras, son of King Birendra's brother Gyanendra, and other relatives. Dipendra was there handed cigarettes laced with a 'black substance' (possibly cocaine), which he had instructed an orderly to bring before leaving the hall. A few minutes later, two servants went to his room, after a close friend, Devyani Rana, alarmed by his slurred speech on the telephone, had alerted his aide-de-camp. They found Dipendra lying on the floor and helped him to the bathroom, but he then ordered them to leave. At around 9 p.m., Dipendra reappeared in the hall wearing combat dress and carrying an array of weapons including a sub-machine gun and an automatic rifle. After shooting his father, he withdrew but returned twice to open fire again. In the space of a couple of minutes he killed outright or fatally injured King Birendra himself, the king's daughter Shruti, brother Dhirendra, sisters Shanti and Sharada, and niece Jayanti, as well as Sharada's husband, Kumar Khadga. Also hit, though not fatally, were Gyanendra's wife Komal Shah, Shruti's husband, Gorakh Bikram Shah, another of Birendra's nieces, Ketaki Chester, and his youngest sister, Princess Shoba. Paras Shah was present in the hall throughout but escaped unhurt, having pleaded with Dipendra not to shoot, and assisted some of the family to hide behind a sofa.

When the shooting began the royal aides-de-camp had been in a room adjacent to the main hall but the connecting door was locked. They moved along the outer corridor towards the entrance which Dipendra was using but fear of coming under fire themselves prevented them from entering by that route. As they finally got the connecting door into the hall open and began tending to the casualties, more shots were heard from the garden

17. King Birendra and Queen Aishwarya in 1990 with their children Princess Shruti, Crown Prince Dipendra and Prince Nirajan (standing in front of them).

between the hall and Dipendra's own quarters. The crown prince had been followed out into the garden by his mother, Queen Aishwarya, and his brother, Nirajan; he apparently shot both of them before turning a handgun on himself. He was taken with the other victims to the Birendra Military Hospital at Chauni, seven minutes drive to the west of the royal palace.

18. King Gyanendra at his formal enthronement on 4 June 2001.

While Birendra was declared dead on arrival at the hospital, Dipendra was still breathing and was placed on a life-support machine. The following morning, following both royal custom and the strict letter of the constitution, the State Council declared the unconscious Dipendra king and appointed as regent his uncle, Gyanendra, who had been brought back from a visit to Pokhara. Detailed accounts of Dipendra's involvement in the massacre, based on non-attributable briefings by palace insiders, had already appeared but Gyanendra announced that the killings had been caused by the 'discharge of an automatic weapon' and the word 'accident' was used in English translations and by the royal press secretary Chiran Shamsher Thapa in a BBC TV interview.

At 3.45 p.m. on Monday 4 June Dipendra died in hospital. Gyanendra was proclaimed king a few hours later and, formally ascended the throne at Hanuman Dhoka palace.[10] It was the second time he had gone through the ceremony, since as a young boy he been placed briefly on the throne by the Ranas in 1950 after Tribhuvan and the rest of his family fled to India (see pp. 71–2). On advice from the state council, Gyanendra immediately set up a commission of inquiry, chaired by the chief justice with a Congress politician, Taranath Ranabhat, and opposition UML leader Madhav Kumar Nepal as members. Although Nepal himself may have been the one who suggested the need for an inquiry rather than a simple announcement of Dipendra's guilt,[11] he was instructed by his party not to serve on the commission. Ostensibly, this was because they felt the inquiry should have been set up by parliament rather than by the king and his advisers. The other two members went ahead with the report, which was released at a press conference on 14 June. It consisted mostly of statements from witnesses, without an attempt to reconcile all discrepancies over timing, but did establish the main sequence of events as outlined above.

The stories circulating immediately after the shooting all linked Dipendra's actions to a clash with his mother over his wish to marry Devyani Rana, the daughter of Pashupati Shamsher Rana, a grandson of the last Rana maharaja and now a leading NDP politician. Queen Aishwarya was supposed to have been particularly hostile to the match but differing explanations were offered for this. One was Devyani's Indian connections: she was a granddaughter of the late raj mata (queen mother) of the old Maratha princely state of Gwalior in western India and had relatives in senior positions in both the Indian National Congress and the Bharatiya Janata Party.[12] Another was caste considerations, including Devyani's descent on her mother's side from C-Class Rana stock and also the supposedly inferior status of Maratha royalty, who were not the genuine Rajputs the Nepalese royal family believed themselves to be. A third possible factor was rivalry between the Juddha branch of the Ranas, to which both Queen Aishwarya and the queen mother belonged, and the descendants of Chandra Shamsher, Devyani's great-great-grandfather. Others claimed that Aishwarya was worried that women in Devyani's family had borne female rather than male children or simply believed that Devyani herself would be too independent. King Birendra was also opposed to the match as, probably, were most others in the royal family. Prince Paras told the inquiry commission that he and Dipendra's younger brother Nirajan had both supported Dipendra, but other sources suggest that Nirajan had later turned against Devyani because her mother was perceived as pushing too hard for the match.[13]

The official inquiry revealed that Dipendra, who had had a passion for guns, had been allowed to take any weapons he liked from the palace armoury and keep them in his room. It also became clear that he had had problems with both drugs and alcohol and, despite his affable public persona, had had a cruel side to his nature. When one remembers the sadistic behaviour displayed by two earlier members of his family, King Rana Bahadur and King Surendra, it becomes quite plausible that resentment against his family did suddenly swell up into murderous rage. Although it appears strange that he could have carried and used accurately so many weapons when a short while earlier he was apparently incapacitated by drink, cocaine is a stimulant which can temporarily offset some of the effects of alcohol. Finally, the fact that the bullet entered Dipendra's head from the left is not inconsistent with self-inflicted injury, since he had regularly practised using guns with both hands.

However, the chief justice's inquiry was tasked only to establish what had happened in the palace on 1 June and did not delve fully into the wider background. In addition, it was never established why it was decided to cremate the royal victims without full post-mortems and the person who might have made the decision, Queen Mother Ratna, was not called to give evidence to the inquiry. As calls for a fuller investigation were ignored, rumours and speculation inevitably continued to flourish. One theory, popular even among some of those with close connections to the Rana–Shah aristocracy, was that Dipendra was indeed the murderer but had planned his actions in advance and intended to declare himself king. According to this version, a failure of nerve or sudden remorse, perhaps after the particularly horrific shooting of his mother, resulted in his final suicide.

In contrast, a majority of Nepalese at the time believed (and many still maintain today) that Dipendra was not the murderer and that the whole affair had been arranged by Gyanendra and/or his son Paras. This belief stemmed from Nepal's long history of court intrigue, from the fact that the massacre brought Gyanendra to the throne, and from the personal unpopularity of both father and son. Described by one foreign academic as 'the brightest, the sharpest and the meanest of the three brothers', Gyanendra had certainly used his official position to make money. In addition, he was thought to have been one of the palace hard-liners urging his brother Birendra to stand firm against protests both in 1979 and 1990. Paras, characterised by one acquaintance as a 'charming, womanising, gun-toting thug', was disliked even more.[14] The previous summer, a vehicle he was believed to be driving while drunk collided with a motorcycle, killing the rider, a popular singer, and there was a large demonstration calling for his royal immunity from prosecution to be lifted. Although another man later came forward and claimed to have been at the wheel, belief in Paras's guilt remained widespread, especially as he had been involved in similar incidents twice before.

In all the circumstances, suspicions were natural, yet, as far as the palace massacre was concerned, almost certainly unfounded. First, there was no solid evidence to back them up, and secondly many of the reasons for doubting the official version were also even stronger reasons for doubting any of the conspiracy theories. Why should any hired assassin weave in and out of the hall three times instead of mowing down all the intended targets right at the beginning? Even if the supposed conspirators had been able to find someone who physically resembled Dipendra (more plausible than supposing all of the royal survivors lied to the inquiry), how could they have been confident the likeness was sufficient to fool family members at close range? And why could they not have arranged a more straightforward terrorist-style attack that could easily have been blamed on the Maoists? Since nobody actually witnessed Dipendra's own death, there does indeed remain a possibility that he was himself actually shot by his younger brother's aide-de-camp, as yet another rumour maintains. A fresh and full inquiry into the whole affair would nevertheless be most likely to confirm the official version of events within the Tribhuvan Sadan.[15]

As with the assassination of President Kennedy and the death of Princess Diana, conspiracy theories are very difficult to lay to rest, and in summer 2001 what mattered most politically was what people believed. Realising this, the Maoists, though themselves unsure of what had really happened, immediately accused Gyanendra of responsibility and alleged he had been part of a plot involving the American CIA and the RAW (the Indian intelligence service). An article by Baburam Bhattarai published in *Kantipur* called on the army to refuse to accept Gyanendra as king and resulted in the newspaper's publisher and editor being briefly detained. A statement issued by Prachanda similarly depicted the massacre as an 'imperialist' blow against the Maoists and claimed that Birendra had been killed for his refusal to allow full deployment of the army against them. There were violent demonstrations on the streets of Kathmandu, involving youths with heads shaven in the traditional style of Hindu mourning. Some of them may have been genuine royalists, but others were most probably Maoist sympathisers who hoped to take advantage of the situation, especially after Baburam Bhattarai had claimed in his article that there had been an 'undeclared working unity' on some matters between Birendra and his own party. Tight security measures nevertheless ensured that the government's position was never seriously threatened.

Although failing to spark an urban uprising, the Maoists nevertheless kept up pressure in the countryside, killing forty policemen on Gyanendra's birthday in July and then abducting another sixty-nine five days later from Holleri in Rolpa district. Koirala now wanted the army to intervene to release them and thought he had the agreement of both Gyanendra and

19. *Naulo Bihani*, a magazine sympathetic to the CPN (Maoist), makes political capital
out of the June 2001 palace massacre. Below a montage of the kings of the Shah dynasty
are shown three Maoist leaders, Prachanda, Krishna Bahadur Mahara and Baburam
Bhattarai. The caption reads: 'After the palace massacre the end of traditional
monarchy in Nepal and the establishment of a republic – preparation of the central
people's government'.

the army commander-in-chief. Troops were helicoptered in and were at first reported to have surrounded the rebels and their captives but the result was a stand-off, with the army commander on the spot apparently deciding he would not be able to use force without the risk of heavy casualties. The policemen were subsequently released by the rebels in batches but in the meantime Girija Koirala submitted his resignation to the king and his Congress rival, Sher Bahadur Deuba, took over.

The Maoists had backed away from peace talks earlier in the year partly because they wished to see if the campaign to remove Koirala, always a particularly resolute foe of the left, would succeed. They responded positively to Deuba's declaration of a ceasefire and three rounds of talks were held between August and November. During his time there were no major clashes between rebels and security forces, but arrests continued and the extortion of money by the Maoists if anything increased, as they now had easier access to urban areas. Although they backed down from earlier insistence on an immediate end to the monarchy, they were still demanding a constituent assembly, and when the government ruled this out Prachanda announced withdrawal from the negotiations. Two days later, on 23 November, the Maoists broke the ceasefire with attacks that for the first time targeted the army as well as the police. In a successful attack in Dang in the western Tarai, they killed over a dozen soldiers and seized a large quantity of weapons. They also announced the setting-up of the 'United Revolutionary People's Council of Nepal' under Baburam Bhattarai. In response, the government declared a nationwide state of emergency and the army was at last fully deployed against the rebellion.

The next fourteen months proved militarily indecisive. The combined strength of the army, regular police and expanding Armed Police Force was over 100,000 as against an estimated force of 5000–10,000 trained guerrillas. The rebels also had the support of a large 'militia', and the security forces had to commit a large proportion of their strength to the defence of fixed positions. Army operations inflicted a large number of casualties but it was unclear how many of these were actual Maoist fighters, how many supporters and how many innocent civilians. By concentrating their forces, the rebels were sometimes able to overrun government positions, as happened at Mangalsen, district headquarters of Acham district in the far western hills in February 2002 and at Sandhikharka, headquarters of Arghakhanchi south-west of Pokhara, the following September. Over 200 army and police personnel died in the two raids. The Maoists accompanied these set-piece attacks with sabotage of the country's infrastructure, including telecommunications installations, local government buildings and hydro-electric plants. The Maoist top leadership, some of whom were believed to have been at least some of the time in Kathmandu over the past five years, now appeared to be in hiding across the open border in India, where the rebels also sought treatment for their injured. But although the Maoists remained the most influential force at village level over much of the country, there seemed no prospect of their being able to take and hold for longer than a few hours even small towns, let alone Kathmandu itself.

Politically, despite disquiet over the security forces' tendency to shoot first and ask questions afterwards, the rebels' action in provoking an extended conflict at first kept parliament largely behind the government. When the state of emergency required ratification in February 2002, a few days after the Mangalsen attack, UML as well as Congress, NDP and Sadbhavana MPs voted in favour. Opposition came only from the minor Communist parties – including the National People's Front (the parliamentary vehicle for Mohan Bikram Singh's Masal Party), the United People's Front and the Nepal Workers' and Peasants' Party, which between them had just seven seats in parliament. From February onwards, however, both the UML and those within Congress opposed to Deuba became increasingly unhappy with the continuance of the emergency, which allowed the army to operate independently of control by the civilian chief district officers. For its part, the army felt it was not getting adequate co-operation from the political parties; ill-feeling was exacerbated by reports (later confirmed) that Koirala and another Congress leader had met the Maoist leader Prachanda in Delhi in March 2002. When the state of emergency came up for renewal again in May, the party organisation ordered Deuba to let it lapse. However, he responded by requesting and obtaining a dissolution of parliament and the holding of elections in November. The emergency was then reimposed by executive ordinance and Congress formally split. When the Election Commission provisionally ruled that Koirala's group was the legal continuation of the original party, Deuba's faction adopted the name Nepali Congress (Democratic).

Deuba's reason for insisting on the emergency was unclear since parliament had already in April 2002 passed a robust Special Powers Act. Possibly he was under pressure from both the palace and the army to ensure the latter's continuing insulation from day-to-day control by civilian officials. However, the dissolution was probably not merely to remove the prospect of the emergency being voted down. Deuba seemed to have been afraid that Koirala and UML leader Nepal were planning to combine against him. In addition, both men had already been discussing amendments to the constitution and Deuba was concerned that the prospect of an attempt

20. Masked Maoist fighters posing for the camera. The female fighter in front is wearing
a scarf emblazoned with the names (and images of) 'Jack' and 'Rose', a rather
unrevolutionary reference to the film *Titanic*.

to reduce royal powers might provoke the king himself into a pre-emptive takeover.

The feasibility of November polls was always in doubt and, after the successful Maoist attack on Sandhikharka in September, Deuba secured the main political parties' agreement to their postponement. Constitutionally, the election had to be held within six months of a dissolution, but Article 127 of the 1990 constitution authorised the king 'to remove difficulties' in its operation. At the beginning of October, Deuba accordingly asked Gyanendra to put the elections back a year to November 2003 and allow his caretaker administration to remain in power until then. Gyanendra responded by dismissing Deuba for failure to hold elections as originally planned, and announced that he was temporarily taking full executive powers himself. He asked the political parties for nominations for a caretaker government but, when they could not agree on a common recommendation, turned instead to Lokendra Bahadur Chand, the trusted royal servant who had been prime minister twice under the Panchayat system and also in 1997. In all this, Gyanendra maintained that he was acting in accordance with Article 127 and that the constitution was still fully operational. In effect, however, power had returned to the royal palace, where it had lain between 1951 and 1990, apart from the interlude of B. P. Koirala's 1959–60 government. The move seemed initially to be welcomed by many ordinary Nepalese, mainly because of widespread disgust with the party politicians. For the longer term, however, polarising the country between royalists and Maoists was a dangerous step both for Nepal and for the monarchy itself.

Informal contacts between the royal regime and the rebels led to a second ceasefire in January 2003, brokered by Narayan Singh Pun, a government minister, who, like the rebels' military commander, Ram Bahadur Thapa, was a Magar. Small-scale violations of the ceasefire by both sides nevertheless continued, and the atmosphere was soured when the Maoists claimed in May that the government had reneged on a commitment to restrict the army to a five-kilometre radius from its bases. The rebels finally withdrew once again from the peace process shortly after the army's apparent execution of nineteen of their cadres arrested in eastern Nepal. The real reason for the breakdown was, however, the Maoists' continuing insistence on a constituent assembly and the government's unwillingness to concede this.

After renouncing the ceasefire in August, the rebels appeared for a time either unwilling or unable to repeat their earlier large-scale attacks on government positions. Although two such assaults did occur in March 2004, targeted killings and ambushes were now the favoured tactic, a trend already indicated by the assassination in Kathmandu of the chief of the Armed Police Force together with his wife and bodyguard just before the January ceasefire had been agreed. By the end of 2003, the conflict had resulted in around 10,000 deaths, the bulk of them since the rebels first attacked the army in October 2001, while at least 100,000 people had fled their homes. The government was proposing to set up a network of 'village defence forces' to counter the Maoists at grassroots level, a step which in other countries had proved effective against insurgencies, but which also greatly increased the danger to the civilian population.

In the meantime, the political parties, except for the National Democratic Party and some smaller factions such as Sadbhavana, were effectively sidelined. Even before the royal takeover, Deuba had effectively ended local democracy by refusing to extend the tenure of existing local bodies, which were mostly controlled by the UML. He transferred their powers to civil servants rather than prolonging their life when it was decided that local elections, due in summer 2002, could not be held as scheduled. The crisis did, though, bring some increase in co-operation between parties. Bamdev Gautam and his followers returned to the UML in January 2002, and in July the United People's Front and the National People's Front merged to form the People's Front. Both these factions, like the Maoists, derived from Mohan Bikram Singh's old Fourth Convention and Singh himself was now once again their accepted leader.

In May 2003, the People's Front, the Nepal Workers' and Peasants' Party and one faction of Sadbhavana joined the two main parties, Congress and the UML, in a campaign of protest against the royal takeover, demanding the formation of a multi-party government or the restoration of the dissolved 1999 parliament. Just as in 1990, Lokendra Bahadur Chand tried unsuccessfully to entice the parties into an expanded government under his leadership. He resigned at the end of May and his place was taken by the other key figure in the National Democratic Party, Surya Bahadur Thapa. The five parties had jointly proposed the UML leader, Madhav Kumar Nepal, as leader of a multi-party administration, but the king rejected this, ostensibly on the grounds that the NDP and Deuba's Nepali Congress (Democratic) had not also approved the choice. Sources close to the palace also suggested that M. K. Nepal would have been unacceptable to one or more foreign powers, or that his cadres were too sympathetic to the Maoists, but the king's wish to keep the reins of power firmly in his own hands was probably the major consideration. Whatever rationales were produced, the fact remained that Koirala's Congress Party had the support of around half of the former Congress MPs and almost certainly a majority of Congress activists. He and M. K. Nepal thus between them clearly represented a majority of the parliamentary forces and so, by rejecting their proposal, Gyanendra showed a determination to rely on the monarchy's own traditional support base rather than forge a broad consensus to confront the crisis.

The international ramifications of the conflict were complex. The initial Maoist attack on the army in November 2001 came only a few weeks after the destruction of the World Trade Center in New York. This timing, in addition to the Maoists' declared ideology, would have ensured full US backing for the government in Kathmandu, even if Deuba's administration had not also formally declared the rebels 'terrorists' – a label which was removed during the ceasefire in 2003 but then re-imposed. The Maoists responded by branding the Nepalese government an American puppet and trying to exploit tensions between the United States and other major powers as they had long exploited tensions between the palace and the political parties. They ceased their denunciations of 'Indian hegemonism' and claimed instead that American logistical and diplomatic support for the government, which continued after Deuba's dismissal, threatened the interests of both India and China.

India's own attitude was not entirely clear. Particularly in view of the links between the Nepalese Maoists and similar groups in India itself, the Indian government regarded the rebellion as a security threat and had in fact started describing the Maoists as 'terrorists' even before the Deuba administration did so. In addition, despite all the publicity over American arms aid to Kathmandu, India was still supplying the Nepalese army with the bulk of its equipment. Nevertheless, many in Nepal pointed to the use of Indian territory by the rebels, and to meetings between Maoist leaders and Nepalese politicians at Siliguri in West Bengal in August 2001 and in spring 2002, several months after the ceasefire had broken down. To some extent, such meetings reflected a lack of capacity on the part of India, rather than deliberate decision, since areas where Maoists chiefly took refuge were often ones where law and order had long been a problem for the Indian government. As the fighting continued, India seemed to be making greater efforts to tighten security near the border. However, some in the Indian establishment did appear to see direct American aid to Kathmandu as a threat to its own regional dominance. Perhaps also some hoped to make the price of full support for the Nepalese government compliance with India's wishes on other matters. This had been the tactic India adopted in 1990 when it pressed the beleaguered Panchayat regime to acknowledge Nepal's inclusion in India's security sphere (see p. 115).

Attitudes varied among Nepal's other main aid donors. China expressed support for the government and condemned the Maoists' use of Chairman

Mao's name, but, as had generally been the case since the 1960s, did not want to play a major role. Most European countries were more worried than the United States about the human rights abuses committed by the security forces, and although a major sale of Belgian small arms to the Nepalese army did go through in 2002, it caused a political crisis within the Belgian government. The British government's line was somewhere between that of the United States and that of most mainland European countries, providing some assistance to the Nepalese army but stressing the human rights aspect more than their American allies.

Despite their differences of emphasis, no government wanted a Maoist victory. Success for the armed rebellion in Nepal might result in instability that could affect both India and China and would also encourage radical groups in other countries across the world with similar problems to Nepal to follow the Maoists' example. Foreign governments generally also wanted a negotiated settlement rather than a fight to the finish but a negotiated settlement would naturally reflect the relative strength of the two sides and would be difficult to achieve as long as both sides felt that continuing the conflict would increase their bargaining power. Both the government and the rebels also understood that many Nepalese, wanting peace and security rather than any particular political outcome, would be likely to give their support to whichever side appeared to be winning.

The constituent assembly issue, on which peace talks twice foundered, was so crucial precisely because it was symbolic of victory or defeat. Simply because the Maoists had been demanding it for so long, securing it would be a signal to the country that they were now truly setting the agenda. For that same reason, the two major parties had been unhappy with the idea and wished to preserve the constitutional order achieved through the 1990 'People's Movement' that they themselves had headed.[16] It was only after the October 2002 royal takeover that significant numbers of people within the UML and Congress warmed to the constituent assembly proposal, and even at the end of 2003 the dominant sentiment in the two parties still remained opposed. On similar logic, Gyanendra was unlikely to agree to the proposal unless the monarchy's position were guaranteed in advance, as the Maoists made no secret that their aim was to use a constituent assembly to achieve a republic.

Even if some compromise formula, such as an expanded version of the 1990 Constitution Drafting Commission, proved acceptable, agreement on the composition of an interim government and on the future of the Maoists' guerrilla force would be another stumbling block. While coy about the exact arrangements they envisaged, the Maoists expected a controlling say, if not actually the formal leadership of an interim government, and also hoped to dominate the round-table conference of political forces they were also calling for. Perhaps most crucially, they wanted either a merger of their forces with the Royal Nepal Army or the replacement of both with some new form of 'People's Militia'. None of this was likely to be acceptable either to the monarchy and the major political parties, or to the army. At the beginning of 2004 there seemed in consequence to be two most likely scenarios. The government's position would slowly strengthen through continued American and Indian support, and perhaps also by some kind of accommodation between the palace and the main parties. Constitutional amendments would be discussed with the rebels, resulting in their re-entering the political process without total loss of face but clearly not as victors in a civil war. The alternative would be for the conflict to continue indefinitely, with the rebels still controlling some areas, the government holding major centres, and much of the country in the grip of warlords or gang leaders nominally aligned with one side or another but in effect running independent fiefdoms. The question would then be how long foreign powers, in particular India, could live with such a situation.

THE FUTURE OF NEPALESE SOCIETY

Destructive as the 'People's War' had been, it should not be allowed to obscure the many other trends operating in Nepal after 1990. Even after the escalation of the violence in 2001, the chance of any one individual being killed or injured is still considerably lower than in many other parts of the world. Before then, opinion polls showed that the average Nepalese thought the problems of unemployment and corruption, not civil war, were the most urgent ones facing the country.

To a large extent, Nepalese society has continued to develop on lines already laid down before 1990. The gulf between town and village remains wide and Kathmandu's special position was highlighted by a December 1998 World Bank report: 'Urban Kathmandu Valley and the rest of Nepal, in effect, are two separate and unequal countries . . . In one, around the capital, where around 5 per cent of the population live, the incidence of poverty is around 4 per cent and illiteracy is 24 per cent; in the rest of the country, poverty is ten times as high and the chance of being literate almost three times lower.'[17] As the 'People's War' intensified, Maoist extortion became a problem even in Kathmandu and arrests of journalists and political activists more frequent, but the concentration of security forces in the Valley has ensured that it has not become a battleground as might villages or small towns elsewhere in the country. Apart from military checkpoints along the ring-road, and clusters of soldiers at some strategic intersections in the city, the average visitor to Kathmandu still sees little sign of the national emergency, unless their visit happens to coincide with one of the *bandhs* or shutdowns called by the Maoists.

The range of goods and services on offer in Nepal's cities continues to expand rapidly. Innovations such as the Internet and mobile phones, as well as further growth in the electronic media, have naturally affected Kathmandu and other major centres more strongly, but the spread of electrification and of the road network has made them available to some in the more prosperous villages. The same can be said of the continuing growth in print and electronic media. The establishment of private sector national dailies, in particular *Kantipur* and its English-language sister publication, the *Kathmandu Post*, together with the arrival of private FM radio and TV channels, have ended the public sector's former dominance of the mass media. Newspapers of any sort are still slow to reach outlying areas, but many of these are now served by a vigorous and growing regional press.

While media developments have largely been positive, problems remain. Governments since 1990 have sought to influence the private press; after the declaration of emergency in 2001 actions against journalists and publications with real or supposed connections to the Maoists have escalated. It is likely that the situation would be even worse if the authorities did not have to worry about the effect on international opinion. While the most influential daily publications are not directly tied to specific parties, weekly publications often do toe a party line and, as before, remain 'viewspapers'. As in other countries, the battle for circulation produces journalistic excesses. The most notorious instance so far was the publication in 2002 of a photograph of a well-known film-star, taken without her consent and showing her semi-naked. Caught between the seedy realities of the film industry and the expectations of a still relatively conservative society, the actress shortly afterwards committed suicide.

Changing standards are also reflected in the increase in substance abuse among young people. The use of ganja (cannabis) has been widespread in Nepal for many centuries and the sale of the drug was in fact legal until banned under US pressure in 1973, but there is now growing use of heroin and also, as dramatically highlighted by the palace massacre, of cocaine. The growing consumption of alcohol has also sparked concern. There is a long-established tradition among the 'tribal' groups of drinking rice- and millet-based beer and spirits, as the old name for these groups – Matwalis (i.e. alcohol-drinkers) – attests. However, since 1990 the production of Western-style alcoholic drinks has boomed, and brewing and distilling now account for around 3 per cent of GDP. This trend has been opposed by a range of groups, including the Maoists, who see it both as a source of social problems but also as convenient issue for winning support from a wider prohibitionist lobby. In 2001 they attacked a number of breweries, and a women's organisation affiliated to them got the government to agree to restrictions on the industry (so far not implemented). In future, if calls for greater decentralisation are heeded, regulation of the commercial production and sale of alcohol may be left to local decisions, as already happens in many countries. However, the underlying problems of alienation and disorientation, evidenced in recent years by a growing problem of suicide among young people, will remain.

Particularly important in the towns has been the continuing expansion of private, English-medium education, which by 2000 was catering for around 20 per cent of the children in secondary schools across the country. The School Leaving Certificate pass rate for such schools averages around 80 per cent, compared with 30–40 per cent in the government institutions. The state-run schools were never particularly good, but politicisation after 1990 has eroded discipline and commitment among the teaching staff even further. Although there certainly are some dedicated professionals among them, teachers are often appointed because of their political connections and often concerned principally with politics. The two-tier system of education is, as has already been seen, a particular target of the Maoists, but has also been criticised by others who think that the private schools' curriculum is too closely modelled on Indian practice. However, any future restrictions on such schools in the interests of equality will penalise the middle class rather than the wealthy, since the latter will still be able to send their children to elite schools in India. The priority should obviously be on upgrading standards in public schools. The Norwegian-funded Basic Education Project, begun in 1991, has been a step in this direction, but real improvement will require the management problem in these schools to be addressed. Very recently, there have been signs of this starting to happen; both donors and government now do seem aware of the need to rebuild links between schools and communities broken when the NESP was set up in the 1970s.

A kind of de facto privatisation has also been under way in the management of development assistance, with foreign donors, and especially international NGOs, often opting to work directly with Nepalese NGOs. By 1997 these were believed to be between 20,000 and 30,000 in number

and the same year they received around \$150 million from abroad, com-
pared with an official aid total of around \$390 million.[18] Cynicism about
the motives and effectiveness of those involved is widespread among members of the intelligentsia not actually working for them, and fears are also
expressed that the state's capacity to co-ordinate and direct development
activities is being undermined. At least some of the NGOs have, however,
been making valuable contributions, for example in raising literacy levels
among the western Tharus, and at village level they are providing opportunities to local people for upward social mobility. Critics are right to point
out that a network of such organisations cannot be a substitute for effective
government institutions but in many cases they are an improvement on
what the government's own system can offer at the moment.

Foreign assistance through whatever channel continues to be of great
importance. During the 1990s Japan and then the Nordic countries were
the leading individual donors, with the World Bank the most important
of the multilateral agencies. The current crisis has increased the interest of
the major powers, particularly that of the United States, but also placed a
question mark over many programmes. Apart from the threat to the safety
of foreign personnel, the suspension of the democratic process and abuses
by the security forces have led some countries to suggest they may have to
curtail their activities. Yet, whoever provides assistance, Nepal's dependence
on it is likely to continue for many years. In 2000–1, it was still providing
around one-third of the government's total budget.

The number migrating within the country or crossing into India has
continued to grow, though it is hard to say how many of those crossing
the border in recent years have done so to escape the fighting and how
many for purely economic reasons. In contrast to the open access to India,
overseas employment normally requires prior payment of huge brokers' fees
and is thus usually an option only for those already relatively well off. The
number of Nepalese living outside South Asia (both legally and illegally) is
nevertheless very large: in 2003 an unofficial estimate put it at 1.2 million
in forty countries, including over 422,000 in the Middle East, 125,000 in
Malaysia and 80,000 in Korea.[19]

The economic importance of remittances from those working abroad
also continued to rise. According to official figures, these had reached US
\$240 million (4.4 per cent of GDP) a year by 2003, but money is mostly
sent back by unofficial channels, and the true total is probably at least
three times as large.[20] Opinions differ on whether dependence on this scale
is healthy, but this may be attributing too much importance to national
borders in an age of globalisation. The state of Kerala in southern India,
which has achieved relatively high levels of education and health care, is

also highly dependent on money sent back from those working outside the state. Should Nepal have to find jobs for all of its citizens within its borders simply because, unlike Kerala, it is a sovereign country?

While most Nepalese abroad are, by host society standards, in low-paid employment, some have done well by any measure. Kantipur Television, a commercial station which began operating in the Kathmandu Valley in summer 2003, was set up with 500 million rupees (US $6.7 million) capital provided by three Russia-based Nepalese expatriates. Taking its cue from the Indian government's wooing of affluent 'non-resident Indians', the Nepalese government hosted a conference for 'non-resident Nepalese' in Kathmandu later the same year. Some Kathmandu intellectuals were offended by the NRNs demand to retain their foreign passports while also being freed from the restriction on foreign ownership of businesses in Nepal, but the conference was a sign of the growing importance of the Nepali diaspora.

One very old link between Nepal and the outside world has, however, weakened with the rundown of Britain's Brigade of Gurkhas. Apart from a battalion on permanent loan to the Sultan of Brunei, the few Nepalese soldiers retained in the British army after Britain's withdrawal from Hong Kong in 1997 are now based in the UK itself. Nevertheless, there are still around 20,000 ex-servicemen in Nepal drawing British pensions. Shortly after the *janandolan*, the newly formed Gorkha Ex-Servicemen's Association[21] began to campaign for these pensions to be made equal to those received by native British soldiers. By agreement with India, Britain originally paid its own Nepalese soldiers at the same level as Indian Gorkha soldiers. After British Gurkhas were deployed in areas where the cost of living was much higher than in South Asia, special allowances were introduced bringing daily salaries into line with their British counterparts, but pensions are still based on the old pay rates. Court cases brought against the British government by GAESO and individual ex-Gurkhas have usually been unsuccessful, but the whole campaign signalled a change in attitude towards Gurkha recruitment by the Communist parties with which many in GAESO are associated. Having earlier simply demanded an end to the whole arrangement, they now still argue for some restrictions on the ways in which Gurkha troops are used but seem ready to accept its continuance on the right terms. In October 2003 a similar pragmatic attitude was displayed (at least for public purposes) even by a Maoist 'area commander'. While briefly detaining a British officer on tour at Baglung in the mid-western hills, he chose to lecture him not on the evils of imperialism but on the importance of recruitment being open equally to all castes and ethnic groups.

Even for Nepalese who remain throughout their lives in their native land, economic links with other countries are of crucial importance. An agreement in 1991 reduced to 60 per cent the proportion of 'Nepalese content' required for duty-free entrance into the Indian market; the 1996 agreement relaxed the restrictions further. Under pressure from its own industries, India nevertheless periodically finds pretexts for restricting imports of particular Nepalese exports, while in any case Nepalese enterprises find it difficult to compete with well-established Indian firms even in Nepal's own domestic market. If the plans for the establishment of free trade between the SAARC countries by 2006 are implemented, Indian dominance is likely to increase even further unless special arrangements are negotiated.

During the 1990s, the proportion of Nepal's trade with countries other than India stabilised at around 70 per cent. As before 1990, the ready-made garment and carpet industries remain the most important manufactured items exported. A decline in the mid-1990s, partly fuelled by concerns over child labour and pollution, was followed by a partial recovery and in 2000 around 150,000 were directly employed in the industries. However, these industries are overwhelmingly dependent on the American and German markets and maintaining sales in the United States will be difficult after the ending of the multi-fibre agreement in 2004 removes Nepal's guaranteed quotas. Even if the industries manage to maintain their current position, there is little prospect of Nepalese industry supplying jobs for more than a small proportion of Nepal's growing population, and those who do not choose temporary or permanent migration will still have to depend on agriculture for their living.

The Agricultural Perspective Plan, the centrepiece of current government policy, aims to boost agricultural productivity on similar lines as before, through the intensification of research and of extension services introducing new techniques to farmers. There is a special emphasis on temperate crops, especially fruit and vegetables, for which the Nepalese hills are naturally suited and which could, if collected and transported in time, find a ready market in northern India. There has in fact already been progress in this direction in the eastern hills (see ch. 5), though this has been jeopardised as the effects of the 'People's War' spread. A principal long-term objective, as in the regional planning approach of the 1970s, is to encourage the development of a network of small towns, dependent on the marketing and processing of agricultural produce but better able than the villages to provide both jobs and services for their inhabitants.

Debate continues over how far this growth-orientated approach should be supplemented by direct action to help the poor. One concrete reform measure, following a long campaign by activists from political parties and NGOs as well as political parties, was the freeing by Girija Koirala's government in July 2000 of the *kamaiyas*. Often ethnic Tharus, they or their ancestors had become bonded labourers after failing to pay off debts to wealthier neighbours. Their emancipation was an important milestone, and proof that change could be achieved by non-violent methods, but they are still left with the problem of earning a living now that their former masters are no longer responsible for feeding and sheltering them. A programme to distribute land to them has been launched but many remained squatters on cleared forest land, without acknowledged ownership rights.

A wider land reform still remains to be put into practice. Sher Bahadur Deuba's 2001–2 government put through parliament a bill reducing the ceilings on land ownership from 17 to 7 hectares in the Tarai and from 4.2 to 2.75 in the hills. The measure was opposed by a minority in Congress as too radical but rejected as inadequate by the UML, whose own inquiry into the problem six years previously had recommended an across-the-board 3-hectare ceiling. Applied nationwide, this lower ceiling would release 304,000 hectares for acquisition and redistribution.[22] Commercial operation of such small holdings would be impossible without adequate provision of credit and fertiliser, and also the exchange of plots on a large scale to consolidate scattered holdings. Implementing such a scheme would require a very high administrative efficiency, especially since, as in the past, families would probably try to avoid giving up land by registering it in the name of relatives or dependents. An alternative approach would be to leave land holdings much as they are and encourage organisation among landless labourers to ensure they get higher share of returns from agriculture. Some form of redistribution is virtually certain, whatever the outcome of the 'People's War', since landowners' influence in their own locality has been reduced by 'outsiders', whether Maoists or soldiers. In some areas, however, the conflict itself has left local elites with some bargaining power. In the western Tarai, the Maoists were reported to have given up attempts to force landlords to take only a third of tenants' crops, since insisting on this would make the former more likely to collaborate with the army.[23] In any case, without a dramatic increase in productivity, even a radical redistribution of resources will provide only a temporary respite. Without such an increase, the long-term solution can only be accelerated migration from the hills towards the Tarai, where allowing the clearing of remaining forest could still release substantial new land for settlement.

Another question for agriculture in Nepal, as in the developing countries generally, is setting the balance between specialisation in cash crops in which the country has a comparative advantage and the encouragement of food self-sufficiency at national or local level. The first strategy offers a chance of higher immediate returns, but many environmentalists argue that it may jeopardise food security if a collapse in export earnings should occur. It is doubtful, however, that any extreme form of autarky would be feasible, and part of the solution must involve some degree of specialisation.

The problem of resources and their distribution is also bound up with the continuing ferment over the religious and ethnic issues which generated so much heat during the drafting of the 1990 constitution. The principle of 'reservations' – quotas for disadvantaged groups – in public employment has now been conceded by all the major parties and, as in India, is likely to play a major part, for good or ill, in Nepal's future politics. In contrast, attempts by local authorities in the Kathmandu Valley and in the east-central Tarai to make their working languages Newar and Maithili respectively were ruled unconstitutional by the Supreme Court in 1998. Activists' demands for education, at least at the primary school level, to be provided in the mother tongue have also not been met, although a government-appointed commission in 1993 recommended this, and there have been some experiments such as a Japanese-funded school in Kathmandu using Newar as the medium of instruction and also some use of Limbu in the eastern hills. The generally slow rate of progress increased resentment at the government's 1993 decision (recently reversed) to make Sanskrit, particularly associated with Brahmans, a compulsory school subject. Languages other than Nepali have, however, been granted greater recognition and the seventeen most widely spoken among them are now regularly heard on the radio.[24] This has helped spread an interest in the language issue beyond the core of committed activists; one campaigner suggested this actually helped Indian Maithils secure the inclusion of Maithili at the end of 2003 in the list of principal languages in the Indian constitution. A greater role for at least some of Nepal's languages is likely in future, and would be in line with the trend seen in Western Europe to reinforce the status of languages such as Catalan or Welsh. However, the global trend is still towards the elimination of smaller languages, and this is also true in China, despite the theoretical commitment to ethnic minority rights that was a feature of the Chinese Communist Party's propaganda before they gained power.

The most radical ethnic demand, endorsed by far left groups including the Maoists, is for different ethnic groups to be granted autonomy on their own territory. At the end of 2003, the Maoists did actually declare an autonomous Magar region centred on their stronghold of Liwang in Rolpa, and this was followed by similar moves for other regions in early

2004. How far this was merely a propaganda move is uncertain, but in any case any comprehensive plan for ethnic autonomy would involve enormous difficulties, because in most districts no single caste or ethnic group constitutes more than half the population (see map 3, p. 100). The only practical solution would be a cantonal system, devolving greater power to villages dominated by one particular group. Since there is agreement across the political spectrum on the need for greater decentralisation once the present crisis is over, this may be the route finally taken. It will be supplemented by some form of guaranteed representation at the centre, most probably by converting the Upper House of parliament into a 'House of Nationalities' as has long been advocated by many ethnic activists.

The demand for Nepal to be declared a secular rather than a Hindu state is at heart an ethnic/caste issue since Hinduism for many symbolises the perceived domination of the high-caste Parbatiyas. After 1990 the proportion of these groups in the legislature, particularly the figure for Brahmans, actually increased, as did the proportion of Brahmans in the senior ranks of the civil service. This is matched by the entrenched position of Brahmans in the hierarchies of the political parties, which in turn reflected the high proportion of Brahmans among the college students from whom political activists were largely recruited. This is likely, however, to be only a temporary blip as the lower castes become increasingly assertive. The trend is a general one across South Asia, beginning before the Second World War with the anti-Brahman movement in South India and felt increasingly in recent years across the areas of North India bordering on Nepal. There was never any possibility that Nepal could remain unaffected by this general movement, and Marxist ideology, seen in its most virulent form in the Maoist movement, is now hastening the end of Hinduism's hierarchical value system.

Less dramatically, Hinduism and other indigenous beliefs are also being undermined by the spread of Christianity. It is possible that in some cases the expansion of one new ideology may be aiding another: one scholar has suggested that clandestine missionary work among the Chepangs may have made them more receptive to Marxist ideas later on.[25] The 2001 census showed a threefold increase in the number of Nepalese Christians from around 30,000 (in 1991) to 100,000. However, both disgruntled Hindus in organisations such as the Hindu Vishwa Parishad and Christians themselves suggest that the latter figure is an underestimate; in any case in certain areas, including some of the 'Tamang belt' north of the Kathmandu Valley, a significant proportion of the population has converted. The process has already led to tension in some villages, though not on the scale of the Hindu/Muslim disturbances that occasionally occur in the Tarai. The majority of Nepalese are still content to accept the 'Hindu' label, but claims from other groups will become increasingly strident and Hinduism itself will have to change fundamentally.

Beyond the immediate issues of Maoist rebellion and ethnic discontents, Nepalese society has to find some way of taming the no-holds-barred struggle for supremacy that operates across the political spectrum and in virtually every institution. This has been displayed in the corruption and instability under the parliamentary system, in the Maoists' own decision to launch their 'People's War' and in many of the actions of the security forces in response to it. There is, of course, no way to guarantee that civil servants will never be improperly influenced by their personal political allegiance or that policemen will see themselves as upholding the law rather than acting as enforcers for particular politicians or local strongmen. However, some way must be found to reduce the present very high levels of politicisation and also to make resource distribution itself dependent on rules, or even on random selection, rather than on the whims of individuals. Constitutional change might go some of the way to achieving this, but the key problem remains not so much the inadequacy of existing rules as a general failure to abide by them and a lack of trust in any institutions that may be set up to enforce them.

Achieving a less personalised and more rule-bound system depends in the long run on increasing the numbers of people who are ready to take an interest in public affairs without requiring an immediate return for themselves. Paradoxically, however, it may depend in the short term on the leadership provided by personalities at the top. Despite the grave weakening of the institution's prestige by the events of 2001, there could still be an important role here for the monarchy, but the king would need to broker agreement among the politicians rather than use their divisions to retain political power in his own hands. Without the monarchy, the burden would be entirely on the shoulders of whatever new political leadership emerged. There would, however, be the grave danger of a Nepalese republic developing on Pakistani lines, with an unstable balance of power between the army, the political parties and (in place of Islamic militants) the Maoists or whatever new extremist group emerges in future.

The role of the gun in Nepalese politics has become increasingly important both because of the Maoists opting for armed revolt and because of the army's increased influence as it takes the lead in countering them. The Maoists' proposal to merge their own guerrilla force with the army will probably not be accepted, but, were it to go ahead, Nepal might find itself saddled with a very large standing army. This would be a continuing drain on resources and also under continuing temptation to intervene in politics. Demobilisation and reintegration into civilian life, though also initially expensive, would be a preferable solution. Alongside this, if it proved politically feasible, consideration might be given again to an old proposal for Nepalese to serve as soldiers in a standing United Nations force.

The search for a solution to these and other deep-seated problems in inextricably bound up with the world beyond the country's borders. Outside influences have always been important in Nepal, even when its policy was avowedly one of self-isolation. Unless the Nepalese themselves now find better ways of settling their own differences, control over their affairs will slip even further into foreign hands, despite the continuing strength of nationalist feeling within the country. Nepal's emergence into the postcolonial world as an independent state was not preordained but the result of a chain of historical accidents. These included both the emergence of a leader of the calibre of Prithvi Narayan Shah at a crucial point in the seventeenth century and also his successors' ability in the following century to adapt sufficiently to the realities of British dominance in South Asia. The country is bound particularly closely to the rest of the region, and particularly to the areas of India that lie, like Nepal itself, east of the line between Delhi and Cape Comorin. The problems of poverty, casteism and corruption found throughout South Asia are here particularly acute: Bihar, for example, if it were not part of India, would be as close as Nepal itself to inclusion on a UN list of failed states. It is questionable whether Nepal can make substantial economic progress without significant development in these adjoining areas. It is even more certain that the political influence of India on Nepal will remain crucial. Throughout Nepal's history, there has been a tendency to beat the anti-Indian drum when in opposition but to seek a closer relationship when in power. This can be seen to some extent in the behaviour of different court factions in the late sixteenth and nineteenth centuries, in party politics since 1951 and also even the Maoists' abandonment of their anti-Indian rhetoric when they decided to take on the Nepalese army in 2001. Despite the statements sometimes made by political mavericks, few Indian politicians are eager to resume full responsibility for Nepal's problems, and the country's formal independence is likely to continue. However, the strength of the reality behind that formal façade remains to be determined.

Genealogical Tables

The Shah dynasty

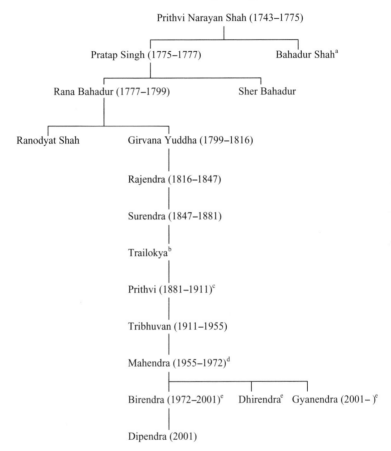

Prithvi Narayan Shah (1743–1775)

Pratap Singh (1775–1777)   Bahadur Shah[a]

Rana Bahadur (1777–1799)   Sher Bahadur

Ranodyat Shah   Girvana Yuddha (1799–1816)

Rajendra (1816–1847)

Surendra (1847–1881)

Trailokya[b]

Prithvi (1881–1911)[c]

Tribhuvan (1911–1955)

Mahendra (1955–1972)[d]

Birendra (1972–2001)[e]   Dhirendra[e]   Gyanendra (2001–)[e]

Dipendra (2001)

Notes:
Kings of Gorkha before the unification of Nepal are omitted; names of kings are followed by their regnal years.
[a] Regent for his nephew, Rana Bahadur, from the death of the king's mother in 1785 to 1795.
[b] Married three of Jang Bahadur Rana's daughters, one of whom became the mother of King Prithvi.
[c] Married two daughters of Bir Shamsher Rana but another wife (from India) was the mother of King Tribhuvan.
[d] Married two granddaughters of Juddha Shamsher Rana.
[e] Married a great-granddaughter of Juddha Shamsher Rana.

The Rana (Kunwar) family

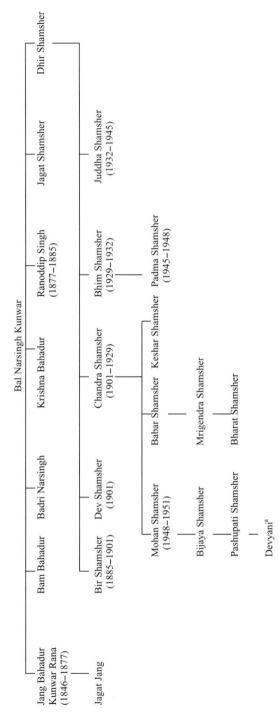

Notes:

Names of maharaja–prime ministers are followed by their years in office. The table omits many individuals who played only a minor historical role. The descendants of Dhir Shamsher normally used 'Shamsher Jang Bahadur Rana' as their full, formal surname.

[a] The woman whom Crown Prince Dipendra reportedly wished to marry despite his parent's opposition.

Biographical notes

Acharya, Tanka Prasad (1910–92): Founding president of the anti-Rana Praja Parishad. As a Brahman he escaped the death penalty when arrested in 1940 but was kept in prison until the end of the Rana regime in 1951. He served as home minister in M. P. Koirala's 1952–4 coalition government and as prime minister in 1956–7, but his party gained only two seats in the 1959 election. He campaigned for the multi-party system ahead of the 1980 referendum and during the 'People's Movement', after which he formally revived the Praja Parishad but did not contest the 1991 election.

Adhikari, Man Mohan (1920–99): Born in Kathmandu but raised in India, he was active in the Communist Party there from 1942 to 1947. A founder member of the Communist Party of Nepal in 1949, he was secretary-general from 1951 to 1956. Imprisoned 1960–9 following King Mahendra's takeover, he later headed his own group, which united with Sahana Pradhan's in 1987 to form the CPN (Marxist). From 1991 he was president of the CPN (Unified Marxist-Leninist) and led the 1994–5 minority government. He died during the 1999 election campaign.

Bhandari, Madan (1952–93): Founder member of the Communist Party of Nepal (Marxist-Leninist) in 1978 and secretary-general from 1989 until his death. An 'underground' worker until the end of the 'People's Movement' in 1990, he was de facto leader of the CPN (Unified Marxist-Leninist) after its formation in 1991 by the merger of his old party and the CPN (Marxist). He was the author of the revised line of 'multi-party people's democracy' formally adopted by the UML in 1993. He died in a controversial accident when the jeep in which he was travelling plunged into a river in May 1993.

Bhattarai, Baburam (1954–): Born in Gorkha district, he was an outstanding student in Nepal before going to India, where he obtained his Ph.D in 1986 and became prominent in left-wing politics amongst the Nepalese community. After returning to Nepal, he was spokesman for the far-left UNPM in the 1990 'People's Movement'. In 1991, he became convenor of the United People's Front, the electoral front for the Unity Centre and, after the 1994 split, a leading member of the CPN (Maoist), frequently acting as its mouthpiece and leading its negotiators in the 2002 peace talks.

Bhattarai, Krishna Prasad (1924–): A founder member of the Nepali Congress, he participated in the 1950–1 anti-Rana struggle. Speaker of the 1959–60 parliament, he was imprisoned after Mahendra's takeover. He was president of Congress from 1976 to 1996 and a member with Girija Koirala and Ganesh Man Singh of the unofficial troika entrusted with party leadership by B. P. Koirala before his death in 1982. He headed the interim government of 1990–1 but failed to win a seat in the 1991 election. He was prime minister again in 1999–2000 but then was ousted by Girija Koirala.

Bijukche, Narayan Man (Comrade Rohit) (1940–): Leader of the Nepal Workers' and Peasants' Party (formerly Nepal Workers' and Peasants' Organisation). He was an early advocate of infiltrating the Panchayat system, his faction gaining control of Bhaktapur town panchayat in the 1980s and putting up candidates successfully in the 1981 and 1986 Rastriya Panchayat elections. After the 'People's Movement', he remained dominant in Bhaktapur town and his party gained four seats in the 1994 election, but he himself was the only member of his party to retain a seat in 1999.

Bista, Kirtinidhi (1927–): A one-time Congress activist, who chose to work in the Panchayat system from 1961, holding numerous ministerial posts, including that of prime minister in 1971–3 and 1997–9. In 1992 he joined M. P. Koirala in setting up the Rastriya Janata Parishad, of which he became vice-president and later president, but the party failed to win parliamentary representation.

Buddha (Siddhartha Gautama) (c. 400–320 BC): Born at Lumbini in what is now the central Nepalese Tarai, he was the son of a chieftain of the Shakya tribal confederacy. He abandoned his wealth and position to seek a cure for human suffering and began his career as a religious leader after attaining enlightenment whilst meditating at Bodhgaya in Magadha (modern Bihar). The legends claiming that he travelled to the Kathmandu Valley are almost certainly false but his followers subsequently brought Buddhism into the Nepalese hills, from where it was transmitted to Tibet.

Chand, Lokendra Bahadur (1939–): Born in Baitadi district in the far west, he became active in Panchayat politics in 1964 and was prime minister in 1983–8 and again for eleven days at the height of the 'People's Movement' in April 1990. In May 1991 he set up the National Democratic Party (Chand), which formed a frequently troubled union with Surya Bahadur Thapa's similarly named party in 1992. He headed a coalition government with the UML in March–October 1997. He was again prime minister for seven months after the dismissal of the Deuba government in November 2002.

Deuba, Sher Bahadur (1946–): Born in the far western Dadeldhura district, he was home minister in the 1991–4 government and headed the Congress-NDP-Sadbhavana coalition government in 1995–7. He became prime minister again in July 2001 and attempted to negotiate with the Maoists, but imposed a state of emergency after the rebels attacked the army in November. With his position under threat from Koirala's faction, he dissolved parliament in May 2002 and later set up the Nepali Congress (Democratic). He was removed from office by King Gyanendra in October 2002.

Gautam, Bamdev (1948–): Pyuthan-born politician, who became a leading opponent within the UML of Secretary-General M. K. Nepal. He was a chief advocate of an alliance with Lokendra Bahadur Chand's wing of the NDP and served as Chand's deputy in the March–October 1997 coalition government. In 1998, together with veteran party dissident G. P. Mainali, he broke away from the UML to re-establish the CPN (Marxist-Leninist). He rejoined the UML in 2002, afterwards allying himself with M. K. Nepal's new rival, Khadga Prasad Oli.

Giri, Tulsi (1926–): A veteran of the 1950–2 struggle and a protégé of B. P. Koirala, he was a minister in the 1959–60 government but resigned in August 1960. After Mahendra's takeover, he became a prominent Panchayat politician, serving as chairman of Council of Ministers in 1961–4 and prime minister in 1975–7. He left Nepal for Sri Lanka in 1986 and moved to South India in 1991.

Khapangi, Gore Bahadur (1945–): Born in Udayapur in eastern Nepal, he was originally a leftist activist but in 1990 set up the Nepal Rastriya Janamukti Morcha (Nepal National People's Liberation Front) to champion the rights of the non-Parbatiya hill peoples. He was electorally unsuccessful but in 2002 became one of two Magars included in the Chand government following Gyanendra's October takeover.

Koirala, Bishweshwar Prasad (B. P.) (1915–82): Educated in India, where his father fled after offending Chandra Shamsher Rana, he played the leading role in the setting-up of the Nepali Congress. After the 1950–1 armed movement, he became home minister in the 1951 Congress–Rana coalition. The party's chief ideologue, he headed the 1959–60 Congress government and was then imprisoned until 1968 after Mahendra's takeover. He subsequently organised armed resistance from India but later returned to Nepal to oppose the Panchayat system peacefully.

Koirala, Girija Prasad (1925–): Younger brother and comrade-in-arms of B. P. Koirala, he led the Congress government elected in 1991 but was weakened by internal disputes and lost the mid-term 1994 general election he himself had called. He became party chairman in 1996, and prime minister again in 1998–9. He assisted his rival K. P. Bhattarai to become prime minister after the 1999 election but ousted him in 2000. He was himself replaced by Sher Bahadur Deuba as premier in 2001 and clashes between the two led to a formal split in Congress in 2002.

Koirala, Matrika Prasad (1912–97): Elder half-brother of B. P. Koirala, he was less popular in the Nepali National Congress but became party president as part of the agreement for merger with the Nepali Democratic Congress in 1950. He was appointed head of the 1951–2 Congress government on King Tribhuvan's insistence but quarrelled with B. P. and in 1953 set up his own Rastriya Praja Party, which was in government in 1953–5. He later rejoined Congress but supported King Mahendra after 1960. He helped set up the Rastriya Janata Parishad in 1992 but did not regain influence.

Lama, Nirmal (1930–2000): Fought in the 1950–1 revolt against the Ranas and joined the Communist Party in 1951. In 1974 he helped Mohan Bikram Singh to set up the Communist Party of Nepal (Fourth Convention) but later expelled him from the organisation. He was one of the drafters of the 1990 constitution and in November merged his party in the Unity Centre, which, as the United People's Front, was third-largest party in the 1991 parliament. Following a split in the party in 1994, Lama remained senior leader of the Unity Centre whilst former colleagues set up the CPN (Maoist).

Mainali, Chandra Prakash (1953–): A member of the Jhapeli group which assassinated 'class enemies' in the early 1970s, he was secretary-general of the Communist Party of Nepal (Marxist-Leninist) from its foundation in 1978 to 1982. After the formation of the CPN (UML) in 1990, he unsuccessfully opposed Madan Bhandari's reformist policy of *bahudaliya janbad*. He was briefly a minister in the 1994–5 UML government but left in 1998 to set up the CPN (Marxist-Leninist). He refused to rejoin the UML when his colleague Bamdev Gautam did so in 2002.

Malla, Jaya Prakash (d. 1769): Last Newar king of Kathmandu, he fought a long and ultimately unsuccessful battle to prevent Prithvi Narayan Shah's conquest of the Valley kingdoms. After the fall of Kathmandu he took refuge with Prithvi Narayan's one-time ally, King Ranjit Malla of Bhaktapur and died of wounds received when the Gorkhalis captured the town in 1769.

Malla, Jayasthiti (d. 1395): An Indian (probably Maithili) prince who married into the politically important Bonta family and became master of the Kathmandu Valley in 1382. His reign saw a strengthening of Hindu orthodoxy in the Valley and also the compilation of the *Gopalarajavamshavali*, the oldest surviving Nepalese *vamshavali* (chronicle).

Manadeva (fifth century AD): Licchavi king of the Kathmandu Valley and surrounding hills. In 465 erected a statue of Vishnu at the temple of Changu Narayan north of Bhaktapur with an inscription recording how he dissuaded his mother from dying on his father's funeral pyre and then consolidated his own power by defeating rebellious feudatories.

Mishra, Bhadrakali (1921–): A minister in the Congress–Rana coalition and, after he had first set up his own Nepal Tarai Congress, in M. P. Koirala's 1953–5 government. He switched to Tanka Prasad Acharya's Praja Parishad but then led one faction of the party in a split in 1958. His Praja Parishad (Mishra) won only one seat in 1959 and after Mahendra's takeover he became a prominent member of the Nepali Congress in exile.

Nepal, Madhav Kumar (1953–): Born in the Tarai district of Rautahat, joined Pushpa Lal Shrestha's faction of the Communist Party in 1966 but became a founding member of the CPN (Marxist-Leninist) in 1978. Became secretary-general of the CPN (UML) in 1992, following the death of Madan Bhandari and was deputy prime minister in the 1994–5 minority UML government. Put forward in April 2003 as consensus candidate for prime minister by the five-party alliance formed to oppose King Gyanendra's takeover.

Pande, Damodar (1751?–1804): A successful military commander in Nepal's wars of expansion, he led the opposition to Rana Bahadur Shah in Kathmandu at the turn of the eighteenth century and pursued a policy of alliance with the East India Company. He was executed on Rana Bahadur and Bhimsen Thapa's return to Nepal in 1804.

Pande, Ranjang (1778?–1843): Son of Damodar Pande, he led the opposition to Bhimsen Thapa as his power weakened in the 1830s. Although initially enjoying the sympathy of the British resident, he encouraged King Rajendra to follow an anti-British line and was removed from office under East India Company pressure in 1840.

Prachanda (Pushpa Kumar Dahal) (1956–): Born in Kaski district, but moving to Chitwan as a child, he became an underground communist activist in 1971. Worked with Mohan Bikram Singh in the Fourth Convention and then in Masal, but broke away in 1985 to set up Mashal. His new party merged with the Fourth Convention in 1990 to form the Unity Centre, which was part of the United People's Front. After a split in 1994 he set up the CPN (Maoist), which launched the 'People's War' in 1996. In 2001, he became chairman of the party and 'Prachanda Path' was adopted as its official ideology.

Pradhan, Sahana (1932–): Born in Kathmandu but spending part of her childhood in Burma, she was involved in leftist and feminist politics from the 1940s. Married Communist leader Pushpa Lal Shrestha in 1953 and took over leadership of his group on his death in 1978, merging it with another group in 1987 to form the CPN (Marxist). Chair of the United Left Front during the 1990 'People's Movement', she was a minister in the 1990–1 interim government. A central committee member of UML from January 1991, she joined CPN (ML) in the 1998 split but returned to the UML in 2002.

Pun, Narayan Singh (1949–): A former lieutenant-colonel in command of the Royal Nepal Army's helicopter wing, he was a minister in K. P. Bhattarai's 1999–2000 Congress government but later set up his own Nepal Samata Party. A member of the Chand government appointed after King Gyanendra's 2002 takeover, he played a key role in securing the January 2003 ceasefire with the Maoists. He led the government delegation in the peace talks but was removed after Chand's resignation in May 2003.

Rana, Bam Bahadur Kunwar (?–1857): Younger brother of Jang Bahadur Rana, he was appointed prime minister in 1856 when Jang resigned the office on being made maharaja of Kaski and Lamjung.

Rana, Bharat Shamsher (1925–): Grandson of Babar Shamsher Rana, the brother of Maharaja Mohan Shamsher Rana, he was a leader of the Gorkha Dal opposing the post-1951 government and was arrested in April on suspicion of planning a coup. He later worked constitutionally through the Gorkha Parishad, which formed the main opposition to Congress in the 1959–60 parliament. Following Mahendra's takeover, he merged the party with Congress and helped organise violent resistance to the royal regime until autumn 1962.

Rana, Bhim Shamsher (1865–1932): Succeeded Chandra Shamsher Rana as maharaja in 1929. He exacerbated tensions within the Rana family by including his illegitimate sons and grandsons on the Roll of Succession after Chandra had barred the addition of such individuals.

Rana, Bir Shamsher (1852–1901): Eldest of Dhir Shamsher Rana's sons, he was a leader in the Shamsher brothers' murder of their uncle Ranoddip Kunwar Rana and Jang Bahadur Rana's son Jagat Jang in 1885, after which he himself became maharaja.

Rana, Chandra Shamsher (1863–1929): One of the sons of Dhir Shamsher Rana, the youngest brother of Jang Bahadur Rana, he became maharaja in 1901. A capable administrator, but staunchly conservative, he supported Britain unreservedly both in its Forward Policy towards Tibet and later in the First World War. He was responsible for the formal abolition of slavery and of *sati* in Nepal. His palace complex, Singha Darbar, now houses the central government secretariat.

Rana, Dev Shamsher (1862–1914): A son of Dhir Shamsher Rana, he succeeded his brother Bir as maharaja in 1901, but his relatively liberal policies alarmed his remaining brothers and he was forced out of office by them after 114 days. He lived until his death in Mussoorie in the Indian Himalayas.

Rana, Dhir Shamsher (c. 1828–84): Youngest brother of Jang Bahadur Rana, whom he accompanied to Europe in 1850, he was the mainstay of the administration of Maharaja Ranoddip Kunwar Rana. His death removed the restraint on the rivalry between his own sons and the sons of Jang Bahadur, and thus paved the way for the 1885 Shamsher coup.

Rana, Jang Bahadur Kunwar (1817–77): In 1846, he was appointed prime minister following the Kot Massacre, in which his troops killed most of the other contenders for power. He engineered the replacement of King Rajendra by Crown Prince Surendra but kept real control in his own hands and secured the predominance of his own family, which assumed the name 'Rana'. He assumed the title of maharaja in 1856. Assisted the British in suppressing the Indian Mutiny in 1857–9, in return for which the western Tarai, ceded to the East India Company in 1816, was returned to Nepal.

Rana, Juddha Shamsher (1875–1952): One of the seventeen Shamsher brothers who seized power in 1885, he became maharaja in 1932. He abdicated in 1945, after the end of the Second World War, in which he had committed Nepal's manpower resources to the Allied cause, and spent the rest of his life in religious retreat in the Indian Himalaya. His statue at the end of Kathmandu's New Road commemorates his contribution to the rebuilding of the city after the earthquake of 1934.

Rana, Keshar Shamsher (1892–1964): Brother of Maharaja Mohan Shamsher Rana, he was perhaps the most capable of Chandra Shamsher Rana's sons. He fought hard to preserve the Rana regime but, after 1951, co-operated loyally with King Tribhuvan, his brother-in-law. He was an avid book collector and his personal library at Keshar Mahal is now open to the public.

Rana, Mohan Shamsher (1885–1965): Son of Chandra Shamsher Rana, he became the last Rana maharaja in 1948. Already known as a hard-liner, he sought to avoid major concessions to the anti-Rana movement through co-operation with India on security and trade matters but, following King Tribhuvan's flight to India, he bowed to Congress military action and Indian pressure by accepting the Delhi agreement of 1951. Served as prime minister of the Congress–Rana administration until its collapse in November 1951. Left Nepal soon afterwards and died in Bangalore.

Rana, Padma Shamsher (1883–1960/1): Son of Maharaja Bhim Shamsher Rana, he succeeded Juddha Shamsher Rana in 1945. Though wanting to preserve the Rana regime, he favoured political reform and with Indian assistance in 1948 adopted a constitution providing for a degree of popular representation. However, he lacked the determination to stand up against Chandra Shamsher Rana's more conservative sons and the same year he resigned and went into self-exile in India.

Rana, Pashupati Shamsher (1942–): Grandson of the last Rana maharaja, Mohan Shamsher Rana, and owner of the Nepal Gas Company, he was active in Panchayat politics from 1975, serving in several governments. Became secretary-general of the united NDP in 1992 and was minister of water resources in the 1995–7 Congress-NDP-Sadbhavana coalition. He became president of the NDP in December 2002. His daughter Devyani's relationship with Crown Prince Dipendra was an important factor in the prince's massacre of his family members on 1 June 2001.

Rana, Ranoddip Singh Kunwar (1825–85): Succeeded his brother Jang Bahadur Rana as maharaja and prime minister in 1877 and eased restrictions on British recruiting from Nepal. Assassinated in 1885 by his Shamsher nephews, who feared he would endanger them by restoring to favour Jang's son, Jagat Jang.

Rana, Rudra Shamsher (1879–1964): An illegitimate son of Maharaja Bir Shamsher Rana he became commander-in-chief on Juddha Shamsher Rana's accession in 1932 but was removed from the Roll of Succession by Juddha in 1934. He was subsequently made governor of Palpa in the central hills and defected with his troops to the Congress insurgents in January 1951.

Rana, Subarna Shamsher (1909–77): C-Class Rana son of Maharaja Bhim Shamsher Rana, he was a major funder of the Nepali Democratic Congress in Calcutta in 1949. After the merger with the Nepali Rastriya Congress in 1950, he had a key role in the 1950–1 anti-Rana movement, and was a minister from 1958 to 1960. He organised armed resistance after Mahendra's coup but called this off when China attacked India in autumn 1962. He reconciled with King Mahendra in 1968.

Rayamajhi, Keshar Jang (1926–): Born in Palpa, he studied medicine in Calcutta, where he joined the Nepal Communist Party in 1949. As the party's secretary-general, he welcomed King Mahendra's 1960 takeover. After a split with the radical wing of the CPN he continued as leader of his own, pro-Soviet faction and was elected to the Rastriya Panchayat in 1986. He was one of two royal representatives in the interim government after the 1990 'People's Movement'.

Regmi, Dilli Rahman (1914–2001): Born in Lamjung district, he was involved in anti-Rana protest as a student in Nepal and then in the Indian nationalist movement. Appointed acting president of the Nepali National Congress in 1947 after B. P. Koirala's arrest in Nepal, he refused to quit the post on B. P.'s release and continued as head of his own faction after B. P.'s larger group had been merged into the Nepali Congress in 1950. He served as a minister in two governments in the 1950s. Regmi was also the author of important but not very readable works on Nepalese history.

Shah, Aishwarya (1949–2001): Great-granddaughter of Maharaja Juddha Shamsher Rana, she married the then Crown Prince Birendra in 1970. Seen as a hard-liner, she became very unpopular at the time of the 'People's Movement', but her reputation recovered somewhat in the 1990s. Her opposition to Crown Prince Dipendra's wish to marry Devyani Rana was probably a key factor in the June 2001 palace massacre, in which she herself died. She wrote and published poetry under the name of Chandni Shah.

Shah, Bahadur (1757–97): Younger son of King Prithvi Narayan Shah, he acted as regent for his young nephew, Rana Bahadur Shah, continuing Gorkhali expansion westwards but provoking a Chinese invasion in 1792 by his aggressive policy towards Tibet. His attempt to secure British diplomatic support helped turn opinion among the courtiers against him and he was removed from office by Rana Bahadur in May 1791. He died in prison six years later.

Shah, Birendra Bir Bikram (1945–2001): Ascending the throne in 1972, he initially continued his father's system but, in response to disturbances in 1979, he called a referendum in which the electorate narrowly endorsed a liberalised Panchayat system rather than a return to multi-party politics. In 1990, he bowed to renewed demands for democracy, though retaining certain reserve powers, in particular de facto control of the military. He died in the June 2001 palace massacre, apparently at the hands of his son, Crown Prince Dipendra.

Shah, Dhirendra (1950–2001): Second of King Mahendra's three sons, he was an influential and reputedly hard-line adviser to his brother King Birendra but resigned his royal title in 1987 after his separation from his wife, Queen Aishwarya's sister, and also the involvement in criminal activity of members of his entourage. He was readmitted to court, though still as a commoner, in the 1990s and was rumoured to have been in contact with the Maoist insurgents on Birendra's behalf.

Shah, Dipendra (1971–2001): Elder son of King Birendra and educated, like him, at Britain's Eton College. He is believed to have clashed with his parents over his wish to marry Devyani Rana, the daughter of Pashupati Shamsher Rana and this, together with the effect of drugs, apparently led him to gun down most of the royal family before himself committing suicide on 1 June 2001.

Shah, Fateh Jang Chautara (?–1846): A *chautara*, or member of a collateral branch of the royal family, he was a political ally of British Resident Brian Hodgson against Ranjang Pande's anti-British faction in 1839–42. He died in the Kot Massacre.

Shah, Girvana Yuddha (1797–1816): Son of King Rana Bahadur Shah by a Brahman mistress, he became king on his father's abdication in 1799 but died in 1816 before he could take over control of the country from his stepmother Queen Regent Lalita Tripura Sundari Shah.

Shah, Gyanendra Bir Bikram (1947–): Youngest son of King Mahendra, he was briefly placed on the throne in 1950–1 after his grandfather's flight to India. He himself succeeded to the throne after the death of King Birendra and his family in the 2001 palace massacre. Following attacks on the army by Maoist rebels in November 2001, he agreed to full military mobilisation against them. In November 2002, he dismissed the government of Sher Bahadur Deuba and effectively reinstated palace control of the country.

Shah, Lalita Tripura Sundari (d. 1832): A junior wife of ex-king Rana Bahadur Shah, she became regent for his son Girvana Yuddha Shah after his assassination and helped Bhimsen Thapa (to whom she may have been related) to maintain control of Nepalese politics for the next twenty-five years.

Shah, Mahendra Bir Bikram (1920–72): Accompanied his father King Tribhuvan in flight to India in 1950 and in his return in 1951 and succeeded him in 1955. He permitted Nepal's first parliamentary election in 1959 but in December 1960 removed B. P. Koirala's Congress government. Helped by the outbreak of the Sino-Indian War in November 1962, he survived a guerrilla campaign against his regime and retained political control in his own hands with the Panchayat system of indirectly elected councils providing a limited façade of representative government.

Shah, Nirajan (1978–2001): Younger son of King Birendra, and reportedly his father's favourite. Apparently killed by his brother Crown Prince Dipendra in the June 2001 palace massacre.

Shah, Paras (1970–): Only son of King Gyanendra, he was spared by Dipendra during the June 2001 palace massacre and was formally declared crown prince in October 2001, despite evidence that he had on at least two occasions caused fatal accidents through drink-driving.

Shah, Pratap Singh (1751–1777): Son of and successor to King Prithvi Narayan Shah, he became king in 1775. Of a non-military disposition and interested in tantricism, his short reign was marked by tension between his favoured advisers and his father's older military commanders.

Shah, Prithvi Narayan (1722–75): Succeeded his father Narbhupal Shah as king of Gorkha in 1743 and established the modern Nepalese state by his conquest of the Kathmandu Valley kingdoms and of the hills as far east as the Tista River in Sikkim. Especially since his descendants recovered political control of the country from the Rana maharajas in 1951, he has been celebrated as father of the nation, but his role has become more controversial in recent years, with a growing debate on whether he should be seen as unifying or simply conquering the country.

Shah, Rajendra (1813–81): Became king of Nepal on the death of his father Girvana Yuddha in 1816. He took charge of the administration after the dismissal of Bhimsen Thapa in 1837 but, after the death of his senior queen in 1841, he was involved in a three-way power struggle with his junior queen, Rajya Lakshmi, and Crown Prince Surendra. This ended in 1847 when Jang Bahadur Rana replaced him with Surendra. Rajendra was arrested when attempting to raise support against the new regime and kept in comfortable confinement in Bhaktapur for the rest of his life.

Shah, Rajya Lakshmi (married 1824): Junior queen of King Rajendra, she appointed Jang Bahadur Rana as prime minister after the Kot Massacre on 15 September 1846. She was forced into exile when she attempted to use him to replace Crown Prince Surendra with her own son as heir to the throne.

Shah, Rana Bahadur (Swamiji) (1775–1806): Became king of Nepal on the death of his father, Pratap Singh Shah, in 1777 and actual ruler in 1794 on dismissing the regent, his uncle Bahadur Shah. Abdicated in 1799 to ensure succession of his son by a Brahman concubine and withdrew to Benares when courtiers resisted his attempt to reassert control. Outmanoeuvred his opponents and returned as *mukhtiyar* (head of administration) in 1804 but was later assassinated by his half-brother Sher Bahadur.

Shah, Ratna (1928–): A granddaughter of Maharaja Juddha Shamsher Rana, she married then Crown Prince Mahendra in 1951 following the death of her sister, Indra Rajya. The match was opposed by Mahendra's father, King Tribhuvan. She had no children of her own and devoted herself to bringing up the future King Birendra and his brothers and sisters. Although present in an adjoining room at the time of the June 2001 palace massacre, she was not called to give evidence to the official inquiry.

Shah, Surendra (1829–81): After the death of his mother, Senior Queen Samrajya Lakshmi, in October 1841, he showed signs of instability and of sadistic behaviour. His demands for his father, King Rajendra, to cede power to him, were theoretically met in 1847 when Jang Bahadur Rana engineered Rajendra's deposition, but real power remained in Jang Bahadur's hands.

Shah, Tribhuvan Bir Bikram (1906–55): Succeeded his father Prithvi as king of Nepal in 1911. He allied with the India-based Nepali Congress in 1950 against the Ranas, fleeing to India and then returned to Kathmandu in February 1951 under an Indian-brokered deal to preside over a Congress-Rana coalition government. He took a more active role after the coalition collapsed, either by ruling directly or by installing governments under his preferred Congress leader, M. P. Koirala. He died in Switzerland whilst receiving medical treatment in March 1955.

Shaha, Rishikesh (1925–2003): Born in Tansen, the son of a hill raja, he worked as a lecturer in Nepali and English at Trichandra College before becoming a founder member of the Nepal Democratic Congress in Calcutta in 1948. He abandoned party politics in 1956 to become Nepal's UN representative. After 1960, he helped write the 1962 Panchayat constitution and served briefly as finance minister and then foreign minister, but became a dissident. He was active as a historian and political essayist and in the field of human rights.

Shastri, Shukra Raj (?–1941): Son of the Arya Samajist reformer Madhav Raj Joshi, he was influenced by Gandhian ideas and set up the Nepal Civil Rights Committee in Kathmandu in 1937. In 1938 he was sentenced to six years in prison but was executed in January 1941 as one of the Four Martyrs, because his teaching was held to have influenced the Praja Parishad conspirators.

Shrestha, Marichman Singh (1942–): Born in Salyan district, he worked initially as a schoolteacher. He entered Panchayat politics in 1960, and served as minister for water resources in 1979 and minister of education in 1980. He was Rastriya Panchayat chairman in 1981–5 and prime minister in 1986–90. Severely criticised for the attempt to repress the 1990 'People's Movement'.

Shrestha, Pushpa Lal (1924–78): Brother of Ganga Lal Shrestha, one of the Praja Parishad members executed in 1940. Secretary-general of the Communist Party of Nepal for its first two years (1949–51), he is regarded as the founding father of the Nepalese communist movement. He remained on the radical wing of the party but after Mahendra's takeover backed the Nepali Congress call for restoration of the 1959 parliament. Remained in India in 1960 and, following a series of splits, set up his own Communist Party at Gorakhpur in May 1968.

Singh, Gagan (?–1846): Confidante of Queen Rajya Lakshmi, he was appointed prime minister after the assassination of Mathbar Singh. His own assassination on 14 September 1846 precipitated the Kot Massacre and the seizure of power by Jang Bahadur Kunwar (Rana).

Singh, Gajendra Narayan (1930–2002): A veteran of the 1950–1 struggle, he was imprisoned in 1960–1 by King Mahendra, then went into self-exile in India until 1979. Imprisoned briefly in 1985 after setting up the Nepal Sadbhavana Parishad (Goodwill Council) to defend Tarai inhabitants' citizenship claims. Elected to the Rastriya Panchayat in 1986. Relaunched Sadbhavana as a political party in 1990 advocating regional autonomy and greater representation in government service for Taraians. Served as minister in coalition governments from 1995 onwards.

Singh, Ganesh Man (1915–97): Son of a senior Newar civil servant, he escaped in 1943 from prison, where he was being held for membership of the Praja Parishad. Re-entering Nepal as a Nepali Rastriya Congress agent, he was reimprisoned until 1951. Held ministerial office alngside B.P. Koirala, then shared imprisonment and exile with him after 1960. He was one of the troika entrusted with leadership by B. P. before his death and was a key organiser for the 'People's Movement'. After the 1990 'People's Movement', he quarrelled with Girija Koirala and withdrew from active politics.

Singh, Kunwar Indrajit (K. I.) (1906–82): Fought in the 1950–1 armed movement against the Ranas in the Bhairahawa region but refused to accept the Delhi agreement and was eventually captured by Indian troops invited into Nepal by M. P. Koirala's government. Freed from custody in Kathmandu during the 1952 Raksha Dal revolt, he fled to Tibet but took a strong pro-Indian line on return to Nepal in 1955. Founded the United Democratic Party and served as Mahendra's prime minister in July–November 1957. Elected to parliament in 1959 and to the Rastriya Panchayat in 1981.

Singh, Mohan Bikram (1935–): Son of a Pyuthan landowner close to King Tribhuvan, he joined the Communist Party of Nepal in 1953 and built up support for it in his area of the western hills. Imprisoned in 1961–70, he set up the CPN (Fourth Convention) in 1974 and then, having lost control of the organisation, Masal in 1983. Masal supported independent candidates in the 1994 election and participated in 1999 under the name National People's Front. He merged Masal with the Unity Centre in July 2002 to form the Unity Centre (Masal), with the United Front (Nepal) as the new party's electoral vehicle.

Singh, Ramraja Prasad (1936–): A Supreme Court advocate, he was elected to the Rastriya Panchayat from the Graduates' Constituency in 1971 but was later imprisoned for continued advocacy of a multi-party system. He founded the Janabadi Morcha (People's Democratic Front) in India and in 1985 claimed responsibility for bomb explosions in Kathmandu. Sentenced to death in his absence, he was amnestied in 1991 and unsuccessfully stood for parliament in that year's general election.

Thapa, Amar Singh (?–1817): Commander of Nepalese forces in the far west in the early years of the nineteenth century, he extended Nepal's frontiers to the Satlaj but was checked from further advance by the Sikh ruler Ranjki Singh. He was compelled to withdraw from Garhwal and Kumaon by Sir David Ochterloney in 1814–15.

Thapa, Bhimsen (1775–1839): One of the courtiers who accompanied Rana Bahadur Shah during his exile in Benares. After Rana Bahadur's assassination in 1806, he installed a junior queen as regent for King Girvana Yuddha Shah and then for Girvana's son Rajendra but himself controlled the administration. His position weakened after the queen regent's death in 1832 and he fell from power in 1837. Later arrested and died of a self-inflicted wound in prison.

Thapa, Mathbar Singh (1798–1845): Nephew and political supporter of Bhimsen Thapa. Appointed prime minister in December 1843 but alienated both King Rajendra and Queen Rajya Lakshmi by his support for Crown Prince Surendra. He was assassinated on royal orders by his sister's son, Jang Bahadur (Rana) in May 1845.

Thapa, Surya Bahadur (1928–): Originally a member of the Nepali Congress, he was an independent member of the Upper House in 1959 and later prime minister under the Panchayat system in 1964–8 but was imprisoned in 1972–4 for calling for political reform. Brought back as prime minister in 1979 ahead of the 1980 referendum, but became a dissident again after losing office in 1983. After 1990 he co-operated uneasily with old rival Lokendra Bahadur Chand in the National Democratic Party. Led a Congress-NDP-Sadbhavana coalition in 1997–8 and was again made premier in May 2003.

Tuladhar, Padma Ratna (1940–): Born in Kathmandu, he worked as a leftist, human rights and Newar cultural activist. He was elected to the Rastriya Panchayat for one of the Kathmandu constituencies in 1986 and served as an intermediary in the negotiations at the end of the 'People's Movement' in 1990. He was elected to parliament in 1991 and 1994 using the party's election symbol and was a minister in their 1994–5 government. Involved from 1999 onwards in attempts to mediate between the government and the Maoist insurgents.

Yogi, Naraharinath (Balbir Singh Thapa Chetri) (1913?–2003): Born in Kalikot district, he left home at the age of thirteen and was later initiated into the Kanphata Yogi sect. In the late 1950s he set up the Karmavir Mandal, a Hindu fundamentalist organisation, and encouraged resistance to the 1959–60 Congress government, with funding from King Mahendra. After 1990 he spoke out against the multi-party system and in favour of traditional Hindu monarchy.

Notes

INTRODUCTION

1 See ch. 1, n. 4.

1 ENVIRONMENT, STATE AND SOCIETY IN THE CENTRAL HIMALAYAS TO 1743

1 Figures from Hagen 1980: 97–103.
2 Whitehouse et al. 2004.
3 Tamu and Tamu 1993.
4 The origin of 'nepa(la)' itself is disputed, but it may derive from the Tibeto-Burman roots *nhet* (cattle) and *pa* (man).
5 Cultivation of maize was widespread in the hills by the 1790s (M. C. Regmi 1972: 17, n. 21).
6 Slusser 1982: 32–3.
7 Jest et al. 2000: 60.
8 This is mentioned in the *Arthashastra,* a treatise traditionally ascribed to Kautilya, minister to the Mauryan empire in the third century BC, but was perhaps actually written in the early centuries AD (Basham 1967: 80).
9 Kirkpatrick 1811: 123.
10 D. R. Regmi 1966: 162–3.
11 Desideri 1932: 316–17.
12 This concept was applied to nineteenth-century Indonesian city-states by Clifford Geertz (1980), and David Gellner (1983) suggests it applies equally well to the medieval Nepal Valley.

2 UNIFICATION AND SANSKRITISATION, 1743–1885

1 See the account by Father Giuseppe reprinted in Kirkpatrick 1811: 380–6.
2 For example, the poets Lalitaballabha and Sundarananda both refer to the incident. See Vaidya 1993: 159.
3 The claims of Nepalese sources are confirmed by one Chinese account. See Rose 1971: 63, n. 38.
4 Michael 1999: 286.

5 M. C. Regmi 1999: 96.
6 Whelpton 1991: 258.
7 Holmberg and March 1999.
8 Vaidya 1993: 283.
9 M. C. Regmi 1988: 56–9.
10 Pradhan 1982: 16.
11 However, there still remain some Khasas who have not become Chetris and who are known as 'Matwali Khasas'. The term 'matwali' (alcohol-drinker) is normally used to refer to the non-Parbatiya tribal 'groups' below the high-caste Hindus in the traditional hierarchy.
12 M. C. Regmi 1999.
13 Pradhan 1991: 192.
14 Bishop 1990: 122–46.
15 M. C. Regmi 1988: 84–5.
16 Lecomte-Tilouine 1993: 31–2.
17 Hamilton 1986 [1819]: 26.
18 Kirkpatrick 1811: 186.
19 In some cases, families may have left the Valley to escape the fighting, as is possibly the case with those from Bhaktapur who settled in the hills to the south-west of Pokhara. See Jest et al. 2000: 61. An inscription in Newar script on a votive lamp shows that Newars had been in the area as early as 1703 (Ramirez 2000b: 136).
20 Kirkpatrick 1811: 152-3.
21 Hamilton 1986 [1819]: 16.
22 An alternative interpretation is that there was no pre-existing core. Instead people from widely varying backgrounds adopted and modified the Thakali spoken by the Thakali mining contractors who employed them (de Sales 1993).

3 NEPAL UNDER THE SHAMSHER RANAS, 1885–1951

1 Gould (1999: 197 and 126) gives the estimates for total serving and for those killed, whilst total Nepalese casualties were put at 24,000 in a 1923 speech by the then British resident at Kathmandu, Lt Col. W.F.T. O'Connor (Uprety 1992: 104). O'Connor also gave the much higher figure of 200,000 for Nepalese contributing to the war effort, but this seems to have been a 'broad-brush' estimate including those in civilian occupations of military relevance.
2 Shaha 1990: II, 49.
3 Juddha's confidence is asserted in many sources but Gurkha veteran Lt Col. John Cross believes he too had doubts and actually at one point asked for the Gurkhas to be kept out of the Burma campaign lest their participation put Nepal in danger of Japanese retaliation (Cross 2002: 10). The author's source (according to a personal communication) was a 1947 conversation with the first secretary at the British embassy, Lt Col. N. M. McCleod 1 GR.
4 The then Nepalese ambassador in London claimed that the British foreign secretary had originally promised him a decision in favour of Gyanendra by

23 November. However, the Indian high commissioner in London believed
he had prevented this by suggesting that both Britain and India should wait
for the outcome of the negotiations between the Indian government and
Mohan's brother and son, who reached Delhi on the 24th (Shaha 1990: II,
222).

5 K. P. Bhattarai, interviewed by Rajesh Gautam (*Himal Khabar Patrika*, 31
December 2000) claimed that the Delhi agreement had been essential for
Congress because of grave indiscipline among its fighters.

6 See ch. 2, pp. 57–58, for the depopulation of Jumla at the end of the eighteenth
century and for mass emigration from the Kiranti areas of the eastern hills in
the nineteenth century.

7 Whelpton 1991: 228.

8 Stiller 1993: 113.

9 Mikesell 1988: 189–90.

10 'Report on the Addas and the Industrial Development of Nepal' (1933?), quoted
in Edwards 1977: 233.

11 Persian, introduced by the Muslim rulers of northern India, had remained a
major official language within India until 1835 and was still used for written
communication between the Nepalese and British Indian governments in the
1890s. Lt Karbir Khatri, who had learnt English from Brian Hodgson at the
residency and later accompanied Jang Bahadur to London in 1850, was probably the first Nepalese to be published in English. The *Illustrated London News*
of 27 July 1850 carried a letter from him concerning Nepal's border with Tibet
(Whelpton 1983: 244). Balaman Singh, who headed the Foreign Office in Ranoddip and Bir's time, is said to have been the first Nepalese graduate of Calcutta
University (Shaha 1990: II, 18).

12 Mojumdar 1975: 53.

13 *Statements of Publications* for Nepali-language registered publications in the
United Provinces, cited in Chalmers 2002: 45–7.

14 Uprety 1992: 94.

15 It is believed by some in the Newar community in Kathmandu that
Ganesh Man would have been executed had it not been for Marichman's
pleading.

16 DesChene 1991: 174–6. DesChene has particularly in mind the leadership of
the All India Gorkha League and dissident Ranas, but similar logic applied to
the Koirala family and their colleagues in Benares.

17 Pamphlet circulated on 7 September 1940, translated in Uprety 1992: 189.
Juddha's habit of virtually abducting any young woman who caught his fancy
on the streets of Kathmandu is confirmed in British residency records (Shaha
1990: II, 127–8.)

18 Fisher 1997: 58.

19 Abhi Subedi (personal communication).

20 Holmberg and March 1999.

21 Stiller 1993: 136–7.

22 Ibid.: 129–30.

23 Whyte 1998.
24 Malla 1989: 457.

4 THE MONARCHY IN ASCENDANCE: DOMESTIC POLITICS AND FOREIGN RELATIONS, 1951–1991

1 Fisher 1997: 180–2. This argument, advanced by Acharya to his biographer in the late 1980s, was possibly influenced by events in Sikkim in 1974, where the clash between the ethnic Nepalese majority and the Lepcha monarchy ended in the kingdom's absorption into India.
2 Proud to Foreign Office, 12 May 1955 (Public Record Office).
3 Holmberg and March 1999: 50.
4 Chatterji 1977: 110.
5 The confusion is even worse in Nepali than in English as the two letters of the Nepali alphabet conventionally transliterated 's' and 'sh' are pronounced identically by most speakers.
6 Andrew Nickson (1992: 371–2) claims Bhattarai would have liked to continue the coalition but that the United States had made it clear to Ganesh Man Singh that support for Congress was conditional on their breaking with the ULF.

5 THE QUEST FOR 'DEVELOPMENT': ECONOMY AND ENVIRONMENT, 1951–1991

1 Figures calculated from Mishra, Uprety and Panday 2000: tab. 18.
2 Khadka 1994: 326–7.
3 'Foreign Aid, Nepal', http://www.1upinfo.com/country-guide-study/nepal/nepal74.html (consulted 18 October 2003).
4 Mihaly 2002 [1965]: 148.
5 'Foreign Aid, Nepal', http://www.1upinfo.com/country-guide-study/nepal/nepal74.html (consulted 18 October 2003).
6 Mihaly 2002 [1965].
7 Rose 1971.
8 D. R. Pandey 1999.
9 Calculated from the figures for agricultural lands given in M. C. Regmi 1976a: 201. They exclude a small additional allowance for residential land.
10 Estimates of the proportion unregistered range as high as 60–80% but this is probably an overestimate (Chaitanya Mishra, personal communication).
11 See NESAC 1998: 118.
12 There are two rivers in Nepal bearing the name Rapti. The more easterly one is part of the Gandaki system and flows through the Chitwan Valley where the Americans ran a resettlement programme in the 1960s. The western Rapti is a tributary of the Gogra (Karnali). See map 2.
13 Stevens (1993) argues that this was the case with the well-known system of forest management amongst the Sherpas of Solukhumbu.

14 Eaton 1993: 156–7.
15 Table reproduced in Khadka (1994: 238–40) which lists 9359 units. Many of these were cottage industries under the government's 1981 classification scheme with machinery, equipment and tools not exceeding 200,000 rupees and fixed assets under 500,000 rupees.
16 *Gorkhapatra*, 21 March 1986, cited in Zivetz 1992: 178. The figure of 20,000 is calculated from the 1986–7 data in Khadka 1994: 238–40.
17 Mahendra Lama, 'Clash of Images', in Baral 1996: 187.

6 LIFESTYLES, VALUES, IDENTITIES: CHANGES IN NEPALESE SOCIETY, 1951–1991

1 Fisher 1997: 196.
2 Upreti 1976.
3 Bishop 1990: 154.
4 In the mid-1990s, by which time numbers had grown substantially, one NGO estimated that there were between 100,000 and 200,000 Nepalese prostitutes in India and that 5000 girls were entering the trade annually (NESAC 1998: 108–9). Some researchers, however, have suggested that these estimates were exaggerated.
5 Ragsdale 1989: 170.
6 Liechty 1998: 89.
7 'Ashok', 'Nepalko Sandarbhma Buddha ra Mao' [Buddha and Mao in the Nepalese context], *Buddha Pravaha*, 1, 1, 1975, quoted in Rawal 1990–91: 71.
8 Ramirez 2000a. See also Gellner 2001.
9 Campbell 1997: 215.
10 The Newar Era was finally given a degree of official recognition in 2003, though the Vikram Era retains its prime place.
11 Perhaps significantly, Maithil representatives were not included. There was an ongoing dispute in the eastern Tarai on whether the dialect spoken there by Tharus was in fact just Maithili, or whether Maithili itself was simply a form of Tharu.
12 Shah 1993: 8.
13 Nepal, National Education Planning Commission 1956: 96–7.
14 Whelpton 1997: 50.

7 DEMOCRACY AND DISILLUSIONMENT: NEPAL SINCE 1991

1 For a no-confidence motion to be successful, Nepal's 1990 constitution (Art. 59(3)) requires it to be passed 'pratinidhi sabhako sampurna sadasya sankhyako bahumatbata' ('by a majority of the entire number of members in the House of Representatives'). This is interpreted as meaning a majority of the House's prescribed strength of 205, although in December 1996 actual strength was only 200 because by-elections had not been held to replace MPs who had died or for

the seats relinquished by party leaders who had stood successfully as candidates in two constituencies simultaneously.

2 The parties involved were: Unity Centre, Masal, Communist Party of Nepal (Marxist-Leninist) and the Nepal Workers' and Peasants' Party, as well as the Communist Party of Nepal (Marxist), Communist Party of Nepal (Marxist-Leninist-Maoist), Communist Party of Nepal (United), Rastriya Janandolan Sanyojak Samiti (a front for the Communist Party of Nepal (Maoist)) and the United People's Front. The CPN (ML) and NWPP were the only parties formally represented in parliament but two nominally independent MPs were actually Masal-backed.

3 Subedi et al. 2000.

4 Nepal, Central Bureau of Statistics 1992, tab. 5.10; Sudhindra Sharma in Mihaly 2002 [1965]: xxv.

5 Govinda Bahadur Shah's remarks to an Amnesty International seminar as reported in the *Kathmandu Post* on 11 September 1999.

6 Gersony 2003: 12–14.

7 Mohan Mainali 2003.

8 Deepak Thapa, 2001.

9 INSEC 1999: 134.

10 This ceremony is not the formal coronation (*rajabhisheka*), which occurs only some years after the beginning of the reign, and involves elaborate preparations and foreign guests. Birendra himself, who became king in 1972, was crowned only in 1975.

11 The chairman of the Raj Parishad, Keshar Jang Rayamajhi, and perhaps Gyanendra himself, had originally wanted simply to announce the details of the killings in a royal proclamation.

12 The BJP had briefly been part of the original Janata Party but was now a distinct organisation.

13 *Himal Khabar Patrika*, 15 June 2001.

14 French 2001.

15 It has been claimed that there were in fact two internal palace inquiries into the killings but the results were not made public (Gregson 2002: 173, 202). Allegedly these revealed that one aide-de-camp had in fact been about to shoot Dipendra before the deaths of his mother and brother but that another aide-de-camp pushed his arm aside. This might possibly be the origin of the story about an aide-de-camp actually killing Dipendra.

16 Krishna Hachhethu (2002: 210) argues that the unexpectedly poor performance in the 1991 elections of the parties led by former Panchayat prime ministers Chand and Thapa stemmed precisely from the fact that Congress and the UML were now seen as the dominant forces.

17 Quoted in *Spotlight* 26 February 1999.

18 Shrestha 2002: 8, 20.

19 Figures compiled by 'non-resident Nepalis' involved in a conference in Kathmandu in 2003 and quoted on nepalnews.com 1 October 2003. Their estimate for Hong Kong (73,000) seems rather high, as the official total is about

23,000 – but a similar figure was already being quoted in Hong Kong several years earlier.

20 Seddon, Gurung and Adhikari (1998) estimate the total receipts at between 13% and 25% of GDP.

21 The technically correct transliteration of the Nepali ('Gorkha') is used by the Association, as well as by the Indian army, but the conventional anglicisation 'Gurkha' is still used by the British army.

22 NESAC 1998: 216–18.

23 K.C. [Khatri Chetri] 2003.

24 These included Hindi, Newar, Rai (Bantaba), Gurung, Magar, Limbu, Bhojpuri, Awadhi, Tharu, Tamang, Maithili, Magarkham and Doteli.

25 Van Driem 2001: 790–2.

Glossary

The list below includes both terms in Nepali or other South Asian languages and names of organisations or institutions that may be puzzling to the general reader.

A-Class Rana   a member of the Rana family born to a high-caste, legitimately married mother and thus, under the system established by Maharaja Chandra Shamsher Rana, eligible for inclusion on the Roll of Succession to the maharajship

anchal   zone (one of the fourteen major administrative units into which Nepal is divided)

Arya Samaj   Hindu reform movement established in Bombay in 1875

aul   virulent form of malaria formerly endemic in the Tarai

Awadhi   language spoken on both sides of the western section of the Nepal–India border

B-Class Rana   a member of the Rana family whose mother, though of high caste, was not married to his father with full rites; normally not eligible for inclusion on the Roll of Succession to the maharajship

Back to the Village National Campaign   body given power under 1975 amendment to the constitution to vet candidates for Panchayat elections

bahadur shamsher jang   brave lion in war (Persian title supposedly given to King Ram Shah of Gorkha by the Mughal emperor)

bahudaliya janbad   multi-party people's democracy (the revisionist line put forward by UML leader Madan Bhandari in place of the Maoist doctrine of 'new people's democracy')

bairagi   desireless one (member of a Vishnaivite monastic order)

baisi   the twenty-two (pre-unification kingdoms in the Karnali basin)

bandh   strike or shut-down as a political protest

banre   generic term for priestly castes (Vajracharyas and Shakyas) of Newar community

bharadar   courtier, member of the political elite serving king or maharaja

bharadari   the *bharadars* as a collective body

bharo   member of the rural nobility in the medieval Kathmandu Valley

Bhojpuri   language spoken on both sides of the central section of the
  Nepal–India border
Bhonta   the Banepa area immediately east of the Kathmandu Valley
Bhotiya   general term for people of Tibetan (or near-Tibetan) language and
  culture (from 'Bhot', Tibet)
bhumigat giroh   underground gang (term coined by Surya Bahadur Thapa in
  the 1980s for an extra-constitutional power elite allegedly directing politics
  under the reformed Panchayat system)
bikas   development
birta   form of tax-free land tenure granted especially to Brahmans and (after
  1846) to members of the Rana family
birtawala   individual holding land under *birta* tenure
Boddhisattva   an individual who willingly remains in the cycle of rebirths to
  assist others to find salvation
Brahman (also Brahmin, *bahun*)   member of the Hindu priestly caste
C-Class Rana   a member of the Rana family born of a low-caste mother and
  thus not eligible for succession to the maharajship
chaubisi   the twenty-four (pre-unification principalities in the Karnali
  basin)
chaudhuri   traditional holder of the revenue-collection right for a *pargana*
  (subdivision of a district); often used as a surname by Tharus who once held
  this position
chautara   originally the title of the senior *bharadar*, later used for any collateral
  member of the royal family
Commission for the Investigation of the Abuse of Authority   official body for
  the investigation and prosecution of corruption
Communist Party of Nepal (Maoist)   name adopted by the faction of the
  United People's Front which abandoned parliamentary politics in
  1994
Communist Party of Nepal (Marxist)   party formed by the merger of the Man
  Mohan Adhikari and Sahana Pradhan (formerly Pushpa Lal Shrestha) factions
  in 1987
Communist Party of Nepal (Marxist-Leninist)   party formed by the former
  Jhapeli group in 1978 and merged with the CPN (M) in 1991 to form the
  CPN (UML); the original name was revived in 1998 by dissidents who left the
  UML, but most of these subsequently returned to it
Communist Party of Nepal (Unified Marxist-Leninist)   Nepal's largest
  constitutional communist party, formed by the 1991 amalgamation of
  CPN (M) and CPN (ML)
Cwasa Pasa   Friends of the Pen (Newar literary association)
Dalit   downtrodden ones (term preferred now for themselves by the
  Untouchable castes of Nepal and India)
Damai   tailor
Dasain   autumn festival commemorating the defeat of a buffalo demon by the
  goddess Durga and seen as renewing the authority of the state

daura-sawal   traditional Nepalese male dress, including tight-fitting cotton trousers and a tunic; usually worn with a Western-style jacket and a Nepalese cap (*topi*)

desha   the 'realm' or area fully subjected to the king's moral and ritual authority

dharmadhikar   righteousness officer (Brahman formerly responsible for enforcing caste regulations throughout the country)

dharmashastra   Hindu science of right conduct; text expounding this

dhunga   stone (used metaphorically for realm or state)

Dibya Upadesh   Divine Counsel (the political testament dictated by Prithvi Narayan Shah shortly before his death)

Dom   local term for members of Untouchable castes in western Nepal and adjoining areas of the Indian Himalayas

Doya   name by which the people of the kingdom of Tirhut (Mithila) were known in the medieval Kathmandu Valley

Dravidian   language family including the major languages of South India; speaker of one of these languages

dvairajya (Sanskrit)   dual kingship, simultaneous rule by two individuals

Dzongkha   language spoken by the dominant Drukpa ethnic group in Bhutan and closely related to Tibetan

filmi git   film song

firangi   European, Englishman

Fourth Convention   communist party established by Mohan Bikram Singh in 1974

gaun panchayat   village panchayat or council (the lowest tier in the pre-1990 Panchayat system)

Gorkha Dal   Rana 'revivalist' organisation set up to oppose the coalition government in 1951

Gorkha Ex-Serviceman's Association   association set up after the 'People's Movement' by veterans of Britain's Brigade of Gurkhas to press for parity of payment with native British soldiers

Gorkha Parishad   constitutional party set up as successor to the extra-constitutional Gorkha Dal in 1952

gosain   member of a Shaivite monastic order

Gurung   Tibeto-Burman ethnic group in the central hills, serving from early on as soldiers for the Thakuri principalities

guthi   form of tax-free land tenure used for the endowment of religious shrines or associations; mutual help association amongst Newars and some other ethnic groups

jagir   originally an assignment of land revenue in lieu of salary

jagirdar   holder of a *jagir*

Jana Hita Sangha   Public Welfare Association (organisation set up in 1960 in opposition to the Congress government's reform measures)

janai   sacred thread worn by Brahmans and other high-caste Hindus

janandolan   people's movement (especially the protest campaign that brought down the Panchayat regime in 1990) *jangi lat*   war lord (unofficial title of the western commanding general, third in the Rana hierarchy, who was in direct command of the army)

jarti (Tamang)   Parbatiyas (Nepali-speakers), especially their higher castes

Jhapeli group   small communist group which attempted the assassination of 'class enemies' in Jhapa district in the early 1970s

jimidar   official responsible for the collection of land revenue in the Tarai at the lowest (*mauja*) level

kalo pani   the black water (referring to the ocean, crossing of which was originally believed polluting for high-caste Hindus)

kamaiya   bonded labourer

Kami   traditionally Untouchable, metal-working caste

Kanphata Yogi   split-eared ascetic (member of order founded by Gorakhnath)

Karmavir Mandal   Hindu traditionalist organisation founded by Naraharinath Yogi to oppose the 1959–60 Congress government

khaja   snack(s)

Kham (Kham Magar)   northern Magar group, with a language mutually unintelligible with other Magar dialects

khancha   youngest son, young boy

Khasa   ethnic group that brought the Nepali language into present-day Nepal

Kilo Sierra 2   police operation against the Maoists in summer 1999

kipat   system of communal land tenure traditional amongst several ethnic groups, especially the Kirantis

Kiranti   Limbu and Rai peoples of eastern Nepal

Kirata   term used in classical Indian references to the Himalayan foothills, probably denoting any member of a Tibeto-Burman group

Kshatriya (Sanskrit)   member of the second (warrior) caste in the Vedic hierarchy

Licchavi   tribal confederation of the Buddha's time, and the title of the (probably related) dynasty ruling the Kathmandu Valley in the early centuries AD

Limbu   ethnic group living mostly in the far eastern hills of Nepal and in Sikkim

Madheshi (Madise)   inhabitant of the Tarai or the North Indian plain

Magar   ethnic group in the central hills closely associated militarily with the *chaubisi* states

Magurali   informal alliance formed by Magar, Gurung, Rai and Limbu activists ahead of the 1980 referendum

mahapatra   equivalent to *patra*

Maharajadhiraj   Great King of Kings (official designation for the Shah kings of Nepal)

Maharjan   formal term for the Newar cultivator caste also known as Jyapus

Mahasabha   Upper House under 1959 constitution

Maithili   language spoken north and south of the Nepal–India border in part of the eastern Tarai

Malla   title both for the rulers of the Nepal Valley from 1200 and also for the rulers of the Khasa empire in western Nepal in the same period

mandales   hoodlums acting as enforcers for the political establishment in the last years of the Panchayat regime

Manka Khalah   Co-operative Group (an association formed in 1979 to press for Newar linguistic rights)

Masal   political party set up by Mohan Bikram Singh after his expulsion from his own Fourth Convention group in 1983

Mashal   political party established in 1985 by former Masal members including the principal leaders of the subsequent Maoist insurgency

Masta   deity (or class of deities) worshipped widely in western Nepal

matwali   alcohol-drinking (generic term for hill ethnic groups regarded as ritually clean but ranking below the Parbatiya high castes)

mauja   basic unit for fiscal administration in the Tarai

Mir Munshi   Chief Persian Secretary (official in charge of diplomatic relations under the pre-1846 and Rana systems)

mit   someone accepted by another as fictive kin

Mughlana   Land of the Mughals (early Nepali term for India)

mukhiya   village headman

mukhtiyar   attorney, minister; used as title of the king's principal minister from the early nineteenth century onwards

muluk   country

Muluki Ain   National (or Civil) Code

Munda   South Asian branch of the Austro-Asiatic language family

Murmi   old Nepali term for Tamangs

National Democratic Front   alliance formed in summer 1959 by parties opposed to the Congress government

National Democratic Party   party of former *panchas*, originating as two separate parties of the same name, under Lokendra Bahadur Chand and Surya Bahadur Thapa, which merged in 1992 (also frequently known as Rastriya Prajatantra Party or United National Democratic Party)

National Development Service   scheme under which students reading for master's degrees in Tribhuvan University had to spend one year living and working in the countryside

National People's Front   electoral front set up before the 1999 elections to allow the Masal communist faction to participate in elections

Nepal bhasha   language of Nepal (i.e. of the Kathmandu Valley) (name for the Newar language preferred by many Newars themselves)

Nepal Democratic Congress   anti-Rana organisation set up by exiled C-Class Ranas in Calcutta in 1948

Nepal Era   system of reckoning years from a starting date in 879 AD

Nepal Magar Sangh   Magar association set up in 1971

Nepal Praja Parishad   anti-Rana organisation set up in 1935 and reactivated as political party in the 1950s; split in 1958 into rival factions under Tanka Prasad Acharya and Bhadrakali Mishra

Nepal Sarvajatiya Manch   left-leaning alliance of ethnic pressure groups established in 1982 (Nepal All-Peoples' Platform)

Nepal Tamang Ghedung   Tamang ethnic pressure group established in mid-1950s

Nepal Workers' and Peasants' Party   Bhaktapur-based Communist faction founded in 1975/6 by Narayan Bijukche (Comrade Rohit) as the Nepal Workers' and Peasants' Organisation

Nepali Congress   major political party established by 1950 merger of the Nepali National Congress and Nepal Democratic Congress (normally referred to simply as Congress)

Nepali Congress (Democratic)   name adopted by the Deuba faction of congress after the 2002 split

Nepali National Congress   anti-Rana party set up in 1947; the faction under D. R. Regmi continued operating under the original name after B. P. Koirala's group merged with the Nepal Democratic Congress in 1950 (also known as Nepali Rastriya Congress)

Pahari   general term for inhabitants of the Himalayan foothills

pajani   annual review of public appointments

pancha   activist in the Panchayat system

panchayat   council of five (one of the elected bodies set up at different levels under the 1962 constitution; also refers to the 1962–90 political system, in which sense it is written in this book with an initial capital letter)

Parbatiya   mountaineer (general term for members of all traditionally Nepali-speaking castes; the word was also used in the nineteenth century for the Nepali language)

pariwar niyojana   family planning, birth control

patra   member of the city nobility in medieval Patan and Kathmandu

People's Front   party formed by the merger of the United People's Front and the National People's Front in July 2002

Pode   Newar sweeper caste

Prachanda Gorkha   clandestine anti-Rana organisation suppressed in 1931

pradhan   equivalent to *patra*

pradhan mantri   prime minister

pradhan pancha   head of a panchayat; hence village leader under the Panchayat system

Prajatantrik Mahasabha   traditionalist party founded by Ranganath Sharma in 1957

pratibandhit   banned, outlawed

Pratinidhi Sabha   Lower House under 1959 and 1990 constitutions

Rai   collective term for a large number of different Kiranti groups living west of the Limbus in the eastern hills

raikar   land on which normal taxes are payable to the government; tenure of such land

rajabhisheka   coronation ceremony

rajguru   royal spiritual adviser

Rajopadhyaya Brahmans   Kathmandu Valley Brahmans who traditionally spoke Newar but now often see themselves as separate from the Newar community

Rajput   ruling caste in western India, some of whose members later fled to the Himalayan foothills

rajyauta   principality whose ruler enjoyed autonomy in return for fealty to the central government

Raksha Dal   Congress militia which fought in the 1950–1 uprising and was later organised as a police force

Raktapat Mandal   clandestine anti-Rana group to which King Tribhuvan belonged in the 1930s (Bloodshed Committee)

Ramayana   story of the adventures of the god Ram

Rastrabadi Swatantra Bidyarthi Mandal   pro-government student organisation under the Panchayat system

rastrabhasha   language of the nation (official status of Nepali in the 1990 constitution)

rastriya bhasha   national language (status afforded to Nepalese languages other than Nepali under the 1990 constitution)

Rastriya Janamukti Party   political party established by Gore Bahadur Khapangi to press the demands of the non-Parbatiya hill ethnic groups

Rastriya Panchayat   national assembly under the Panchayat system

Rastriya Praja Party   party set up by M. P. Koirala in 1953 after his expulsion from Congress (also known as the National Democratic Party but not connected with the post-1990 party of that name)

Roll (of Succession)   list of order of succession to the Rana maharajship

Sadbhavana Party   Tarai regionalist party originally established in 1985 as the Sadbhavana (Goodwill) Council

salwar-kamiz   Panjabi-style female dress, with tunic and loose-fitting trousers

samanta   feudatory, powerful courtier

sanskritisation   changes in diet, marriage practices etc. aimed at bringing a lower-status group more into line with high-caste Hindus; (with an initial capital letter) incorporating Sanskrit loanwords into a modern South Asian language

sarangi   Nepalese-style fiddle

Sarki   cobbler caste

sati   virtuous woman (widow burned alive on her husband's funeral pyre; the custom of widow burning)

satyagraha   civil disobedience (campaign)

Sen   surname used by the Hindu dynasty established in medieval Bengal and also by the royal lineage originally established at Makwanpur in the central Nepalese hills

Shaivite   connected with Shiva

Shakya   ethnic group to whom the Buddha belonged

shankaracharya   senior priest at one of the four Shaivite religious centres supposedly established by the ninth-century philosopher Shankara; full designation of Shankara himself *shiksa niyojana*   education control (ironical phrase coined by opponents of the government's New Education System Plan by analogy with *pariwar niyojana*, 'family limitation' or 'birth control')

Shiva   the Hindu god of destruction and renewal

Shrestha   Newar Hindu caste claiming Kshatriya status

Shri Panch Sarkar   Five Times Illustrious Ruler (title used by the Shah kings)

Shri Tin Sarkar   Three-Times Illustrious Ruler (title used by Rana maharajas)

sthiti   arrangements, regulations or customs

subba   senior civil service rank, chief district administrator; also used as a title for Limbu headmen who traditionally exercised revenue and administrative functions for the central government

talukdar   local revenue-collector

Tamang   ethnic group found principally in the hills around the Kathmandu Valley

tapain   you (polite form)

Tarai   belt of plain lying between the hills and the Indian border

Tarai Congress   Tarai regionalist party formed in 1953

Thakali   ethnic group originally living in the Kali Gandaki Valley south of Mustang

Thakuri   Parbatiya caste to which the rulers of the hill states of central and western hills (including Gorkha) generally belonged

Tharu Welfare Society   Tharu ethnic organisation established in 1949 (also known as Tharu Kalyankari Sabha)

Therevada   conservative form of Buddhism practised in Sri Lanka and South Asia and less ritually elaborate than the Himalayan variety

thulo manche   influential person (literally, 'big person')

Tibeto-Burman   language family including most of the indigenous languages of the Nepalese hills excluding Nepali

timi   you (familiar form)

topi   Nepalese cap

Tripura   name of a palace in medieval Bhaktapur and of the influential royal family associated with it

ubayarajya   dual kingship under which each ruler is responsible for a separate half of a kingdom

umrao   chief, headman, military leader

United Democratic Front   alliance between Congress, the Nepali National Congress and the Praja Parishad formed in 1957

United Democratic Party   party established in 1955 by former Congress radical K. I. Singh in 1955

United Front   alliance of Praja Parishad and Communist Party of Nepal against Congress in 1951

United Left Front   grouping of communist factions which co-operated with Congress to launch the 1990 'People's Movement'

United Mission to Nepal   association of Protestant churches jointly operating medical and other services for the Nepal government

United National People's Movement   grouping of radical communist groups
that organised protests during the People's Movement independently of
Congress and the ULF

United People's Front   established in 1991 as an electoral vehicle for the
extra-parliamentary Unity Centre communist group

United Revolutionary People's Council of Nepal   provisional 'government' set
up by Maoists after they attacked the Nepalese army in autumn 2001

Unity Centre   communist group formed in 1990 by the merger of the Fourth
Convention, Mashal and some smaller groups

upanayan   initiation ceremony at which a Brahman boy is invested with the
sacred thread

Uray   highest Newar Buddhist lay caste

Utpidit Jatiya Utthan Manch   pressure group established in 1987 to advance
interests of Parbatiya Untouchable (Dalit) castes (Oppressed People's
Upliftment Platform)

Vaishnavite   connected with Vishnu

Vajracharya   the highest Newar Buddhist caste

Vajryana   form of Buddhism involving the use of Tantric rituals

vamshavali   genealogy, chronicle

Vedas   the earliest Hindu scriptures, many of them dating from before 1000 BC

vihara (Sanskrit)   Buddhist monastery

Vishnu   Hindu god of preservation

yogi   spiritual adept, ascetic

Bibliography

Adams, Vincanne. 1998. *Doctors for Democracy: Health Professionals in the Nepal Revolution*. Cambridge: Cambridge University Press. [On the role of health workers in the 1990 'People's Movement'.]

Adhikary, Surya Mani. 1988. *The Khasa Kingdom: A Trans-Himalayan Empire of the Middle Ages*. Jaipur: Nirala.

Ahearn, Laura. 2002. *Invitations to Love: Literacy, Love Letters, and Social Change in Nepal*. Ann Arbor: University of Michigan Press.

Allen, Nigel J. R. 1997a. '"And the Lake Drained Away": An Essay in Himalayan Comparative Mythology', in A. W. Macdonald (ed.), *Mandala and Landscape*, pp. 148–61. Delhi: Printworld.

——— 1997b. 'Hinduization: The Experience of the Thulung Rai', in Gellner, Pfaff-Czarnecka and Whelpton 1997: 303–23.

Alsop, Ian. 1996. 'Christians at the Malla Court', in Siegfried Lienhard (ed.), *Change and Continuity: Studies in the Nepalese Culture of the Kathmandu Valley*, pp. 123–35. Alessandria, Italy: Edizioni dell'Orso.

Bajracharya, Badra Ratna. 1992. *Bahadur Shah: The Regent of Nepal (1785–1794 AD)*. New Delhi: Anmol Publications.

Baral, Lok Raj. 1977. *Oppositional Politics in Nepal*. New Delhi: Abhinav. [Valuable survey of dissident politics in the early Panchayat era.]

——— 1993. *Nepal: Problems of Governance*. Delhi: Konark Publishers. [An analysis by Nepal's leading political scientist, based on developments up to the election of the Congress government in 1991 but correctly anticipating some later problems.]

——— 1996. *Looking to the Future: Indo-Nepalese Relations in Perspective*. New Delhi: Anmol Publications. [Papers by leading authorities from both countries, the Nepalese contributions providing a good picture of establishment thinking on the issues.]

Basham, A. L. 1967. *The Wonder that Was India*. London: Sidgwick and Jackson. [General background to early Hindu civilisation.]

Bhattarai, Baburam. 2003. *The Nature of Underdevelopment and Regional Structure of Nepal: A Marxist Analysis*. Delhi: Adroit Publishers.

Bishop, Barry. 1990. *Karnali under Stress: Livelihood Strategies and Seasonal Rhythms in a Changing Nepal Himalaya*. Chicago: University of Chicago Press. [Though mainly focusing on conditions in the 1960s, this includes a good summary of the development of Parbatiya society in the western hills from early times.]

Bista, Dor Bahadur. 1987. *The People of Nepal*, 5th edn. Kathmandu: Ratna Pustak Bhandar. [Useful introduction to the major ethnic groups, though weakened by not dealing with their inter-relationship under the old caste hierarchy.]

    1991. *Fatalism and Development: Nepal's Struggle for Modernization.* Hyderabad: Orient Longman.

Blaikie, Piers, John Cameron and David Seddon. 1979. *Peasants and Workers in Nepal.* Warminster: Aris & Philips.

    1980. *Nepal in Crisis: Growth and Stagnation at the Periphery.* Oxford: Oxford University Press. Revised and enlarged edition, Delhi: Adroit Publishers, 2001.

Bore, Ole, Sushil R. Panday and Chitra K. Tiwari. 1994. *Nepalese Political Behaviour.* New Delhi: Sterling.

Bouillier, Véronique. 1998. 'The Royal Gift to the Ascetics: The Case of the Caughera Yogi Monastery', *Studies in Nepali History and Society* 5(2): 213–38.

Brown, Louise T. 1996. *The Challenge to Democracy in Nepal: A Political History.* London and New York: Routledge. [Study of political developments in Nepal from 1951 to 1995, focusing particularly on the 'People's Movement' of 1990.]

Burghart, Richard. 1978. 'The Disappearance and Reappearance of Janakpur', *Kailas* 6(4): 257–84.

    1984. 'The Formation of the Concept of Nation-State in Nepal', *Journal of Asian Studies* 44(1): 101–25.

Cameron, John. 1998. 'The Agricultural Perspective Plan: The Need for Debate', *Himalayan Research Bulletin* 18(2): 11–14.

Campbell, Ben. 1997. 'The Heavy Loads of Tamang Identity', in Gellner, Pfaff-Czarnecka and Whelpton 1977: 205–35.

Caplan, Lionel. 1970. *Land and Social Change in Eastern Nepal.* Berkeley: University of California Press (Himal Books reprint with postscript, additional photos, 2000). [Describes how Brahman settlers gradually became the main landowners on land previously held by the Limbus under communal tenure. Based on fieldwork in Ilam but illustrates a transformation that occurred, with local variations, over much of the country.]

    1995. *Warrior Gentlemen: 'Gurkhas' in the Western Imagination.* Oxford: Berghahn. [Covers similar ground to DesChene but focuses much more on British attitudes.]

Chalmers, Rhoderick A. M. 2002. 'Pandits and Pulp Fiction: Popular Publishing and the Birth of Nepali Print-Capitalism in Banaras', *Studies in Nepali History and Society* 7(1): 35–97.

    2003. 'We Nepalis: Language, Literature and the Formation of a Nepali Public Sphere in India, 1914–1940'. University of London Ph.D thesis.

Chatterji, Bhola. 1967. *A Study of Recent Nepalese Politics.* Calcutta: World Press. [Strongly pro-Congress account of the armed movement against the Ranas and of political developments until the early 1960s. The author was one of the Indian socialist politicians who helped B. P. Koirala procure weapons.]

1977. *Nepal's Experiment with Democracy*. New Delhi: Ankur.

1980 *Palace, People and Politics: Nepal in Perspective*. New Delhi: Ankur. [A collection of interviews with B. P. Koirala conducted whilst he was living in India in the 1970s.]

1990. *B. P. Koirala: Portrait of a Revolutionary*, 2nd edn. Calcutta: Minerva.

Corvinus, Gudrun. 1985. 'Report on the Work Done on the Project of Quarternary and Prehistoric Studies in Nepal', *Ancient Nepal* 86–88: 1–6.

2000. 'The Prehistory of Nepal after Ten Years of Research', in Ram Pratap Thapa and Joachim Baaden (eds.), *Nepal: Myths and Realities*, pp. 537–64. Delhi: Book Faith India.

Cross, John. 1986. *In Gurkha Company: The British Army Gurkhas, 1948 to the Present*. London: Arms and Armour. [Enthusiastic account by a retired Gurkha officer.]

2002. *Whatabouts and Whereabouts in Asia*. London: Serendipity.

DeLancey, Scott. 1987. 'Sino-Tibetan Languages', in Bernard Comrie (ed.), *The World's Major Languages*, pp. 799–810. New York: Oxford University Press.

DesChene, Mary K. 1991. 'Relics of Empire: A Cultural History of the Gurkhas 1815–1987'. Stanford University, Ph.D thesis. [Excellent account of the development of the brigade and of the differing perceptions of British officers and enlisted Nepalese, based on both archival research and oral interviews.]

Desideri, Ippolito. 1932. *An Account of Tibet: The Travels of Ippolito Desideri of Pistoia, SJ, 1712–1727*. Edited by Filippo De Filippi. London: Routledge.

Devkota, Grishma Bahadur. 1979. *Nepalko Rajnaitik Darpan* [Political mirror of Nepal], 3rd edn., vol. II. Kathmandu: Dhruva Bahadur Devkota.

Dhakal, D. N. S. and Christopher Strawn. 1994. *Bhutan: A Movement in Exile*. New Delhi and Jaipur: Nirala.

Dhungel, Ramesh K. 1999. 'Nepalese Immigrants in the United States of America', *Contributions to Nepalese Studies* 26(1): 119–34.

Dhungel, Ramesh and Aishwaryalal Pradhananga. 1999. *Kathmandu Upatyakako Madhyakalik Artik Itihas* [Medieval economic history of the Kathmandu Valley]. Kathmandu: Centre for Nepal and Asian Studies.

Diamond, Jared. 1998. *Guns, Germs, and Steel: The Fates of Human Societies*. New York: Norton.

Dixit, Kanak and Shastri Ramachandaran (eds.). 2002. *State of Nepal*. Kathmandu: Himal Books.

Dollfus, P., M. Lecomte-Tilouine and O. Aubriot. 2003. 'Les cultures à l'épreuve du temps: esquisse d'une histoire de l'agriculture en Himalaya', in J. Smadja (ed.), *Histoire et devenir des paysages en Himalaya*, pp. 273–316. Paris: CNRS.

Douglas, Will. 2002. 'The Fifteenth-Century Re-invention of Nepalese Buddhism'. University of Oxford Ph.D thesis.

Driem, George van. 2001. *Languages of the Himalayas: An Ethnolinguistic Handbook of the Himalayan Region*. Leiden: Brill.

Eaton, Richard M. 1993. *The Rise of Islam and the Bengal Frontier, 1204–1760*. Berkeley: University of California Press.

Ebert, Karen H. 1990. 'On the Evidence for the Relationship Kiranti–Rung', *Linguistics of the Tibeto-Burman Area* 13(1): 57–78.

Edwards, Daniel. 1977. 'Patrimonial and Bureaucratic Administration in Nepal: Historical Change and Weberian Theory'. University of Chicago Ph.D. thesis.

Egli, Werner M. 2000. 'Below the Surface of Private Property: Individual Rights, Common Property, and the Nepalese *Kipat* System in Historical Perspective', *European Bulletin of Himalayan Research* 18: 5–16.

English, Richard. 1985. 'Himalayan State Formation and the Impact of British Rule in the Nineteenth Century', *Mountain Research and Development* 5(1): 61–78.

Evans, C., J. Pettigrew and Y. Tamu. 2000. 'The Kohla Project: The First Season of Excavation. Report to the McDonald Institute for Archaeological Research'. Cambridge.

Fisher, James F. 1990. *Sherpas: Reflections on Change in Himalayan Nepal.* Delhi: Oxford University Press. [Describing changes between 1964 and 1988, the author argues that the Sherpas have been able to take advantage of tourism and other changes to strengthen rather than weaken their distinct identity.]

1997. *Living Martyrs: Individuals and Revolution in Nepal.* Delhi: Oxford University Press.

Frederick, John. 1998. 'Deconstructing Gita', *Himal* 11(10) (October): 12–23. [Argues that, rather than being the unknowing victims of traffickers, families often know their daughters are being taken into prostitution but feel poverty leaves them no alternative.]

French, Patrick. 2001. 'Mad, Bad and Dangerous', *Telegraph Magazine*, 25 August: 32–7. [Account of Dipendra and the palace massacre, based on extensive interviews with individuals close to the palace.]

Fujikura, Tatsuro. 2001. 'Emancipation of Kamaiyas: Development, Social Movement, and Youth Activism in Post-Jana-Andolan Nepal', *Himalayan Research Bulletin* 2(1): 29–35. [Interesting study of how Tharu activists organised effectively by alternately working the international aid establishment and taking direct political action.]

Gaborieau, Marc. 1977. *Minorités musulmanes dans le Royaume hindou du Népal.* Nanterre: Laboratoire d'Ethnologie.

1978. *Le Népal et ses populations.* Brussels: Editions Complexes.

Gaenszle, Martin. 1997. 'Changing Conceptions of Ethnic Identity among the Mewahang Rai', in Gellner, Pfaff-Czarnecka and Whelpton 1997: 351–73.

2000. *Origins and Migrations: Kinship, Mythology and Ethnic Identity among the Mewahang Rai of Eastern Nepal.* Kathmandu: Mandala.

Gautam, Rajesh. 1989–90. *Nepalko Prajatantrik Andolanma Praja Parishadko Bhumika* [The role of the Praja Parishad in Nepal's democratic movement]. Kathmandu: the author.

Geertz, Clifford. 1980. *Negara: The Theatre-State in Nineteenth-Century Bali.* Princeton: Princeton University Press.

Gellner, David. 1983. 'Review Article: *Negara: The Theatre-State in Nineteenth-Century Bali*', *South Asia Research* 3(2): 135–40.

1986. 'Language, Caste, Religion and Territory: Newar Identity Ancient and Modern', *European Journal of Sociology* 27: 102–48.

2001. Review of P. Ramirez, *De la disparition des chefs: une anthropologie politique népalaise. Contributions to Nepalese Studies* 28(1): 125–9.

(ed.) 2003. *Resistance and the State: Nepalese Experiences*. New Delhi: Social Science Press.

Gellner, David, Joanna Pfaff-Czarnecka and John Whelpton. 1997. *Nationalism and Ethnicity in a Hindu Kingdom: The Politics of Culture in Contemporary Nepal*. Amsterdam: Harwood.

Gellner, David and Declan Quigley (eds.). 1999. *Contested Hierarchies: A Collaborative Ethnography of Caste among the Newars of the Kathmandu Valley, Nepal*. Delhi: Oxford University Press.

Gersony, Robert. 2003. 'Sowing the Wind . . . History and Dynamics of the Maoist Revolt in Nepal's Rapti Hills'. Report for Mercy Corps International. Portland, OR: Mercy Corps International. [Includes interesting detail on the rise of Maoist influence in their core area on the Rukum–Rolpa border.]

Ghimire, Vishnuprasad. 1988. *Palpa Rajyako Itihas* [History of the Kingdom of Palpa]. Kathmandu: Srimati Padma Ghimire.

Glover, Warren W. 1970. 'Cognate Counts via the Swadesh List in Some Tibeto-Burman Languages of Nepal', in Austin Hale and Kenneth Pike (eds.), *Tone Systems of Tibeto-Burman Languages of Nepal*, part II, *Lexical Lists and Comparative Studies*, pp. 23–6. Urbana: University of Illinois Press.

Gould, Tony. 1999. *Imperial Warriors: Britain and the Gurkhas*. London: Granta. [Excellent survey, drawing both on the author's own experiences as a Gurkha officer and on the analyses of social scientists.]

Gregson, Jonathan. 2002. *Blood against the Snows: The Tragic Story of Nepal's Royal Dynasty*. London: Fourth Estate.

Guneratne, Arjun, 2002. *Many Tongues, One People: The Making of Tharu Identity in Nepal*. Ithaca: Cornell University Press.

Gupta, Anirudha. 1993. *Politics in Nepal 1950–1960*. Delhi: Kalinga Publications.

Gurung, Harka. 1989. *Regional Patterns of Migration in Nepal*. Honolulu: East–West Centre. [Scholarly but readable analysis by a geographer and former minister who also led the commission that produced a controversial report on the citizenship issue in 1984.]

1994. Nepal: *Main Ethnic/Caste Groups by Districts Based on Population Census 1991*. Kathmandu: the author.

1998. *Nepal: Social Demography and Expressions*. Kathmandu: New ERA. [A wealth of statistical information bearing particularly on the situation of the ethnic minorities.]

Gyawali, Dipak and Ajaya Dixit. 2001. 'How Not to Do a South Asian Treaty', *Himal* 14(4) (April): 8–19. [An analysis of the process leading to the ratification of the Mahakali treaty, arguing that the agreement was not in Nepal's national interest. Also includes a discussion of earlier water-sharing agreements.]

Gyawali, Shambhu Prasad. 1999. *Vyakti ra Vichar: Ek Vakilko Sansmaran ra Chintan* [Individuals and thoughts: reminiscences and reflections of a lawyer]. Patan: Jagadamba Prakashan.

Hachhethu, Krishna. 2002. *Party-building in Nepal: The Nepali Congress Party and the Communist Party of Nepal (Unified Marxist-Leninist)*. Kathmandu: Mandala. [Detailed study of the functioning of the political parties at local level. The author summarises his argument in his contribution to Gellner 2003.]

Hagen, Toni. 1980. *Nepal: The Kingdom in the Himalayas*, 3rd edn. New Delhi: Oxford and IBH. [Lavishly illustrated general introduction to the country including a detailed account of stages in the formation of the Himalayas. The 2000 reprint by Himal Books includes updating of his account of changes since the first visit to the country by the author, a Swiss national who conducted a geological survey of Nepal in the early 1950s and later helped set up the carpet industry.]

—— 1994. *Building Bridges to the Third World: Memoirs of Nepal 1950–1992*. Delhi: Book Faith India. [Includes material on the author's role in setting up the Tibetan-style carpet industry in Nepal and also a critique of development assistance.]

Hamal, Lakshman B. 1994. *Economic History of Nepal: From Antiquity to 1990*. Kathmandu: Ganga Kaveri Publishing House.

Hamilton, Francis Buchanan. 1986 [1819]. *An Account of the Kingdom of Nepal*. New Delhi: Asian Educational Service. [Reprint of the 1819 original edition of the book by a British writer attached to the staff of Capt. Knox, East India Company resident in Kathmandu in 1802–3. Especially valuable for details of the history of the *chaubisi* and *baisi* kingdoms.]

Hasrat, Vikram. 1970. *The History of Nepal as Told by Its Own and Contemporary Chroniclers*. Hoshiarpur: V. V. Research Institute. [Translations from Brian Hodgson's papers of indigenous accounts of the pre-unification period together with summaries of later events by British residency officials.]

Hitchcock, John. 1979. 'An Additional Perspective on the Nepali Caste System', in James F. Fisher (ed.), *Himalayan Anthropology*, pp. 111–20. The Hague and Paris: Mouton.

Höfer, Andras. 1979. *The Caste Hierarchy and the State: A Study of the Muluki Ain of 1854*. Innsbruck: Universitätsverlag Wagner. [Combines a detailed study of Jang Bahadur Rana's law code with anthropological data.]

Hoftun, Martin, William Raeper and John Whelpton. 1999. *People, Politics and Ideology: Democracy and Social Change in Nepal*. Kathmandu: Mandala.

Holmberg, David. 1989. *Order in Paradox: Myth, Ritual and Exchange among Nepal's Tamang*. Ithaca: Cornell University Press. [Concerned particularly with Tamang religion but includes more general information on the group and the evolution of their place in Nepalese society.]

Holmberg, David and Kathryn March. 1999. 'Local Production/Local Knowledge: Forced Labour from Below', *Studies in Nepali History and Society* 4(1): 5–64.

Human Rights Watch/Asia. 1995. *Rape for Profit: Trafficking of Nepali Girls and Women to India's Brothels*. New York: Human Rights Watch/Asia. [Sees the problem as predominantly one of girls being forcibly abducted or tricked into prostitution.]

Hunter, Sir William W. 1896. *Life of Brian Houghton Hodgson, British Resident at the Court of Nepal*. London: John Murray. [Very readable but eulogistic account by a personal friend.]

Hussain, Asad. 1970. *British India's Relations with the Kingdom of Nepal 1857–1947*. London: Allen and Unwin.

Hutt, Michael (ed.). 1994. *Nepal in the Nineties*. New Delhi: Sterling. [Includes accounts of the 'People's Movement', the constitution drafting process, the 1991 elections, development prospects and the future of Britain's Brigade of Gurkhas.]

(ed.). 2003a. *Himalayan 'People's War': Nepal's Maoist Rebellion*. London: Hurst.

2003b. *Unbecoming Citizens: Culture, Nationhood, and the Flight of Refugees from Bhutan*. Delhi: Oxford University Press. [On the flight of refugees from Bhutan into Nepal in the early 1990s but also including a detailed account of the development of the Lhotsampa (ethnic Nepalese) community of southern Bhutan from the late nineteenth century onwards.]

INSEC [Informal Sector Service Center]. 1999. *Human Rights Year Book 1999*. Kathmandu: INSEC.

Ives, J. D. and B. Messerli. 1989. *The Himalayan Dilemma: Reconciling Development and Conservation*. London: United Nations University Press/Routledge.

Jacobson, Calla. 2000. 'Glimpses from a Margin: Images of Caste and Ethnicity in Nepal's Middle Hills', *Bulletin of Himalayan Research* 20(1–2): 31–41.

Jest, C., J. Galodé, M. Lecomte-Tilouine and P. Ramirez. 2000. 'The Populations of Gulmi and Argha-Khanci', in Ramirez 2000c: 51–74.

Joshi, Bhuvan Lal and Leo E. Rose. 1996. *Democratic Innovations in Nepal: A Case Study of Political Acculturation*. Berkeley: University of California Press. Reprint, Kathmandu: Mandala, 2004.

Justice, Judith. 1986. *Politics, Plans and People: Culture and Health Development in Nepal*. Berkeley: University of California Press.

Karan, Pradyumna Prasad and Hiroshi Ishii. 1996. *Nepal: A Himalayan Kingdom in Transition*. Tokyo: United Nations University Press.

Karki, Arjun and David Seddon (eds.). 2003. *The People's War in Nepal: Left Perspectives*. New Delhi: Adroit Publishers. [An edited collection including some of the Maoists' own documents and contributions by leftists critical of their methods.]

K.C. [Khatri Chetri], Sharad. 2003. 'Naya Jamindarko Rupma Maobadi' [The Maoists as New Zamindars], *Himal KhabarPatrika*, 17 November.

Khadka, Narayan. 1991. *Foreign Aid, Poverty and Stagnation in Nepal*. New Delhi: Vikash Publishing House.

1994. *Politics and Development in Nepal*. Jaipur: Nirala. [Useful as a guide to the thinking on Nepal's economic problems of the man who was to become economic adviser to Sher Bahadur Deuba.]

1997. *Foreign Aid and Foreign Policy: Major Powers and Nepal*. New Delhi: Vikash Publishing House.

Kirkpatrick, William. 1811, *An Account of the Kingdom of Nepaul*. London: W. Miller. [Written by the leader of the 1793 British mission to Kathmandu, this is the earliest full-length Western work on Nepal. Regularly reprinted in India.]

Koirala, B. P. 2001. *Atmabrittanta: Late Life Reminiscences*, transl. Kanak Mani Dixit. Kathmandu: Himal Books.

Kölver, Bernard and Hemraj Sakya. 1985. *Documents from the Rudravarna-Mahavira, Patan*, vol. I, *Sales and Mortgages*. Sankt Augustin: VGH Wissenschaftsverlag.

Kumar, Dhruba (ed.). 1995. *State, Leadership and Politics in Nepal*. Kathmandu: CNAS. [A good survey of problems with the political process emerging in the early 1990s.]

(ed.). 2000. *Domestic Conflict and the Crisis of Governability in Nepal*. Kathmandu: CNAS. [Essays by leading Nepalese scholars, including the Maoist and ethnic problems.]

2003. 'Sankatko Nikas: Sainya Katauti'. *Himal Khabar Patrika*, 18 April.

Landon, Perceval. 1928. *Nepal*, 2 vols. London: Constable. [Commissioned by Maharaja Chandra Shamsher Rana and thus rather partisan, but a valuable portrait of the country in the early twentieth century.]

Lecomte-Tilouine, Marie. 1993. *Les dieux du pouvoir: les Magar et l'hindouisme au Népal central*. Paris: CNRS.

2000. 'The Two Kings of Musikot', in Ramirez 2000c: 143–70.

2002. 'La désanskritisation des Magar: ethno-histoire d'une group sans histoire', *Purusartha* 23: 297–327.

2003. 'The History of the Messianic and Rebel King Lakhan Thapa: Utopia and Ideology among the Magar', in Gellner 2003: 244–77. [Revised version of an article in *European Bulletin of Himalayan Research*, 19 (2000).]

2004. 'Regicide and Maoist Revolutionary Warfare in Nepal: Modern Incarnations of a Warrior Kingdom', *Anthropology Today* 20(1): 13–19. [Links Maoist tactics with a tradition of violence within Nepal and with the position of the Magar ethnic group.]

Lecomte-Tilouine, Marie and Catherine Michaud. 2000. 'From the Mine to the Fields: History of the Exploitation of the Slope in Darling (Gulmi)', in Ramirez 2000c: 222–63.

Leuchtag, Erica. 1958. *With a King in the Clouds*. London: Hutchinson. [Memoirs of a physiotherapist employed in King Tribhuvan's household in 1948.]

Levy, Robert I. 1990. *Mesocosm: Hinduism and the Organization of a Traditional Newar Society in Nepal*. Berkeley: University of California. [Examines perceptions of their society amongst Hindu Newars in the Kathmandu Valley's third city.]

Liechty, Mark. 1998. 'The Social Practice of Cinema and Video-Viewing in Kathmandu', *Studies in Nepali History and Society* 3(1): 87–126.

2003. *Suitably Modern: Making Middle-Class Culture in a New Consumer Society*. Princeton: Princeton University Press.

Macfarlane, Alan. 1976. *Resources and Population: A Study of the Gurungs of Nepal*. Cambridge: Cambridge University Press. [A Malthusian account, still of value although the author now admits he failed to allow for the safety valve provided by migration to the towns and for remittance income. 2nd edn. Kathmandu: Ratna Pustak Bhandar, 2003.]

Mainali, Kashi Kanta. 2000. *Political Dimensions of Nepal 1885–1901*. Kathmandu: Radhika Mainali.

Mainali, Mohan. 2003. 'One Country, Two Systems', *Nepal Times* (on-line edition), 20 June.

Malla, Kamal Prakash. 1979. *The Road to Nowhere*. Kathmandu: Sajha. [Reflections on Nepal's intelligentsia by a prominent Nepalese linguist.]

——— 1981. 'Linguistic Archaeology of the Kathmandu Valley: Preliminary Report', *Kailash* 8(1–2): 5–23.

——— 1983. 'Epigraphy and Society in Ancient Nepal: A Critique of Regmi', *Contributions to Nepalese Studies* 13(1): 57–94.

——— 1989. 'Language and Society in Nepal', in K. P. Malla (ed.), *Nepal: Perspectives on Continuity and Change*, pp. 445–66. Kirtipur: CNAS.

Manandhar, Triratna. 1986. *Nepal: The Years of Trouble*. Kathmandu: Purna Devi Manandhar. [The fullest account of court intrigue under Maharaja Ranoddip Singh.]

Michael, Bernardo. 1999. 'Statemaking and Space on the Margins of Empire: Rethinking the Anglo-Gorkha War of 1814–1816', *Studies in Nepali History and Society* 4(2): 247–94.

Mihaly, Eugene Bramer. 2002 [1965]. *Foreign Aid and Politics in Nepal: A Case Study*. London: Oxford University Press.

Mikesell, Steven. 1988. 'Cotton on the Silk Road'. University of Wisconsin Ph.D thesis.

——— 1990. *Class, State, and Struggle in Nepal: Writings 1989–1995*. New Delhi: Manohar.

Mishra, Chaitanya, Laya Prasad Uprety and Tulsi Ram Panday. 2000. *Seasonal Agricultural Labour Migration from India*. Kathmandu: CNAS.

Mishra, Shanti. 1994. *Voice of Truth: The Challenges and Struggles of a Nepalese Woman*. Delhi: Book Faith India. [Memoirs of the librarian who set up Tribhuvan University's central library.]

Mishra, Tirtha Prasad. 1991. *The Taming of Tibet: An Historical Account of Compromise and Confrontation in Nepal–Tibet Relations (1900–1930)*. Jaipur: Nirala.

Mojumdar, Kanchanmoy. 1973. *Indo-Nepalese Relations, 1877–1923*. New Delhi: Munshiram Manoharlal.

——— 1975. *Nepal and the Indian Nationalist Movement*. Calcutta: Mukhopadhyaya.

Nepal, Central Bureau of Statistics. 1992. *Statistical Pocket Book*. Kathmandu.

——— 1993. *Nepal Census of Population*. 15 vols. Kathmandu.

Nepal, National Education Planning Commission. 1956. *Education in Nepal*. Kathmandu: College of Education.

NESAC [Nepal South Asia Center]. 1998. *Nepal Human Development Report 1998.* Kathmandu: Nepal South Asia Centre.

Nickson, R. Andrew. 1992. 'Democratisation and the Growth of Communism in Nepal: A Peruvian Scenario in the Making?', *Journal of Commonwealth and Comparative Politics* 30(3): 358–86. [Prescient paper which forecasts the outbreak of the 'People's War' later in the decade.]

Noonan, Michael. 1996. 'Fall and Rise and Fall of the Chantyal Language', *Southwest Journal of Linguistics* 15(1–2): 121–36 (also at www.uwm.edu/~noonan/LANGLOSS.pdf).

Ogura, Kiyoko. 2001. *Kathmandu Spring: The People's Movement of 1990.* Kathmandu: Himal Books.

Oldfield, Hector Ambrose. 1880. *Sketches from Nepal.* London: W. H. Allen. [Posthumously published writings of the surgeon at the Kathmandu residency fom 1850 to 1873, who became a personal friend of Jang Bahadur Rana. Reprinted, New Delhi: Cosmo, 1974.]

Oliphant, Laurence. 1852. *A Journey to Kathmandu with the Camp of Jung Bahadur.* London: John Murray.

Onta, Pratyoush. 1994. 'Rich Possibilities: Notes on Social History in Nepal', *Contributions to Nepalese Studies* 21(1): 1–43.

——— 1996. 'Creating a Brave Nepali Nation in British India: The Rhetoric of *Jati* Improvement, Rediscovery of Bhanubhakta and the Writing of *bir* History', *Studies in Nepali History and Society* 1(1): 37–76.

Oppitz, Michael. 1983. 'The Wild Boar and the Plough: Origin Myths of the Northern Magar', *Kailash* 10(3–4): 187–226.

Ortner, Sherry B. 1989. *High Religion: A Cultural and Political History of Sherpa Religion.* Princeton: Princeton University Press. [Examines how income from wage labour in Darjeeling and mountaineering enabled the foundation of the first celibate monasteries in Solukhumbu in the early twentieth century.]

Pandey, Devendra Raj. 1999. *Nepal's Failed Development: Reflections on the Mission and the Maladies.* Kathmandu: Nepal South Asia Center. [By a former civil service head of the Finance Ministry, who was finance minister in the 1990–1 interim government.]

Pandey, Ramniwas. 1987. 'Paleo-environment and prehistory of Nepal', *Contributions to Nepalese Studies* 14(2): 11–24.

——— 1989. 'Ancient History', in K. P. Malla (ed.), *Nepal: Perspectives on Continuity and Change*, pp. 51–76. Kathmandu: CNAS.

Pemble, John. 1971. *The Invasion of Nepal: John Company at War.* Oxford: Clarendon Press.

Perlin, Frank. 1981. 'The Precolonial Indian State in History and Epistemology: A Reconstruction of Societal Formation in the Western Deccan from the Fifteenth to the Early Nineteenth Century', in H. J. M. Claessen, and Peter Skalnik (eds.), *The Study of the State*, pp. 275–302. The Hague: Mouton.

Perry, Cindy L. 1997. *Nepali around the World: Emphasising Nepali Christians of the Himalayas.* Kathmandu: Ekta.

Petech, Luciano. 1984. *Mediaeval History of Nepal c. 750–1482*, 2nd edn. Rome: ISMEO. [A work for specialists, mainly concerned with establishing regnal dates but with a little information on social and economic history.]

Pinch, William R. 1999. *Peasants and Monks in British India*. New Delhi: Oxford University Press.

Poffenberger. Mark. 1980. *Patterns of Change in the Nepal Himalaya*. Delhi: Macmillan. [Succinct account of the roots of Nepal's 'population explosion'.]

Pokhrel, Durga. 1996. *Shadow over Shangri-la: A Woman's Quest for Freedom*. Washington, DC, and London: Brassey's. [Memoirs of a college lecturer frequently imprisoned for Congress activities between 1974 and 1982. She now (March 2004) heads Nepal's Women's Commission.]

Pradhan, Kumar. 1982. *Pahilo Pahar* [First phase]. Darjeeling: Shyam Prakkashan.

— 1991. *The Gorkha Conquests: The Process and Consequences of the Unification of Nepal with Particular Reference to Eastern Nepal*. Calcutta: Oxford University Press.

Prasad, Ishwari. 1975. *Biography of Juddha Shumshere J. B. Rana*. New Delhi: Ashish. [A partisan account by a personal friend.]

Quigley, Declan. 1993. *The Interpretation of Caste*. Oxford: Oxford University Press.

Ragsdale, Todd. 1989. *Once a Hermit Kingdom: Ethnicity, Education and National Integration in Nepal*. Kathmandu: Ratna Pustak Bhandar. [Examines the impact of the New Education System Plan on a Gurung village and its school.]

Raj, Prakash A. 2001. *'Kay Gardeko?': The Royal Massacre in Nepal*. New Delhi: Rupa. [Brief but clear account of the killings and their background.]

Ramirez, Philippe. 2000a. *De la disparition des chefs: une anthropologie politique népalaise*. Paris: CNRS.

— 2000b. 'From the Principality to the Nation-State: Gulmi, Argh-Khanci and the Gandaki Kingdoms.' In Ramirez 2000c: 103–40.

— (ed.). 2000c. *Resunga: The Mountain of the Horned Sage*. Kathmandu: Himal Books. [Study by a team of anthropologists of the present condition and earlier history of Arghakhanchi district and adjacent areas in the hills south-west of Pokhara.]

— 2000d. 'Subjects and Citizens.' In Ramirez 2000c.

Rana, Prabhakar S. J. B., Pashupati S. J. B. Rana and Gautam S. J. B. Rana. 2003. *The Ranas of Nepal*. New Delhi: Timeless Books. [Particularly in its account of the Ranas today, this is more like a family scrapbook than a serious analysis, but it is valuable for its excellent selection of historic photographs and paintings.]

Rawal, Bhim. 1990–1. *Nepalma Samyabadi Andolan: Udbhav ra Bikas* [The communist movement in Nepal: rise and development]. Kathmandu: Pairavi Prakashan.

Reed, Horace B. and Mary J. Reed. 1968. *Nepal in Transition: Educational Innovation*. Pittsburgh: University of Pittsburgh Press.

Regmi, Dilli Rahman. 1966. *Medieval Nepal*, vol. I. Calcutta: Firma Mukhopadhyaya.

— 1969. *Ancient Nepal*, 3rd edn. Calcutta: Firma Mukhopadhyaya.

— 1975. *Modern Nepal*. Calcutta: Firma Mukhopadhyaya.

1983. *Inscriptions of Ancient Nepal*. Delhi: Abhinav. [Aimed primarily at specialists but useful for the English translations of the inscriptions.]

Regmi, Mahesh Chandra. 1972. *A Study in Nepali Economic History 1768–1846*. New Delhi: Manjushri.

1976a. *Land Ownership in Nepal*. Berkeley: University of California. [The best overall summary of the results of research by Nepal's leading economic historian.]

1976b. 'Some Questions on Nepali History', *Contributions to Nepalese Studies* 3(2): 1–5.

1978. *Land Tenure and Taxation in Nepal*. Kathmandu: Ratna Pustak Bhandar. [Foundational study of the subject; originally published in 4 vols., 1963–8, by University of California Press.]

1988. *An Economic History of Nepal 1846–1901*. Varanasi: Nath Publishing House.

1999. *Imperial Gorkha: An Account of Gorkhali Rule in Kumaun (1791–1815)*. Delhi: Adroit Publishers. [Argues the essentially colonial nature of Gorkhali rule in this area.]

Riccardi, Theodore Jr. 1996. 'Change and Continuity in the Kathmandu Valley: The Archaeological Perspective', in S. Lienhard (ed.), *Change and Continuity in the Nepalese Culture of the Kathmandu Valley*, pp. 16–22. Turin: Edizioni dell'Orso.

Rose, Leo E. 1971. *Nepal: Strategy for Survival*. Berkeley: University of California Press.

Sales, Anne de. 1993. 'When the Miners Came to Light: The Chantel of Dhaulagiri', in G. Toffin (ed.), *Nepal Past and Present*, pp. 91–7. New Delhi: Sterling.

Salter, Jan and Harka Gurung. 1996. *Faces of Nepal*. Lalitpur: Himal Books.

Schetenko, Prof. Dr. 1977–8. 'The Outcomes of the Scientific Mission to Nepal in Brief', *Ancient Nepal* 43–5: 1–2.

Seddon, David, Ganesh Gurung and Jagannath Adhikari. 1998. 'Foreign Labour Migration and the Remittance Economy of Nepal', *Himalayan Research Bulletin* 18(2): 3–10.

Sever, Adrian. 1993. *Nepal under the Ranas*. Delhi: Oxford and IBH.

Shah, S. 1993. 'Throes of a Fledgling Nation', *Himal* 6(2): 7–10.

Shaha, Rishikesh. 1990. *Modern Nepal: A Political History 1769–1955*, 2 vols. New Delhi: Manohar.

1992. *Ancient and Medieval Nepal*. New Delhi: Manohar.

Sharma, Dilli Raj. 1988. 'Archaeological Remains in the Dang Valley', *Ancient Nepal* 106: 8–12.

Sharma, Prayag Raj 1972. *Preliminary Account of the Art and Architecture of the Karnali Region, West Nepal*. Paris: CNRS. [In addition to discussing the physical remains of the Khasa (or western Malla) empire, this includes a reconstruction of its political history.]

1974. 'The Divinities of the Karnali Basin in Western Nepal', in Christoph von Fürer-Haimendorf (ed.), *Contributions to the Anthropology of Nepal*, pp. 244–60. Warminster: Aris Philips.

1983. 'The Land System of the Licchavis of Nepal', *Kailash* 10(1–2): 11–62.

1997. *Kul, Bhumi ra Rajya: Nepal Upatyakako Purba-Madhyakalik Samajik Itihas* [Lineage, land and state: early medieval social history of the Nepal Valley]. Kathmandu: CNAS.

Shrestha, Celayne Heaton. 2002. 'NGOs as *Thekadars* or *Sevaks:* Identity Crisis in Nepal's Non-Governmental Sector', *European Bulletin of Himalayan Research* 22: 5–36. [Examines the two faces of NGOs as social activism and as simple entrepreneurship.]

Siddika, Shamina. 1993. *Muslims of Nepal.* Kathmandu: Nurun Nahar.

Sidky, H., James Hamill, Janardan Subedi, Ronald H. Spielbauer, Robin Singh, J. Blangero and S. Williams-Blangero. 2000. 'Social Organisation, Economy and Kinship among the Jirels of Eastern Nepal', *Contributions to Nepalese Studies*, Jirel Issue: 5–22.

Skinner, Debra, Alfred Pach III and Dorothy Holland (eds.). 1998. *Selves in Time and Place: Identities, Experience, and History in Nepal.* Oxford: Rowman & Littlefield.

Slusser, Mary Shepherd. 1982. *Nepal Mandala.* Princeton: Princeton University Press.

Stevens, Stanley F. 1993. *Claiming the High Ground: Sherpas, Subsistence and Environmental Change in the Highest Himalaya.* Berkeley: University of California Press.

Stiller, Ludwig. 1968. *Rise of the House of Gorkha.* Ranchi: Patna Jesuit Society.

1973. *The Silent Cry: The People of Nepal 1816–1839.* Kathmandu: Sahayogi. [On economic and social conditions under Bhimsen Thapa and also his skilful handling of the East India Company after Nepal's military defeat.]

1981. *Letters from Kathmandu: The Kot Massacre.* Kathmandu: CNAS. [Collection of correspondence from the British residency archives illustrating events in Nepal from 1840 to 1847.]

1993. *Nepal: Growth of a Nation.* Kathmandu: Human Resources Development Research Centre.

Subba, Tanka B. 1992. *Ethnicity, State and Development: A Case Study of Gorkhaland Movement in Darjeeling.* New Delhi: Dhar Anand.

Subedi, Janardan, Sree Subedi, H. Sidky, Robin Singh, J. Blangero and S. Williams-Blangero. 2000. 'Health and Health Care in Jiri', *Contributions to Nepalese Studies*, Jirel Issue: 97–104.

Tamu, Bhovar Palje and Yarjung Kromchhe Tamu. 1993. 'A Brief History of the Tamu Tribe', in Bernard Pignède, *The Gurungs* (English edition by Sarah Harrison and Allan Macfarlane), pp. 479–93. Kathmandu: Ratna Pustak Bhandar.

Temple, Mark. 1991. 'Population Growth and Labour Shortage in Nepali Agriculture', Paper presented at the Himalayan Forum, University of London.

Thapa, Deepak. 2001. 'India and the Maoists'. *Nepali Times*, 14 December.

Thapa, Deepak with Bandita Sijapati. 2003. *A Kingdom under Siege: Nepal's Maoist Insurgency, 1996–2003.* Kathmandu: The Printhouse.

Thapa, Shankar. 2001. *Peasant Insurgence in Nepal 1951–1960*. Kathmandu: Nirmala K. C.

Thapar, Romila. 1984. *From Lineage to State: Social Formations in the Mid-First Millennium BC in the Ganga Valley*. Delhi: Oxford University Press.

Toffin, Gérard. 1999. 'The Social Organization of Rajopadhyaya Brahmans', in Gellner and Quigley 1999: 186–208.

Tucci, Giuseppe. 1956. *Preliminary Report on Two Scientific Expeditions to Nepal*. Rome: Istituto Italiano per il Studio del Medio ed Estreme Oriente.

  1962. *The Discovery of the Malla*. London: Allen & Unwin. [Account for the non-specialist of the author's discovery of the remains of the western Malla or Khasa empire.]

Turin, Mark. Forthcoming. *The Thangmi Language*. Leiden: Brill.

Unbescheid, Günter. 1980. *Kanphata: Untersuchungen zu Kult, Mythologie und Geschichte Sivaitischer Tantriker in Nepal* [Kanphata: investigations into the culture, mythology and history of Shaivite Tantricists in Nepal]. Wiesbaden: Franz Steiner.

Upreti, Bedh Prakash. 1976. 'Limbuwan Today: Process and Problems', *Contributions to Nepalese Studies* 3(2): 47–70.

Uprety, Prem R. 1984. *Nepal: A Small Nation in the Vortex of International Conflicts*. Kathmandu: Pugo Mi. [An account of Nepal's involvement in the two world wars and other conflicts through its alliances with British India and then with independent India.]

  1992. *Political Awakening in Nepal: The Search for a New Identity*. New Delhi: Commonwealth Publishers.

Vaidya, Tulsi Ram. 1993. *Prithvi Narayan Shah: The Founder of Modern Nepal*. New Delhi: Anmol.

Vajracarya, Dhanavajra and Kamal Prakash Malla. 1985. *The Gopalarajavamsavali*. Wiesbaden: Franz Steiner. [Text and translation of this fourteenth-century work, the oldest of the Kathmandu Valley chronicles.]

Waterhouse, David M. (ed.). 2004. *The Origins of Himalayan Studies: Brian Houghton Hodgson in Kathmandu and Darjeeling 1820–1858*. London: Royal Asiatic Society. [Includes discussions of Hodgson's work in natural history and Buddhist studies as well as his critical role in relations between Britain and Nepal and his influence on internal Nepalese politics.]

Watters, David E. 1975. 'The Evolution of a Tibeto-Burman Pronominal Verb Morphology: A Case-Study from Nepal', *Linguistics of the Tibeto-Burman Area* 2(1): 45–79.

Webster, P. 1981. 'To Plough or Not to Plough? A Newar Dilemma', *Pacific Viewpoint* 22: 99–135.

Whelpton, John. 1983. *Jang Bahadur in Europe: The First Nepalese Mission to the West*. Kathmandu: Sahayogi Press. [Annotated translation of a travelling companion's account of the first Rana prime minister's 1850 visit to Britain and France.]

  1990. *Nepal*. Oxford: Clio Press.

1991. *Kings, Soldiers and Priests: Nepalese Politics and the Rise of Jang Bahadur Rana, 1830–1857*. New Delhi: Manohar.

1997. 'Political Identity in Nepal: State, Nation and Community', in Gellner, Pfaff-Czarnecka and Whelpton 1997: 39–78.

1999. 'Nine Years On: The 1999 Election and Nepalese Politics since the 1990 *Janandolan*', *European Bulletin of Himalayan Research* 17: 1–39.

Whitehouse, Paul, Timothy Usher, Merritt Ruhlen and William S. Y. Wang. 2004. 'Kusunda: An Indo-Pacific Language in Nepal', *Proceedings of the National Academy of Sciences*, 101(15): 5692–5.

Whyte, Timothy. 1998. 'The Legacy of Slavery in Nepal', *Studies in Nepali History and Society* 3(2): 311–39.

Witzel, Michael. 1993. 'Nepalese Hydronomy: Towards a History of Settlement in the Himalayas', in Gérard Toffin (ed.), *Nepal: Past and Present*, pp. 217–66. New Delhi: Sterling.

Zivetz, Laurie. 1992. *Private Enterprise and the State in Modern Nepal*. Madras: Oxford University Press.

Index

Note: Readers seeking information about particular individuals or events should also consult the 'Key events' (pp. x–xviii) and 'Biographical notes' (pp. 238–51) sections. The index also omits names of ethnic groups or castes which appear only in table 1.1 (pp. 9–10).

Index

trade, 27–8, 76–7, 113, 123, 146, 152–3, 229–30
  across the Himalayas, 19, 27–8
  see also India
Tribhuvan International Airport, 139
Tribhuvan Rajpath, 90, 130, 132, 137, 138
Tribhuvan Sadan, 211–16
Tribhuvan University, 166–7, 185–6, 189–90
Trichandra College, 64, 66, 67, 83, 166
Tripura family, 21–2
Trisuli dam, 132
Trisuli River, 18, 35, 39
trolleybus system, 133
Tsangpo, 6, 13
tuki system, 143
Tuladhar, Padma Ratna, 110, 182, 209
Turks, 15

ubayarajya, 19
UK, *see* Britain
UML, *see* Communist Party of Nepal (Unified
  Marxist-Leninist)
UNCTAD, 152
unemployment, 137
United Democratic Front, 93
United Democratic Party, 92–3, 94, 96, 97
United Front (of 1951), 88
United Left Front, 113–14, 115–17
United Mission to Nepal, 135
United National People's Movement, 114
United Nations, 127, 130
United Nations Development Programme,
  128
United People's Front, 119, 121, 175, 203
  post-1991 street agitation, 189–90
  1994 split, 192
  2002 merger, 222
  opposition to state of emergency, 219
United Revolutionary People's Council of
  Nepal, 218
United States, 69, 94, 97, 134
  and 1991 election, 95
  aid programme, 103, 126, 128–30, 131, 133, 136,
    137, 138, 143
  economic relations, 148–9, 230
  and Maoist insurgency, 223, 225
  resettlement programme, 141
  support for Kampas, 103

United States Operations Mission, 130
Unity Centre, 203
universities, 63–4, 108, 166–7
Untouchables, 11, 31, 84, 156–7, 163
Uray, 31, 155
urbanisation, 123
Utpidit Jatiya Utthan Manch, 183
Uttar Pradesh, 39
Uttaranchal, 39

Vaisali, 18
Vaishnavism, 52
Vajracharyas, 30, 31, 60, 155–6
Vajryana, 30, 155–6
vamshavalis, 13, 29, 30
Vedic period, 18
vegetable oil, 77
Vietnam, 15
Vietnamese language, 12
viharas, 29
Vijaypur, 24–5
Vikram Era, 182
Village Defence Forces, 222
village development, 130, 131, 132
Vishnu, 34, 52, 84, 175
Vrijis, 19

water resources, 132, 139–40, 189
West Bengal, 112
Western Europe, 123, 129
wheat, 16, 140
WHO, 135
women, status of, 158–9, 164
Women's Commission, 107
wool trade, 27, 28, 148–50
work permit system, 112
World Bank, 127, 128, 130, 135, 142, 143, 147, 193,
  228

Yadav caste, 110
yaks, 27–8, 134
Yogi, Naraharinath, 98
Younghusband expedition, 64, 76, 82
Yugoslavia, 101
Yunnan, 13

Zhou Enlai, 133